REIMAGINING AMERICAN THEATRE

REIMAGINING AMERICAN THEATRE

Robert Brustein

ELEPHANT PAPERBACKS

Ivan R. Dee, Publisher, Chicago

 This book was originally published in 1991 by Hill and Wang and is here reprinted by arrangement with the publisher.

First ELEPHANT PAPERBACK edition published 1992 by Ivan R. Dee, Inc. 1332 North Halsted Street, Chicago 60622. Manufactured in the United States of America and printed on acid-free paper.

Library of Congress Cataloging-in-Publication Data:
Brustein, Robert Sanford, 1927–
Reimagining American theatre / Robert Brustein
— 1st Elephant pbk. ed.
p. cm.
Originally published: 1st ed. New York : Hill and Wang, 1991.
"Elephant paperbacks."
Includes index.
ISBN 0-929587-99-5 (alk. paper)
1. Theater—United States. 2. Theater—United States—Reviews.
3. American drama—20th century—History and criticism. I. Title.
[PN2232.B7 1992]
792'.0973—dc20 92-16024

This volume is dedicated
to DANIEL and MAX . . .
who are reimagining the future.

PREFACE

This book is a reflection on the American theatre of the eighties through the agency of selected articles and reviews written largely, though not exclusively, in my capacity as drama critic for *The New Republic*. Despite my own skeptical and even pessimistic nature, despite the radical problems I see confronting the American theatre today, the tone of the volume is essentially positive. I believe, as my title suggests, we are in a period of theatrical renewal and change. Other observers may interpret the same signs I find promising as tokens of disintegration. And it is possible to dismiss my uncharacteristically sunny mood as an effort to maintain my faith in the form I have devoted my life to. Still, the reason the stage matters is that people are still trying to improve and redirect it. A country without a theatre is a country without a soul.

In order to focus on the issues of the American theatre, I have generally omitted discussion of theatre from abroad. Not always. A musical such as *The Phantom of the Opera* exerts too great an influence on our own musical theatre to be ignored, just as the productions of Peter Brook must be covered because of their significant impact on the direction of the American classical theatre. Also, I have occasionally included a visiting production when it formed an interesting contrast to one of our own, and I have discussed the British stage in order to compare it with what I consider to be our underestimated native product.

The book is divided into three sections. The first—"Plays"—is primarily devoted to new American works; the second—"Productions"—

to new versions of revivals, usually by institutional theatres; and the third—"Polemics"—to the various issues underlying, or impeding, the development of an American dramatic art. I apologize for the cantankerous evangelical note that occasionally enters my prose, especially in the third section, which deals with the obstacles to artistic freedom, notably the federal government, once so promising an ally, now such a daunting adversary. The reinvention of our theatre will not proceed until these blocks to progress are "burnt or purged away."

CONTENTS

FOREWORD REIMAGINING THE AMERICAN STAGE 3

PART I PLAYS

INTRODUCTION REIMAGINING THE DRAMA 19

Post-Naturalist Triumph (*Balm in Gilead*) 33
One-Person Shows (*Sex and Death to the Age 14; Mistero Buffo*) 36
The Hit of the Building (*The World According to Me!*) 40
Look Back with Nostalgia (*Anything Goes; Into the Woods*) 44
The Shape of the New (*Geniuses; Edmond*) 49
Poisoned Airwaves (*Talk Radio*) 52
The Shlepic (*The Phantom of the Opera*) 54
Transcultural Blends (*The Gospel at Colonus; M. Butterfly; Juan Darien*) 57
The Last Refuge of Scoundrels (*Speed-the-Plow*) 62
The Best Play of Which Year? (*A Walk in the Woods; Boys' Life*) 65
The Voice of the Eighties (*Reckless; Without You I'm Nothing*) 69
Running on Empty (*Miracolo d'Amore*) 72

An Evening of Last Rites (*Jerome Robbins' Broadway*) 74
Women in Extremis (*The Heidi Chronicles*) 78
Orpheus Condescending (*Orpheus Descending*) 81
Plays for People Perhaps (*Gypsy; Other People's Money*) 85
Political Theatre: The Havels and Have-Nots (*Some Americans Abroad; Crowbar*) 89
Prelude to a Fairy Tale (*Prelude to a Kiss*) 94
Soured Grapes (*The Grapes of Wrath*) 96
The Lesson of *The Piano Lesson (The Piano Lesson)* 99
She-Plays, American Style (*Machinal; Abundance*) 104
End-of-Season Notes (The Tonys; *Six Degrees of Separation*) 108

PART II PRODUCTIONS

INTRODUCTION REIMAGINING THE CLASSICS 115

Three Years after "1984" (*1984*) 123
A Tribute to Robert Penn Warren (*All the King's Men*) 127
Headline Hunting (*The Front Page*) 130
Clowns and Vaudevillians (*The Comedy of Errors*) 134
The Longest Journey (*The Mahabharata*) 136
Breaking the Frame (*The Mistress of the Inn*) 140
The Definitive Production (*A Midsummer Night's Dream; The Cherry Orchard*) 143
The Limits of the Auteur (*The Cherry Orchard*) 147
The Ultimate Broadway Transfer (*Our Town*) 151
Shakespeare with an American Accent (*The Winter's Tale*) 155
Kid Coriolanus (*Coriolanus*) 159
Much Ado about Something (*Much Ado About Nothing*) 162
Diderot's Yuppie (*Rameau's Nephew*) 164
Phèdre with Pilaf and Pekoe Tea (*Phaedra Britannica*) 167
Godot in LaLa Land (*Waiting for Godot*; *Cafe Crown*) 171
Jewish Metaphysics (*The Tenth Man*) 175
Fairy Tailspin (*Cymbeline*) 178
The Hero of the Nursery (*Peer Gynt*) 182

Transforming Actors and Star Personalities (The Death of Olivier; *Twelfth Night*) 186
Actors Directing Actors (*Macbeth*) 190
Post-Modern Prophecies (*Woyzeck; Baal*) 194
In the Midst of Death (*A Celebration of Samuel Beckett*) 197
How to "Serve" Shakespeare (*On Directing Shakespeare*) 201

PART III POLEMICS

INTRODUCTION REIMAGINING THE PROCESS 209

The Legacy of the Group Theatre 217
Notes on the Bottom Line 221
Theatre and the Individual Talent 225
Lighten Up, America 227
Designs for Living (Rooms) (*The Theatre of Boris Aronson*) 230
An Actor Prepares (*The 1988 Democratic National Convention*) 234
All in the Family Ties (*The 1988 Republican National Convention*) 237
A Theatrical Declaration of Independence 240
Dreams and Hard-back Chairs 248
Dangerous Books 252
Arts Wars 257
    Disaster at the NEA 257
    The NEA Belly-Up 260
    Artistic Freedom and Political Repression 264
As the *Globe* Turns 272
Politics and Theatre 280

ACKNOWLEDGMENTS 293
INDEX 295

REIMAGINING AMERICAN THEATRE

FOREWORD

Reimagining the American Stage

The theatre, usually at odds with reality, seems to be imitating nature in one important regard: its cycles of death and rebirth. Something seems to be dying, and as with all seasonal changes, something new is struggling to be born. The death of the theatre has been celebrated so many times now that nobody bothers to mention it anymore. Instead, the print and broadcast media are behaving as though grass is already growing on its grave. In the past, the state of the theatre's health would be argued in intellectual magazines, popular newspapers, and trade journals, in living rooms and bars, even in the songs of Simon and Garfunkel. Today, the question is treated with a vacuous and rather bored silence. The Arts and Leisure section of *The New York Times*—who remembers when it was once called the Theatre section?—can barely squeeze out an article about the stage once every two or three weeks, infrequently on its front page. Nor does discussion often focus on the American theatre. The *Times* has three full-time reviewers, and another two or three part-time contributors, but considering how seldom they appear in the daily cultural pages—once or twice a week at most—it would be more economical to pay them an hourly wage.

Newsweek has drastically reduced the space of its regular theatre critic, Jack Kroll, so that he rarely appears in print unless covering some monumental event, like Peter Brook's *Mahabharata* or the London theatre season. *Time* magazine is more generous to its reviewer, William Henry III. Most New York newspapers feature reviews that read like telex copy, not much different in kind from the encapsulated asides of the coiffured pundits of TV. *The Village Voice* still makes an effort to cover most New York theatre events (so does *Variety* from another perspective), and its writers constitute the largest reviewing staff on any current newspaper. But even that lively enterprise is now being buried under ads and personals, a considerably eviscerated effort in contrast to an era when half the paper was devoted to the stage.

As for the serious magazines, neither *Harper's* nor *The Atlantic* has carried a theatre article in years—an exception was David Denby's *Theaterophobia*, a savage attack on the stage. I'm still writing in *The New Republic*, but my once weekly column now appears monthly, by editorial decree. John Simon continues to rage weekly at helpless moving objects in *New York* magazine, but that's less a species of criticism than blood sport, to be recorded in the annals of bullbaiting. There was a time when every serious magazine reserved considerable space in order to examine what was happening in theatre—when Mary McCarthy and Susan Sontag were reviewing for *Partisan Review*, when Elizabeth Hardwick was covering theatre for *The New York Review*, when the *New Leader* featured Albert Bermel, *The Nation* had Harold Clurman (later Alan Schneider and Richard Gilman), and Wilfrid Sheed and Richard Gilman were writing for *Commonweal*. Even *The Hudson Review* had regular reviewers, John Simon among them, where he had the opportunity to be more reflective than reflexive. And *Commentary*—in the years before the editors began to see Reds in every dressing room—was noted for its sociological overviews of the American stage. Indeed, at one time virtually every American intellectual felt a compulsion to express an opinion on the state of Broadway theatre.

Well, what happened? The chief thing was the decline of Broadway. We were having such a great time hurling stones at a seemingly invincible commercial target that we were unprepared when that muscular Philistine fell flat on his face before the assaults. I'm not suggesting it was our little slingshots that brought Goliath down. The issues were far more fundamental than that. But when you're flailing away against the mediocrity and meretriciousness of a powerful adversary and it suddenly falls down, the effect can be disorienting. Surely, something unsettled many of the writers I've just named, because they soon abandoned theatre criticism and returned to literary pursuits, thus ending that golden period, in the early sixties, when literate theatre critics were having an impact. Why, *The New York Times* asked even me, a notorious highbrow, to become its daily drama reviewer, undoubtedly responding to the discontent then being expressed by the intelligentsia toward the newspaper's cultural personnel. I refused the temptation, pleading my inability to write coherent reviews in less than three days (the real reason was a hesitation to exercise instant life-and-death power over productions that took months to prepare). I recommended Stanley Kauffmann for the post. He held it for less than a year, and still hasn't forgiven me.

The end of concerted intelligent reflection on the state of our theatre coincided, as I said, with the deterioration of the commercial stage and the loss of a central platform for aspiring American theatre artists. This left our New York–based critics with very little to write about, apart from the inferior quality of Broadway stagecraft. And how often can you write about that without falling into rage or repetition? Frank Rich is often assailed for destroying Broadway, and there's no question that sour critical judgments in the *Times* directly affect the barometric pressure of theatre economics. But it's not necessary to agree with his opinions, or even his aesthetic, to conclude that his only critical alternative to ferocity is mendacity—or finding a less damaging place to express his views. Largely for money reasons, Broadway *has* degenerated into an arena for the tried and true: huge, numbing musicals; Neil Simonized comedies; or, at best, imports from Britain and transfers from American resident theatres. The new American play—once the proud staple of the commercial theatre in the thirties, forties, and fifties—has virtually disappeared from producers' agendas, unless it can be marketed as a variant of affirmative action, alleviating liberal guilt toward minorities or the handicapped. And the day of the genuinely original American musical is over, too, eclipsed by such grinding British juggernauts as *The Phantom of the Opera* and *Les Misérables*.

Ticket prices are clearly the main issue. The high level of producers' greed, artists' royalties, expensive theatre-leasing arrangements, and union featherbedding has made a couple of seats to a Broadway show—if you add in transportation, restaurants, parking, and babysitting—cost as much as a couple of shares of IBM; and when the evening's over, you don't even have a dividend to show for it. At such prices, any theatregoer is going to stay home unless he's promised a blockbuster. Consequently, what was once the theatre center of the world no longer has a regular theatre audience. Look around the Majestic or the Winter Garden the next time you visit Broadway and see if you can recognize anybody you know. It's an audience of tourists and expense accounters, commuters traveling via bridge and tunnel. But that gabby, feisty, noisy, demanding New York audience that used to mob the Broadway box office is a thing of the past. Oh, you'll probably see a few natives at the revival of *Gypsy* or at *Cat on a Hot Tin Roof*. But most commercial producers recognize that they haven't the slightest notion who their customers are.

And it's for that reason, I think, that so much of the current Broadway product is trite and banal. Where the criterion for staging shows once was originality and surprise, now it is the capacity to repeat successful formulas from the past. Sometimes this works. All of Andrew Lloyd Webber's big mechanical musicals sound exactly alike to people like me, but every one of them (*Aspects of Love* excepted) somehow manages to start a box-office stampede. The same is true of Neil Simon, each of whose recent hit plays is just another chapter in his romanticized autobiography, tinted with rose-colored water and studded wtih contrived gags. It is more likely, however, that any theatre work based on some previous success will seem desiccated and tired, unless it has an infusion of new artistic energy. And that energy is just what frightens conventional Broadway producers these days. You don't risk four to ten million dollars on the unknown.

But in failing to trust their audiences, the Broadway producers have been encouraging audiences not to trust *them*, with the result that living-room conversation these days is never about the latest play; it's about the latest movie or miniseries. Attendance is down, though box-office income continues to rise, inflated by astronomical ticket prices. Each new season is pronounced more horrible than the last. Because of these reasons—and because there's so little youth, vigor, excitement, or new ideas on the Broadway stage—the theatre as a whole is now considered moribund. And because the intellectuals have deserted it as well, no strong voice in this country is calling attention to the fact that, far from being dead, the American theatre throughout the nation may today be more advanced and more dynamic than at virtually any other time in its history.

I realize this is a large and unsupported claim. But it might seem less preposterous once it is recognized that the idea of theatre has undergone a profound change during the past two decades—in its definition, its structure, its purpose, its geography. Being a market for proven commodities rather than a source of new forms, New York has been among the last areas in this nation to acknowledge this fact. Until recently, the new theatre has been seen only around the city's periphery—at the Brooklyn Academy of Music or at Ellen Stewart's La MaMa or at the Kitchen—though the presentation of performing artists at Lincoln Center called "Serious Fun" suggests a growing awareness at its midsection.

But what a provincial village New York has become in regard to the arts. This is clear enough in opera, where the Met continues to roast old chestnuts and the City Opera is devoting more and more of its repertory to light opera and musical comedies of the past. If you want to see a new American opera, you have to fly to Chicago, Philadelphia, Santa Fe, Houston, Saint Louis, Louisville, or—this is a bigger scandal—to the Netherlands and Germany, where most of Philip Glass's work has been premiered. The first-string music critic for the *Times*, who seems to believe that opera consists of divas clunking downstage, facing the audience, and warbling arias *in situ*, will invariably attack any operatic methods that depart in any way from conventional practices of composition and production. This may explain why a recent issue of the magazine *Daedalus* was wholly devoted to asking why New York has lost its place to Europe and regional American cities as a hospitable arena for new musical expression.

What is less commonly noticed is that the same thing is true of the stage. Decades ago, a number of theatre leaders—Tyrone Guthrie and Zelda Fichandler were the first—recognized that if theatre was going to survive in this country, it was going to have to be decentralized and based on a system motivated by art, not profits. Fichandler went to Washington and founded the Arena Stage. Guthrie—rejecting Boston because it was too close to New York—went to Minneapolis, where he not only founded a fine theatre but helped to make that city into the most progressive in the land for philanthropic support of the arts.

The earliest resident theatres in this country were formed on such British repertory models as the Old Vic, the Royal Shakespeare Company, and the National Theatre, staging staple classics mixed with the occasional new play, performed in an acting style influenced by the great English performers (Gielgud, Olivier, Richardson). But some of the newer companies were later to explore other forms of inspiration. The Theatre of Living Arts, founded in Philadelphia by André Gregory, developed a radical, boisterous approach to the works of Beckett and Anouilh; Joe Papp's New York Shakespeare Festival and Public Theater, especially in their early days, encouraged new American plays and began experimenting with a peculiarly American Shakespeare, based on rough-hewn styles borrowed from broad movie farces. And, if I'm permitted to mention it, the Yale Repertory Theatre, after its founding in 1966, was turning to a blend of Brecht and cabaret in approaching little-known classics and satiric new works. At the same time, The

Open Theatre and later Mabou Mines and The Wooster Group—performance groups reflecting the influence of the Living Theatre—were exploring a whole new approach to acting in their evolution of new works for the stage.

The sixties and early seventies were a high point for the resident theatre movement, though it must be acknowledged that after a time—largely as a result of a funding crisis caused by dwindling private foundation support and the too slow growth of the National Endowment for the Arts—many of these theatres began to grow stale and conventional, losing their initial radical thrust. One of the proudest things about this movement in the early stages was its independence from the commercial New York stage. Now many were returning to an old role as tributaries, generating products for Broadway. Of course, a good play deserves a longer life in many different venues, and there's no reason why New York should not be one of the pit stops. But this is different from actually choosing plays in order to move to Broadway, or restaging past Broadway and Off-Broadway successes. *A Chorus Line*, though it saved Joe Papp from bankruptcy and enabled him for a while to preserve his dedication to unpopular new plays, was an early harbinger of the misalliance between nonprofit theatres and the commercial stage. Before long, resident theatres would be trying out the comedies of Neil Simon, or circulating productions of August Wilson and *Into the Woods* to other resident theatres as tryout stations on the way to New York.

This made good sound fiscal sense. It brought an infusion of royalties to hard-pressed institutions and created celebrity for its artistic directors, directors, playwrights, and actors. But as the media wheeled around to applaud this new breed of American theatre people, and turn them into stars of the week, the institutions themselves began to sicken and even die. The first casualty was the idea of a permanent resident company. How could an ensemble remain together when so many of its members were performing in New York? As a result, there are not more than three or four major resident acting companies still in place in this country, because its members—once happy to join a group with clearly defined goals—have largely decamped for Hollywood and New York. Another casualty was the ideals and aspirations of these once-committed institutions. Institutional theatres originally devoted to developing their own style and their own artists began competing with each other over projects they thought might have the legs to walk to Broadway.

A little of this is understandable and probably inevitable. But it has presently grown so widespread and endemic that it is discrediting the entire movement. In a culture which worships success, few are prepared to cry out against this progressive deterioration. Quite the contrary, it is being encouraged, largely by critics interested only in results, with less interest in the process by which these results are achieved. The effects, however, are more noticeable in England, which currently provides so much fodder for our own commercial stage—and our noncommercial stage as well. The two large companies responsible for much that was forceful and original in English theatre lost their prime artistic leaders a few years ago—Trevor Nunn of the Royal Shakespeare Company and Peter Hall of the National. Both were under fire for having abandoned their original purpose in order to profit personally by their commercial ventures. If anyone had said, a decade ago, that the leading purveyor of blockbuster musicals to Broadway and the West End was going to be the head of the Royal Shakespeare Company, he would have been pilloried for impugning the honor of British culture. Yet Trevor Nunn is now enriching himself with such factory items as *Cats* and *Starlight Express*, while Peter Hall is spinning off star-studded revivals of Shakespeare and Tennessee Williams to Broadway. Meanwhile, the companies they once led are devoting more and more of their repertories to new and old musicals, and American producers and critics are shopping for new products along the corridors of established classical theatres.

A *New York Times* article on this subject, noting the predominance of English talent in the American musical theatre, was entitled "The Empire Strikes Back." A better title would have been "The Empire Strikes Out." Certainly, the American resident theatre movement has also been striking out lately, to the point where, in many cities of this country, it is barely distinguishable from the commercial theatre in any way except its 501-C3 nonprofit designation.

Before I leave this rather depressing issue, let me cite one more possible reason for the disappointing record, recently, of the once-promising resident theatre movement: Time itself. The initial leaders of this movement were usually men and women who had founded their theatres and provided them with structure and vision. Their enthusiasm managed to attract not only a group of like-minded artists but patrons from the community ready to support their work in a crucial moral and financial way. Now that the movement is over thirty years old, many of its leaders have either died, burned out, or retired, with the result that power over the theatre has shifted not to their artistic successors but rather to their managing directors and their boards. Board members hold the purse strings; they also hold the power to hire and fire. But whereas old warriors like Tyrone Guthrie and Joseph Papp and William Ball usually had the capacity to keep a board at bay, if not productive and friendly (Adrian Hall once fired a board when it started to get rambunctious), their young artistic director replacements are considerably more subject to the whims and caprices of financial advisors. In most cases, this second artistic generation is composed of gifted and imaginative directors. But since they didn't found their theatres and, in most cases, have abdicated fund-raising to development people, they are often much less involved with the fiscal health of the institutions they run. In economic terms, they are more like employees than independent leaders. In psychological terms, they are rather like sons and daughters who accept their allowance without feeling any particular responsibility for keeping the family bank account in balance.

In consequence, their jobs are always at risk if subscriptions falter or unearned income drops, and their theatres become accountable not to the exigencies of artistic exploration but rather to the vagaries of the box office. This puts the resident theatre—to borrow a term from Jean Genet—back in the brothel, and explains why so many of its leaders have begun to lose heart and desert it. Adrian Hall, the brilliant artistic director of Trinity Rep and, later, of the Dallas Theater Company, is only the latest casualty of the general anomie. An eloquent and dedicated spokesman for nonprofit companies, as well as one of our most imaginative creative artists, he has now abandoned the movement to seek personal satisfactions in freelance theatre directing and moviemaking. And who can blame him when the system proceeds, so remorselessly and inexorably, to suck the idealism and adventure—and pleasure—out of any promising theatrical venture.

I may be exaggerating the extent of the rot, but even if what I say is only partially accurate, it is a pretty depressing account of theatre in this country. And, under these circumstances, you may ask, how in the world can I claim that American theatre has rarely been stronger in the quality and vision of its creative artists? The conditions I have been trying to describe are hardly congenial for a renaissance of this beleaguered art. Yet something like a renaissance has nevertheless been brewing over the past five or six years—and perhaps the crisis has been partly responsible.

Take playwriting. Everybody remembers a golden time when the

American theatre could boast a succession of dramatists renowned throughout the world, beginning with O'Neill and continuing through Odets, Hellman, Miller, Williams, and Albee. By contrast, today it is generally assumed that playwriting is in decline. I am nevertheless convinced that the young writers working on the contemporary stage have the capacity to equal, if not surpass, most of those I have just named. Admittedly, they are more obscure. Few have had a major success on Broadway. But that is more a condition of a faulty system than of their own intrinsic talents. Sam Shepard, for example, has contributed a body of plays—chief among them *Buried Child* and *True West*—that will stand comparison with virtually anything written in the last twenty years, though it is true that he spends less time writing these days than acting in such movies as *Baby Boom*. David Mamet—also a part-time Hollywood writer and director—is another major playwright of the period: *American Buffalo* and *Glengarry Glen Ross* are masterpieces, but all his plays come from the hand of a master. David Rabe's *Hurlyburly*—in its full-length version, not the truncated comic mechanism greased for the stage by Mike Nichols—can compete, in power and rage, with the late plays of O'Neill. Christopher Durang, a deadly scorpion, with poison leeching into his writing hand, is one of the most powerful satirists our stage has ever seen. And Ronald Ribman continues to write with a surrealist bite and poetic penetration that makes most of the domestic drama of the past look declarative, linear, and obvious.

Many other distinctive writers—Arthur Kopit, Craig Lucas, Howard Korder, David Ives, Tom Babe, Richard Nelson, Wendy Wasserstein, William Hauptman, Lanford Wilson, Eric Overmyer, John Guare, August Wilson, Alfred Uhry, Harry Kondoleon, Allan Havis, David Henry Hwang, Marsha Norman, Wallace Shawn, Keith Reddin, George C. Wolfe, A. R. Gurney, Jr., Charles Mee, Jr., Jon Robin Baitz, dozens more—have all done redoubtable work. The numbers alone suggest that something unusual is happening, but the general intelligence and seriousness of their plays are the real measure. Because they so rarely have Broadway hits, few of these playwrights have been celebrated by the media, so their existence is not a significant fact in the public mind. But this may be why they continue to write with such obdurate intensity, with such astonishing unpredictability. Obscurity has advantages as well as disappointments, just as sudden fame can prove to be an enemy of promise—as it did with our more celebrated playwrights in the past, many of whom faltered in trying to repeat their early successes.

Today's playwrights may not have as much chance as yesterday's to enjoy the rewards of American success. But they have a better shot at something more elusive and satisfying—to last the course with dignity, without exhausting their creative wills.

And most of them have found congenial directors: Jerry Zaks, Gregory Mosher, Ron Lagomarsino, Michael Engler, Norman René—who mount their plays tastefully and faithfully, though the more interesting directors today are essentially auteurs who, following Peter Brook and Jerzy Grotowski, work best with material devised in concert with actors and dramaturges. The rise of the auteur director is another recent American theatrical phenomenon worthy of note—a movement which parallels, without often meeting, the movement in playwriting. The grandiose creations of Robert Wilson, just beginning to be recognized and appreciated in this country, though long celebrated in Europe, are among the most startling and original theatre works ever devised by an American: *Einstein on the Beach*, created in collaboration with Philip Glass (a composer whose valuable contributions to the modern stage have yet to be measured); *Death Destruction & Detroit*, parts I and II; and, above all, the monumental *The CIVIL WarS*. These creations are making theatrical history at a time when the theatre is no longer thought to have a history.

The work of Richard Foreman with the Ontological/Hysterical Theatre, Lee Breuer and JoAnne Akalaitis with Mabou Mines, Elizabeth LeCompte with The Wooster Group, Andrei Serban with a variety of theatres, Anne Bogart, Robert Woodruff, Peter Sellars, Michael Greif, Des McAnuff, Julie Taymor, Ping Chong, and countless others—usually in collaboration with a cadre of gifted designers and composers and performance artists—testifies to an auteur vitality unique in our theatre history. And with the probes of the dancer Martha Clarke into theatrical territory, in conjunction with the composer Richard Peaslee and the designer Robert Israel, the borders have been breached between theatre and dance through such stunning creations as *The Garden of Earthly Delights*, though her subsequent works are admittedly less impressive. These artists, fighting for recognition and grants in our own country, have almost all been recognized in Europe and Asia as people who make our experimental theatre the envy of the world—at the very moment when the funeral notices are being posted by our own critics and reviewers.

Two new departures should be noted: the growing interest of auteur directors in classical drama and, even more unexpected, new American plays. Lee Breuer was among the first to try his hand at such work, after experimenting with the short pieces of Beckett, first with his *Lulu* at the American Repertory Theatre (a compound of Wedekind's *Earth Spirit* and *Pandora's Box*), then with a controversial *Tempest* at the New York Shakespeare Festival, then with a modern retelling of *Oedipus at Colonus*, adapted for gospel singers and retitled *The Gospel at Colonus*, and, most recently, with a less successful deconstruction of *King Lear* with Ruth Maleczech in the title role. JoAnne Akalaitis has also been working with texts, first from the modern period—with her *Endgame* and *The Balcony* at the American Repertory Theatre—then with such classics as Büchner's *Leonce and Lena* and Genet's *The Screens* at the Guthrie, then with Ford's *'Tis Pity She's a Whore* at the Goodman Theatre in Chicago, and most recently with Shakespeare at the Public Theater. Also notable among recent auteur-driven classics are Richard Foreman's *Woyzeck* at the Hartford Stage and Robert Woodruff's *Baal* at Trinity Rep. A few seasons ago, Robert Wilson was persuaded to direct his first classical text—Euripides' *Alcestis*—preparatory to his work on the Gluck opera *Alceste*. The results were strong enough to win a prize as Best Foreign Production in France when the production traveled to the Festival d'Automne in Paris.

Andrei Serban, who has been working with classics all his creative life, undertook his first new American play some years ago—Ronald Ribman's *Sweet Table at the Richelieu*, which, despite its idiosyncratic approach, the author declared the finest production his plays had ever had. In the same season, Richard Foreman turned for a moment from his own scenarios to direct a radical production of Arthur Kopit's *End of the World (with Symposium to Follow)*. These, along with other such ventures by experimental directors, while no doubt fraught with potential battles between authors and auteurs, promise to close up one of the few remaining gaps in our theatre process—the once unbreachable division between living playwrights and independent directors.

Let me mention one more element in this new awakening—the public. Audiences, once either sleepy or pious before American efforts to create a serious theatre, have suddenly come alive. There is a huge and growing following for the more radical artists in our midst, and once again, the audience at a play includes many young people who lend an air of freshness and vitality to the theatre event. The Next Wave Festival at BAM (the Brooklyn Academy of Music), featuring some of the most advanced art in the world, plays most of its performances to sold-out houses. Not all experimental theatres can boast of similar success with the public. But it has become increasingly clear that those who keep faith with the audience's intelligence will ultimately win out with a little persistence. It is a far better gamble than cynicism or fear.

Two major problems remain for the American theatre, one concerning actors, the other involving critics. Most American actors seem to have lost interest in the stage, and those that remain are riddled with uncertainty and self-doubt. All the pressures of our success-crazed society tell the actor he's a fool to remain with a profession that promises little money and less fame when those enticements are continually beckoning from LaLa land. As a result, and with a great sense of sadness, the resident theatre movement has watched some of its most gifted performers end up in a vapid TV series or, at best, a feature film, while the great stage roles go begging. What also goes begging is their creative spark in a meat-market culture which values only their easily digestible personal qualities for a moment before they are left on the scrap heap, bemoaning the waste of spirit in an expense of shame.

And then there are those who evaluate our stage, leaving the only permanent record of an ephemeral art which disappears the moment the curtain falls. It may well be our critics and reviewers, a handful of honorable exceptions noted, who represent the major failure of contemporary American theatre, though only history will be able to measure how much responsibility they bear for the lapses and failings of the art they continually belabor. For very few of our critics have adapted to the primary recent changes in our theatre structure—its institutionalization and decentralization. The New York critics still remain largely in New York, where the structure is falling apart. And those few that travel, and even most of those who regularly work in other cities, still tend to evaluate production on a show-by-show basis, as if the resident theatre were a commercial house with no identity of its own as an organic institution. As a result, most dedicated theatre people feel they are laboring in a vacuum, which adds to their sense of frustration. How many theatre critics are prepared to examine the relationship between one company production and another, or to admit they've seen a resident actor before in an entirely different kind of role, or to watch the development of a director, a playwright, a designer in a sequence of creations, or to prod a theatre which seems to be failing its own declared purposes? No, the repertory critics who would spur the new movement—whose aesthetic and energies are tied to an entirely different form of alternative theatre—have not materialized in any significant numbers, and as a result, the American stage is currently being evaluated on the basis of minimal evidence and false cues.

Still, as I said, a large and growing public exists for the kind of work I have been trying to describe, and that gives strength to us in difficult times. The public may be slow in responding to new developments, but with a little courage and patience on the part of theatre boards, audience members eventually come around. They must. For it is in the memory of the public that any lasting theatrical achievement will be recorded until that time when critics and reviewers again assume their full responsibilities to this provisional art.

PART I

PLAYS

INTRODUCTION

Reimagining the Drama

In the second act of Ibsen's *The Master Builder*, Halvard Solness endeavors to explain to his young admirer, Hilda Wangel, the origin of his peculiarly lucky career as a builder. It had all begun with a fire in his own house, a fire which caused the death of his children and turned his wife into a living corpse, but which gave him his first chance to exercise his building talents. The curious thing about the scene is the manner in which he describes the cause of that fatal blaze.

> SOLNESS: You see, the whole business revolves about no more than a crack in a chimney.
>
> HILDA: Nothing else?
>
> SOLNESS: No; at least not at the start. . . . I'd noticed that tiny opening in the flue long, long before the fire. . . . Every time I wanted to start repairing it, it was exactly as if a hand was there, holding me back. . . . So nothing came of it.
>
> HILDA: But why did you keep on postponing?
>
> SOLNESS: Because I went on thinking. . . . Through that little black opening in the chimney I could force my way to success—as a builder.
>
> (tr. Rolf Fjelde)

So far, nothing unusual. The passage looks like a perfectly conventional piece of exposition, with the playwright demonstrating how the past influences the present—how Solness began his career and acquired his guilty conscience. A crack in the chimney, leading to a dreadful fire. An opportunity to subdivide the burnt-out area into building lots. A new reputation as a builder of suburban homes.

But then something extraordinary happens in the scene, as Ibsen proceeds to demolish his own very carefully fashioned causal construction.

> HILDA: But wait a minute, Mr. Solness—how can you be so sure the fire started from that little crack in the chimney?
>
> SOLNESS: I can't, not at all. In fact, I'm absolutely certain it had nothing whatever to do with the fire . . .
>
> HILDA: What!
>
> SOLNESS: It's been proved without a shadow of a doubt that the fire broke out in a clothes closet, in quite another part of the house.

Hilda's exclamation of astonishment is shared by a chorus of readers and spectators, for the play seems to have taken a very mischievous turn. But Ibsen is not being perverse here. Quite the contrary, what he is suggesting is entirely consistent with his poetic apprehension of reality and with the metaphysical impulse animating all his plays, including his so-called social-realistic drama. The determination of guilt and its expiation may still constitute the moral quest of his characters, but Ibsen obviously believes that the sources of this guilt are not easily accessible to the inquiring mind.

What Ibsen is anticipating in this passage is the significant turn that the theatre was to take sometime around the end of the nineteenth century, in common with similar developments in science, philosophy, and literature—the universal departure responsible, in part, for the movement called modernism, which influenced the work of the major European dramatists, among them Strindberg, Pirandello, Beckett, Ionesco, Handke, and Heiner Müller.

For Ibsen has quietly proceeded to undermine a basic assumption of the naturalist universe—namely, that cause A precedes consequence B, which in turn is responsible for catastrophe C. Isn't it possible, he is suggesting, that A has nothing whatever to do with B, much less with C, regardless of the apparent evidence? Isn't it possible that events are so multiple and complex that the human intelligence may never be able to comprehend the full set of causes preceding any situation, consequence, or feeling? Ibsen, in short, is attempting to repeal the simple, fundamental law of cause and effect, which had been an unquestioned statute at least since the Enlightenment—the law that ruled the linear, logical, rationalistic world of literature and, in particular, the Western literature of guilt. In its place, he is reconfirming the unknowable, ineffable secrets underlying the will of Nature.

All of Ibsen's plays contain religious elements, but *The Master Builder* is clearly his most religious play since *Brand*. What the playwright is trying to do through the character of his ruthless, guilty hero, Solness, is to challenge the orthodox pieties at the same time that he is preserving the romantic mysteries. The purpose of the universe, the structure of character, the nature of sin—all are beyond the reach of traditional concepts; they can be determined only through the artist's intuition, and then only obscurely. And the task of the modern artist is to help humankind move beyond the sterile cycle of guilt and expiation, which is one of the offshoots of cause-and-effect thinking. Hilda exhorts Solness to challenge God by developing a robust Viking conscience. Ibsen exhorts us to become gods by transcending our sense of guilt, through a gargantuan effort of the will and the inspired intelligence. Whether this is finally possible is open to serious doubt. But one thing is certain: the old rationalistic assumptions will no longer serve the modern understanding. Indeed, they can only compound ignorance and point us toward false paths.

Ibsen's proposals are revolutionary. They challenge not only conventional theatre but established religion, established psychology, established social theory as well. Nevertheless, these proposals are actually a return to the assumptions of an earlier age of mystery, which held sway before the advent of Newtonian physics, Cartesian logic, and behavioral psychology. The drama of the Greeks and Elizabethans, for example, is rarely causal in our modern sense: human motives are sometimes so numerous that latter-day commentators are hard put to find the characters credible. Clytemnestra offers not one but five or six reasons for killing Agamemnon; Iago mentions so many motives for hating Othello that Coleridge was obliged to speak of the senseless motive-hunting of a "motiveless malignity"; and T. S. Eliot criticized Shakespeare for failing to give Hamlet an "objective correlative," meaning that he found Hamlet's feelings to be in excess of his situation.

While contemporary social scientists are busy rooting around in search of causal explanations for poverty, crime, neurosis, depression, and madness, great artists have traditionally understood that the true explanations are beyond concepts of blame. As Shakespeare's Edmund puts it, in *King Lear*, "This is the excellent foppery of the world, that, when we are sick in fortune—often the surfeit of our own behaviour—

we make guilty of our disasters the sun, the moon, and the stars. . . . 'Sfoot! I should have been that I am had the maidenliest star in the firmament twinkled on my bastardizing."

European drama has managed to recapture this biological understanding of motive, dating from a period in the last century. It was then that Ibsen—along with Nietzsche, Kierkegaard, and Freud—threw down a gauntlet, not only before orthodox religion, but before the prevailing liberal ideology of the nineteenth and twentieth centuries, meanwhile reducing the middle-class living room to a pile of rubble and exposing domestic realism as a cardboard illusion.

A quick look at the history of our own theatre reveals that American drama has been very slow in rising to this challenge, or even in showing any awareness of it. Just as the dominant strain of our religious life has been a tradition of Judaeo-Christian puritanism, and the dominant strain of our politics (at least before the eighties) a form of liberal reform democracy, so the dominant strain of our stage has been social, domestic, psychological, and realistic—which is to say, *causal*—and its dominant theme, the excavation, exposure, and expiation of guilt. The fires that burn through most American plays have been caused by that crack in the chimney, and the guilty conscience of their central characters can usually be traced to a single recognizable event.

This is particularly striking when one considers how many playwrights in the mainstream of American drama have thought themselves to be writing consciously in an Ibsenite tradition. And I speak now not just of the dramatists of the pre–World War II period—such social-minded writers as Clifford Odets, Sidney Howard, Maxwell Anderson, Robert Sherwood, Lillian Hellman, Irwin Shaw, and John Steinbeck—but also of the postwar "mood" playwrights—including such psychological writers as Tennessee Williams, Arthur Miller, William Inge, Lorraine Hansberry, Paddy Chayefsky, William Gibson, Frank Gilroy, and, more recently, Lanford Wilson, Mark Medoff, Richard Greenberg, Michael Cristofer, and August Wilson.

Even the progenitor of our drama, Eugene O'Neill—though he began writing under the strict influence of Nietzsche and Strindberg—became a causal dramatist in his last plays, when he was writing under the influence of Ibsen. In his greatest play, indeed the greatest play ever written by an American, *A Long Day's Journey into Night*, O'Neill proceeds to weave a close fabric of causality. Every character is suffering pangs of conscience and every character is trying to determine the root cause of his guilt. If the blighted house of Tyrone is misbegotten, then every member of the family is implicated in the other's hell. Each separate action ramifies outward into myriad branches of effects, and characters interlock, imprisoned in each other's fate.

My point reflects not on the quality of the play, which is a masterpiece, but rather on the fact that *A Long Day's Journey* is so remorselessly American in its concentration on the sources of guilt, and on the painful confrontations between parents and their children. These emphases are also evident in the work of an even more conscientious disciple of Ibsen—Arthur Miller—who, along with Tennessee Williams, has been the most celebrated postwar American dramatist, and the strongest influence on the American realist theatre. Miller first broke upon the contemporary consciousness, in fact, with a play that leans heavily on such middle Ibsen works as *The Wild Duck*, *Pillars of Society*, and *An Enemy of the People*—namely, *All My Sons*. Located in a middle-class living room around the end of World War II, this play has the task of identifying the guilt and establishing the responsibility of its elder protagonist, a wealthy manufacturer named Joe Keller. Keller has served a short term in the penitentiary, having been convicted of increasing his profits by manufacturing faulty cylinder heads for aircraft engines; these have caused the deaths of a number of American fighter pilots. Keller's older son, Larry, is missing in action and, at one point, the characters consider the possibility that the same faulty parts may have caused his death as well. By the play's end, we learn that the causal connection exists, but in indirect form: upon discovering that his father was responsible for the death of his comrades, Larry committed suicide by purposely crashing his plane. After a confrontation with his surviving son, Chris, Keller is forced to recognize that he is responsible for more than the lives of his immediate family—that the victims are "all my sons." He expiates his guilt through his own suicide.

It is easy enough to score points on Miller's dramaturgy, which often seems as faulty as Joe Keller's airplane parts. But my quarrel is not with the farfetched plotting of a young and relatively inexperienced writer; his work is to grow considerably more persuasive as his career progresses. No, my point is, rather, that *All My Sons* is based on assumptions and conventions which, regardless of how the playwright matures, remain central to his work, not to mention mainstream American drama as a whole—assumptions and conventions which are virtually anathema to Ibsen. For Miller is wedded to simple theatrical causality, whether the sequential links are direct or indirect, and his plays never escape the kind of connection he establishes in *All My Sons*, between Joe Keller's crime and Larry Keller's air crash. The action A precedes the consequence B, which leads inevitably to the guilty catastrophe C.

And the catalyst in this mixture is almost invariably the protagonist's son, who manages to bring the plot from a simmer to a boil. In fact, the typical Miller drama has a code which might be deciphered thus: The son exposes the father's guilt and shows him the way to moral action, and sometimes inadvertently to suicide. Take Miller's most famous play—often called the finest tragedy of modern times—*Death of a Salesman*. The well-known plot concerns the false values of Willy Loman, but the character who confronts Willy with the fraudulence of his own life is Biff, Willy's older son. Once extremely close to his father, Biff has now grown estranged from Willy, for reasons that Miller chooses to keep hidden until the end of the play. Something has happened between them, something which has affected not only their relationship but Biff's entire adult life; he has broken off a promising high-school sports career and become an aimless drifter. This, in turn, has had a powerful influence on Willy's life, since Biff once represented his main hope for the future. Ineluctably, the play brings us toward the revelation buried inside this family mystery: coming to visit his father in Boston one day, Biff discovers that Willy has a woman in his room.

Clearly, Miller is willing to risk a great deal of credibility in order to establish a moral showdown between father and son. Consider how much of the plot, theme, and character development hinges on this one climactic hotel-room encounter. *Death of a Salesman* purports to be about false American values of success, but beneath the sociological surface lies the real drama—a family drama of guilt and blame. The object of Biff's hero-worship, the model for his own life and behavior, has been discovered in Boston cheating on Mom.

In short, the premises underlying Miller's themes and actions are not Ibsenite in the least. They belong to the eighteenth century, which is to say the age of Newton, rather than to the twentieth, the age of Einstein. And Miller's theatrical Newtonianism remains an essential condition of his style, whether he is writing about Salem witch-hunts, or about the guilt and responsibility of those implicated in the crimes of the Nazis, or about self-destructive glamour queens, or about East European dissidents. In each of Miller's plays—indeed, in most of the plays of his contemporaries and disciples—every dramatic action has an equal and opposite reaction. It is the crack in the chimney that sends the house up in flames.

So prevalent is this pattern in mainstream American drama that even now, at the beginning of the nineties, our most highly acclaimed dramatists are still shaping their works to sequential diagrams. The style of our drama has admittedly undergone something of an exterior change; its causal pattern is occasionally more elliptical than in Miller's work; and the familiar fourth-wall realism is frequently broken by stylistic or supernatural devices. But these are changes touching the surface rather than the heart of these plays. More often than not, American mainstream drama continues to explore the causes behind the effects; the event to be excavated is still the guilt of the (generally older generation) protagonists; and the drama retains the air of a courtroom, complete with investigations, indictments, arraignments, condemnations, and punishments.

Take August Wilson, perhaps the most typical and highly esteemed of the current crop of playwrights. The winner of numerous prizes, Wilson has often been compared with Eugene O'Neill—but a perfunctory glance at his accomplishments soon reveals that he has a closer relative in Arthur Miller. Like Miller, Wilson is essentially a social dramatist, fashioning attacks on the inequities of the social system; like Miller, he identifies the nexus of corruption through a process of family conflict; and like Miller, he will occasionally make modest departures from domestic realism in order to force an indictment of national crimes as a whole.

In Wilson's case, these crimes are invariably linked with racism, not surprisingly, since he is partly black; and his work thus far has been a decade-by-decade examination of the way white society has managed to oppress the Afro-American minority and ignore the black experience. Take *Fences*, perhaps the most tightly written play in the cycle thus far. It concerns Troy Maxson, a hard-drinking family man, now reduced to "hauling white folks' garbage," though he was once a gifted baseball player who hit forty-three home runs in the Negro Leagues. Although he has served time in the penitentiary for robbery and murder, Troy prides himself on his capacity to support his family. He loves his wife, Rose, but is continually locked in quarrel with his second son, Corey. Corey, in emulation of his father, shines in sports and has been offered a college football scholarship. Troy would rather he took a job in the A&P. When Troy reveals to Rose that he has fathered a child with another woman, the unity of the family is shattered; and after

Troy manhandles Rose, Corey threatens him with a baseball bat. The last scene, six years later, takes place at Troy's funeral, where Corey, now an enlisted man in the Marines, reflects on the relationship they might have had and the man Troy might have been.

Wilson's larger purpose depends on his conviction that Troy's potential was stunted not through "surfeit of his own behavior" but by centuries of racist oppression. Just as he is reduced to being a lifter rather than a driver because he is black, so the color of his skin has blocked him, like Satchel Paige, from entering the major leagues (the play mostly takes place in the fifties, just when color barriers in sports were falling). To support his racial subject, however, Wilson concocts a straightforward family drama built on overworked baseball images, about the confrontation between an erring father and his indignant son, with a crisis almost identical to the climactic scenes in *All My Sons* and *Death of a Salesman*. Like Willy Loman, Troy has a long-suffering wife, a son with ambitions to be a football player, a crony with whom to share his confidences, a climactic infidelity, and the obligatory back yard. The play even ends with a funeral—again like *Death of a Salesman*—giving the characters a chance to discuss the protagonist's futile dreams against the background of the nation's false values.

Despite these similarities, Wilson has claimed for the "black experience" in *Fences* an exclusive privilege, insisting that only a black director should film the play (he has also assailed George Gershwin for the "tremendous audacity" of "bastardizing our music and our experience" in *Porgy and Bess*). Yet, for all his sense of black uniqueness, his recurrent theme is the familiar American charge of victimization. What is remarkable is the way in which audiences sit still for their portion of guilt, not only failing to rise to such baited challenges, but conferring fame, fortune, and Pulitzer Prizes on the writers who denounce them the most. At least one member of this audience—himself a gifted black writer named George C. Wolfe—has refused Wilson's indictment. In parodying the theatre of guilt, Wolfe suggests one of the directions our drama might take, were that crack in the chimney ever to be repaired. Wolfe's play, *The Colored Museum*, is a satire that runs roughshod, not only through the conventions of plays like *Fences*, but through many of our prevailing social pieties and assumptions.

The Colored Museum is lively and loud and full of fiery jive. The Brandenberg Concerto which opens the show is soon undercut by reggae, New Orleans jazz, gospel, and snatches of Ellington, Satchmo,

Miles Davis, Billie Holiday, Bessie Smith, and the Supremes. This suggests that Wolfe has something cogent to say about both the clash of cultures and the awkwardness of black assimilation, voluntary or involuntary, into the white world. Some of this is provocative: an opening sequence aboard a "Celebrity Slave Ship" flying at high altitudes where "shackles must be worn at all times" and earphones can be purchased for "the price of your first-born male"—or a skit involving a prosperous member of the black bourgeoisie carrying a Saks shopping bag who plops everything connected with his past (his first pair of Converse All Stars, his autographed photo of Stokely Carmichael) into a dumpster, finally adding to the pile a contemptuous street kid representing his repressed rage ("Being black is too emotionally taxing; therefore I will be black only on weekends and holidays"). Other sketches are thinner, less coherent, overextended.

But "The Last Mama-on-the-Couch Play" displays the felicities of the piece as a whole, and its freedom from orthodox thinking. Subtitled "A searing domestic play which tears at the very fabric of racist America," this is a satire on the whole range of serious black drama and commercial black musicals, though its ostensible target is Lorraine Hansberry's *A Raisin in the Sun*. An omnipresent stage manager hands Mama an award when she slaps her son across the room for doubting the existence of God, and all the actors slip into cultivated Shakespearean cadences ("What's gotten into you?" "Juilliard, good brother"). The malcontented Walter-Lee-Beau-Willy, always bellyaching about "the Man," is convicted of overacting and shot. The stage manager cushions his head with a pillow, saying, "If only he could have been born into an all-black musical." In response, the entire family is resurrected, singing and dancing, no doubt in *Raisin*.

Although it bravely pinpoints the creaky conventions and tired themes of Broadway-bound black protest, *The Colored Museum* doesn't always rise above the level of a drama school takeoff. Still, the piece is significant as a genuine advance beyond the clichés of black realism and the imperatives of black pride. It is easy enough to satirize white attitudes toward racial issues (a staple of black drama since the war). What is considerably more difficult—and more courageous—is to satirize black attitudes as well. Richard Pryor has done this, though admittedly with more wit and intensity; so, with more energy, has Eddie Murphy. And the TV program *In Living Color* has made black satire a witty staple of the home screen. But *The Colored Museum* remains a tonic for an ideologically choked age which, like most suppressed things exhumed from underground, helps us breathe the unpolluted air of freedom.

Insofar as Wolfe belongs to a time-honored satiric tradition, he breaks no new formal ground. One dramatist who has turned over the theatrical topsoil is Sam Shepard, a writer who has devoted most of his time to the movies after completing an usually large body of mythic material. In common with a number of playwrights today, Shepard has explored shortcuts through the habitual terrain of plot, character, and theme, primarily through the use of legendary material, borrowed from the myths and magic of the movies, including gangster films, horror films, and science fiction. By bringing recognizable figures onto the stage from popular culture, Shepard and his followers have been able to dispense with illusionary settings and obligatory exposition, fashioning instead a drama which is mystical and mysterious, with the ambiguous reverberations of a poem.

In one of his later plays, *Buried Child*, Shepard enters the terrain of family drama—but what a family! Set somewhere in the Middle West, the work features Ma and Pa Kettle, or their post-modern equivalents, raging, feuding, mean-spirited. Shepard here develops an entirely new form of domestic drama, enmeshed and entwined with the stuff of American myth. As the title suggests, there is a child interred in the back yard which represents the secret of the household, possibly of America itself. "That corpse you planted last year in your garden," wrote T. S. Eliot in *The Waste Land*, "Has it begun to sprout?" Shepard's buried child is threatening to sprout throughout the play.

One of the mysteries of the play is the paternity of the child. But this mystery (never resolved) is less important than its vegetable significance. It is associated with images of birth and renewal and seasonal change. The older characters, Dodge and Hallie, live in a dust bowl. But Tilden, their idiot son, is continually entering with armfuls of produce which he dumps over Dodge as if anointing him as a vegetable god. It is an entirely weird family, the only "normal" characters being Tilden's son, Vince, and his girlfriend, Shelley, who enters with the convictions that this family are typical Americans: "Dick and Jane and Spot and Mom and Dad and Junior and Sissy." But Tilden doesn't recognize his own son, and neither do his parents. In fact, the only physical contact between these young people and the family occurs when Bradley, a second son, brutally thrusts his hand into Shelley's mouth.

The attempt to bring the family secret into the light is a process of exhumation, the same process that drives Ibsen's *Ghosts*, but in this case the process is literal, since the secret is literally buried. Dodge announces his last will and testament and expires. Hallie has a vision of corn sprouting in the fallow garden. And Tilden enters with his last gift of rebirth and fertility—a bundle of rags and bones in his arms, the remains of the dead child.

There is no simple explanation for this powerful final image. It is the family secret—possibly all our family secrets—being exposed to common view. Or it could be a symbol of the failed promise of our native country—a land so full of possibility, where humankind could start afresh, whose hopes have now been buried, existing only as the rotting corpse of a child. Like much of Shepard's work, the play is a hallucination and therefore not readily available to logical explanation. But in the act of disintegrating the causal conventions of realistic family drama, Shepard has managed to reinterpret the conventional drama of guilt. For *Buried Child* takes the form of a self-accusation, rather than an indictment, in which guilt becomes the price we pay for being alive.

With Sam Shepard, the American theatre takes a step beyond the Newtonian universe into a world of dream, myth, and inner space. With Robert Wilson, it leaps into the universe of Einstein, developing new dimensions of outer space and inner time.

My reference to Einstein's universe is not gratuitous. All of Wilson's bizarre theatre pieces involve a relativity-influenced temporal and spatial sense, and one of his earlier works—the dance-opera-drama piece he created with the composer Philip Glass—was actually entitled *Einstein on the Beach*.

This five-hour meditation showed the influence of Einstein both in its physics and in its spirit. Every one of the actors was made up to resemble Albert Einstein (dressed in suspenders, gray pants, and tennis shoes), and the principal soloist, like Einstein a violinist, had a flowing white mane and a bushy white mustache.

The opera brought us from the world of the locomotive, which is to say the machinery of the Industrial Revolution, to the world of the spaceship, Einstein's culminating gift (along with the atomic bomb) to the twentieth century. Built around three separate settings—a train, a courtroom, and a field—connected by little dialogues in front of the curtain called "knee plays," the work dramatized (so subtly one absorbed it through the imagination rather than the mind) the change in perception—especially one's perception of time—that accompanied this technological development. The interminable length of the performance, therefore, became a condition of its theme, as did the strange schematic settings, the vertical and horizontal shafts of light, and the apparently meaningless snatches of dialogue.

A later creation called *The Forest*, one of many pieces Wilson created with German subsidy (in return for draining Germany's lavish arts treasury, it may very well be the most Teutonic of his works), extended his debt to Einstein even further. An epic adventure in fractured time devised with the musical connivance of David Byrne, *The Forest* was based on the Babylonian story of *Gilgamesh*, a Mesopotamian epic written in cuneiform on clay tablets around the second millennium before Christ (it was discovered only last century among the ruins of Nineveh). The piece paid homage to these mind-boggling spans of time through a kind of Wagnerian fusing of music, theatre, art, history, sociology, and myth. As one would expect, Wilson and his literary collaborators (Heiner Müller and Darryl Pinckney) deconstructed the story. But despite a radical adaptation which broke the causal narrative of epic and placed the action in the nineteenth century, *The Forest* contained more coherence than most Wilson works, signifying his growing interest in text.

Wilson and his collaborators interpreted the rivalry between Gilgamesh and the wild man Enkidu as a clash of culture and nature, urban versus nomadic life, the raw as opposed to the cooked, by translating the epic into a visual commentary on the rise of German industrialism, glancing sideways at its effect on the destruction of the Black Forest. The evening—which lasted almost four hours—was structured in seven acts, separated by two knee plays. In typical Wilsonian fashion, the acts paralleled each other (one and seven; two and six; etc.), with Act IV forming a solitary, ambitious centerpiece. Visual parallels abounded as well. The bars on the drawing-room windows, separating the industrialist Gilgamesh from his lobotomized workers, for example, resembled bars that fell over the opening of Enkidu's cave.

Those privileged to see *The Forest* were rewarded with a wealth of dazzling, exquisitely executed dream images which remained imprinted on the mind's eye long after the curtain fell: the splitting of the sun into planets, revealing a beached monster on the sand while a child played with a model of a small city; factory workers laboring on huge ladders near massive gears as Gilgamesh smoked in his chair, attended by eerie domestics and a weary lion; the golden Enkidu in his cave, accompanied by an armored knight, a figure in doublet and hose, a man cooking himself in a vat, an outsized porcupine; the slow-motion seduction of Enkidu by a lipstick-stained whore as animals and trees paraded across the stage in stately procession; the rock and ice landscapes of the concluding acts, where the two men joined battle with a dragon. It was a piece designed with such beauty that each stage picture constituted a work of art, reinforcing Wilson's position as one of our greatest visionary artists.

These, then, are some of the dramatic artists who have virtually demolished the "tasteless parlor" of illusionistic theatre, and not simply through the let's-pretend devices associated with, say, the theatre of Thornton Wilder. Wolfe, in an excess of satiric glee, knocks down the walls of the family home; Shepard walks his characters through these walls with vegetation in their arms; and Wilson investigates the outer reaches of the expanding universe. By leaping beyond the physical confines of the kitchen, the bedroom, and the living room, these writers are transcending the thematic limitations imposed by those rooms as well. Artists working in other forms have been responsive to the kinds of advances now affecting the modern consciousness—relativity theory, indeterminacy theory, black holes, quasars, bends in time, anti-matter, ESP, and the like. Now the theatre is showing some sign that it has not remained impassive before the liberating new possibilities of the imagination.

And that has been the destiny of all great art—whether theatrical, literary, visual, or musical, whether ancient or modern—to expand rather than constrict the structure of the imagination. The strict laws governing so much modern drama provide an atmosphere of safety and predictability, but only at the cost of severe limitations on the possibilities of creation. To live in uncertainty in such insecure, inchoate times as ours is to live in fear and trembling. But what the poet Keats called the "negative capability"—meaning our capacity to function with doubts and ambiguities—remains an essential condition of the poetic imagination. Like Molière's Monsieur Jourdain, we are beginning to discover that we have been speaking prose all our lives—and we have been listening to too much prose as well. But the nonlinear theatre fulfills some of the conditions of poetry by introducing us to the unexpected and by bringing us beyond the prosaic formulas of our social-psychological universe.

For it dredges a channel through which artists find their way to a hidden reality inaccessible to barren explanations and causal links. I hope it is obvious that I am not arguing here for obfuscation or obscurantism. If excessive rationalizing is the bane of modern theatre, then there is an equal danger in formulating mystery for its own sake, as I believe Edward Albee and Harold Pinter are sometimes prone to do. The true dramatic poet understands that symbols are a tool with which to reveal rather than to obscure, the key to turn those locks that remain impervious to conceptual thought.

And finally, this noncausal, nonlinear theatre will help to free us from the facile guilt-mongering of our accusatory playwrights. Rhetoric—as W. B. Yeats said in a famous passage—proceeds from the quarrel with others, poetry from the quarrel with ourselves. The rhetorical indignation so familiar to twentieth-century drama is a result of a failure to understand that the accusing finger may not belong to a blameless hand. Master Builder Solness denounced himself for failing to repair that crack in the chimney, even though he knew full well it had nothing to do with the fire that destroyed his house. Thus, he accepted his own guilt—a condition of being human—and thus, he transcended it—a condition of being an artist. Only through this double responsibility could he preserve the mysteries without losing his humanity, and go on to create a penetrating new art.

(1978; revised 1990)

Post-Naturalist Triumph

(*Balm in Gilead*)

In 1959, in my maiden piece for *The New Republic*, I reviewed *The Connection*, a play with music about derelicts and junkies by a young Chicago playwright named Jack Gelber. The first significant production of the 1984 New York season is the Circle Rep revival at the Minetta Lane of Lanford Wilson's *Balm in Gilead*, another play with music about derelicts and junkies, as directed by a young Chicago actor from Steppenwolf named John Malkovich. This might suggest that progress in the American theatre has been minimal over the past quarter of a century, and *Balm in Gilead*, first produced in 1965, just six years after *The Connection*, is certainly derivative of Gelber's work. Nevertheless, Wilson's sketchy, aimless investigation of underground Americans is presently providing the occasion for a brilliant piece of theatre, one which may well be remembered as a landmark of the post-naturalistic stage.

Post-naturalism (forgive the neologism, but one needs a term to describe this phenomenon) has been with us at least since the earlier days of the Living Theatre, the first company to mix Pirandellian and Brechtian theatrical devices with an exacting documentary style. It represents an effort to reproduce on stage the details of a plotless verisimilitude at the same time that its dramatic characters are wandering through the auditorium, haranguing and badgering the audience and otherwise exposing the illusionistic nature of the event. This is the theatre's last-ditch effort to salvage a tradition recently expropriated by visual media (especially the movies) infinitely better equipped to simulate a documentary reality. Never permitting the audience to forget it is watching an artificial rather than a real event, post-naturalism manages to preserve what is unique about the theatre—its immediacy and danger—while still fulfilling naturalism's mandate to explore the habits and habitations of an abandoned underclass.

Using Wilson's text as a scenario for improvisation, Malkovich creates a stylistic triumph with this technique. *Balm in Gilead* is a work from the playwright's early period, before a wistful romanticism began to soften his writing. It is a closely observed sociological study of hookers, hustlers, pimps, pushers, and dopers of every sexual persuasion converging on each other in an all-night coffee shop on Halloween—Gorky's *Lower Depths* transferred to Upper Broadway. For most of its length, the play avoids plot, theme, or purpose, but eventually two figures break free from this sketchily drawn crowd of twenty-nine characters to make a story: Joe, a part-time heroin pusher who wants to escape his profession, and Darlene, a good-time girl from Chicago. At the climax, after mating briefly with Darlene in her hotel room, Joe is stabbed to death by a hood sent by the gangster for whom he works, an event barely noticed by the denizens of the coffee shop. A casual murder, it emerges nonetheless as a highly melodramatic event, one which seems contrived when contrasted with the usual low pressure of the narrative. Like all naturalistic works, *Balm in Gilead* is persuasive and authentic only as long as it is pointless and meandering.

Without ever violating the spirit of Wilson's play, Malkovich discharges a directorial function that almost amounts to co-authorship. The suggestions of post-naturalist devices in the written text—music, for example, and an announcement of an intermission by one of the characters—Malkovich turns into an occasion for his own invention. First, he orchestrates a "sound design" that invades the overlapping dialogue, much of it improvised, enhancing it with thrilling sonic rock (the final Bruce Springsteen number literally rattles the seats of the theatre). And supplementing the single non-illusionistic break for coffee in the lobby, he employs a character named Dopey to conduct and stage-manage the entire evening with a lighted cigarette. Dopey (played by fellow Steppenwolf member Gary Sinise, who directed Malkovich in *True West*) is a chain-smoking bearded Afro-haired junkie in dark glasses who wanders through the action for no apparent purpose other than to announce the post-nuclear triumph of cockroaches over civilization. The first stoned raisonneur in theatrical history, Dopey controls the music, lights, and action of the show, waving his cigarette like a baton to call the characters to attention and activate their specials and spots.

But even before the play begins (post-naturalists know that plays should never "begin"), some of these derelicts are stumbling through the audience, selling lyrics for a sing-along, taking Polaroid shots of the spectators, nodding off in a corner. "Let's roll, man" brings the lights down in the auditorium and up on a seedy broken-down diner with plastic booths and graffiti walls where two homosexuals are ogling a male hustler named Tig and a couple of lesbians are quarrelling over an anorexic whore with corn-row runs in her stockings. Slumped over the counter is Babe, a character who utters no more than two or three lines in the whole evening but whose static drugged state, as enacted in the highly concentrated performance of Debra Engle, rivets your attention ("This piece of meat is done," observes one of the few who notice her, "take it off the fucking stove"). In short, none of the actors in this awesomely large cast (by Off-Broadway standards) is anything less than splendid or original, with the possible exception of the transvestite, Franny, played like a clone of John Lithgow in *Garp*.

The first and more convincing act is essentially local color filtered through a heroin-tinted spectrum. Following the intermission, the show is mostly monologues, the longest (five closely spaced pages of printed text) belonging to Darlene. In factual content, her tale is little more than an account of how she and her boyfriend once bought a marriage license and then neglected to get married. But in emotional content, as performed by Laurie Metcalf, her monologue is a complete history of a soul who, though blighted by life, never quite loses faith in existence despite all the evidence of her senses. Miss Metcalf is also a member of Steppenwolf (as is the gifted Glenne Headly, playing the dazed hooker whose ear she bends). Looking a little like a Barbie doll in a miniskirt, acting with a slight lisp and an authentic Chicago accent, laughing through her own witticisms, relating how "the license got shuffled up with a lot of other things, and got a bend across it, all bent up," she eventually builds the character into a shattering emotional breakdown.

Music comes up under the end of her speech; a spot is held on her anguished features; the audience answers with applause—an unnecessary coda, one of the director's few false moves. But the moment is followed immediately by an ugly encounter, where Malkovich pulls no punches, between the transvestite Franny and Tig, the hustler—surely one of the most explicit and brutal homosexual scenes ever seen in the

American theatre. And when Joe is stabbed in the midst of a children's Halloween revel—an event Wilson wants repeated three times—Malkovich stages the killing in a manner worthy of a streetwise choreographer, brutality and grace in fusion, a sanguinary dance of death.

"And I don't know," says Darlene, not even looking at the dead body of her lover. "Everyone was so tired and so down, and I thought, Christ, aren't we even moving? You know?" It is a decisive No answer to the questions asked in the Book of Jeremiah, from which Wilson took his ironic title—"Is there no balm in Gilead? Is there no physician there?"—and both playwright and director would seem to have provided an unflinching view of unmediated, unmedicated reality. Yet Wilson's play, for all its strengths, still falls short of being a satisfying work of art—not just because it fails to transcend its own naturalism and not because it is formally abrupt and incomplete, but because it somehow manages to contradict its own impulses. Wilson is almost Saroyanesque in his treatment of the lost and the dispossessed—whatever their habits and failings, almost all of his characters are basically goodhearted, with the exception of the hood who kills Joe. As in Saroyan's Manichaean *Time of Your Life*, this is a contained society disrupted by external evil; the romantic sentiment hidden in the tough shell of Wilson's later plays, beginning with *Hot l Baltimore*, is just one step away.

Still, whatever the seeds it may be planting, *Balm in Gilead* is neither sentimental nor romantic, and it has inspired a fine production, so let us be grateful. It has also established John Malkovich as a galvanizing director in the post-naturalist style and reconfirmed the talents of the Chicago Steppenwolf company, now unhappily disbanded and scattered. I long to see them in reunion soon, at work again with Malkovich on a great play from this tradition. How about O'Neill's *The Iceman Cometh*?

(1984)

One-Person Shows

(*Sex and Death to the Age 14; Mistero Buffo*)

Because the commercial theatre is presently too enfeebled to generate any trends, theatre critics have no material for end-of-season generalizations. I mean, it's bad enough that shows are closing and attendance is down, but pretty soon reviewers will be joining actors on the unemployment line—which may strike some as a form of poetic justice. In a slightly desperate effort to keep my job a little longer, I'm going to try and identify what I perceive to be a relatively new fashion in contemporary theatre: the one-man and one-woman show.

The multiplication of these offerings is, of course, a direct consequence of Broadway's celebrated economic woes. At a time when conventional forms of theatre are sinking under burdensome costs, one-person shows offer the precious advantage of reasonable budgets, supporting but a single Equity actor and very little in the way of physical production except for a table, a microphone, a change of costume, and a glass of water. Furthermore, the featured performer often functions as his own writer and director, which reduces not only royalties but the opportunity for disputes between stars and collaborators. What a blessing in the matter of program and poster billing alone!

The vogue of one-person shows, which started last year with Whoopi Goldberg, is now threatening to become epidemic. So far, the 1985–86 New York theatre season has featured Lily Tomlin winning a Tony for *The Search for Signs of Intelligent Life in the Universe*, Eric Bogosian doing contemporary character riffs in *Drinking in America* at the American Place, Dario Fo and Franca Rame alternating dazzling virtuoso evenings at the Joyce Theater, and Spalding Gray unfolding a trilogy of monologues at Lincoln Center's Mitzi E. Newhouse. The essence of theatre being conflict conveyed through dialogue and action, the one-person show probably belongs more to narrative than to drama (even the solo actor Thespis had a chorus to keep him company on the stage). Still and undeniably, there is dramatic satisfaction in watching a splendid actor shedding characters like skins while creating scenes and telling tales in ancient bardic fashion.

Spalding Gray is not so much a character actor as an engaging human being with what appears to be total recall about his life. I'd enjoyed his work on tour, but I dropped down to the Mitzi E. Newhouse to take another look at *Sex and Death to the Age 14*, the earliest of his autobiographical monologues. I wanted to see how he worked a New York audience, which is to say a disjointed group from hither and yon, with no particular geographical center. The absence of a core community made Gray's presentation somewhat nervous—he spoke faster than usual and with some uncertainty. Otherwise, he kept his customary charm and intimacy. Gray is an attractive man in his late forties with brown-gray hair and diabolical eyebrows, a former actor with The Wooster Group who for the past seven years has been accumulating an oral history of his time. Dressed in a Sears, Roebuck checked shirt, blue jeans, and black Reeboks, he appears on stage with the houselights up and, after diffidently greeting the audience, sits down at a table and unrolls memories, using a loose-leaf notebook as his prompter.

Sex and Death is the story of his childhood in Barrington, Rhode Island, and his evolution into sexual awareness behind the stern repressive backs of his Christian Science family. It is also a history of dead pets, from one cocker spaniel which continually took chunks out of his flesh to another, which got killed chasing cars, to a series of cats, most of them named Mittens, which ended up in various states of *rigor mortis*. Gray recounts his early experience of animal deaths with the same awed innocence he uses to describe his mother washing his "tinkler" ("I never knew it could be pleasurable until much later when I got to do it myself"). It is intriguing how this "normal" small-town childhood—the familiar bucolic material of so many plays and movies—could be so full of dread and ignorance. Kenneth Tynan once wrote a parody of *Our Town* that had the Stage Manager musing on lynching and Jew-baiting, but Gray suggests that Thornton Wilder ignored these social issues probably because they were virtually unknown in New England villages: "I never saw a black, a Jew, or a double bed until I moved to Boston."

What Wilder really censored from his small-town portraits, however, were the erotic components, and Gray generously fills in the lacunae. Telling of his first book of pornographic photos—it showed a man putting his semi-erection into a glass of water being drunk by a girl ("Did our parents do this in order to have us?")—then of a friend who amused himself by displaying his rectum, then of his petting sessions with Judy Brooks ("What?" asked an outraged friend, "you touched the place she pees out of?"), and finally of his first ejaculation after masturbating with a Davy Crockett beaver cap, Gray creates an erotic history of early adolescence that does for New England Protestants what Lenny Bruce and Philip Roth did for Brooklyn and New Jersey Jews. The piece ends with Gray, a rebellious teenager with "attitudinal problems," informing the headmaster of a private school that "since they invented the H-bomb, there is no more future."

Dario Fo has been called the funniest man in the world and to judge from *Mistero Buffo* (*Comic Mystery Play*), his title is thus far unchallenged. While his wife, Franca Rame, a passionate, handsome actress, is performing contemporary skits about the subjugation of women in *Tutta Casa, Letto e Chiesa* (*It's All Bed, Board, and Church*), Fo is fully engaged with an ancient historical tradition: he is the direct heir of those medieval Italian iconoclasts known as *giullàri*. To watch Fo perform is to see the glue that connects great Western comedy through the ages, from its roots in the satire of the goliards (and later Rabelais) on the excesses of the Church through *commedia dell'arte* and Molière, to its modern culmination in such cinematic clowns as Chaplin, Keaton, and the Marx Brothers.

Fo uses an improvised language he calls *grammelot*, a hodgepodge of dialects, peasant idioms, and invented sounds based on his parodic imitations of French, British, or American speech. Costumed in anarchist black slacks and shirt, with Marxist red socks, the white-haired Fo, with his chipmunk teeth and twinkling eyes, introduces his skits with quasi-historical discourses (translated on stage by the amiable Ron Jenkins) before launching into hilarious *grammelot* character sketches, rendered (rather unnecessarily) by English supertitles. These vary from night to night, according to the audience and the whims of the actor, but usually begin with his great acting triumph, the impersonation of a *zanni* so ravenously hungry that he consumes his own intestines as if they were spaghetti (he then proceeds to gourmandize a fly). Here Fo demonstrates comedy's indebtedness to mime, as he munches, slurps, chews, and digests imaginary objects, exalting his appetites in a grumbling basso voice. In his next piece, following a lecture on Molière's debt to Italian *commedia* traditions, he describes French fashions during the age of Louis XIV, informing us that the enormous wigs of the period were determined by the Sun King's small head, and that the mincing walk and court minuet resulted from the difficulty of urinating through masses of French lace.

Fo's most indignant satire is reserved for the second part of the evening, the mystery play itself, where he speaks from the standpoint of a disappointed believer mourning the betrayal of the hierarchy of spirit by the hierarchy of office. Ridiculing the vice of indulgences—the sale of absolution for profit by greedy clerics—and the medieval passion for collecting sanctified relics (the bones of one saint were later discovered to be the remains of a woolly mammoth), Fo proceeds to create a comic reconstruction of the resurrection of Lazarus as seen from the perspective of the hawkers and concessionaires. This Monty Pythonesque number segues into a ferocious attack on the medieval

Pope Bonifacio VIII, who consolidated the temporal power of the Church, a vicious sadist who nailed monks by their tongues to city doors. And, finally, he turns his attention to the modern Church, with a skit featuring John Paul II, a Pope with a passion for kissing babies, not to mention the ground of every country he visits—which concludes with an irreverent reenactment of his attempted assassination.

Fo sprinkles all this with pseudo-scholarly asides about the origin of capitalism, the relationship between Elizabethan English and the language of a state he calls "South Virginia," and the stereotypical American notion of Italians as skirt-chasers with beards, sideburns, and black-and-white shoes. What drives this comedy is not just amusement over the absurdity of life but a profound political and religious outrage. Fo is equally indebted to Karl and Groucho Marx, which is to say, to political radicalism and comic anarchism. He is not only a one-man show but, however collective his hidden agenda, a one-man revolution—the revolution of the individual against institutions, of common sense against official piety, of the body against the soul. Represented previously in New York only by a weak production of his play *Accidental Death of an Anarchist*, periodically barred by the State Department on suspicion of heresy and subversion, Dario Fo has now burst onto our shores in all his gargantuan glory, and neither comedy nor politics will ever be the same. The genie is out of the bottle; the release is liberating us all.

(1986)

The Hit of the Building

(The World According to Me!)

The Jewish comedian Jackie Mason is a big hit at the Brooks Atkinson—a theatre which lately has been harboring mostly British imports (*Steaming, Edmund Kean, Noises Off, Benefactors*). Mason is an import from an entirely different tradition. "It's a pleasure to meet me," he modestly admits upon entering the stage. "I'm the star of this building." I suspect that's what the Brooks Atkinson represents to Mason—a *building*, not significantly different from the Las Vegas nightclubs and Borscht Belt hotels he's played in the past. And among the many refreshing things about his show, *The World According to Me!*, is its total lack of cultural piety. Having improbably won a Tony, Mason is now playing to 100 percent capacity. It was nice to catch his act after he had had the time to reflect on his totally unexpected success. "I'm glad I'm a hit," he confides to the audience. "My career stunk till now . . . now I'm too big a star to talk to anyone." Sitting on the edge of the stage, describing his early life as a rabbi (bored, he started telling jokes to the congregation and soon began charging cover and a minimum), Mason testifies to the ecstatic pleasures of postponed popularity.

A great deal of his appeal is nostalgic. How long has it been since we heard a comedian, matjes herring resonating in his voice, taking so for granted the Jewish identity of his audience? I was reminded of the glory days of Tamiment, where I first encountered the frenetic humor of Sid Caesar, of Grossinger's and the Concord before they became convention sites. I remembered the burlesque comedians at the Old Gaiety, the insult humor of Milton Berle, the high-stepping musicals starring Bobby Clark or Phil Silvers, Mel Brooks' *2000 Year Old Man*, the rude jostling waiters at Ratner's and Rappaport's. As a matter of fact, Mason's humor is redolent of restaurants; it stimulates the salivary glands; much of it concerns food. He is a comedian unafraid of stereotyped ethnic or racial generalizations, chief among them the assumption that Gentiles like to drink and Jews like to eat. As for Puerto Ricans: "They brought back something to this country that we almost lost—cockroaches." Gentiles don't have them because "Just how much can a cockroach drink?"

Cheerfully insisting that he abhors ethnic jokes, Mason devotes the greater part of his act to outrageous, usually prohibited, ethnic characterizations. Italians are tough street fighters; blacks are snazzy dressers ("They got no closets, they wear everything at once"). Poles are dumb; Hispanics strip cars (he travels to Puerto Rico every year "just to visit my hubcaps"). Yet Mason is far from being a Jewish chauvinist; his most telling satire is reserved for arrivistes and suburbanites, which is to say most of the coreligionists out front. For him, every Jew is neurotically devoted to status symbols—the plush apartment lobby, the Muzak-filled elevator, the Mercedes he can't afford to gas, the yacht he's never learned to sail ("Is there a bigger shmuck on earth than a Jew with a boat?"), or—a Jew's most precious possession—his car telephone ("The Gentiles are crashing from drinking, Jews are crashing from dialing"). The Gentile worships his boss and will sell his soul for a key to the toilet; the Jew thinks "the man is a shmuck," and will settle only for a key to the vault.

The Jew is embarrassed to work with his hands, he can't even turn on his VCR, while "there's nothing happier than a Gentile with a broken car . . . On Sunday, you can't find them, they're all under their cars." As for the Jewish wife, when she says *I do*, "that's the last thing she does." She hasn't cooked a meal in nine years and he's "shlepping garbage." The transformation of the Jewish husband into a Japanese wife explains the popularity of Chinese restaurants (an anomaly, since you never see a Chinese husband in a delicatessen). Jews change their names, they cut off their noses, they give French names to their Miami condos—all as a result of what Mason calls the "Identity Crisis of Minorities in This Country." What he means is Jews. When the show is over, the Gentiles will always tell him how funny he was. "You know what the Jews will say? Too Jewish."

Rude as his humor is, Mason knows exactly how to work his largely Jewish audience to love his insults. Ambling onto a stage which features a star-studded cyclorama and a revolving globe ("There's no furniture in this show—that is the main quality; when you go into a furniture store, do they show you a comedian?"), Mason looks like the offspring of Edward G. Robinson and Joe Papp, with his flat face, large lips, hooded eyes, and modified Afro. His Yiddish-inflected Sten-gun delivery is illustrated with hand motions close to his waist which saw and slice the air. Within seconds, he has established an atmosphere of nightclub intimacy in a house of considerable dimension, largely by identifying some unfortunate innocent in the first row as the mute target of his caustic asides ("Did you come here just to get even with the Jewish people?"). A projection of the famous Hollywood sign and the Beverly Hills Hotel ("Now it looks like a show") follows his warm-up, initiating a turn on the pretensions of the West Coast, where everyone's a producer, talking deals and handing out business cards ("That's all they produce—cards"). Mason is offended by the prevalence of sex scenes in movies ("They say, Doesn't everyone have sex? I say, Doesn't everyone have soup?"), and even more by the paleolithic mutterings of such movie stars as Sylvester Stallone. "I talk poifect, I can't make a living. Who is he to make such a fortune when I have to talk to a shmuck like this?"

Mason's priceless parody of the inarticulate Stallone, followed by equally cogent riffs on Alfred Hitchcock and James Cagney, establishes him as a gifted impersonator with a strong satiric bent. And when the projection changes to a map of the world, he demonstrates a powerful capacity for political commentary as well. Noting that the world is made up of two-thirds water ("Do we really need all this water? Maybe the Gentiles need it, but the Jews have a swimming pool"), he proceeds to take on all the nation's leaders, starting with Reagan ("A great President, it just so happens this is not his field"). Mason is delighted with Reagan's unfailing cheerfulness—always laughing, though nobody knows the joke. He just can't believe he got the job. All the other recent Presidents have always looked "nauseous." But this guy always goes "Ha, ha, ha." Maybe he's proud of the fact that Grenada has never attacked this country, or of his continually failing memory—"The only thing I remember about Iran is that I forgot."

Kennedy and Kissinger (also savagely imitated) can't be understood because of incomprehensible Boston and Viennese accents. Gary Hart's campaign manager, when he returns to the campaign, will be Dr. Ruth. Ollie North turns out to be a guy "who never made more than $85 a week and is controlling the whole world." As for Nixon, "I love a crook who knows his business . . . Every week they caught him and every week somebody else went to jail." In perhaps the wildest moment of the show, Mason offers his own diagnosis of Nixon's physical afflictions while in office. He had syphilis. "You can't screw 200 million people and end up with phlebitis." Inspired by his own medical acumen, he characterizes Reagan's visits to the hospital as those of an ailing Pinocchio. "Every time he says he never heard of the Contras, he gets another nose operation."

This, I submit, is political analysis of the highest order, and it becomes high geopolitical analysis during his observations on Israel. Mason epitomizes the American Jew's astonishment over Israeli pugnacity. Israel's tough army ("I thought Puerto Ricans drove the Jewish tanks") baffles a man who always believed that Jews were incapable of street fighting or terrifying other races ("I never saw four black people say, Watch out, there's a Jew over there"). Guns are not for Jews—"unless there's coffee and cake." Yet the Israeli military triumphs in the Middle East fill him, like most Jews, with a secret pride—why, Israel only turned back from taking the Suez Canal because it didn't have a boardwalk.

Curiously, Mason's wit falters when he turns to show business. His Al Jolson, Sinatra, and Crosby impersonations seem a little fatigued, though he taps considerable energy out of his virulent hatred of folk singers ("There's nobody on earth who's lower—and I say this with the highest respect. They're always saying 'Everybody'—you sing and they make the money"). And his impersonation of Ed Sullivan—so stunned by Mason's Jewish humor that for the rest of his life he couldn't move his shoulders—brings back memories of a great vaudeville age. Jackie Mason is the last of a vanishing species, a species of unafraid Jewish comedians and unashamed Yiddish culture. Catch him before it vanishes altogether.

(1987)

Look Back with Nostalgia

(*Anything Goes; Into the Woods*)

The American musical has become the El Dorado of the Broadway theatre—that lost paradise of total gratification where artists and backers once disported on golden meadows to the sound of ringing cash registers. A character in *42nd Street* elegizes musical comedy as "the most beautiful words in the English language," but there's a mournful obsolescent ring to those words now, as if they were already being cycled into archaic language. Once hyperbolized as "our greatest native art form," the American musical has fallen into disrepair, and the success of Andrew Lloyd Webber's glitz machines only heightens the miserable condition of our own maladroit contraptions. Just as the Japanese and Koreans have surpassed the United States in the mass-produced technology first created by Henry Ford, so the British have usurped the only theatrical form ever invented (or respected) on Broadway. The glories are all in the past, which may account for the spate of musical theatre histories on publishers' current lists.

It may also account for the pervasive aura of nostalgia that surrounds the recent offerings, whether revivals or new works. How many American musicals today take place in the present or deal with issues even remotely meaningful? It is no accident, as the Marxists used to say, that the remake of Cole Porter's *Anything Goes* opened at the Vivian Beaumont in the same week as the stock-market crash. First produced during the Depression, it helped then to avert American eyes from the breadlines, the apple stands, and the pinstriped bodies hurtling out of corporate windows. The revamped production at the Lincoln Center

Theater is beautifully engineered to provide us with the same insouciant distractions.

Equipped with a new book by Timothy Crouse and John Weidman, based on an original script by Guy Bolton, P. G. Wodehouse, Howard Lindsay, and Russel Crouse—and dominated by Cole Porter's enthralling music and lyrics—*Anything Goes* still possesses that enchanting quality of total irrelevance that made it so appealing in the thirties. If anything, it is even more irrelevantly appealing today. Set in the luxury-class quarters of an ocean liner when, in our own age, cruise ships exist mainly to carry tourist groups to the Caribbean for duty-free shopping, populated with types that vanished from popular culture soon after Fred Astaire and Ginger Rogers stopped dancing the carioca, *Anything Goes* functions as a voyage through the high seas of the past in the interior of a time boat, the theatrical equivalent of two hours spent watching reruns in a repertory movie house.

Under Jerry Zaks's shrewd direction, it's an artful reconstruction. Tony Walton's sets and costumes alone deserve a place in a retrospective exhibit of Musical Comedy Memorabilia. Ornamented with the round silvered curves of Art Deco, the S.S. *American* cruises the silver seas featuring a white piano bar, a red-white-and-blue smokestack, and a ship's orchestra performing on the top deck. As for the characters, they are off the streamlined Art Deco rack as well—a Yale alum drinking his way across the ocean, a goofy gangster posing as a minister, a square British lord, dowagers and debutantes, camera-toting reporters in checkered coats, long-legged chorines in flared sailor pants and high heels, the hard-boiled siren Reno Sweeney making out with all available males, the feckless hero Billy Crocker wooing his rich lady love in disguise and ending up with both the girl and a zillion dollars. Fox-trots up and down the gangways, choral tap dances that rattle the decks, gypsy turns and tangos, production numbers by the entire crew and officer staff—*Anything Goes* recycles everything from the halcyon days of the Astaire-Rogers shipboard romances. The only characters missing are Eric Blore and Edward Everett Horton.

What is also missing is a book. The Crouse-Weidman revamping improves on the jerry-built original, but the jokes are feebly dependent on the incompatibility of British elegance and American slang ("Bring me my tea and step in it") and the plot remains a crude comedy of disguise and misunderstanding. Still, the books for these musical comedies were never more than scaffolding for songs, and Porter's songs retain all their melodic surprise and lyrical wit. It's odd to be reminded that such classics as "I Get a Kick Out of You," "You're the Top," "It's Delovely," "Easy to Love," "Blow, Gabriel, Blow," or even the eponymous "Anything Goes," not to mention the eleven other superb numbers, were once show tunes—not just because they have all achieved an enduring independent life, but because today our musical comedy hits are fortunate to feature just one memorable song, not to speak of seventeen. Porter's songs emerge out of nowhere in *Anything Goes*—the occasion for music is determined by time, pace, and mood, rather than plot requirements—but they represent the essence of the show. The orchestra, under the bright direction of Edward Strauss, plays these tunes smartly, and they are well sung by virtually everyone in the cast. Patti LuPone, especially, brings a sharp energy to the role of Reno Sweeney, her red velvet slack suit and auburn hair handsomely framing her generous, slightly cruel mouth. And Howard McGillin is an attractive Billy Crocker, though he dances like a four-letter man at the senior prom and his baritone range doesn't easily accommodate the countertenor tones he's often forced to produce. All in all, *Anything Goes* is a pleasant pastime for those who have the time to pass. If I sound a bit resistant to its charms, well, I'm getting older and my time is somewhat limited.

The talented pair who brought forth *Sunday in the Park with George* have now created another musical. It's called *Into the Woods* and is playing at the Martin Beck. Stephen Sondheim, who wrote the music and lyrics, and James Lapine, who wrote the book, are both highly sophisticated gentlemen of considerable wit. But I looked in vain for the animating impulse behind this new work, apart from the desire to collaborate on a new conversation piece. *Anything Goes*, and other thirties musicals, exist to showcase wonderful tunes. *Into the Woods* doesn't have much to contribute in the way of music—it is Sondheim at his most tuneless and doggerel, trying his hand at nursery songs—so I suppose we're meant to be satisfied with the concept. Still, the evening lacks conviction, the concept seems forced. I sat through this thing, fidgeting in my seat, a witness once again to the will trying to do the work of the imagination.

Into the Woods is structured in two acts—the first a fairly conventional rendering of familiar fairy tales, the second a mordant commentary on the afterlife of its characters, with a glance at Bruno Bettelheim's Freudian analysis of fairy tale and myth, *The Uses of Enchantment*. Lapine's interest in psychiatric material was first evident in *Twelve Dreams*, his theatricalized version of a Jungian case study about a young girl tortured by prophetic dreams concerning her own premature death. But this sort of commentary is invariably thinned, if not vulgarized, on the Broadway stage. As in *Sunday in the Park with George*, which followed a stunning first-act tableau with a self-conscious Chromolume coda, the overintellectualized conclusion of *Into the Woods* is an excrescence on material which is the more powerful the less it is explained.

The Grimm fairy tales have already been sensitively adapted to the stage in Paul Sills's *Story Theater*, not to mention the Philip Glass–Robert Moran–Arthur Yorinks opera *The Juniper Tree*, both of which, through simple fidelity to the source material, allowed their deeper meanings to resonate. *The Juniper Tree*, for example, with its account of stepmother infanticide, parental cannibalism, beheadings, resurrections, and reconciliations, contains enough mythical material to fill a dozen psychiatric casebooks, a slew of religious and classical mythologies. But its power lies in permitting the spectators to see these correspondences for themselves. The Sondheim-Lapine adaptation, on the other hand, even in its relatively straightforward opening act, lacks innocence, as if a couple of urban intellectuals were remembering their childhoods through a haze of cocktail parties and couch sessions.

Into the Woods starts with projections of the first pages of two familiar Grimm Brothers tales, "Cinderella" and "Jack and the Beanstalk," plus one, "The Baker and His Wife," invented by Lapine. Along with the tales of "Rapunzel" and "Little Red Riding Hood," these are then woven into a consecutive narrative through the device of a witch who exhorts the baker to seek for objects (Jack's beans, Rapunzel's locks, etc.) that will cure his wife's childlessness. In the dark woods, very little is permitted to remain implicit. The Wolf in "Little Red Riding Hood," for example, is a fully sexual animal, complete with a hint of genitals, and when he devours her ("a full day of eating for both"), the erotic implications are made fully manifest. Too often, the stories are show-busied up with winks and smirks ("I'm afraid I was rude, now I'm being pursued, and I'm not in the mood," sings Cinderella), while the characters seem drawn more from musical comedy—Jack from *Big River*, Riding Hood from *Annie*, the Baker's Wife from *Oklahoma!*—than from the pages of children's literature. Still, the first act at least retains a semblance of respect for the conventions of fairy tales, including the happy endings.

In the second act, however, Grimm turns grim, as Lapine and Sondheim demonstrate what happens to such people *afterward*, when their wishes are granted. The wife-swapping Prince is unfaithful to Cinderella, Rapunzel becomes a screeching nag, the Baker's wife is killed, and when the Giant's widow comes to take revenge for the murder of her husband by Jack, the whole world turns nuclear, bathed in an orange glow. The moon is covered in smog, the trees are blasted, the woods are ashen—punishment, apparently, for the participation of fairy-tale characters in the sexual revolution. Cinderella and Riding Hood find each other in the mist to sing "You Are Not Alone," a song reprised by the Baker to Jack, though minutes before he was going to feed him to the Giantess. In this world, one suspects, consistent motives are less important than plugging the ballad, even one suspiciously reminiscent of "You'll Never Walk Alone." At the end, everyone pairs off, regardless of their previous relationships, and the blasted woods return to their former dark glory. We are left with the musical moral: "Careful the things you say / Children will listen," which may be a warning against reading anything to kids at bedtime besides health manuals or mail-order catalogues.

Tony Straiges' leafless bowers and vine-encrusted scoop are a handsome complement to the production, though the setting seems a little derivative for such an original stage artist. Bernadette Peters, as the Witch, manages to preserve her enticing powder-puff pout under the obligatory warts and frizzle, Robert Westenberg is a stalwart Prince, and Kim Crosby's Cinderella has the naïve beauty and innocent grace one seeks in vain throughout the rest of the show. It is not the fault of Chip Zien or Joanna Gleason as the Baker and his Wife that they come on like Chico Marx and Ado Annie, or of Tom Aldredge that he is featureless in the part of the Narrator (in *Story Theater*, at least, narrators are allowed to transform into characters). The actors are stuck in a world where urban cynicism alternates with nostalgic sentiment, where show-biz tinsel glitters on the bark of fairy-tale trees.

(1987)

The Shape of the New

(*Geniuses; Edmond*)

If anything as amorphous as American drama can be said to have a shape, it is possible to detect a pattern in the new plays of the eighties; at least, a number of their authors share similar values, characteristics, and backgrounds. In their twenties and thirties, many of them sons and daughters of Harvard and Yale, they have recently settled near such enterprising producing agencies as Playwrights Horizon, the Second Stage, the Manhattan Theatre Club, and the Ensemble Theatre Company. What unites them is a wry, jaded, urban sensibility, and a fascination with their own college-educated, overpsychoanalyzed, media-saturated generation. The dexterity with which they perform sociological CAT scans suggests that they are also the children of Jules Feiffer and Garry Trudeau, though they have yet to show the interest of their mentors in moral or political issues.

The school of playwrights I am describing includes, among others, Christopher Durang (*Beyond Therapy*), Wendy Wasserstein (*Uncommon Women and Others*), Ted Talley (*Coming Attractions*), James Lapine (*Table Settings*), and Deborah Eisenberg (*Pastorale*), all of them writing in a cogent, amusing, often acid style. To this list, we can now add the name of Jonathan Reynolds, whose new play, *Geniuses*, has had a successful debut at Playwrights Horizon. Reynolds has based his plot on the circumstances surrounding the making of Francis Ford Coppola's epic near-debacle *Apocalypse Now*, though the subject of the film has been changed from the Vietnam War to the conflict in Angola. Here called *Parabola of Death* and twenty-eight days behind schedule, the plague-ridden movie is being shot in a small village in the Philippines; when the play begins, it is clear why it is so far over the budget. The screenwriter is demolishing his typewriter because he can't think up an ending, the art director is shooting crippled water buffalo, the Playboy bunny has dysentery, the makeup man is wrestling with the delusion that he is Ernest Hemingway, and the set is being battered by a typhoon.

These are the ingredients of farce, and for the first two acts Reynolds displays the manipulative skills of a literate farceur, Ben Hecht with an honors degree in English. The play seems like a rewrite of *Twentieth Century*, its subject being the capricious rule of imperial "genius" directors—today invested with the means to create their own nations, even their own wars. What this playwright tells us is that the contemporary American film world is significant, not as an arm of culture, but rather as an extension of venture capitalism, possibly even an alternative form of government. For Reynolds' bankable prodigy, Milo McGee McGarr, "the deal is the only exciting thing about making a movie—five points, ten cases of Guinness, my own chopper." In short, the prime dividend of films is *making* money—not having it or spending it: "There is nothing as creative or romantic as business in America."

Reynolds regards this with a detached air, alternately awed and amused by the monster he has uncovered. He is equally neutral toward Milo's cowering, typhoon-locked underlings—particularly Jocko, the screenwriter—as they scurry about trying to hold on to their jobs, their Stolichnaya, and the half-exposed buttocks of Skye, the Playboy bunny with whom they share their wicker quarters. Skye's tempting *pulkes* motivate the only action in the play. A quintessential West Coast loony, having gone through est, actualization, and primal screaming before being converted to "wattage therapy," she has a passion for her place of origin exceeded only by Jocko's contempt for it ("I don't hate L.A., where the smog creeps in on little rat's feet"). Their arguments over the relative merits of the two coasts form the basis for a witty, if somewhat loquacious, sexual debate. But the plot grows darker when Skye is badly beaten by the sadistic art director whose advances she has spurned.

Although Skye's colorfully bruised face is hugely admired by the makeup man (he is always looking for fresh inspiration), it is potentially dangerous to Milo when that worthy finally makes his appearance late in the play. He needs his art director; she wants to imprison him for life. The impasse is broken with a deal. In return for a huge sum of money, tax-free, a part in Milo's next picture, the privilege of pummeling the art director's private parts, and the possibility of becoming the next president of Paramount, she agrees to return to her beloved Pismo Beach—and Jocko, abandoning the picture before he is fired from it, agrees to meet her there for three glorious days of sex and wattage therapy.

With its frenetic pace and rough masculine bantor, *Geniuses* never quite decides whether it wants to be social satire or commercial farce, the movie of *Mash* or its incarnation as a television series. The production, under the well-controlled direction of Gerald Gutierrez, shares some of the same ambivalence, vacillating between hyperactive door slamming and dark character portraiture. I was impressed by the actors—particularly Joanne Camp as the lubricious bunny, Peter Evans as the mordant Jocko, and Kurt Knudson as a Falstaffian makeup man—and the sound, lights, and special effects are very deftly executed and designed. But the ambiguity of attitude plunges the play into a moral vacuum—an uncertainty of tone so typical of the playwrights of the eighties, so reflective of their confused, unanchored world.

David Mamet is a playwright of the seventies, and ever since his brilliant debut with *American Buffalo* and *Sexual Perversity in Chicago* he has been having a little difficulty getting a purchase on the problems of this decade. With his new play, *Edmond*, now being performed in a semi-workshop production at the Goodman Theatre in Chicago, he has accomplished something of a breakthrough. As directed by Gregory Mosher, *Edmond* is a remarkably cruel play—ruthless, remorseless, unremittingly ugly. Written in that terse banal naturalism that has become Mamet's staccato trademark, it follows the spiritual journey of a stocky middle-class young man who wakes up one morning to tell his wife that he is deserting her. Leaving the safety of his home, he embarks on a terrifying odyssey through the urban landscape, looking for sexual and other satisfactions but instead finding violence and fraud. Beaten up and robbed, he buys a knife for protection. Mugged by a pimp, he turns on his attacker and kills him.

In his developing madness, Edmond becomes one with the hostile world he has invaded, until in a particularly brutal scene he stabs to death a waitress who has taken him home. His whole being now is riddled with hatred—of blacks, of women, of humankind itself: "This world is a piece of shit. There is no law. There is no history."

Eventually, Edmond is apprehended and imprisoned. His cellmate, a gigantic sleepy-eyed black man, listens stoically to Edmond's philosophizing before unzipping himself and forcing Edmond to commit an act of fellatio ("Right now, Jim, and you'd best be nice"). When the victim reports it to the authorities, he is told: "It happens." In the final scene, Edmond is on the lower bunk talking to his cellmate above about the nature of God and the universe ("Maybe we're here to be punished . . . Do you think we go somewhere when we die?"). When he is finished with this primitive, oddly affecting metaphysics, he reaches up, in the last gesture of the play, to hold the hand of the man who sodomized him and kiss him good night.

What Mamet has written is a version of *Woyzeck* in the modern city, displaying not only Büchner's hallucinatory power but also the same capacity to show compassion for lowly inarticulate wretches without mitigating their awful fates. He has pushed our faces into a world which most of us spend our waking hours trying to avoid, finding a kind of redemption in the bleakest, most severe alternatives. I don't think he will be thanked much for this, but I for one want to thank him—for the play, even in its current rough state; for the production, even though it lacks a scenic strategy; and for the brave performances of the entire company, particularly Paul Butler as the prisoner and Colin Stinton as Edmund Burke—the namesake of the man who wrote *The Vindication of Natural Society.*

(1987)

Poisoned Airwaves

(*Talk Radio*)

Talk Radio at Joseph Papp's Public Theater belongs to a growing list of theatre works (others are David Mamet's *The Water Engine* and Richard Foreman's *Film Is Evil: Radio Is Good*) which tap the radio medium as a source of social commentary and cultural revelation. Entirely composed of talk, denied any visual distractions, radio has the capacity to penetrate the secret corners of the national spirit, and *Talk Radio*, as written by Eric Bogosian after an original idea by Tad Savinar, is a cruel probe into the dark corners of modern America. It is an effort to do for the stage in the eighties what Nathanael West did for the novel in the thirties—to give expression to the disenfranchised, benighted, desperate millions who seek salvation in a world where God has been displaced by folk such as Jerry Falwell. Barry Champlain, a popular talk-show figure on an all-talk station, monitors the calls of the sleepless booboisie, the frightened, demented, and suicidal, listening in a state of blank anomie before silencing their threats and complaints with a cut-off button or a vicious rejoinder. Chain-smoking, dissipated, deeply depressed himself, sinking deeper into hatred for his listeners and his own behavior, Champlain is sucked against his will into the swamps of human suffering—like West's Miss Lonelyhearts, a man poisoned by the misery of the world he lives off.

Champlain blows bored smoke rings while callers rave about pollution, transvestism, "the mess this country is in," our lack of patriotism. He listens to a pregnant girl trying to track down her lover, a whacked-out druggie who claims to have killed his girlfriend with an overdose. An anti-Semite accuses him of being Jewish, another bigot calls him a homosexual. Champlain responds with icy sarcasm ("Are you on drugs or is this your naturally normal voice?"), when he is not flipping the cut-off button or taking breaks from the flow of venom and suffering in the calm trough of a commercial.

In somewhat superfluous monologues by his producer, his assistant, and his researcher, the play tries to provide a motivating background for Champlain, though he is more interesting just behaving. An ex-actor, he first went into "subversive" radio having discovered that "talking is thinking out loud." He knew how to pull secrets out of people, and his producer—Dan Woodruf—learned how to market this gift to the networks. At the moment Woodruf is worried (so is the sponsor) that the felonious druggie who called—Barry has invited him to come to the studio—is going to create a scandal on the air. When the hophead arrives, giggling, shaking his legs, wired to the breaking point, Champlain eyes him wearily: "I sincerely hope you do not represent the future of this country." The kid is a fraud; he invented the entire murder story just to get on the air. Barry considers quitting, going back to Akron. Catatonic, he commits the one impermissible act of radio—silence. After forty-five seconds of dead air, he admits to his listeners, "I guess we're stuck with each other," and signs off. The new host arrives for the next show—a female psychologist, a jaundiced version of Dr. Ruth, poised to offer slick solutions to her listeners' sexual problems.

There isn't much story or character development in this piece, apart from Champlain sinking into his own self-disgust, but at times it cuts very deeply. Bogosian plays Champlain—his eyes hooded, his curly black hair bedizening his head like an Armenian Harpo Marx—with a ferocious intensity. He is an actor who suffers for his craft, and he is abetted by a very able cast, particularly Mark Metcalf as Woodruf and Michael Wincott as the druggie. Frederick Zollo has contributed sharp uncompromising direction, though allowing abstract projections to accompany the radio dialogue shows a certain distrust for the material. *Talk Radio* is engrossing enough without illustrations. In fact, the disembodied nature of our national poisons—the acid in the ether—is precisely its point. As for David Jenkins's glass-and-linoleum setting of the radio studio, it provides a plush contrast to the rot and deterioration confirmed by the play.

(1987)

The Shlepic
(*The Phantom of the Opera*)

It could be argued that we no longer have theatre on Broadway, we have only Events. And the blame for this rests squarely at the door of economics and the media. Recognizing that few people today are prepared to meet the soaring costs of theatregoing unless assured of a blockbuster, the press, television, and radio have been devoting more and more space to hyping special large-scale attractions. Anything that promises big sales through advance publicity receives massive pre-opening and post-opening coverage—features, double reviews, interviews, follow-ups, even audits of the income of its creators—until we are smothered under an avalanche of information we have no desire to know. This is a variant on the morphology of the hit, but it has grown to extravagant proportions. As Russell Baker noted in a recent column, people will buy tickets only to a show they can't get into. Success in the Broadway theatre is based on a culture of scarcity.

By this measure, there would be a run even on Edsels were there a shortage of parts, and lots of theatrical Edsels have gone on the market lately masquerading as Rolls-Royces. Under such conditions, what can criticism do but fall into lockstep, praising what it has no power to alter? Even with bad reviews, the blockbuster continues to play to full houses and huge advance sales; even when heaped with scorn, the lachrymose engineer who manufactured the Event can row through his tears to the bank. By the end of the run, he probably owns the bank.

The critic-proof Event has resulted in a whole new theatre genre which I call the "Shlepic." Often originating in England, and always costing millions, it takes New York by storm and runs for centuries to standing ovations. The earliest of these Shlepics was *Cats*, followed hard upon by *Les Misérables* and *Starlight Express*, with *Chess* and *Carrie* still to come. (Is it possible that *The Mahabharata* is an avant-garde version of the Shlepic?) The latest, and by far the most successful, in this series is *The Phantom of the Opera* by the onlie begetter of the genre, Andrew Lloyd Webber. This musical generated $17 million in advance sales before it even opened, and now you can't buy a ticket until next Tish'a b'Av. Costing $8 million to produce, *The Phantom of the Opera* is not a musical play so much as the theatrical equivalent of a corporate merger. We follow the plot with less interest than its box-office reports; we can barely hear the music above the jingle of its cash register.

There are people moving around the stage of the Majestic, but the star of the show is obviously the chandelier. I've sometimes spoken of leaving a musical singing the set; this is the first time I've gone home singing the chandelier. What a piece of work! It may look like an ordinary object, sitting there lumpishly on the floor as you enter, but just when you're wondering why the set looks so drab, it rises laboriously from its moorings, like Old Deuteronomy's neon-flashing tire in *Cats*, and sails over your head to take its place amid transformed scenery, to the gasps of the audience. I'll say this for *The Phantom of the Opera*: You're never in doubt about where the production budget went. Most of it was lavished on this redoubtable piece of stage machinery, which makes another entrance at the end of the first act, gliding over our heads, executing a few barrel rolls and Immelmanns, then dropping gently if anticlimactically to the stage. I was disappointed when it failed to take a personal bow at the curtain call.

The Phantom of the Opera, as you doubtless know, is based on Gaston Leroux's 1911 variant on "Beauty and the Beast." As a literary work, it has as much value as the novels of Paul de Kock, but Leroux's feverish melodramatic plot was perfect material for silent films, where it gave Lon Chaney an opportunity to display one of his thousand faces. The hideousness of that disfigured face, as Chaney pumped and pounded away at his underground organ, is still the most memorable feature of the movie; and mimed silence is still the most appropriate medium for the plot. In the musical, the Phantom is allowed to express himself in song, through the overheated lyrics of Charles Hart and the supercharged music of Mr. Lloyd Webber, and while it is true that anything too silly to speak can be sung, I couldn't help longing for Mr. Chaney's golden silence. *The Phantom of the Opera* passes itself off as an opera about opera. It not only takes place in an opera house, it features nonstop singing and revolves around scenes from operatic works. But although this strategy gives the production designer (Maria

Bjornson) ample opportunity to create some monumental sets and glittering costumes for simulations of works by Mozart, Verdi, Meyerbeer, and Massenet, Lloyd Webber's music, though also presumably based on operatic models, somehow always comes out sounding like a Puccini score clotted with damp Parmesan cheese. Here, the composer is still hung up between writing theatrical music and devising songs that might hit the charts. As usual, he delivers one such overplugged tune—in *Cats*, it was "Memory," in *The Phantom of the Opera*, "The Music of the Night"—that lifts itself lyrically for a moment from the gluey mass of kitsch.

But *The Phantom of the Opera*, like other obnoxious offspring, is really meant to be seen, not heard. The story of a little girl from the *corps de ballet* who steps in and becomes a star when the diva resigns in a huff was more amusing in *42nd Street*. And the heroine's relationship with the Phantom—"a lonesome gargoyle who burns in hell"—is a weak variant on the story of Svengali and Trilby, with a sidelong glance at the Dracula myth. The plot also peeks at the myth of Pandora when, at the end of the first act, our overly curious heroine lifts the white plastic half-mask of the monster, who dragged her to his lair in the bowels of the opera house, to reveal his ghastly face. Maybe this is a latent reference to exposing the "ugly" hidden parts of the male anatomy; anyway, it had half the women in the audience swooning. The other half, I suspect, were fuming. The cheap perfume that permeates the evening comes from masochistic romantic novels, with their assumptions that women relish being ravished, dominated, and controlled.

Anyway, I think the heroine is meant to relish it, though in Sarah Brightman's impassive performance it is hard to know exactly what she is feeling. At the moment when the Phantom, placing a red noose around the neck of her bleached-blond boyfriend, is preparing to hoist him to the chandelier, Miss Brightman impulsively plants a wet kiss on the mug he calls ugly enough to "incur" even "a mother's fear and loathing." Dynamite! His vengeful heart melting, his hatred relenting, the Phantom frees the lover and sends the couple away, in a boat apparently borrowed from the prop shop of *Tales of Hoffmann*. Then, weeping copious tears over his gruesome topography, he sings "It's over now, the music of the night." Not quite over. Surrounded by pursuers, with all his exits blocked, the Phantom vanishes in a chair—leaving only his mask on the pillow and his character still available for the Shlepic sequel, *The Phantom Returns*.

Michael Crawford manages to play this operatic Elephant Man not only with a straight face, which is no small thing, but also with considerable passion, though I found his voice a little thin and reedy in the upper registers. The even more straight-faced Miss Brightman has a pleasant soprano, and the rest of the cast performs with that confident complacency that bespeaks certainty of extended employment. The contributions of the director, Harold Prince, and his lighting designer, Andrew Bridge, to this orgy of special effects have been properly celebrated. If you're a fan of laser-lighting shafts, flames shooting up from the floor, musty crypts, trick mirrors, stage elephants and bull-faced sphinxes, boat rides through a fog-shrouded lake festooned with glowing lights, and, above all, aeronautical chandeliers, it will be hard to find two more accomplished technical magicians in this hemisphere. But I remember a time, not long ago—in a Lloyd Webber musical called *Evita*, for one thing—when Prince owed more to the Berliner Ensemble than to Industrial Light and Magic, when he was able to astonish us with simple Brechtian elements rather than multimillion-dollar stage mechanisms. *The Phantom of the Opera* is a vulgar glitzorama, a parade of conspicuous consumption, a display of fake rococo for a transoceanic audience glutted with material goods. It suggests that something much more dangerous than a chandelier might be crashing onto the stage.

(1988)

Transcultural Blends

(*The Gospel at Colonus; M. Butterfly; Juan Darien*)

Three productions in New York draw strength (some weakness, too) from crossing cultural boundaries, providing additional evidence that American theatre is awakening from its traditional isolationism. In past years, it was Europe that tried to jump our theatrical borders; today it is Latin America and Asia. The new influences stem partly from the ease of world travel, partly from visiting foreign troupes, partly from our increasingly multiracial society, with its rich Hispanic, black, and Asian heritages. The doors of our theatre have opened to a whole new breed of once-exotic performers and performance styles.

As with all such blends (Peter Brook's recent work is an example), the mixture is not always digestible when seasoned with too many diverse elements, and not all the shows under review here are models of *integritas* or wholeness. But even when the meal is imperfect, the taste is still appealing, perhaps because even overspiced dishes are preferable to stale white bread. A very zesty, if somewhat muddled, example of these recent transcultural works is *The Gospel at Colonus*, Lee Breuer's deconstruction of the aged Sophocles' lovely play of old age, *Oedipus at Colonus*. It is Breuer's fanciful notion to set the action in a Pentecostal black church, turning the dialogue into a series of sermons and benedictions, and the choral odes into a medley of gospel songs, jazz, rock, and jive arias. He has resolved the usually vexing problem of how to modernize the Greek chorus; I'm not certain he has successfully modernized the play.

I liked this production better when I first saw it at the Brooklyn Academy of Music some years ago, possibly because the opera house venue was more congenial than a Broadway theatre to the concert style of the presentation. At the Lunt-Fontanne, however, *The Gospel at Colonus* is obliged to masquerade as an American musical rather than a series of rousing gospel numbers bridged by dialogue. And while Breuer has added a few theatrical effects—thunder and lightning and smoke during Oedipus' apotheosis—the minimal staging coupled with the declamatory nature of the acting and the static action burden the piece with occasional *longueurs* that vitiate its considerable power.

Moreover, I'm not convinced that the story of the blinded, feeble Oedipus—exiled to an Attic deme near Athens, visited by his daughters, Ismene and Antigone, harassed by Creon, enraged by his son Polyneices, and finally blessing Theseus' Athenian state with his death at Colonus—is entirely compatible with the rituals of Christian evangelism as practiced in a black church. Admittedly, Western and Greek theatre both originated in religious ceremonies, and one can find parallels between the Passion and Resurrection of Jesus and Oedipus' self-maiming and mysterious transfiguration. But if Afro-American rituals were capable, over a period of years, of assimilating the Synoptic Gospels, they cannot absorb Greek dramatic myths as readily over the course of a single evening. Here one witnesses cultures not so much blending as being banged forcibly together.

The confusion begins with the setting—a garishly painted cyclorama depicting Icarus falling by degrees from the sun, and a series of Ionic columns, built out of plaster and wire. What are these doing in a Pentecostal church? Why would a black congregation participate in the performance of a non-biblical text? What do they put in the collection plate—obols and drachmas? Why would men of the cloth agree to play pagan characters during ceremonies normally devoted to the Christian sacraments? And does the myth of Oedipus, with its roots in the mysteries of Dionysus, Adonis, and Osiris, really aspire to be a fifth Gospel?

Happily, such questions become irrelevant as soon as the music starts, for when the thirty-one-member chorus of the Institutional Radio Choir launches into the thrilling "Stop, Do Not Go On," or the J. D. Steele Singers perform the tremulous "Numberless Are the World's Wonders," or Clarence Fountain and the Five Blind Boys of Alabama—singing the role of Oedipus in identical white suits and dark glasses—break into "No Never," all accompanied by the strongly syncopated brass and woodwind rhythms of Little Village Band, we are transported by inspired musicians into ecstatic realms. What one feels during such musical numbers is less an inclination to quibble with Breuer than to express gratitude to him for creating the conditions in which such artists can display their gifts. Deserving of more gratitude is Bob Telson, the composer, who also conducts the performers from his piano, his hair flying wildly as he rocks and pounds. Robert Fitzgerald's limpid translation of the verse (most lovely his rendering of the third choral ode) is not delivered with much grace, and the sequencing of dialogue and music robs the play of its compacted theatrical force. But if *The Gospel at Colonus* lacks power as drama, as a concert it is one of the more spectacular events of the decade.

David Henry Hwang's *M. Butterfly* is an effort not so much to mix cultures as to demonstrate how and why they clash. Played on a modified Kabuki stage—a large red surround equipped with travelers and screens and circular walkways—it is the story of a French vice consul who falls in love with a performer from the Peking Opera and ends up in prison for revealing diplomatic secrets. Although based on an actual espionage trial, the spy story interests Hwang a good deal less than the love affair—not surprising when you consider that the French diplomat lived with his little "Butterfly" for over twenty years, and even had a child by "her," without ever realizing that "she" was a man.

The playwright seems as bemused by the diplomat's obtuseness as we are, and accounts for it only by suggesting, through his characters, that darkness and feigned modesty obscure the fact that humans have more than one orifice for sexual pleasure. Considering that René Gallimard (as this would-be Pinkerton is called) also photographed sensitive documents for his lover without asking why, he must be considered excessively stupid even by Western diplomatic standards. As for Song Liling (the name of his Chinese Butterfly), he seems unusually cunning even by stereotypical standards of inscrutable Oriental shrewdness. Since it is hardly a secret that women in Peking Opera are played by men, the most convincing explanation is that Gallimard was unconsciously aware of his beloved's sex from the start.

Using Puccini's opera as a parallel reinforcing plot, Hwang exploits the story for its political, cultural, and sexual implications, his theme being that Western treatment of the East—Vietnam included—is motivated by myths of male domination and female passivity; in short, by the same relationships to be found in *Madama Butterfly*. According to Gallimard, who adores playing Pinkerton ("Very few of us would pass up the opportunity," he smirks at the audience), "Orientals will always submit to a greater force." But, as another character suggests, the Western use of "greater force" stems from a fear of sexual impotence; "the whole world is being run by men with pricks the size of pins."

The danger of such large cultural generalizations is to replace one form of stereotype with another. Hwang's sexual-racial explanation of Western imperialism leaves unexplained Mrs. Thatcher's policies, not to mention any number of atrocities committed by the more feminine East (though he does identify Red China as a macho society that refuses to recognize homosexuality). Gallimard nevertheless atones for his sexist stupidity by putting on Butterfly's kimono and makeup, and committing hara-kiri—Song Liling, in a Western business suit, is given Pinkerton's final cry of "Butterfly" over the corpse. That the towering John Lithgow, as Gallimard, looks in this garb more like the harridan Katisha in *The Mikado* is only one of the problems of the evening. John Dexter's production is overwrought and ponderous; and failing to fuse Eastern and Western styles, he has stranded some very good actors mid-ocean, including the usually dependable Mr. Lithgow, who spends most of his stage time posing with fist in back pocket and bellowing lines—when he is not, along with B. D. Wong (fetching and sinuous as Song Liling), painting his face and changing his clothes.

As for the play, it is notable more for its intentions than for its execution. Hwang has an excellent subject, and he has obviously thought a lot, if not very originally, about the origins of racism and imperialism. But the work has no subtext and lacks the gift of language. These are serious flaws in a piece so full of direct address, for without language the oratory grows tiresome, the characters lose depth, and the romantic story sheds its pathos. T. S. Eliot once complained about another playwright of ideas, Bernard Shaw, that the poet in him was stillborn. David Henry Hwang's poetic ovum hasn't even been fertilized yet and even his prose could use some ripening. He's got an eye for a good story; when he develops a better ear, we may have another good playwright.

Juan Darien, produced by the Music-Theatre Group at St. Clement's Church, is a blending of a Uruguayan story and the most sophisticated visual and musical techniques. Julie Taymor has always been a highly imaginative puppet-maker and mask designer, honing her own original talents with extensive research in Indonesian theatre. Here, in coordination with her usual musical collaborator, Elliot Goldenthal, she has created a striking spectacle based on Latin liturgical texts and the poems of Horacio Quiroga. It is the tale of a tiger cub whose mother has been killed by hunters. Suckled by a woman who has lost her own child, he transforms into a human himself. When his adopted mother dies, he seeks comfort in the cages of captured tigers and, suspected of being a wild animal by the tiger-tamer, is tortured, whipped, and semicrucified on a bamboo platform. As "Juan," the boy shares his mother's grave, but as a resurrected tiger, he continues to live in the jungle with his own kind, killing the tiger-tamer and joining the others in feeding on his flesh.

The story is encumbered by pathetic fallacies (animals with the innocent natures of saints), not to mention specious Jesus parallels, and puppetry is too frozen and inexpressive a form to support much emotional depth. But as a pretext for the wonderful fairy-tale theatricality of Miss Taymor's designs and Mr. Goldenthal's music, it is extraordinary. The opening moments are typically beautiful, as falling fronds transform the bare stage of the church into a jungle, and a succession of lizards, birds, fireflies, moths, toucans, and forked-tongued snakes slither through the undergrowth. The Latin American village Miss Taymor has devised is equally haunting, a mound on which miniature huts are illuminated to reveal the shadows of their inhabitants, all presided over by a huge black buzzard (the village has suffered a plague), by funeral processions and huge masks of grief-stricken women. Mimed and sung rather than acted, the piece doesn't probe as deeply as it should—nor does the whispering, percussive music, which remains at a level of melancholy theatricality—but it is nevertheless a fine example of transcultural blending, a splendid feast for ears and eyes.

(1988)

The Last Refuge of Scoundrels

(*Speed-the-Plow*)

Speed-the-Plow consolidates David Mamet's place in the pantheon of major American dramatists, representing another of his remorseless anthropological probes into the underlife of *Homo Americanus*. Like *American Buffalo* and *Glengarry Glen Ross*, the play establishes friendship between males and personal loyalty among the corrupted as virtually the last remaining values in an increasingly hypocritical and decaying society. And it insinuates this theme in an insidious, subterranean manner, using the terse, taciturn minimalism for which he has become famous. Mamet's ear for language has never been more certain or more subtle, but what distinguishes him from other playwrights with a natural control of the American idiom (Paddy Chayefsky, for example) is the economical way he can advance his plot, develop his characters, and tell his jokes without departing from, or announcing, his strong social-moral purpose.

Speed-the-Plow is the deftest and funniest of Mamet's works, and the airiest, too, since the characters are playing for relatively low stakes. In *American Buffalo*, *Edmond*, and *Glengarry Glen Ross*, men are fighting for their very existence. In *Speed-the-Plow*, they are skirmishing over movie deals and percentages of the gross. Charlie Fox offers his friend Bobby Gould—recently promoted to Head of Production—the opportunity to "greenlight" what used to be called "a good safe stinker" featuring a bankable movie star. The script, a prison-buddy movie, is a dog. What inspires these self-described "two old Whores" is the chance to make a "shitload of money." Fox and Gould are masters of movie business cant ("*Fuck* money . . . But don't fuck 'people' . . . 'Cause people . . . are what it's All About"), which they also recognize as absolute bullshit. The key thing is to get rich and "kick the ass of a lot of them fuckin' people."

The studio head has asked Gould to give a "courtesy read" to a pretentious novel about radiation and the end of the world by an "Eastern sissy writer" (not Jonathan Schell—this author believes that radiation is a God-invented medium for salvation). In an effort to seduce his new secretary—an office temp named Karen, who can't even work the telephones—Gould lets her be the reader. Karen professes to be overwhelmed by the inspirational and idiotic message of the book. And over Gould's objections that his job is to "make the thing everyone made last year," she argues that in promoting a prison picture "degrading to the human spirit," he has been neglecting a masterpiece. Naturally, she is willing to make herself available to help produce it.

Gould's conversion to higher movie values occurs, in Chekhovian fashion, between the acts, which is also where he gets to sleep with Karen. When Fox returns to close his deal with Gould, he finds a born-again idealist, prepared not only to break his word to a friend but to ruin his own career by making a $10 million bomb about finding God in rads and roentgens. It is difficult to know what leaves Fox more incensed—the loss of a profitable deal, the girl's chicanery, his friend's disloyalty, or the sheer stupidity of the entire situation. But before the end of the play, he has forced the girl to admit she used her sexual wiles for her own advancement. He has also made Gould face up to his own delusions: "I wanted to do Good," he confesses. "But I became foolish."

Reconciled, Fox and Gould conclude that their only earthly purpose is to make movies, preferably with their names above the title, and that, despite their jokes, they're in a "People Business" after all. *Speed-the-Plow* is not, as some critics have misconstrued it, just a satire on movie hucksters. Mamet finds Fox's cynical commercialism infinitely more acceptable than Karen's fake idealism. The play is, rather, an almost Hemingwayesque tribute to people who perform their tasks with wit and grace, no matter how tawdry or empty—a further development of Mamet's belief in personal loyalty as the only cement in an unstuck public world. Like the real-estate salesmen in *Glengarry Glen Ross*, like the petty thieves in *American Buffalo*, Fox and Gould ultimately prove superior to the hypocrites and timeservers around them because they recognize their own shortcomings and respect the bonds of friendship. For it is friendship, not patriotism, that is the last refuge of Mamet's scoundrels, whose epitaph might be "Never give a sucker an even break, but never cheat a friend."

The nonprofit Lincoln Center production of *Speed-the-Plow* has opened in a Broadway theatre, a Mamet play-within-a-play we'll get to in a moment. Using a simple wall-less set by Michael Merritt, consisting primarily of pink-champagne drapes and furniture pieces covered by sheets when not in use, Gregory Mosher has directed the action with the precision of a master machinist, orchestrating its rhythms as if he were tuning an experimental car. Joe Mantegna as the hapless Bobby Gould, his sharp features and hooded eyes working beneath a shock of patent-leather hair, brings a dour tenor snap to his deal-making scenes, and manages his almost religious conversion with a kind of glazed transcendence. Ron Silver as Charlie Fox, a half-growth of beard festooning his good-natured features, is a center of primal energy and colloquial fluency, whether rushing across the stage and literally kissing Gould's ass or blistering him for his treachery with a furious stream of invective ("You squat to pee"). These performances are impeccable, possibly the most powerful acting to be seen on the American stage this year.

It is a pity they are compromised by the female star. Madonna is a charismatic pop singer with an electric performing style and a huge following (including my son). She is not a qualified actress. Her performance is becomingly unshowy, but her modesty subdues her. Her hair dyed a mousy brown, her voice halting and sometimes inaudible, her face inexpressive, her gestures and movements oddly hesitant, she virtually disappears from the stage in an important supporting role—and gives a new dimension to the meaning of the word "flat." Karen should dominate the center of the play; in Madonna's hands, the center does not hold. The production is weak and flaccid whenever she's on the stage, the senior show at Secaucus High instead of a professional New York premiere.

Even were Madonna a more finished actress, she would have been an unfortunate choice for the part. Her celebrity was bound to attract the wrong kind of attention to the play. Doubtless, the producers felt they needed a star to ensure a Broadway success. But to reason thus is to create an almost Pirandellian event, with one of the play's themes—the cynical manipulation of art for commercial purposes—being enacted behind the scenes. While I'm on the subject, I should mention that *Speed-the-Plow* was produced first on Broadway instead of in the Mitzi E. Newhouse Theater at Lincoln Center because the financially successful *Boys' Life* has been occupying that stage for months. Another Lincoln Center hit, the Cole Porter *Anything Goes*, although a more appropriate choice for Broadway, has been sitting in the Vivian Beaumont Theater all year, blocking additional productions. I am full of admiration for the theatrical expertise of the people who run this institution, whom I also count among my friends. But I always thought the purpose of a subsidized theatre (in contrast with the Broadway stage) was to produce a sequence of ambitious plays, not hunker down with commercial bonanzas. Or perhaps that's to fall into old-fashioned idealism. Perhaps in a time of ethical relativism and moral decay, it is, as Mamet suggests, sufficient simply to be good at your job.

(1988)

The Best Play of Which Year?

(*A Walk in the Woods; Boys' Life*)

Some plays are born out of their time, and it is a paradox that this can account for either a quick demise or a successful run, depending on what seems dated, the substance or the form. August Wilson's *Fences* was voted Best Play of 1987 by virtually every award committee extant. But with its tidy structure, linear realism, back-yard ferment, and father-son confrontations, it's actually the Best Play of 1947, being a tendril of Arthur Miller's *Death of a Salesman*. Lee Blessing's *A Walk in the Woods* might have been a worthy competitor for Best Play of pre-*glasnost* 1982. But since its political agenda failed to keep pace with current events, it was obsolete before it opened and may not have the stamina to last the course.

A Walk in the Woods is a two-character, one-set show about a couple of arms negotiators holding a series of private heart-to-heart talks on a park bench in a forest near Geneva. Reputedly, the play is based on conversations held away from the conference table, seven years ago, by Paul Nitze and Yuli A. Kvitsinsky, when these Russian and American delegates reached an unofficial agreement regarding disarmament, only to see it subsequently rejected by both their governments. The idea of two citizens of adversary nations trying to inject some sense into the official proceedings, before being blocked by Cold War politics, has a poignant potential; and the play proceeds in its earnest, well-intentioned, if plodding, fashion to demonstrate the ultimate ineffectuality of their melancholy labors. But *glasnost* and Gorbachev's surprising capacity to conclude an arms control deal with Reagan, despite the resistance of the President's right-wing supporters and, presumably, his own Defense Department, consigns the play to a historical wastebasket.

The playwright makes little effort to accommodate recent developments, apart from one skeptical reference to "the new openness." It's not hard to see why. He displays an obstinate pessimism about transactions between governments as opposed to the possibility of positive dealings between men of goodwill, perhaps in the liberal delusion that long-standing ideological conflicts are merely the result of misunderstanding or suspiciousness, rather than the consequence of genuine differences, and that if governments could display the same benevolence toward each other as private individuals, they would quickly resolve the issues that divide them. *A Walk in the Woods* reminds me of all those movies and miniseries that conclude with Russian and American citizens ruefully shaking hands while their rulers prepare to press the buttons that will blow them to smithereens.

It is at least possible that ruling systems are administered by the same species of human beings as those amiable and judicious creatures who sit on park benches to discuss affairs of state. And if Gorbachev is presently the most interesting figure in world politics, it is because he has demonstrated how a powerful individual can change, even if only temporarily, the inexorable course of history—not through hands-across-the-sea sentiments so much as by recognizing that his system will collapse if it continues on its present course. "Friendship," on the other hand, is the taproot of the relationship between Andrey Botvinnik and John Honeyman, the fictionalized Russian and American negotiators of *A Walk in the Woods*. The play is really a flirtation on a park bench—a solemn and discursive version of *Key Exchange*—where two affectionate characters risk the wrath of their superiors in order to deepen their relationship. Botvinnik is represented as a genial clownish sophisticate with an aphoristic flair ("Formality is simply anger with its hair combed," "History is geography over time"), while Honeyman is characterized as a driven, somewhat humorless man determined to create a diplomatic breakthrough. Both are charged with the difficult task of keeping our interest alive over the space of two hours, when the outcome of their efforts is foreordained before the curtain even rises.

Blessing is clearly less interested in the details of their proposals than in the courtship. "Do you like me?" asks the Russian, and though the American replies that "I'm here to make a treaty with you, not a friendship," it is their personal interaction that fills the interstices of the play. Botvinnik tries to persuade Honeyman to be more frivolous, to talk about Mickey Mouse or country-and-Western music, while Honeyman tries to induce Botvinnik to submit a new proposal to his superiors, saying, "If you don't do this, we will never be friends." Botvinnik agrees and, when the U.S. government rejects it, resigns from the peace table. "Will you miss me?" he asks Honeyman. "The new man will not be you" is the answer. They fail to kiss, but the play concludes with the two men sitting quietly, if hopelessly, in the lap of nature, pledging eternal friendship.

This sentimental contrast between private sensitivity and public intransigence takes place over four seasons, marked by falling leaves and flowers blossoming through the fake moss—the seasonal transitions being accompanied by the graceful woodwind music of Michael S. Roth (the temptation to use Vivaldi must have been strong). Des McAnuff has directed the event with pace and understanding. If he has also directed it with false climaxes and artificial comedy, the impulse is understandable considering that he is charged with feeding political porridge to pretty much the same Diners Club that gobbles *Cats* and *The Phantom of the Opera*. Robert Prosky plays Botvinnik with a thick Russian accent and a coy sententiousness, though he is always a strong presence, and Sam Waterston's priggish, agonized Honeyman is full of passion, though he still seems to be choking back vestiges of guilt over deserting Dith Pran in *The Killing Fields*. Considering that all this play needs is a park bench, I admired the way Bill Clarke supplemented the space with birch and linden trees, enhanced by a suggestive painting upstage of another part of the forest, and the way Richard Riddell's lighting lent mystery to an otherwise excessively declarative evening.

Howard Korder's *Boys' Life* at the Mitzi E. Newhouse Theater (Lincoln Center) may not prove to be the Best Play of 1988, but at least it belongs to our time, having been written by a very interesting new playwright with a thoroughly contemporary sensibility. Korder writes under the influence of David Mamet—his play is being performed by members of the Atlantic Theatre Company, a group of Mamet's former students who also act in his movies. Under the direction of W. H. Macy, another Mamet regular, *Boys' Life* bears a certain resemblance to *Sexual Perversity in Chicago*. Still, the imitation is far from slavish. Korder's voice is singular and true. The most valuable thing he has learned from Mamet is to let his themes and characters emerge through action rather than announcement.

Boys' Life is a series of vignettes revolving around three listless young studs, motivated exclusively by sexual desire, their energies aroused only by women. Don (Jordan Lage) takes up with a waitress who wants to be a sculptor, only to betray her with a casual kook on a one-night stand; Phil (Steven Goldstein) manages to connect with a girl at a party who can't decide whether to sleep with him or to go home with her escort; Jack (Clark Gregg) tries to seduce a female jogger while keeping one eye cocked toward his child on the jungle gym. These are men (boys really, hence the enigmatic title) without futures, without pasts, without purpose or sense of history. Asked to free-associate about the seventies, all the "post-modern nut" Don can remember is Watergate and the Sex Pistols. "From campus cutups to wasted potentials"—that is the progress of their shared lethargy. Don hangs out in his underwear because "I like to be prepared for sleep." Phil is losing his hair "and that really sucks." Jack, pretending to be a movie producer, offers to star a potential pickup in a movie about "a generation that had it all, and didn't know what to do with it."

The play seemingly tracks along as aimlessly as its characters, all the while preparing for a climax riddled with affectlessness. Confronted by his girl with evidence of his unfaithfulness (a pair of strange panties), Don declares his love and marries her. Jack—a marginal guest at the wedding, seated near the men's room, wearing a tuxedo jacket and torn jeans—can think only of finding an apartment where he can cheat on his wife. To the shocked Phil, he says, "It doesn't matter what you do because nobody's watching." The only real affection he feels is for his buddies; yet he can't help alienating them as well. Hugging Phil and claiming that he loves him, Jack adds, "So can I have the apartment?" At the end, Jack is alone with his wife amid the detritus of the wedding, pouring sugar into the champagne to make it fizz. She's drunk and as desperate as he. "You're not the worst man in the world," she concludes. "I'm afraid you're just not—but you'd like to be."

This is the characteristic tone of the eighties—affectless, weightless, purposeless, stoned. Jack's sarcasm, though it suggests self-hatred, never falls over into self-pity. He represents a generation that believes personal fulfillment to be an illusion of past times ("Happiness? That was the sixties"). In its insinuating, impressionistic way, *Boys' Life* contains a more eloquent political statement than anything to be heard in *A Walk in the Woods*, for all its clamorous speechifying and ponderous declamation. But its implicit message is infinitely more disturbing and discordant. In the words of one of Korder's characters, "Everybody's worried about the world getting blown up, right? But what if it doesn't?"

(1988)

The Voice of the Eighties

(*Reckless, Without You I'm Nothing*)

This decade was preparing to close without an identifying mark other than a mindless smirk plastered across a simpering yuppie face. Suddenly there are signs of social definition. You won't often find these in American movies where, reflecting the illusory optimism of Reaganism, the typical motif is wish fulfillment through supernatural agencies—altering family destiny (*Back to the Future*), extricating old people from unpleasant situations with extraterrestrial help (*Cocoon 1 and 2*, *Batteries Not Included*), accelerating the age of children (*Big*), exchanging the identities of adults and kids (*18 Again*, plus a half-dozen movies whose names I've blocked). But if Hollywood continues to be in thrall to fantasy, the American stage is once again assuming a traditional obligation to measure and challenge the form and pressure of the time.

In recent months, Howard Korder's *Boys' Life* anatomized the weightless malaise of bored young studs; David Mamet's *Speed-the-Plow* tested the limits of friendship as the last refuge of decent conduct; and now Craig Lucas' *Reckless* is analyzing the disintegrating boundaries of human relationships. *Reckless* is the most radical of the three. In the fractured perspective of Loy Arcenas' design—a Magrittish field of blue decorated with birdlike clouds—the lineaments of a dream are used to contour a terrifying spiritual reality, evoked, under Norman René's expert direction, in a hallucinatory manner by the Circle Repertory Company (a theatre normally associated with a rather damp naturalism).

Reckless begins with a couple in bed watching TV ("It's just the news—it's not real"), while Bing Crosby sings "I'll Be Home for Christmas." Babbling contentedly under her flowered comforter, Rachel tells her husband, Tom, of her unspeakable happiness ("I'm having one of my euphoria attacks"). He responds by announcing he's taken out a contract on her life; in five minutes, he says morosely, an assassin will stage her "accidental" death. Feeling belated remorse, he helps her escape, in bathrobe and slippers, through the bay window into the falling snow. And thus begins her strange odyssey through a dimension where every day is Christmas and every town is named Springfield. Rachel, attended by six female psychiatrists (all played winningly by Joyce Reehling) who invariably think her story a dream, is plunged into a series of phantasmagoric experiences—alien encounters which parallel the conditions of a totally mad country.

Rachel takes refuge in the home of Lloyd (John Dossett) and his wife, Pooty (Welker White), a paraplegic who also pretends to be deaf. In love with the needy, Lloyd works in a benevolent organization called Hands Across the Sea. Like everyone in the play, Lloyd has a shameful history—he abandoned his first wife and stole $35,000. Rachel tells him, "The past is irrelevant—it's something we wake up from," but for him, "It's the nightmare you wake up *to* every day." In order to repay the theft and obliterate this Joycean nightmare, all three appear on a TV game show called *Your Mother or Your Wife*—Pooty pretending to be Lloyd's mother, Rachel his wife. And to the accompaniment of ear-splitting studio audience screams, he wins $100,000 by correctly guessing how the women answered such questions as "If Lloyd were a salad dressing, what flavor would he be?"

During another Christmas celebration, one year later, Pooty and Rachel's returned husband, Tom, die drinking champagne, poisoned by a disgruntled employee in Lloyd's organization. Rachel and Lloyd escape. Lloyd, still wearing his Santa costume, turns inward, breaking his silence to tell the gabby Rachel to "shut the fuck up." Capable only of watching TV and sipping champagne, he dies of anorexia. Rachel lands in a madhouse, also bereft of speech. Her analyst takes Rachel to a TV interview show, partly to relieve her delusion that someone is trying to shoot her. Someone is, though the bullet intended for Rachel lodges in the forehead of the guest personality. In the final scene, Rachel has also become an analyst—in snowy Alaska, where it's always Christmas. The patient she treats is her own son. He doesn't recognize her and she doesn't reveal her identity.

Determinedly disjointed and disorienting, the play contains its own crafty logic. As played brilliantly by Robin Bartlett with Madeleine Kahn-like shrieks of high-pitched merriment, Rachel is the embodiment of misplaced American optimism. The contrast between her Pollyanna cheerfulness and the catastrophic world she encounters is reminiscent of the jarring views of life represented in the movie *Blue Velvet*, where artificial images of serenity were also juxtaposed against scenes of brutality, sudden death, and sexual corruption. Rachel is a daytime spirit in a Nighttown of the soul, her conventional notions of happy suburban life and healthy family values continuously undercut by greed, mayhem, murder, inane media displays, and a therapeutic discipline grown insensitive to the implacable darkness hidden within the folds of existence. In its illogical plotting and lobotomized atmosphere, *Reckless* is a deeply political play, possibly the most fundamental criticism we are likely to get of the American Dream as marketed by the ad agencies and the mass media, and, incidentally, of the contemptible jingoism being peddled by the Bush campaign.

Sandra Bernhard is another voice of the eighties and I'm glad I managed to hear its caustic melodies on the final night of her show (*Without You I'm Nothing*) at the Orpheum Theatre. Performing in front of a bank of lights, a few tarps, and an entirely disreputable punk band, Bernhard combines stand-up comedy, show-biz impressions, personal confessions, and belted rock-and-roll to mirror and criticize her age. Bernhard is a sometime actress (you may remember her as the demented groupie in Scorsese's *King of Comedy*). Coming on like a hip yenta in her black leotard and backlit red hair, she is a virtual encyclopedia of celebrity personalities, fashion labels, and brand names. Yet, she manages to distance herself from the values of the commodity culture, partly by snarling at our hero worship and her own lapses into sentiment. Wonderfully foulmouthed, totally unbuttoned, she bases her act on a love-hate relationship with the audience. She sure knows how to work it—how to abuse it, too, calling the customers "meatheads, screwballs, motherfuckers," when they fail to give her band enough applause.

Bernhard is unashamedly Jewish, with the aggressive confidence of Lenny Bruce rather than the apologetic mildness of Woody Allen. She fantasizes being Gentile, having a brother named Chip, wearing Laura Ashley clothes, eating Christmas dinner. Although she comes on as a new woman, she has a traditional Jewish girl's obsession with finding a good husband, not a promising possibility when *Newsweek* has told her the odds "ain't too damn good" for women over thirty-five. At the same time, she's too jaundiced to care and too dejected to look: "There will be no more lovers and very few friends!"

Bernhard's gloomy nature was apparently shaped by her parentage—"My father's a proctologist, my mother's an abstract artist, that's how I view the world." Her jaded views extend, refreshingly, to her own bad notices. She tears Clive Barnes apart for calling her a "butch Carly

Simon," and she mentions how the *Village Voice* reviewer phoned and asked for a favor after panning her act (she plays this recorded conversation back to the audience). Shining a flashlight in the eyes of the audience, she evaluates the customers, even grabbing a woman's pocketbook and assessing her character through its contents. She reads magazines aloud, satirizes the ads, castigates a celebrated photographer's inclination to "accessorize" his female subjects, fantasizes about L.A. after a nuclear holocaust where only the strongest—Tina Turner and Madonna—have survived, and laments the failure of her own career ("You know you're in trouble when you start resenting Linda Hunt").

As this suggests, her references are exclusively pop, even though she says she regrets the disappearance of all those "liberal intellectuals who once made the city a center of art and thought." Still, she knows about the corruptions of pop culture, too—the rock singers who try to hire their black backup singers as maids after the show, the gushing starlets who say they "really want to make this film," the endless stream of newly discovered Marilyn Monroe photos. She does her final number in a black ranch mink, then strips down to her underwear to perform some Jane Fonda exercises. The raw contrast is symbolic. She obviously hates the age of which she is the product, hates the goals she aspires to achieve. But what she hates most is the strong-arm hypocrisy of the powerful. "Don't let them fuck you over," she says in parting counsel, "fuck *them* over," which is Sandra Bernhard's way of rephrasing Norman Mailer's conviction that the shits are killing us. Her act is vulgar, excessive, overamplified—but her rage is pure and purgative, perhaps the best response of defenseless people to the affronts of a dismal decade.

(1988)

Running on Empty

(*Miracolo d'Amore*)

Miracolo d'Amore (New York Public Theater) is the fourth in a series of theatre-music pieces that Martha Clarke has been devising in collaboration with the composer Richard Peaslee and the design artists Robert Israel (sets and costumes) and Paul Gallo (lights). Having assembled one of the most brilliant creative teams in America, as well as a fine dance company, she has had a rare opportunity for continuous, organic artistic development. Yet, rather than growing in strength, Miss Clarke's work, since her masterly and astonishing *The Garden of Earthly Delights*, has been getting progressively more diffuse.

Miracolo d'Amore is the least satisfying of the series. Handsome and powerful though it was, *Vienna: Lusthaus* suffered, in my opinion, from Miss Clarke's failure to assimilate the verbal rhythms of Charles Mee, Jr.'s text; *The Hunger Artist*, for all its eerie atmosphere and surrealist imagery, lacked a convincing stage equivalent for Kafka's febrile imaginings; and *Miracolo d'Amore*, despite some gorgeous music and striking visual properties, is a curiously empty and sometimes pretentious exercise in choreographic calisthenics. At the same time that her technical vocabulary is growing, Miss Clarke's creative energies seem to be flagging a bit. She tends to repeat images from her other work, sometimes accompanied by a morbid cuteness.

In a cogent article in *The New York Times*, Michael Kimmelman has hinted at a reason for these limitations—her relationship to her source material. Martha Clarke has always been indebted to other artists—Hieronymous Bosch in *The Garden of Earthly Delights*, Klimt and Schiele in *Vienna: Lusthaus*, Kafka in *The Hunger Artist*. Here, she is looking for theatrical inspiration in the canvases of Tiepolo and Grandville, but without finding anything she can call her own. It is a style that Kimmelman astutely identifies as "Mannerism"—"Its inspiration is art, not experience." The result is fifty minutes of *longueurs*. It's like looking at a painting, all right—looking at it dry.

Miss Clarke has the capacity to create a very beautiful painting, of course, which Paul Gallo has textured with shafts of gorgeously sculpted light. Robert Israel has contributed a precariously balanced set of skewed flats and slanted windows and Doric doorways, while dressing the men in white ruffed harlequin suits and conical hats to resemble Tiepolo's humpbacked Punchinellos. As for the women, they appear in various states of nudity. One lissome girl pulls a seashell out of another's pubic area and listens to its sounds. A nymph opens her bodice and, presented with a flower, presses it to her bosom. A naked lady sits in a window with a skeleton and combs her hair with its bony fingers.

One man costumed like Jesus in a white loincloth is fed pasta by a child holding a basket (better treatment, I suppose, than vinegar sponges). Rising from his cross, he distorts his stomach, hobbles across the stage, puts his crippled arms behind him like a vulture's wings, and crows. A naked man wearing a large fish head appears in a gathering fog, and rolls in it. It is not long before these Punchinellos turn mean, like the post-lapsarian brutes in *The Garden of Earthly Delights*. Two coneheads aim flintlocks at innocent birds, then at each other. One man falls to the ground with a hand in his eyes, and is mauled and kicked; his throat is cut with a thumb. A nymph is attacked by a short man, resists him, and is throttled. Familiar scenes of men brutalizing women and each other. Rape and murder. The miracles of love.

But these juxtapositions of violence and beauty, meant to surprise, inspire instead a sense of *déjà vu. Miracolo d'Amore* is accompanied by lovely sounds—notably Peaslee's Monteverdi-like music, snatches of Petrarch, and some verbal interpolations in Italian. Yet, for all its visual and aural appeal, the piece is dull. Its form virtually obliterates its content, its images seem random and arbitrary. I am reminded of what Julian Beck of the Living Theatre once said about a piece of his own: "All very beautiful, but what does it mean?"

It is a fact of our culture that artists are always expected to follow a success with a new triumph, pressures not always compatible with the unpredictable pace and leisurely process of creative gestation. Like Tennessee Williams, who felt the need to bring forth a play every year, ready or not, Miss Clarke has been producing annual events with steadily diminishing results. It is said that *Miracolo d'Amore* took months to rehearse. Would that it had taken months to prepare. My entirely unsolicited and no doubt unwanted advice to this hugely gifted artist is to abstain from public presentation until her artistic resources are replenished, until the experience tank refills, until personal rather than media pressures compel her to create.

(1988)

An Evening of Last Rites

(*Jerome Robbins' Broadway*)

The torrent of gratitude that critics and the public have been pouring over the choreographic genius behind *Jerome Robbins' Broadway* would suggest that he's discovered a new form. Actually, he's reconstructed an old one—the dance/ballet musical—a species of musical comedy invented by Agnes de Mille in *Oklahoma!* and then perfected by Gower Champion, Bob Fosse, and Robbins himself, beginning with *On the Town* in 1944. This genre has been in eclipse for a number of years, probably dating from the time, twenty years later, when Robbins retired from the stage following *Fiddler on the Roof*. By abandoning Broadway at the height of his success in order to return to full-time work with the New York City Ballet, he managed to achieve something approaching legendary status, which may explain why the audience starts applauding this show even before the curtain goes up. They're like shoeless peons in search of a leader, with Robbins reappearing like Emiliano Zapata on a white horse riding down the mountain to stir a conservative musical stage with memories of a discarded revolution.

The title of his "new" show says it all. When theatre marquees light up at the end with the titles of Robbins' shows throbbing in neon (a minor theft from *42nd Street*), you realize what a driving force he was in musical comedy, whether using choreographic, directing, or conceptual skills. This Broadway really *did* belong to Robbins, and it was a lot more healthy as a result of his classical dance influence than the quasi-operatic cat-and-chandelier Broadway of Andrew Lloyd Webber. For one thing, you were likely, in a Robbins show, to look at the lineaments of the human form rather than at spectacular machinery, masks, or makeup. And you were treated to an infinite variety of style and movement, not just monotonous incantations of Puccini souped up with tremulous tonal climaxes.

Actually, the sets for the ten shows represented in *Jerome Robbins' Broadway*, though designed by very gifted artists, are the tackiest thing in the evening (Boris Aronson's *Fiddler* excepted). But that's not important, because the designs serve as backgrounds for dance and song rather than as actors competing for audience attention. Furthermore, by abstracting the high moment of each show—generally the centerpiece dance number—Robbins manages to divert attention from the basic weakness of musical comedy, namely the book, and emphasize the glories of its music and motion. To be sure, this is achieved at the cost of some jerkiness. None of the shows—not even *West Side Story*, represented by a twenty-five-minute segment—is allowed to unravel in consecutive fashion. And as the evening whips us from New York in the forties (*On the Town*) to New York in the twenties (*Billion Dollar Baby*) to New York in the fifties (*West Side Story*), then back to Plautine Rome (*A Funny Thing Happened on the Way to the Forum*), turn-of-the-century America (*High Button Shoes*), Siam (*The King and I*), fairyland (*Peter Pan*), and the Polish shtetl (*Fiddler on the Roof*)—before concluding with a reprise of *On the Town*—one is likely to feel imprisoned in a particularly cantankerous time-space machine incapable of setting down firmly in any historical period.

The best way to regard *Jerome Robbins' Broadway* is not as a Broadway musical but as a celebration of choreography, rather like a benefit evening at the New York State Theater. Even the rather synthetic overture is devoted to songs about dancing, where the rhetorical question "Shall we dance?" is immediately answered by the angular Sailor Ballets in *On the Town*. Although the most high-spirited number is "On a Sunday by the Sea" from *High Button Shoes*, with ballet music by Jule Styne, it is clear that Robbins was most consistently inspired by his collaboration with Leonard Bernstein. It was their work on the ballet *Fancy Free* that eventually developed into *On the Town*, and the nervous, spasmodic, dynamic, oddly syncopated Bernstein music proved perfectly suited to the angular sliding, leaping, and somersaulting of Robbins' choreography. *On the Town* looks curiously innocent today—gobs and girls in the Big Apple—especially in contrast to the urban angst of *West Side Story*. Stephen Sondheim's lyrics for the later work brought a new sophistication to the musical (a quality missing from Arthur Laurents's rather soupy book), and it stimulated a new energy in Robbins, especially in the wonderful "America" number, where jazz and Latin American rhythms combine in a frenetic Hispanic debate over the dubious attractions of San Juan. It could also stimulate a certain utopian sappiness, as in the sentimental dream sequence ("There's a Place for Us"), when the Jets and the Sharks stop fighting to hold hands, gaze into each other's eyes, and contemplate a future of love and peace instead of bicycle chains and ashcan lids.

It is in numbers like this, and to some extent in the finger-snapping rumble sequence, that Robbins' choreography tends to romanticize reality. *West Side Story* was never a convincing study of racial conflict or street violence, but its glamorized warriors of indeterminate origin make it look today like a dead artifact of liberal sociology in a world of freeway snipers, skinheads, teenage hustlers, crack wars, and movies like *Colors*. There are clearly some subjects that musicals don't handle very well—the choreographed pogrom in *Fiddler on the Roof* is another such, though Robbins has mercifully excluded it from the current show. He's much more comfortable adapting his energized vision to images of American innocence—the "Charleston" sequence in *Billion Dollar Baby*, for example, with its hoodlums in pinstripe suits, flappers in pearls, and swells in pink raccoon coats—or to images of American innocence seen through exotic eyes, such as the Siamese version of *Uncle Tom's Cabin* ("The Small House of Uncle Thomas") in *The King and I*. In both these cases, Robbins follows Brecht's admonition to make the familiar strange and the strange familiar, often by using techniques borrowed from Kabuki, Noh, and Balinese theatre.

For Robbins' brilliance as a choreographer is partly due to his skill as a director. That is what distinguishes the opening number ("Comedy Tonight") of *A Funny Thing*, a contribution said to have saved George Abbott's show after its disastrous reception on the road (it employs the most comical use of a curtain since Picasso's *Desire Trapped by the Tail*). Robbins' directorial skill also distinguishes *Gypsy*'s "You Gotta Have a Gimmick," where the blowsy strippers blow trumpets and display illuminated bras and G-strings in a bump-and-grind ballet. It is Robbins' knowledge of acting that makes Jason Alexander look like something more than a rubber-stamp Zero Mostel as Pseudolus and Tevye, though he lacks Zero's gargantuan talent. And it is Robbins' gift for histrionic dynamics that gives such performers as Robert La Fosse, Charlotte D'Amboise, Scott Wise, and the others such a powerful presence on stage when a lesser artist might have made them look like mere hoofers. Aside from "Mr. Monotony," an Irving Berlin number dropped from a couple of shows for what now appear to be perfectly sound reasons, only the *Peter Pan* sequence fails to impress, largely because it depends more on (very expert) aerial technology than on situation, timing, and character.

Jerome Robbins' Broadway momentarily makes the musical comedy an American possession again—but at what a price! The piece cost $8 million to produce and was six months in rehearsal, with sixty-two performers, fourteen designers, and five producers, including the Shubert Organization and the Suntory Foundation. It will be years before they can recoup their investment, even at $55 a seat. We've come a long way from the "astronomical" prices ("They're paying $4.40 a ticket out there!") bemoaned by Julian Marsh in *42nd Street*. And while it's a tribute to Jerome Robbins' fabled reputation that he was allowed to spend so freely on what is effectively a homage to himself, the cost of the enterprise makes it clear why the American musical has become as extinct as the dodo bird and the woolly mammoth. There are creative reasons, too. The great composers represented here—Morton Gould, Leonard Bernstein, Richard Rodgers, Jule Styne, Moose Charlap, Irving Berlin, Jerry Bock—have all, with the exception of

Stephen Sondheim, either died or retired from the stage, and so have the great choreographers. In the meantime, a passion for extravaganzas—probably to justify the exorbitant ticket prices—has replaced the clean, lithe leap of creative inspiration. *Jerome Robbins' Broadway* is a celebration of golden oldies, an exercise in nostalgia, an anthology of past triumphs. It represents not so much a reawakening of the American musical as a great big fun-filled wake, a rousing ceremony of final rites.

(1989)

Women in Extremis

(The Heidi Chronicles)

I saw Wendy Wasserstein's *The Heidi Chronicles* at the Plymouth when it was still playing next to Richard Greenberg's *Eastern Standard* at the Golden. The two plays clearly belonged together on the same street, but they offer instructive and contrasting insights into how to fashion a serious comedy for the eighties. Both were developed in nonprofit theatres by Yale School of Drama graduates, though of different generations. Both revolve around ambitious young people from the middle class engaged in careers, seeking relationships, troubled by nagging social questions. Both are composed with wit and a certain amount of bile by writers contemporary with their yuppie characters, who, to some extent, share their problems. And both demonstrate what an empty exercise is life without a passionate calling or an overarching commitment.

The difference is that Greenberg does this unwittingly, while Wasserstein makes it the thematic center of her work. *Eastern Standard* satirizes its liberal protagonists for their failure to take life seriously. But being more interested in advancing his romantic Philip Barry plot than in addressing the worrisome issues he raises in his play (AIDS and homosexual love, poverty and the homeless), Greenberg ends up looking more unserious than any of his benighted characters. Wasserstein, though she shares Greenberg's weakness for facile banter, clearly has more of a personal investment in her material. This imparts a certain melancholy to the proceedings and elevates her play above the level of sociological entertainment.

The Heidi Chronicles is not the work of a fully mature playwright, but it is a giant step beyond the cute dating games of *Uncommon Women and Others* and *Isn't It Romantic.* Wasserstein has a wry, self-deprecating humor which helps her avoid righteousness without losing her sting. And while her heroine is both more self-conscious and self-aware than the various self-deluded types she encounters on her spiritual journey, she is a charter member of her own generation. The playwright is old enough to have experienced the protest movements of the sixties along with the disillusionment of the seventies and the cynicism of the eighties. This experience endows her play with themes of nostalgic retrospection. *The Heidi Chronicles* could be considered *The Big Chill* of feminism and of failed American dreams.

Instead of using the device of a reunion, Wasserstein creates an episodic backward-and-forward history, beginning in Chicago in 1965 and ending in present-day New York, designed to dramatize the gulf between the ideals and actions of her Baby Boomer characters. Following a 1989 prologue, where Heidi, a professor of art history, lectures on the neglected art of women, we encounter her as a high-school student at her first dance, as a college peace marcher during the Vietnam War, as a graduate student member of a consciousness-raising feminist rap group, as a protester against the exclusion of women artists from museums—which is to say, in most of the radical postures of the passing decades. During these episodes, she meets a variety of militant women and two recurrent male friends—one a homosexual pediatrician, the other a womanizing lawyer—and in virtually every case witnesses the idealist causes she joined, however marginally, being transformed into opportunism, careerism, and compromise, not to mention marriage without love.

In a typical scene, Heidi is approached by two old friends—formerly feminists, now absorbed in media manipulation. They want her as consultant on a TV sit-com ("All we need is three pages—who these people are and why they're funny"), not because of her intrinsic talents, but because "sit-com is big—art is big—and women are big." Later, addressing an alumni group, she breaks down, finding it unbearable that her generation made so many mistakes. She tells the women she feels stranded—and "I thought the whole point was that we wouldn't feel stranded." The growing emptiness of her world is symbolized by her empty, unfurnished apartment. Unable to connect with a man—there is always an unconsummated relationship with some shadowy editor in the background—she becomes the single mother of an adopted child, hoping its generation will grow up better than hers.

Throughout this odyssey, Heidi remains a bemused outsider with one eyebrow raised at the absurdity of her contemporaries. She has no answers—neither does the playwright—except to maintain a degree of grace and style in the face of the general disillusionment. Wasserstein is an acute social observer. She seems to recognize that despite the typically American hunger for total fulfillment, it's just not possible to have it all. She also seems to suggest that the feminist movement, instead of reforming society, has succeeded largely in introducing women to the ravening competitiveness of the given circumstances, which is to say it has encouraged women to imitate the worst qualities of men.

This is not a conclusion destined to please the sisterhood, but it is a lot more honest and courageous than the moral of, say, *Working Girl*, where the heroine's ascent up the Wall Street ladder is cheered on by virtually everyone, except those being pierced by her stiletto heels. Despite her disenchantment, Heidi will no doubt continue to battle on behalf of her sex for equal rights and recognition. And her slide lecture, like Wasserstein's play, makes a convincing case for women artists achieving the same ready acceptance as men. But Heidi's argument for true equality also demands that women be assessed by the same ethical criteria as men, which makes *The Heidi Chronicles* less a celebration of the yuppie standard of values than a subterranean assault on it.

Wasserstein's handling of female character is as deft as her treatment of feminist ideology, and her collective of lesbians, career women, radicals, and professionals is amusingly drawn, especially in the rap session, when the militant women end up hugging each other and singing camp songs, as well as in a talk-show sequence featuring a vacuous blond hostess with a coffee cup who keeps repeating, "Boy, I'm impressed." Where I still sense theatrical immaturity is in the playwright's dialogue—not from a lack of wit, but from an excess of it. Wasserstein's characters, all of them educated, are almost ferociously epigrammatic. Their weakness for wisecracks makes them seem shallower than intended and undercuts the seriousness of the work. It remains to be seen whether in her next play Wasserstein will manage the infinitely more difficult task of *not* being clever.

Dan Sullivan's production is careful and competent and occasionally more. Tom Lynch's witty use of projections and sliding panels, though somewhat lost on the large Plymouth stage, is nevertheless ingeniously simple, while Pat Collins's lighting nicely manages to localize the playing area. There are some casting weaknesses, but Joan Allen brings a bent-frame sense of awkwardness, earnestness, and irony to the title role; and Ellen Parker, Anne Lange, and Joanne Camp display a transforming variety in other female portraitures. Among the men I was impressed by Boyd Gaines as the anguished pediatrician and, though he struck me as somewhat hyperactive, by Peter Friedman as the sell-out radical who, after joining a corporate law firm, begins publishing a celebrity magazine for Baby Boomers. All of these characters are clearly perceived and cleanly acted. What they lack at present is the deeper emotional range that would catapult the play off the platform of contemporary commentary into a sphere of dimensioned art. Perhaps that will be the next stage of this promising writer's development.

(1989)

Orpheus Condescending

(*Orpheus Descending*)

Tennessee Williams' *Orpheus Descending* was originally staged in 1957, seventeen years after the failure in Boston of his first commercially produced play, *Battle of Angels*. With the exception of Eliot Norton, who saluted the young author's unusual talent, none of the Boston critics managed to recognize the sound of a new theatrical voice, and the play abruptly closed, despite Williams' offer to make radical revisions. Williams, who did not take kindly to failure, stubbornly persisted in his desire to rewrite the play: *Orpheus Descending* is the belated result. Produced on Broadway under the direction of Harold Clurman, with Cliff Robertson and Maureen Stapleton in leading roles, the new play failed as well, though for different reasons. By this time, Williams' work was being criticized less for unconventionality than for predictability. After a series of well-deserved triumphs, the playwright was beginning to repeat himself.

The major character alteration Williams made in the intervening years was to transform the heroine from a retiring Southern housewife (Miriam Hopkins in *Battle of Angels*) into a lusty Italian virago. The female lead in *Orpheus Descending* was written for Anna Magnani, who wouldn't commit to a stage run but later appeared with Marlon Brando in the film version, *The Fugitive Kind*. Williams kept the subplot involving the sensitive ex-gigolo, Val Xavier, and the neurotic aristocrat, Carol Cutrere (an early version of Blanche DuBois). And he preserved the melodramatic conflict between the bright angels of sexual freedom and the dark angels of Southern repression. But if, as Williams claimed, 75 percent of the writing was new, most of the additions were fat injections—bloated metaphors regarding the corruption of innocence by the forces of darkness.

These capsize the play. Instead of proceeding from the action, Williams' windy images seem like the burps of literary indigestion. Clearly, *Orpheus Descending* is more about mythmaking than playmaking. Whenever someone is poised to advance the (preposterous) plot, the character stops to describe the significance of snakeskin jackets or the purity of legless birds that never touch the earth. Val Xavier bears the name of two Catholic saints, and is confused by a female visionary with Jesus Christ (the play takes place just before Easter, with Val acting as a surrogate sacrificial object). Yet this Lawrentian "fox in a chicken coop" is also endowed with the capacity to "burn down a woman," to run a temperature as high as a dog's, to hold his breath for three minutes, to stay awake for forty-eight hours, and to go a whole day without passing water.

In other words, emblems of Christian renunciation are continually colliding with images of macho muscle-flexing, and all are undermined by the mythological symbolism suggested in the title. In *Battle of Angels*, Val expressed his artistic inclinations by writing a book; in *Orpheus Descending*, he is a musician, toting a twelve-string guitar signed by Leadbelly and other blues greats. The analogy with Orpheus' lyre is obvious enough, and Val's descent into the depths of Southern bigotry to redeem the benighted Lady Torrance is designed to mirror Orpheus' descent into Hell to rescue Eurydice. Yet I suspect that Williams' fascination with the Orpheus myth was stimulated more by a Dionysian variant, described by Robert Graves, where this demi-god is pursued by maenads for engaging in homosexual practices (the maddened women tear him to pieces, then watch his severed head floating down a river singing beautiful songs). Among the many false things about plays like *Orpheus Descending* is that Williams—like William Inge and for similar reasons—was not prepared to reveal to a Broadway audience his real theme: the violent fate of the homoerotic artist in an intolerant patrilinear society.

The same kind of reticence marred such plays as *Sweet Bird of Youth* and *Cat on a Hot Tin Roof*—also Oedipal revenge stories weakened by fake phallic posturing and camouflaged references to sexual corruption. Williams' men and women may engage in passionate embraces, but the true heat of his plays is provided by the punishing father figure—Boss Finley or Big Daddy or Jabe Torrance—when he threatens the hero with real or symbolic castration. However melodramatically conceived, this character carries the weight of genuine threat; and it is not until Jabe Torrance lumbers down the stairs in the final scenes of *Orpheus Descending* that the play begins to develop dramatic tension. It is the same tension described by Freud in *Moses and Monotheism*, where he interprets the ritual of circumcision as the father's warning to the potentially incestuous son that if he makes a move on Mom, he'll chop off the rest.

This may explain why, despite the rampant sensuality in his work, Williams almost invariably associates eroticism with mutilation or death: his later plays are comprehensible only as disguised family romances. Williams' habit of pairing off sexually ravenous older women and sexually available young men—and this combination appears in at least seven of his plays—may reflect his own unhappy experiences in the markets of rough trade, but it also suggests the courtship of a seductive mother and her mother-fixated son. Which may be why the vindictive daddy is usually lurking in the wings brandishing his pruning shears.

Peter Hall dredges this unconscious theme to the surface in the final scene, when he shows the hapless Val being led naked to his doom by a redneck sheriff carrying a blow torch. It is one of many Expressionist interpolations in the English production he has restaged at the Neil Simon Theatre. *Orpheus Descending* is hardly a realistic play, but this Freudian nightmare is so supercharged it makes Elia Kazan look like a minimalist. The ominous opening moments are punctuated by pouring rain, barking dogs, and groaning music, as if credits were about to roll on *The Omen* or *The Entity*. Automobile headlights continually rake the windows of the Torrance General Store—is everyone in town using this street for U-turns?—while the electricals change so often you'd think Stanley Kowalski was upstairs getting the colored lights going with Stella. A coterie of prattling women deliver the tedious exposition directly to the audience, characters materialize from corners of the room, and a series of overloaded performances blow the fuses of an already overloaded play.

Vanessa Redgrave, I fear, is the biggest circuit breaker. I wasn't a fan of her Lady Torrance in London, where her accent seemed more Polish than Italian (now it's a combination of Polish, Swedish, and Irish), but by contrast with what she's doing on Broadway, her previous acting was a model of decorum. There's no quiet in this woman, no sensuality, ultimately no truth; even the breathless radiance of her curtain call struck me as false. I suspect this restless overwrought performance may be a form of compensation. Rather than swelling the ranks of great Williams heroines, as some have said, she's been seriously miscast. Lady Torrance is juicy, fleshly, curvilinear, passionate, a woman who acts from the groin and the soul; Redgrave is angular, dry, edgy, hoarse, hysterical, a woman who acts from her bones, muscles, and nerves. Redgrave is unafraid to take chances on stage or to look unattractive—in one scene she appears in a hairnet, wearing no makeup. But even her risks seem ostentatious. She's always on, always exploding with anger, and the botched accent, rather than being a technical glitch in an otherwise fine performance, is a constant reminder that she's engaged less in a form of acting than in a species of impersonation.

The supporting performances represent an unsuccessful effort to sustain a shape in this sandstorm. These are all competent American actors, but few are allowed to stand up to the star. An exception is Tammy Grimes as the sheriff's goofy wife. Not an actress usually celebrated for restraint or understatement, she has some subtle and powerful moments, especially when, telling a story about holy water, she almost seems internally burned. Another is Marcia Lewis as a mean-spirited nurse. And Anne Twomey, as a pasty-faced Carol Cutrere, looks like, though she lacks the power of, Picasso's *Repasseuse*.

But Brad Sullivan, an actor who usually plays weaklings, doesn't capture the brutal Oedipal menace of Jabe Torrance, and Kevin Anderson, though an attractive performer, lacks the experiential weight for Val Xavier. Anderson certainly has more sexual energy than his weak counterpart in London, but he's too innocent for the part and there's simply no electricity flowing between him and Redgrave. Their relationship is all talk, and without sufficient pressure from a strong male actor, nothing can stop Redgrave from chewing the scenery.

As a result, this *Orpheus Descending* seems to me like a long, tedious circumnavigation of Williams' dream life, with a plot not far removed from soap opera (a spinoff of *General Hospital* called *General Store*). Its endlessly reiterated theme could be compressed within a single sentence: "We are the fugitive kind, tainted with corruption but wild in the country, who want to live, live, live, and fly high above the earth like legless birds in our snakeskin jackets." If you can bear listening to this kind of boozy music for three hours, you'll like the show. But you should also weigh my dyspeptic response against a critical reception that has been virtually unqualified in praise of play, production, and leading actress. In short, mine is an opinion you're perfectly free to ignore. I didn't like *Batman* either.

(1989)

Plays for People Perhaps

(*Gypsy*; *Other People's Money*)

Two recent productions are giving audiences the kind of pleasure one rarely finds in the New York theatre anymore. Arthur Laurents' book for *Gypsy* and Jerry Sterner's Wall Street satire, *Other People's Money*, both center on people with deep moral deficiencies, which means they are rooted in character rather than levitated by mechanical spectacle. And Jule Styne's melodious score for *Gypsy* reminds us of how exhilarating Broadway show music once was, before being smeared with Andrew Lloyd Webber's patented brand of oleomargarine.

Gypsy also reminds us of what an inspired lyricist Stephen Sondheim is—or was, before he began composing his own scores. His stunning *West Side Story* debut had already established him as a shrewd master of ironic verse. "Officer Krupke," particularly, with its abrupt transitions, unexpected internal rhymes, and street-smart wit, and "America," with its demythologizing of tropical island fantasies, were in refreshing contrast to Laurents' book, a sudsy reduction of *Romeo and Juliet* into interethnic soap opera. In *A Funny Thing Happened on the Way to the Forum*, he displayed an equally warm affinity for the raucous rhythms of vaudeville and burlesque, even though his score for that musical, sprightly and exuberant as it was, struck me as somewhat superfluous to an event that already had integrity as straightforward Plautine farce. As Sondheim's musical ambitions escalated, I imagine, his lyrics lost some of their edge, becoming their least congenial in the blurry aesthetic editorializing of *Sunday in the Park with George* or the chic urban doggerel of *Into the Woods* (de-da-de-da). Sondheim has surely written some wonderful songs. But his compulsion to marry serial music and *Sprechstimme*, not to mention furrowed (middle) brow themes, to the conventions of musical comedy has resulted in compositional forms that not only etiolate his scores but also denature his literary wit.

In *Gypsy*, however, he is inspired—both by the characters Laurents based on the show-business memoirs written by the principals and by Styne's genius for melodic line. The man responsible for the original rhyme schemes of "Small World," the comic confusions of "Mr. Goldstone," and the ecdysiast enthusiasms of "Gotta Have a Gimmick" is riding some very special wave that lifts the whole occasion. As an experimental auteur, Sondheim has sometimes been plagued by mannerism and pretentiousness, but as a lyricist of Broadway show tunes, he still has no peer.

The narrative strength of *Gypsy* does not lie in its title character. This is not so much the story of an Ugly Duckling as that of a Stage Hen—a species of ambitious American mother who at the premiere in 1958 was to become the subject of musical comedy for the very first time. Rose is the heart of the work, the only character endowed with any complication, and her single-minded, sometimes brutal determination to turn her older daughter, Baby June, into a star makes her sacrifice not only her own love life but the happiness of her other daughter, Louise. Professionally ignored and a little disdained by Rose, Louise enjoys a fabled metamorphosis—not into a swan (though she brandishes swan feathers), but into the stylish stripper Gypsy Rose Lee. Baby June becomes the actress-playwright June Havoc. In the memoirs both women wrote, Rose is a less affectionate and forgivable figure. But the same qualities that seemed somewhat repellent to her children make the revival timely. In her independence of mind and her refusal to be cowed or domesticated, Rose satisfies certain feminist requirements that make her more acceptable to her sisters than to her daughters. What may also have influenced her treatment is the relationship of the musical's three male Jewish creators to their own mothers. They invest what might otherwise be considered a monstrous maternal drive with exculpatory grit and courage.

What lends *Gypsy* real color, though, is its theatrical wrap-around. Kenneth Foy's basic set is a universal backstage and all human events become a subspecies of show business ("Don't you know there's a Depression?" "Of course, I know. I read *Variety*"). Appearing in a number of broken-down vaudeville houses in a number of depressed cities, Baby June in her blond curls, white rolled stockings, and gold shoes leads her four newsboys (Louise included) through numberless choruses of "Let Me Entertain You," punctuated by handstands, splits, baton twirling, and Jerome Robbins' wonderfully satiric choreography. Eventually, time intervenes—abetted by a celebrated strobe-light transformation—to change Baby June first into Dainty June and then into a June Bride after she walks out on the act to get married, leaving Mom to belt out "Everything's Coming Up Roses" through clenched teeth at the fall of the first-act curtain.

After failing to fill June's golden shoes as a vaudeville star, Louise enjoys her own transformation when she learns she's not only beautiful but can stimulate men with arch commentary while removing long white gloves. It is Rose who coaches her to be grand and elegant ("with that classy lady-like walk"), but her willingness to expose Louise to the male leers of the burlesque house is enough to make her boyfriend take a walk. Louise, now a headliner at Minsky's (I used to sneak in to ogle her there at the age of eleven), declares her own independence, while in "Rose's Turn" the abandoned mother expresses defiant self-pity, before receiving absolution from her daughter on the way to a party.

This is all sure stuff and it is played to the hilt by Tyne Daly and a strong supporting cast under Laurents' knowing direction. Daly doesn't age a year through the decades of the action—she is always the good-natured, if portly, *Cagney and Lacey* wisecracker in a page-boy—and she often seems less to be singing songs than announcing station stops. Still, she's a more polished, more romantic actress than Merman, and by using the piercing top notes of her speaking voice, abetted by clever amplification in the songs, she manages to simulate the loudmouth requirements of the classical belter. Where she fails, and the whole enterprise falls down, is in acknowledging the coarseness and ruthlessness that motivate a stage mother's ambitions for her children. But one shouldn't look too hard for Mother Courage's wagon on the stage of a Broadway musical.

Other People's Money is about another redeemable monster in the American vein. Closer to the ethical ambiguousness of Mike Nichols' *Working Girl* than to the moral firmness of Oliver Stone's *Wall Street* or Caryl Churchill's *Serious Money*, Jerry Sterner's play is the "Let Me Entertain You" of arbitrages, substituting the arcane mysteries of inside trading for the inside dope of show business. Ostensibly an examination of predatory financial practices, replete with definitions of "white knights," "shark repellents," "poison pills," "golden parachutes," and other current terms in the corporate lexicon, *Other People's Money* is really a celebration of the Romance of Capitalism, whose hero is magically transformed before our eyes from an object of disgust into a heroic icon.

As played by Kevin Conroy, with matted hair and beard, stained suit, spreading paunch, disappearing neck, hunched back, and red suspenders, "Larry the Liquidator" Garfinkle makes his first appearance as a singularly obnoxious Jew. He is visiting a Rhode Island wire-and-cable company with the intention of gobbling it up, and by contrast with the honest New Englanders who run the place in their cardigan sweaters and modest suits, he behaves as if he's competing for Vulgarian of the Year. "Haven't seen a place this shitty since I left the Bronx," he announces to the startled office staff, which recoils, along with the audience, before his repulsive mannerisms. Responsive only to dogs, dough, and doughnuts (not of course those baked with honey or whole wheat), Larry at first seems like a walking vindication of anti-Semitic prejudice.

On the narrative surface, the play is about the extinction of the old business values—employers who loved their workers and their product—by the new predatory arbitrageurs who love only money. But while Larry is perfectly willing to admit he is motivated by greed ("I don't need the money, I *want* the money. Money is unconditional acceptance"), the playwright is really more interested in pulling off a theatrical stunt familiar to us from such works as *The Phantom of the Opera*—turning the monster into the love interest, making the audience embrace the object of its initial disgust. The moment the beautiful female lawyer, Kate Sullivan, sets out to battle Larry on behalf of the company, you realize that the play is to be a romantic comedy rather than a social satire, with Larry and Kate playing Beatrice and Benedick. He may destroy the company and put all its employees out of work, but Kate somehow finds him irresistibly charming, and by the close of the curtain, she has become first his lawyer, then his partner, then his wife (their two kids are called "Little Bear" and "Little Bull").

"Whatever happened to that brave young girl who set out to do battle to heal all the world's ills?" her mother pauses to ask while trying to comfort the ethical employer before he dies (two years later) from the struggle. Apparently, that brave young girl has gone into the office shredder, along with John F. Kennedy's inaugural address and remaindered copies of *Born Yesterday*. One has to admire how the playwright and the production carry off this act of moral equivocation. Conroy, who played *King John* in Central Park for Papp (here he seems to be playing *Richard III*), is a bit overblown in the opening scenes—his blustering performance is better suited for the Winter Garden than the intimate Minetta Lane—but the actor's high obnoxiousness soon gives way to a steadily evolving charm. Sterner apparently regards Garfinkle's counterparts—Ivan Boesky, Carl Icahn, Irving Jacobson—as "modern gunslingers" in the tradition of John Wayne and Gary Cooper, and like all such heroes who square off on a dusty road, Garfinkle certainly has his appeal. So does spunky Kate in the pungent performance of Mercedes Ruehl (all the parts are vigorously acted). But the real triumph of the evening is how *Other People's Money* manages to make the skewed values currently turning us into a second-rate nation the object of consent and applause.

(1989)

Political Theatre: The Havels and Have-Nots

(*Some Americans Abroad*; *Crowbar*)

The accession of a playwright, Vaclav Havel, to the Presidency of Czechoslovakia may not portend a new era of philosopher-kings, but it certainly reflects the links that have historically existed in Europe between politics and art. Elizabeth I of England wrote verses; so did Frederick the Great of Prussia; even the current Pope squeezed out a few youthful plays. Richard Brinsley Sheridan served in Parliament, W. B. Yeats was a "smiling public man" in the Irish Dáil, and Bernard Shaw stood for election as a Fabian candidate. It is true that American writers occasionally run for office, but only our movie stars manage to get elected. If Ronald Reagan or Clint Eastwood were ever to be libeled with the name of artist, they'd probably reach for a Colt or Magnum. We value performance, not intellect or imagination; that's the reason our writers turn into performers, too. In Europe, however, the creative artist remains a hugely influential figure, which explains why so many of them, including Havel, have spent so much time in jail or exile. It is a truism that the European writer *matters* in a way that the American writer does not, though the latter works in an atmosphere of considerably more freedom.

Despite his delicacy of temperament and powerful ironic intellect, Havel is not in my opinion a dramatist of the first rank. He has expended his energies less in refining his art than in bearing witness to the oppressive conditions of his own country. Consequently, like Athol Fugard (who would be a valuable addition to any new South African government), he is notable as the embodiment more of stirring humanistic convictions than of inspired revelations. Havel's incredible media exposure will no doubt result in numerous productions of his plays about which little truth will be spoken. But in becoming Czechoslovakia's President he has finally found his true calling—to help in the task of reshaping his disfigured nation into a work of democratic art.

Havel's plays suffer the fate of all engaged dramaturgy—untidy reality is sometimes shunted aside by the force of strong political convictions. American plays usually suffer from the opposite condition, lacking any political content at all. Our playwrights are often criticized for wanting a public dimension, for choosing to write what the English critic Benedict Nightingale calls "diaper plays" about personal family relationships. For that reason, two current works are unusual—each tries, with varying degrees of success, to generalize its plot into a study of the American character.

Richard Nelson's *Some Americans Abroad* at Lincoln Center's Mitzi E. Newhouse Theater was first commissioned by the Royal Shakespeare Company. Like not a few of our dramatists (David Mamet included), Nelson presently seems to be finding a more congenial home in England for his work. An impressionist study in the Russian manner about a group of American academics on a British theatre tour, *Some Americans Abroad* may very well be Nelson's most focused play yet, and it is receiving a subtle, well-acted production in the hands of Roger Michell. There are few direct confrontations in this work. It is Nelson's transparent assumption that the American professoriate is either too timid or too cowardly to engage each other honestly. But, as in Chekhov, careers are being ruined and lives are being broken as people engage in the customary rites of everyday life.

Chief among these are eating and theatregoing, both symbolized in the setting—a group of suspended dining tables and lawn furniture, backed by a large blowup of memorial verses to Shakespeare. Collected around lunch at Luigi's in Covent Garden are a sextet of students and teachers, discussing disarmament, the death penalty, and *Major Barbara*, their section leader being the department chairman, Joe Taylor. A bearded former radical and chief defender of Shaw's "intellectual honesty," Taylor is entrusted with the task of telling Henry McNeil, a dowdy nontenured Milton scholar, that he has no future at the college. But he lacks the "intellectual honesty" to admit he's offered McNeil's job to another.

Many lunches and play visits later, after two of the teachers (one of them married) have started an affair, Taylor is confronted with another academic crisis: a female student has dropped out of the tour to sleep with an Amherst boy. Taylor's handling of this apparently momentous dereliction is as bungled as his treatment of McNeil. And when the girl, "to save her butt," accuses another teacher of touching her breasts, Taylor accepts the charge without sufficient investigation. At the last dinner of the tour, after everyone has thoroughly tired of three-and-a-half-hour British productions, the retired chairman of the department—a forthright outspoken conservative—tells McNeil he hears he has to "move on," while the embarrassed Taylor, fumbling with the bill, tries to find some tactful way of saving the department the expense of an invited guest's meal.

Filling out this undersketched plot are group recitations of Wordsworth's "Westminster Bridge" under umbrellas (followed by off-key renderings of "God Save the Queen"), and considerable postprandial chat—as the academics scrape their spumoni cups and wave their breadsticks—about the splendors of the British stage and the vulgarity of (other) American tourists. The satire on the typical Anglophilia of our cultivated elite is quite delicious, and it is deliciously fashioned in the Horatian manner, through indirection and representation. Nelson may have overestimated the current importance of the *loco parentis* function, not to mention the scandal power of college amours (sexual harassment excluded) in an age of comparative erotic freedom. But he has certainly nailed the hypocrisy, timidity, and expediency of certain university administrators, not to mention the pretentiousness and snobbery of educated middle-class Americans abroad.

As director, Michell begins each scene by lowering another prop from the ceiling to set the stage, and flashing the lights briefly, as if each episode were a photo opportunity. He also handles the cast with discretion and authority. Colin Stinton as Taylor captures the weak, flabby nature of a weasel who uses his intelligence to escape reality rather than confront it (in one scene, he tells an obnoxious American tourist: "I'm British, I'm a naturalized British citizen; I tutor at Oxford"), and Bob Balaban's McNeil is appropriately reticent, panicked, and armored against reality. Kate Burton, as his embittered wife, fixes Taylor with eyes that are lasered with hate, and Henderson Forsythe, playing the conservative chairman, comes on looking and sounding like a latter-day Ezra Pound. John Bedford Lloyd and the always dependable Frances Conroy are the clandestine lovers. And Richard Nelson, who virtually never repeats himself from play to play, may very well have found his theatrical identity as the American David Lodge.

Mac Wellman's *Crowbar* is a blunter work than *Some Americans Abroad* and its social ideas are cruder—but it deserves some marks for ambition, if not for originality. *Crowbar* is not only being performed at the Victory Theatre—a newly renovated house on Forty-second Street. It is, in effect, a history of that theatre, first called the Republic when owned by Oscar Hammerstein, then named for David Belasco after he refurbished it for his spectacular productions (starting with *Sag Harbor* in 1900), then renamed the Republic when it featured movies, burlesque, and porno films, and finally dubbed the Victory, having reverted to its former legitimate glory. Besides being a history of the theatre, *Crowbar* also serves as something of a theatre tour, minutely examining, with floodlights and flashlights, every corner of the ancient stage and auditorium, and especially the gorgeous, cupid-decorated overhead dome. The audience is seated both on stage and to the side, with most of the action in the orchestra and balconies, providing a clear view of the actors—and of a daily critic snoozing in his chair.

Billed as a "pataphysical compilation" culled from newspaper stories around the turn of the century (the date of *Sag Harbor*'s opening), *Crowbar* is intended as a ghost story, its dust-covered spirits being the various suicides, homicides, infanticides, and lunatics of the time. A mostly female chorus stomps through the house like a spectral chain gang, a limber figure with a saxophone (Reg E. Cathey) provides the exposition, a Polish woman (Elzbieta Czyzewska) wails about the changes in management over the past ninety years and the plight of her poor benighted country (which "doesn't exist most of the time"), her bewildered husband (Omar Shapli) tells us that "America is an empty theatre and all theatres are haunted," and finally David Belasco (Yusef Bulos) materializes to extol his ingenious technical improvements and to regret "the infamy of consuming time."

Although well executed, the production spinoffs of *Marat/Sade* and *The Phantom of the Opera* tire one rather quickly, and so does the inflated style of the dialogue (one is tempted to ask, along with one of the characters, for "a little reduction of the garrulity"). Because they are content to substitute rhetorical tirades for dramatic speech, Wellman's historical ghosts never manage to escape their tabloid origins. And the wider theme seems to have a tabloid imprint, too. I'm not certain how much more I know about my country after being told it's an empty haunted theatre. I'm not even sure how much more I know about the theatre after hearing it described as "a kind of big place—with red walls—like the inside of a human heart—but not as empty." Let me admit, however, with blushes, that I have never been numbered among those who grow wet-eyed about the past history of endangered Broadway houses. For while I am delighted whenever such legitimate theatres as the Victory in Times Square and the Majestic in Brooklyn are rescued from urban decay and porno nude shows, I confess to being much more interested in what goes on inside these buildings than in the ghosts and ornaments of their past.

What's going on inside the Victory at the moment is a riot of environmental techniques, performed with all the enthusiasm, and some of the limitations, of an advanced drama school exercise. This En Garde Arts production seems imitatively avant-garde. Mr. Wellman possesses, at times, a certain daffy Joycean eloquence which augurs well for future better-formed plays, and Richard Caliban's direction shows control of mood, effects, and movement. But in view of all that's happening in the world these days—during a time when at least one playwright has things on his mind urgent enough to dominate the affairs of an entire country—*Crowbar* seems peculiarly theatre-enclosed. For all its technical ambitiousness, it's another melancholy sign of how little American art seems to matter in the universe at large.

(1990)

Prelude to a Fairy Tale

(*Prelude to a Kiss*)

Craig Lucas has the power to make us see things his way, which is the mark of an artist. He peers at the world through thick ground lenses, exposing warts and blemishes undetected by the naked eye. He shares this magnified vision with the filmmaker David Lynch. Indeed, Lucas' best work, *Reckless*, was a kind of homage to Lynch's disturbing film *Blue Velvet*. Both were stories of twisted sex, gratuitous violence, unexpected revelations. Both focused on the blisters beneath the Pepsodent, the malignant crawling things that lurk behind the smiling surface of billboard America. And both seemed wholly original, yet almost wholly persuasive in their documentation of the dark underside of life.

Blue Velvet tended to lose its hypnotic hold on us whenever Lynch felt compelled to define its mysteries. The snake-like hose that moved in torment through the undergrowth was a more shocking image before it was analogized into the stroke being suffered by the hero's father, just as the severed ear discovered in the bushes was hauntingly suggestive so long as we didn't know its origin. I found *Reckless* somewhat more consistent in sustaining its atmosphere of disorientation. The play isolated us in a kindless, airless, gravity-less world, tangential to our own, yet possessed of its own special properties. If Lucas had offered to explain why the heroine's husband had taken out a contract on her life, or why every town she visited was called Springfield and every day was Christmas, he would have sacrificed poetry for clarity. The alchemy of the unconscious, of hallucination or dream, is to turn images and characters from waking reality into elusive chimerical forms. Explanation and analysis are the reductive tools of the rational scientific mind, not of the visionary imagination. They belong to the tradition of social-psychological realism.

Lucas' new play, *Prelude to a Kiss*, is hardly a work of realism. Still, it fails when it explicates a poetic premise into a prosaic fable. Highly entertaining and also deeply disappointing, the play will advance the playwright's reputation through a regression in his art. Lucas has lost little of his abrupt, declarative intensity. What he has lost (let us hope temporarily) is the capacity to remain in doubt and ambiguity, the courage to surrender one's need for absolute certainty.

Before posing its tantalizing hypothesis, *Prelude to a Kiss* begins with a conventional courtship, as romantic as the title-inspired song that Ella Fitzgerald is singing when the lights come up. Two young people meet at a party and fall in love. Rita is a part-time bartender in a chic club who claims she hasn't slept an hour since she was fourteen, a socialist who doesn't want to bring babies into an evil world. Peter, a literate young man who works in a publishing firm, spends a lot of time in Europe. After discussing their histories, literary tastes, and sexual preferences, they agree to marry. And when her dentist-father and housewife-mother give their approval, the suburban wedding takes place.

The wedding festivities, however, are interrupted by the appearance of a disreputable old man who insists on kissing the bride. The set goes gray; the old man staggers and kneels at the feet of Rita's father, saying, "Daddy, it's me." At this point the play becomes intriguingly Lucas-skewed. On honeymoon in the Caribbean, Peter begins to believe that Rita has changed. His socialist bride has bought a $1,500 gold bracelet and is indifferent to the poverty of Jamaica. She sleeps soundly every night. She claims she hasn't read Freud, when they discussed his case histories before they were married. She is eager to bear a child. She doesn't know how to make his favorite drink. She seems vague about the history and makeup of her own family. In short, "a different Rita."

Nobody else seems to notice any difference, but Rita's presumed alteration and her lack of patience with Peter's suspicions cause marital problems. The couple quarrel, and Rita's father removes her things from the apartment. Is Peter paranoid? Has Rita really changed?—or is this a parable about the strangers who meet in marriage? "They're always changing," one character tells us. "That is life. Things are always shifting, growing." The first act closes in a shroud.

Which the second act unfortunately unveils. Peter's wife and the old man have exchanged souls through the kiss. Seeking Rita, Peter finds her trapped within a feeble male body, reflecting on old age and forgetfulness and the death of friends ("And as a final reward for all this, you disappear"). But Peter has married for better or for worse; he still adores his wife; and in a genuinely touching moment, he kisses the old man on his wrinkled lips. In the happy-ever-after conclusion, Rita recovers her soul from the usurper, who reverts to his avuncular self.

As a parable about the spiritual, platonic nature of love, *Prelude to a Kiss* has charm and sweetness. But what promised at first to be a penetrating glimpse into the heart of darkness is thinned into a slight fable about the transmigration of souls. The play reminded me of *Ladyhawke*, a movie about two lovers separated by a curse—transformed into a falcon and a wolf, they assume human shape at different times of the day. It reminded me even more of Carlo Gozzi's *The King Stag*, where a king—his body usurped by a villainous minister—is forced to win back his wife in the shape of a sickly old man (like Peter, she finds that true love is more powerful than the lineaments of physical beauty).

I don't wish to appear indifferent to the appeal of fable or fairy tale, but Lucas promises something deeper in *Prelude to a Kiss*. Although approving critics are mining it for autobiographical clues, the play is basically an escapist fantasy, which may be why Hollywood is already bidding for the property and beckoning the actors. And, meticulously directed by Norman René in this Circle Rep production, the acting is very good: the romantic fervor of Alec Baldwin as Peter, the silken appeal of Mary-Louise Parker as Rita, the crusty humor of Barnard Hughes as the Old Man, and the satiric edge of Joyce Reehling in a variety of roles. I also liked Loy Arcenas' setting—focused like most of the author's plays on a mysterious Magritte-like window, surrounded by crawling branches that augur a darker, more resonant experience than Lucas has managed this time to create.

(1990)

Soured Grapes

(*The Grapes of Wrath*)

The Steppenwolf company of Chicago is identified by a realistically acted, socially committed, emotionally accessible style of production, which may be why so many of its actors and products have entered the mainstream. It is not inappropriate to find its epic version of *The Grapes of Wrath* on Broadway, though its fate is uncertain. Ensconced at the Cort to high critical praise, the Steppenwolf production doesn't seem to be drawing an audience. I'm sorry about that, but not entirely surprised. The production is admirable, but like most Broadway shows the play is seriously out of date.

With economical means and considerable imagination, Frank Galati (the director and adapter) has created a conceptually brilliant work, brimming with integrity and extremely well acted. It is also rather extraneous except as a homage to Steinbeck's inspirational novel about an Oklahoma family's odyssey to California in quest of migratory work. Possibly, the production is meant to point to parallels with the plight of today's homeless and dispossessed. But one quick look at the sidewalks of New York is enough to suggest how inadequate are the author's eulogies to the indestructiveness of the "little people." Like Brecht's Mother Courage, Steinbeck's Joads display what Paul Tillich called the "courage to be" in the face of circumstances that would otherwise suggest extinction. But Brecht had the artistic sense to endow his heroine with the complicated moral qualities enjoyed by all humanity, while Steinbeck (as Lionel Trilling observed) makes poverty synonymous with nobility and wealth with malevolence. To dispense vices and virtues according to income is the stuff of Marxist melodrama—not an uncommon form in the thirties, but tiresome even to Soviet critics today.

Equally ennobled in *The Grapes of Wrath* are the union organizers, and while nobody will deny the historical importance of the labor movement, it is not so likely today to excite such unqualified admiration in the minds of audiences. For every idealistic César Chavez advancing the interests of the fruit pickers, there have been at least fifty fat-cat mob-related Jimmy Hoffas stealing from pension funds, if not sending goons with baseball bats in battle against their own constituents. One looks a little wryly at the sacrifice of Steinbeck's Preacher Jim Casy in light of the future development of the movement he died for. The same problem blights our appreciation of Odets' *Waiting for Lefty*.

The Grapes of Wrath, therefore, has value largely as a fable—a fable of the American family holding together against all odds. It is also a mythical evocation of a more innocent age before our hopes for social reform foundered on the rocks of violence, greed, and selfishness. These dark qualities are abundant enough in Steinbeck, but seem shadowy and aberrant. More prominent are resounding affirmations of social optimism and human goodness. Modeled on Exodus, featuring a two-thousand-mile trek across the nation to find the Promised Land, the story supports enough catastrophes to daunt the most intrepid Moses—evictions, floods, murders, and mayhem. Yet its characters remain forever indomitable. "We're the people that live," says the indomitable Ma Joad, "and we ain't goin' to get wiped out. We're the people that go on." And the indomitable Tom Joad, affirming that "a man's gotta do what he's gotta do," adds, "Wherever there's a cop beating up a guy, I'll be there." All this indomitability is heart-stirring, but the homely wisdom tends to grow a bit sticky. And I ain't seen many white working-class folk around lately protesting police brutality.

One must resist the impulse to parody this work, and it is to Galati's credit that he takes it so seriously. Indeed, that's why the production works. Enacted on a simple platform with five inner prosceniums suggesting infinite space, where the actors form images from paintings by Hopper, Wyeth, and Grant Wood, the action proceeds against a country-and-Western aural surround performed on guitar, violin, and jew's harp—only an unfortunate piece of choreography out of Agnes de Mille's *Oklahoma!* mars the authenticity. The focal image is a truck—employed like Mother Courage's wagon as the mobile home containing all the possessions of the itinerant characters. And as with Courage's wagon, the truck's inhabitants are gradually decimated by fateful happenings.

Galati's other image is water—the great Colorado River, in which the characters playfully disport, and the frightening flood that threatens to evict them from their temporary home. (I haven't seen so much rain on stage since *The World of Suzie Wong*.) But the most striking image in the play is the pastoral Pietà that ends it, where Rose of Sharon, her infant having died in childbirth, offers her breast to a starving man. That the unemployed suckler on stage is black—and that earlier in the play the migratory Okies share a campfire with other black people—arouses a suspicion that there's something ahistorical about this historical re-creation, considering the fact that segregation was still very much in force in Depression America, even among such virtuous models as the Joads.

Still, the actors perform with such sincerity and conviction that you tend to ignore such anachronisms, and if the definitive John Ford movie is not quite obliterated from memory, the play creates more of a sense of journey in its panoramic picture of poverty. Gary Sinise's laconic, wide-eyed Tom Joad is less appealing than Henry Fonda's, but somehow seems more authentic, though Lois Smith's vaguely neurotic Ma Joad lacks the maternal stoicism of Jane Darwell's. I also liked Terry Kinney's Jim Casy without losing my affection for John Carradine's sly old preacher in the film. And Lucina Paquet and Nathan Davis added cartoon amusement as Granma and Grampa.

So qualified congratulations to Frank Galati and Steppenwolf for committing so much artistry to such an obsolete project. Since Steinbeck wrote *The Grapes of Wrath*, we have experienced corrupt unionism,

World War II and the Holocaust, Korea and Vietnam, desegregation and race riots, political assassinations and abdications, Watergate and Iran-Contra, ten years of conservative politics, the death of liberalism, and the systematic dismantling of the advances of the New Deal. One can hardly demand foresight of a writer. Still, Brecht did predict the coming of the Nazis, and the greatest artists have always known enough about the human heart to keep their works alive regardless of how history misbehaves.

(1990)

The Lesson of *The Piano Lesson*

(*The Piano Lesson*)

There are reasons why I didn't review the three previous August Wilson productions that moved from the Yale Repertory Theatre to Broadway. Lloyd Richards, who directed them all and guided their passage through a variety of resident theatres en route to New York, succeeded me as Yale's Dean and Artistic Director eleven years ago, and protocol required that I hold my tongue about the progress of a theatre I founded and the conduct of my successor. I broke my resolve in a general article for *The New York Times* regarding the role of Yale and other resident theatres in what I viewed as the homogenization of the nonprofit stage. * I called this process "McTheatre"—the use of sequential nonprofit institutions as launching pads and tryout franchises for the development of Broadway product and the enrichment of artistic personnel. Since the universally acclaimed Broadway production of *The Piano Lesson* at the Walter Kerr brings this process to some kind of crazy culmination—and raises so many troubling cultural questions—I'm going to break my silence once again.

First, let's take a look at the Wilson phenomenon. *The Piano Lesson* is an overwritten exercise in a conventional style—to my mind, the most poorly composed of Wilson's four produced works. None of the previous plays was major, in my opinion, but they each had occasional firepower, even some poetry lying dormant under the surface of their kitchen-sink productions. I don't find much power or poetry at all in

* See "Reimagining the Process," p. 209.

The Piano Lesson, though the play has earned Wilson his second Pulitzer Prize and inspired comparisons with O'Neill (one critic likened him to Shakespeare!). In a sense, the O'Neill comparison is apt. Wilson also has epic ambitions, handicapped by repetitiousness, crude plotting, and clumsy structure. But whereas O'Neill wrote about the human experience in forms that were daring and exploratory, Wilson has thus far limited himself to narrow aspects of the black experience in a relatively literalistic style.

Before his death, O'Neill determined to compose a nine-play cycle about the progressive degeneration of the American spirit (only *A Touch of the Poet* was completed to his satisfaction). Wilson's four plays also have a historical plan—each attempts to demonstrate how the acid of racism has eaten away at black aspirations in the various decades of the twentieth century. *Ma Rainey's Black Bottom*, set in the twenties, shows how black musicians were prevented from entering the mainstream of the American recording industry; *Fences*, set in the fifties, shows how black athletes were prevented from participating in major league baseball; *Joe Turner's Come and Gone*, set in 1911, shows how blacks were reduced to poverty and desperation by the chain-gang system; and *The Piano Lesson*, set in the thirties, shows how black ideals were corroded by slavery. Presumably, Wilson is preparing to cover at least five more theatrical decades of white culpability and black martyrdom. But while this single-minded documentation of American racism is a worthy if familiar social agenda, and no enlightened person would deny its premise, as an ongoing artistic program it is monotonous, limited, locked in a concept of victimization.

In comparison with the raging polemics of Ed Bullins or Amiri Baraka, Wilson's indictments are relatively mild. His characters usually sit on the edge of the middle class, wearing good suits, inhabiting clean homes. Securely shuttered behind realism's fourth wall, they never come on like menacing street people screaming obscenities or bombarding the audience with such phrases as "Black power's gonna get your mama"—which may explain further Wilson's astounding reception. It is comforting to find a black playwright working the mainstream American realist tradition of Clifford Odets, Lillian Hellman, and early Arthur Miller, a dignified protest writer capable of discussing the black experience without intimidating the readers of the Home section of your Sunday newspaper. Still, enough radical vapor still floats over the bourgeois bolsters and upholstered couches to stimulate the guilt glands of liberal white audiences. Unable to reform the past, we sometimes pay for the sins of history and our society through artistic reparations in a cultural equivalent of Affirmative Action.

On its three-year tryout road to Broadway, *The Piano Lesson* could have benefited from some more honest criticism; in present form, it represents a backward step. Like *Fences* a family drama, it lacks the interior tension of that work (not to mention the riveting presence of James Earl Jones), and at three hours it's about an hour and a half too long for its subject matter. Buried inside much tedious exposition is a single conflict—between Boy Willie and his sister, Berneice, over a carved piano. Boy Willie wants to sell the piano and buy some farming land down south. Berneice wants to keep it as a token of the family heritage (their mother polished it every day for seventeen years). A repetitive series of confrontations between the two adds little about the conflict but a lot more about the piano as symbolic heirloom. It belonged to Sutter, a slave owner, who sold members of their family in order to buy it for his wife as an anniversary present. Eventually, their father stole it back from Sutter, and was later killed in a box-car fire, while Sutter fell or was pushed down a well.

Wilson pounds this symbolic piano a little heavy-handedly. Like Chekhov's cherry orchard, it is intended to reflect the contrasting values of its characters—Berneice (Madame Ranevsky) finds it a symbol of the past while Boy Willie (Lopakhin) sees only its material value. But Chekhov's people are a lot more complicated than their attitudes; and because Wilson's images fail to resonate, the play seems like much ado about a piano, extended by superfluous filler from peripheral characters. Frying real food on a real stove, turning on real faucets with real hot-and-cold running water, ironing real shirts on real ironing boards, and flushing real toilets (how David Belasco would have loved this production), these colorful supernumeraries natter incessantly on a variety of irrelevant subjects, occasionally breaking into song and dance. This is partly intended as comic relief and *The Piano Lesson* has been praised for its humor. But the domesticated jokes, most of them about watermelons, are about at the level of *The Jeffersons*—even the audience laughter seems canned. As for Wilson's highly lauded dialogue, his language here lacks music—except for one potentially strong speech by Boy Willie about his daddy's hands—usually alternating between the prosaic and the proverbial ("God don' ask what you done. God asks what you gonna do").

What ultimately makes this piano unplayable, however, is the ending, which tacks a supernatural resolution on an essentially naturalistic play.

Sutter's ghost is (inexplicably) a resident in this house, his presence signified from time to time by a lighting special on the stairs. In the final scene, Boy Willie, after numerous efforts to remove the piano (after three hours, I was prepared to run on stage and give him a hand), is blown off his feet by a tumultuous blast. He rushes upstairs to do battle with the ghost, now represented through a scrim by flowing, glowing window curtains. Returning, Boy Willie renounces his desire to take the piano from the house, while the supernumeraries laugh and cry and Berneice praises the Lord. Willie adds, "If you and Maretha don't keep playin' on that piano, me and Sutter both likely to be back." Curtain.

This ending, though arguably less ludicrous, is considerably more forced than the version I saw three years ago at one of the play's numerous station stops. There Willie rushed upstairs as the curtain fell on the illuminated portraits of his slave ancestors in the attic. Either way, the supernatural element is a contrived intrusion. When ghosts begin resolving realistic plots, you can be sure the playwright has failed to master his material, and he has not been helped to shape it by the director. In the hands of his mentor Lloyd Richards, the production manages to exaggerate the flatness and familiarity of the play while submerging whatever could have been distinctive or unique. Instead of urging the author to cut out the fat, Richards (to judge from his interview citing Peter Hall's three-hour *Merchant of Venice* as a precedent) apparently encouraged him to treat every line as holy writ. While the set is crammed with realistic artifacts, the pacing is that of commercial farce. Everyone speaks at top volume with similar rhythms, especially Charles S. Dutton, a capable and powerful actor, who bellows his part at the same pitch and tempo throughout the entire play. (Others—S. Epatha Merkerson, Rocky Carroll, Lou Myers—make strong first impressions without being allowed to develop their characters.) There is no silence in this house, no moments to pause, but despite the relentless tumult, the show seems static—much of the dialogue is spoken around a kitchen table. Characters sometimes walk through the invisible wall between the kitchen and the living room, neglecting the doorway arch the designer (E. David Cosier, Jr.) provided for passage. And the crude handling of the ghost effects reminded me of the creaky TV soap *Dark Shadows*.

August Wilson is still a relatively young man with a genuine if not yet fully developed talent. O'Neill's early plays were just as highly praised, though he wrote nothing truly great until the end of his life. Premature acclaim was actually one of the obstacles to his development; only by facing the demons in his heart at the end of his days, a sick lonely man in a shuttered room, was he able to write with total honesty about his true subject. To judge from *The Piano Lesson*, Wilson is reaching a dead end in his examination of American racism, though another play on the subject (appropriately entitled *Two Trains Running*) is now gathering steam at Yale on its way through the regional railroad depots to its final Broadway destination. It will probably be greeted with the same hallelujah chorus as all his other work. But if he wishes to be a truly major playwright, he would be wise to move on from safe popular sociology and develop the radical poetic strain that now lies dormant in his art. It is not easy to forsake the rewards of society for the rewards of posterity, but the genuine artist accepts no lower standards than the ones he applies to himself.

Speaking of rewards, I have a last word to say about the way this play has been marketed. In the past, resident theatres were usually content to leave their Broadway-bound shows in the hands of commercial producers, collecting a small percentage of the gross for their home institutions. In at least one case (*I'm Not Rappaport*), Dan Sullivan returned his director's fee to the Seattle Rep, believing it was the rightful property of the originating theatre. (The Washington State Supreme Court, arbitrating Sullivan's divorce settlement, agreed with him.) Now look at the producing credits above the title of *The Piano Lesson*:

Lloyd Richards
Yale Repertory Theatre, Center Theatre Group/Ahmanson Theatre
Gordon Davidson and the Jujamcyn Theaters
with Benjamin Mordecai, Executive Producer
in association with
Eugene O'Neill Theatre Center, Huntington Theatre Company
Goodman Theatre and Old Globe Theatre
present

I will refrain from commenting on the propriety of nonprofit directors drawing substantial artistic fees for commercial versions of plays originally funded by subsidized institutions. I will simply ask how much attention such an artistic director can pay to his own institution when he has spent the last three years staging a single play in five different theatres, before producing and directing it on Broadway?

(1990)

She-Plays, American Style

(Machinal; Abundance)

Two plays by and about women have appeared recently on the New York stage, separated by sixty-two years of sexual politics. They suggest how the passage of time can affect the themes, if not the quality, of female literature. In Sophie Treadwell's *Machinal* (1928) at the New York Public Theater, a passive heroine seeks freedom through an act of murder; in Beth Henley's *Abundance* (1990) at the Manhattan Theatre Club, a more active heroine seeks freedom through a burst of careerism. Both are preoccupied with issues confronting women in a masculine world. Both have more interest as sociological artifacts than as works of art.

Of the two, *Machinal* is the more engrossing, partly because of a well-orchestrated production by Michael Greif. I was not overly fond of this play when reviewing its previous Off-Broadway revival (could it have been thirty years ago?). Then, as now, I thought it had value largely as a parade ground for the precision marches of an imaginative director (Gene Frankel in the 1960 version). *Machinal* has all the mechanical simplicity of early American Expressionism—the style that came to us via Germany, through the plays of Georg Kaiser and Ernst Toller. Unlike the expressionistic work of Strindberg, who invented the form as a means of exploring his dream life, German Expressionism was propelled primarily by social-political considerations. And it was these implicit Marxist critiques of the system that were to inform later American manifestations, most notably Eugene O'Neill's *The Hairy Ape* and Elmer Rice's *The Adding Machine*.

Like Rice's Mr. Zero, Treadwell's Miss A (otherwise known as Young Woman) is identified by a generic name, and like Mr. Zero, she works at dehumanizing tasks. After the stagelights go on, industrial lamps are raised, and a stertorous voice announces "Episode One: To Business" over a large radio mike, the various automatons comprising the office work force begin their mechanical functions: typing, adding, telephoning, mimeographing. Miss A is late ("All those bodies pressing—had to get out in the air"), and when she arrives—a pert little thing in black bobbed hair—her tender ears are assailed by a cacophony of homilies ("The early bird catches the worm," "Haste makes waste").

Machinal is based on an actual story, the Ruth Snyder murder case. Snyder was the first woman to die in the electric chair—and the *Playbill* displays a photograph of the execution taken from the front page of the *Daily News* (the headline screamed "DEAD!" in monstrous capitals). This celebrated case inspired a number of fictional works, including James M. Cain's *The Postman Always Rings Twice* and an unproduced play by William Styron and John Phillips called *Dead: A Love Story.* Male authors tend to treat Ruth Snyder as a ruthless lech who persuaded a hapless lover to murder her wealthy husband. Treadwell, ignoring the complicity of the lover, treats her as a neurotic victim of sexual and social oppression, driven to murder as the only alternative to madness and despair.

Miss A is loved by Mr. J, the vice president of the firm, who repels her, possibly because he can converse only in industrial maxims (her choppy conversation, by contrast, seems designed for Western Union: "Kisses? No. I can't"). Still, he represents the one avenue of escape from her uncaring home and unfulfilling work. During their honeymoon, as the hotel chanteuse sings, "I kiss your hand, madam," he tells her dirty jokes and explains the secret of his success ("learning to relax"). In a scene of revulsion and disgust, performed to the sound of drilling as she cries "I want my mother," she is forced to submit to his advances, and later bears him a child. When she meets an attractive young man who kills bandits in Mexico (a part originally played by Clark Gable), she falls for him. Her tensions soften; her language changes from telegraphic messages to consecutive sentences. Nevertheless, the lover decides to return to Mexico. Why? "*Quíen sabe,*" he shrugs. Increasingly rattled by reality, she conks her husband on the head with a bottle filled with stones, is tried, convicted, and led to the chair, while a black prisoner sings spirituals ("I'm gwine up to heaven," as Lenny Bruce once parodied such racial slurs and movie stereotypes, "goin' to find out what a 'gwine' is").

When Miss A is asked in the courtroom why she didn't choose divorce rather than murder, she answers, "I couldn't do that. I couldn't hurt him like that." It is the only startling thought in the play. Otherwise, this tale of a sensitive plant wilting in the age of the machine is declarative, predictable, simplistic. What remains vital and lively, however, are the theatrical possibilities, and Greif sniffs these out like a pig in search of truffles. Jodie Markell as the delicate heroine and John Seitz as the gross good-natured husband both bring drive and conviction to their parts, while the supporting cast performs its choral duties like a well-oiled industrial machine. This *Machinal* has value less as the revival of a forgotten play than as a reconstruction of a forgotten age. Enhanced by David Gallo's setting and Kenneth Posner's lighting, the historical evocation is sufficient to keep us engaged for most of its length.

Both the audience and I were squirming, however, at Beth Henley's *Abundance*. The play makes no sense at all, and when I look at my notes, I can't make sense of them either. I sat through this affair in a vague delirium, keeping awake only by watching two women signing the dialogue for the deaf (they were actually more animated and convincing than the two leading actresses). Perhaps the whole thing should have been mimed. Henley had the interesting idea to write a play about a pair of mail-order brides in the Wyoming Territory during the 1860s. This is hardly well-explored ground, but it is so trampled with self-conscious literary ostentation, so overembellished with self-conscious eccentricity, that it seems indistinguishable from the playwright's more contemporary fandangos.

Bess Johnson (Amanda Plummer) and Macon Hill (Tess Harper) meet in a railroad station on their way to join two husbands they've never seen. They take an instant liking to each other and vow to be friends—not surprising, since they share the same overheated language ("I'm drunk with Western fever," "I love the ocean; it never stops moving," "I can smell destiny; one day I'll write a novel about it"). The men they meet, on the other hand, have none of their imagination or warmth. Bess's husband (Jack) is a brute who knocks her down and terrorizes her with a pistol, while Macon's (William) is a one-eyed farmer whom, though kinder, she finds physically repulsive. Macon teaches Bess to chase falling stars (" 'cause I know we can catch one of them"). She also teaches Bess how to whistle, not an inconsiderable achievement, considering Bess's uncertain wits. These soon deteriorate: "For no apparent reason, she seems to have lost her mind." When her child dies, she dresses up a prairie dog in the child's clothes. Jack is also in "an insane condition." In addition to threatening Bess's life, he sets fire to their cabin, which makes her long "for the flutter of angels' wings." Both take refuge with Macon and William. But although William gets a new eye and a new mustache to please his indifferent wife, and although Jack continues to act coarsely (he eats William's pound cake), Macon has an affair with her friend's husband, which Bess discovers when she sees Macon give him her combs to hold.

With me so far? Okay, but I may lose you now. Bess goes off into the night and is captured by Indians. When she returns nine years later, partially scalped, speaking in tongues, tattooed on arm and chin, we learn she has been the wife of a chief. Persuaded to write a book about her adventures, she soon becomes a best-selling author. The talk of the town; 60,000 copies. Dion Boucicault inquires about adapting it "into a hit play" (!). Her husband, Jack, is now infatuated with her; she treats him like a slave. Macon needs fifty dollars to prevent repossession of her house. Bess refuses. At the end, Bess, having acquired "abundance," comes upon Macon again, a syphilitic crone selling health remedies. She remembers Bess once wanted to reach out and touch a falling star. "Do you still whistle?" she asks. "No," Bess answers. They whistle together at the play's end.

I wouldn't bore you with so much synopsis except that *Abundance* has been respectfully received in some critical quarters and I wanted you to understand my puzzlement. I found the plotting so random, the characters so arbitrary, and the theme so cloudy that I couldn't imagine why it was written or performed. Ron Lagomarsino's production is only a little less inept than the play. One redeeming feature is Adrianne Lobel's setting—an entirely wooden sculpture of walls and floor that transforms into railroad tracks, cabins, and Western horizons. But Amanda Plummer, with her feral demeanor and nagging voice, plays Bess like Butterfly McQueen refusing to birth a baby, and Tess Harper's Macon has the kind of shrill reedy delivery that makes dogs weep. I guess the intention of this play was to show that women are more bonded to each other than they are to their brutish husbands, and that sexual betrayal therefore violates a sacred covenant. Bess says she loves Macon "so much more than anyone else," but it takes about sixteen years for her to forgive the episode of the combs.

In the eighteenth century, the English invented a form called "she-plays." Although written by men, such plays featured not vigorous heroes and active heroines but errant husbands and suffering wives, while taming the tragic themes of drama into stories of domestic inconvenience. *Machinal* and *Abundance* are examples by female writers of modern she-plays bearing many of the same domestic themes. Although both playwrights are fixed on the victimization of women, however, at least Sophie Treadwell is capable of leavening her perception of the predatory masculine world with a passion for social justice. For Beth Henley, the Wild West is mostly a backdrop for intermarital affairs and monosexual friendships. In her cute eccentric way, she has domesticated a savage episode of American history into a story of broken hearts and damaged hearths, where even the Indian wars are an occasion for discussing "relationships." Implicit in the myth of the West was a dread that civilizing women, with their bustles and combs, would soon come to bridle the male capacity for adventure and heroism (*pace High Noon*), an emasculating process already thought to be in force in the effete East. *Abundance* seems to reinforce that myth from the feminine perspective.

(1990)

End-of-Season Notes

(The Tonys; *Six Degrees of Separation*)

Each June, the League of American Theatres and Producers, and its accountants, declare the current Broadway season to be the most successful in history. This is usually less a judgment of quality than an audit of the balance sheets. With ticket prices rising steadily, the Broadway box office is likely to break records, even with attendance dropping off. In the 1989–90 season, attendance showed a slight rise because the year included an additional week (without it there would have been a slight drop). Still, this year the league was able to boast not only about its bank account but also about the number of "serious" plays (not to mention the number of stars) to be found on the Great White Way.

The same bravado characterized the Tony Awards. Almost all the presenting celebrities, beginning with Mistress of Ceremonies Kathleen Turner, had acted on Broadway this season—unlike the bejeweled and bespangled luminaries usually shuttled in from Hollywood to boost the ratings and the sequin content of the evening. And instead of those tiresome paeans to the glories of the Broadway musical, the focus was on the contributions of the Actor. Kevin Kline, Morgan Freeman, and Philip Bosco were actually given the opportunity to read some Shakespearean verse between production numbers from the nominated musicals and plays.

The evening was also salted with tributes to the nonprofit theatre movement for providing the "serious" product. Ron Silver even extemporized a salute to the National Endowment for having funded three of the four Best Play nominees (the funding actually went to the originating theatres). As compared with the previous season, when *The Heidi Chronicles* had no serious contenders, the Best Play competition was unusually stiff this year. The winner, Frank Galati's adaptation of John Steinbeck's *The Grapes of Wrath*, beat out *Prelude to a Kiss*, *Lettice and Lovage*, and *The Piano Lesson*. I agreed with the choice without being satisfied by any of the nominated works. *The Grapes of Wrath* was a hostage to its outdated source material. *Lettice and Lovage* was a compact car stretched into a limo to accommodate an outrageously campy performance by Maggie Smith (who won Best Actress in a Play). *Prelude to a Kiss* bobbed up from the depths of a mysterious premise to become a surface fairy tale. And *The Piano Lesson*—well, let's not get into that again.

As well as sharing the flaw of every award system (subjecting dissimilar creative acts to comparative standards), the Tony competition has a notorious limitation: it considers only Broadway productions. Testifying to nonprofit achievement is all very well, but the Tony policy ignores the great body of work being done throughout the country, as well as much of the noteworthy Off-Broadway material produced in New York City, unless marked for commercial transfer. Thus, it is unsurprising that two of the most interesting plays of the season were either not nominated or not eligible for awards: Richard Nelson's *Some Americans Abroad* and John Guare's *Six Degrees of Separation* (though the latter arrived too late for consideration anyway). I've already commented on the Nelson play; let me say a few words about the Guare.

Six Degrees of Separation at Lincoln Center's Mitzi E. Newhouse Theater is not a very radical piece of writing, but it is still the most contemporary thing John Guare has produced since *The House of Blue Leaves*. Claiming to have been mugged outside their building, a black con artist named Paul wins the confidence of a prosperous New York art dealer, Flan Kittredge, and his wife, Ouisa. Pretending to be a classmate of their children at Harvard, passing himself off as the son of Sidney Poitier (currently making a film of *Cats*), he dazzles the couple with stories of his father and his knowledge of Orwell, Salinger, and Russian film festivals. After being invited to dinner (he cooks the spinach pasta), where he delivers a moving oration on the virtues of the imagination, he is given the keys to the house. But when Flan and Ouisa discover Paul humping a male hustler in the guestroom, they kick him out, learning later from their children that they don't know Paul from Adam.

Soon, the Kittredges are comparing notes with other prosperous victims of Paul's ingenious scam: "The common thread linking us all is an overwhelming need to be in the movie of *Cats*." But the common thread is suggested more seriously by the title—everyone in the world is separated by only six shared acquaintances. One of these is an MIT computer hack named Trent Conway, who, in return for Paul's sexual favors, had agreed to educate him into an eagerly sought-after young sophisticate (this Eliza repays his Henry Higgins by stealing his stereo, skis, and laser printer). Paul, however, doesn't confine himself to manipulating the social conscience of the rich. He also conspires to steal the meager savings of a poor aspiring actor, who commits suicide after Paul seduces and abandons him.

It is at this point that the play shifts its satiric sails and makes for emotional shores. Paul phones Ouisa to express remorse for the suicide of the boy. By this time, he is calling himself Paul Poitier-Kittredge ("It's a hyphenated name"), and Ouisa, motivated by concern and affection rather than anger and revenge, suggests he turn himself in. She offers to be a friendly witness when the police arrive but, caught in New York traffic, comes too late. Paul disappears into the vast bureaucracy of the penal system. Since the Kittredges are not family members (they don't even know his real name), they're not able to identify him as the prisoner who committed suicide in Rikers Island. "He wanted to be us," Ouisa muses in an epilogue, "all we are in the world . . . He did more for us in a few hours than our children ever did." By the end, recognizing that her life has had color without any real structure—rather like the Kandinsky painting that forms the visual metaphor of the play—Ouisa is ruefully acknowledging the randomness and emptiness that characterize her existence.

All this is delivered with Guare's characteristic wit and whimsy and goofy charm. The play also contains astringent commentary, especially when the liberal parents are being savaged by their yuppie kids. If it finally softens at the edges, well, a little sentimentality is understandable given the delicacy of the subject. *Six Degrees of Separation*, like David Henry Hwang's *M. Butterfly*, is a totally implausible story which happens to be true. Both plays are based on actual newspaper events. Unfortunately, both playwrights unsettle this reality by using the Captain Queeg Maneuver—reversing our attitude toward an unappealing character in order to accommodate an emotional climax. Guare is dealing with important and sensitive contemporary issues—the extent to which the affluent classes are obligated to the poor, the vulnerability of liberal whites to black mythologizing, the capacity of the underclass (in Tom Wolfe's pungent phrase) to Mau Mau the Flak Catchers. If he hasn't seen these issues through to an honest conclusion, then neither has society.

Jerry Zaks directs the play like a satiric farce, with a snappy pulse that never lets the action flag. I'm not certain it's the best strategy for Guare's cinematic structure to keep most of the scenes anchored, regardless of the setting, near the same two sofas in the Kittredge living room. But the Newhouse admittedly is not the most flexible of theatres. Zaks, however, has managed to collect a very accomplished cast and guide them toward incisive performances—notably James McDaniel as Paul, John Cunningham as Flan, Kelly Bishop as Kitty, and, especially, Stockard Channing as Ouisa. Miss Channing is that rare thing, a comic actress with genuine emotional depth. In this production, she is obliged to transform, in a matter of minutes, from a dizzy hostess into a woman of sympathy and sensibility, and the way she makes her mouth crumple and her cheeks sag is a signal demonstration of the actor's art.

(1990)

PART II

PRODUCTIONS

INTRODUCTION

Reimagining the Classics

The most controversial issue in the theatre today continues to be the reinterpretation or "deconstruction" of celebrated classical plays by conceptual directors. There is no theatrical activity that more inflames purist sensibilities in criticism and the academy—nothing that stimulates as many caustic generalizations about the debasements of modern culture. Perhaps because "deconstruction," as an assonant noun if not as a method, is so perilously close to "destruction" and "desecration," the standard purist posture is that of Switzers before the gates of the Vatican, defending sacred texts against the profanations of barbarians. The irony, in this contemporary war between the ancients and the moderns, is that both sides are really devoted to the same aesthetic purpose, which is the deeper penetration of significant dramatic literature. The difference is in the attitude. Is reinterpretation of classics a reinforcing or a defiling act—a benign or a malignant development in the history of modern theatre?

My own position is a qualified vote of support for conceptual directing. I have long believed that if dramatic classics are not seen with fresh eyes they grow fossilized—candidates for taxidermy. Even the most harebrained textual reworking may open up new corridors into a play, while the more "faithful" version is often a listless recycling of stilted conventions. That is why I continue to echo Artaud's call for "No more masterpieces"—great plays can be "desecrated" by excessive piety as much as by excessive irreverence. Although I champion a radical auteurism in directing, not all examples of this process have the same integrity of purpose, however. One can support the idea of classical reinterpretation without defending all its forms or ignoring the fact that what passes for originality is sometimes merely another kind of ego-tripping.

Let me refine my position by distinguishing between two common methods of reworking the classics—one that depends largely on external physical changes and one that changes our whole notion of the play. It is a distinction that can be illustrated through analogies with figures of speech—the prosaic *simile* and the poetic *metaphor*. Directors who are fond of similes assume that because a play's action is *like* something from a later period, its environment can be changed accordingly. Directors with a feeling for metaphor are more interested in generating provocative theatrical images—visually expressed through physical production, histrionically through character and relationships—that are suggestive rather than specific, reverberant rather than concrete.

Simile directing is a prose technique. Its innovations are basically analogical—providing at best a platform for ideas, at worst an occasion for pranks. Metaphorical directing attempts to penetrate the mystery of a play in order to devise a poetic stage equivalent—a process considerably more radical in its interpretive risks, since the director "authors" the production much as the author writes the text. Naturally, this process is controversial: critics—though somewhat more tolerant of simile directors, who change only the period—invariably accuse metaphorical directors of arrogance and distortion. Nevertheless, it is the metaphorical approach, I believe, that has the greater potential for rediscovering the original impulses and energies of the material. Which is not to say that all simile directing is without value or that metaphorical directing doesn't have its meretricious side as well.

The simile approach is the more familiar, at least to New Yorkers, because it is often used by visiting British companies and by Joseph Papp's Shakespeare Marathon. But the tradition extends back at least as far as the thirties. Orson Welles's celebrated *Julius Caesar* was an early example, transforming Shakespeare's tragedy of assassination and retribution into an indictment of totalitarianism. Welles accomplished this by updating the text—always the hallmark of simile theatre—exchanging Roman togas for Italian black shirts and turning Caesar into a Fascist leader. Tyrone Guthrie was also a proponent of simile directing long before he inaugurated the Guthrie theatre with a Victorian *Hamlet*. I still have vivid memories of his Old Vic production of *Troilus and Cressida*, set in the early twentieth century, with Helen reinterpreted as a seductive torch singer and Thersites as a Brady-like photographer of the battlefield. The Old Vic also staged an updated *Much Ado About Nothing* (directed by Franco Zefferelli), complete with peanut vendors, carabinieri, and Italian accents, while the Royal Shakespeare Company and the Royal National Theatre produced a variety of modernized classics, including *The Taming of the Shrew* on motorcycles. Perhaps the most consistent updating was done at the now defunct American Shakespeare Festival in Connecticut: a *Much Ado* set in Spanish Texas during the time of the Alamo, a *Measure for Measure* in nineteenth-century Vienna, and a *Twelfth Night* in Brighton at the time of Horatio Hornblower.

All of these productions were known inside the trade as "jollying Shakespeare up," a practice much admired by directors who (overdosed on the Bard) streamlined their assignments with decorative environments as an antidote to creative fatigue. But it was rarely more than a novelty of surfaces, skin-deep and marred by traces of voguishness; critics were right to carp. Recently, A. J. Antoon staged an attractive example of the genre with *A Midsummer Night's Dream* at the New York Public Theater set in the Bahia province of Brazil and featuring priests and priestesses of the Umbanda cult. And Gerald Freedman recently jollied up the much jollied-up *Much Ado About Nothing* in New York's Central Park by updating it to the Napoleonic wars. Freedman's *Much Ado* had the advantage of a fine cast, including Kevin Kline and Blythe Danner as a ripening Benedick and Beatrice; but its novel setting lent nothing especially original to the interpretation, apart from a few cannon blasts, Empire clothes, and Kline's grenadier mustaches.

It was not long before directors found operas as convenient to modernize as plays. Peter Sellars, for example, has often used the metaphorical approach in his theatre work, but his productions of Handel and Mozart are clear-cut examples of simile directing. Setting *Orlando* in Cape Canaveral and *Julius Caesar* near the Nile Hilton, transporting *Così Fan Tutte* to a modern diner and *The Marriage of Figaro* to the Trump Tower, Sellars managed to coat the original libretti with a visual varnish that created more flash than clarity. Sellars' operatic work is usually spirited and impish, but what he tends to substitute for any deep probing of the material is technical dazzle and anachronistic high jinks—inventions that distract attention from the composer and librettist while attracting it to the director. (Sellars' work with contemporary opera—*Nixon in China*, for example—is, by contrast, considerably more forthright and uncluttered.)

Updating is a shorthand way of showing how the material of a classical play has topical meaning for contemporary audiences. And when directors use this approach for thematic rather than ornamental purposes, it can be valuable and illuminating. But simile productions are never as powerful as those that try to capture the imaginative life of a classic through leaps into its hidden, sometimes invisible depths. And while updating may be a component of metaphorical theatre, it is rarely the basic device. Perhaps what I am trying to describe is a difference in national temperament. Whereas simile theatre originally comes from England, metaphorical directing—which originated with the Russian Meyerhold—is usually associated with Continental Europe. It is true that the English-born Peter Brook devised at least two fine examples of metaphorical theatre with his Beckettian *King Lear* and his circus-oriented *Midsummer Night's Dream*. But Brook's chief influences in those days were Brecht, Beckett, and Artaud, and his subsequent work was largely developed in Paris.

Brecht himself, though celebrated as playwright, was also a metaphorical auteur director as daring as any who today raises purist hackles. His work is virtually a pastiche of plundered literature ("In literature as in life," he admitted, "I do not recognize the concept of private property"). These thefts, paradoxically, were authorized by Shakespeare, a writer also notable less for originality of plot than for originality of conception. And just as, say, *Hamlet* was a reworking of an earlier play, probably by Thomas Kyd, so the great bulk of Brecht's dramas were conceptual revisions of classical material—*The Threepenny Opera*, to take just the most famous example, being an adaptation of John Gay's *Beggar's Opera*.

Brecht revised these plays in order to make them conform to a political purpose: he even began an adaptation of *Coriolanus* in which the emphasis was shifted from a story of human fallibility to a study of the economic problems caused by the rising price of corn. The uncompleted *Coriolan* at the Berliner Ensemble was a brilliant example of metaphorical theatre, where Marcius and Aufidius stalked each other like Kabuki warriors and Menenius aged before our eyes.

Partly under the influence of Brecht, partly under the influence of

Meyerhold, a horde of metaphorical directors soon arose in Rumania—among them Liviu Ciulei, Andrei Serban, and Lucian Pintilie. Each of these men turned to the great classical tradition in their efforts to reinvent the modern theatre, each doing much of his work in the United States. Ciulei's reworking of Shakespeare, Büchner, Ibsen, and Wedekind—Serban's of the Greeks, Molière, Beaumarchais, Gozzi, Chekhov, and Brecht—Pintilie's of Molière, Ibsen, and Chekhov—are among the most powerful and controversial classical productions of our time. And it is possible to argue that, for all their liberties with texts and deviations from received notions, they come the closest to the spiritual core of the plays.

Rumanian productions invariably impress us with sharp memories of striking tableaux: Serban's *Cherry Orchard*, with its circular images of confusion and disorder, and his maze-like *Uncle Vanya*, with its atmosphere of mechanization and imprisonment; Ciulei's *Midsummer Night's Dream*, with its themes of sexual strife and contention emotionally reinforced by an angry Chinese-red surround; Pintilie's *Wild Duck*, with its climactic scene of eggs falling from the loft above, followed by Hedvig's body smashing to the floor—each provides suggestive visual stimulations in order to generate strong new visions of the play.

For me, the most brilliant recent expression of metaphorical reinterpretation was Ingmar Bergman's *Hamlet* during its brief run at the Brooklyn Academy of Music. Rethinking every character, every scene, every moment of the text, Bergman managed to invent not just a fresh approach to the title role reflecting the current style of a generation (the actor-oriented pattern of English Hamlets), but rather a comprehensive and original reading of the entire work that prophesied the nightmares of the future. Performed on a bare stage decorated only with an arc of lights, the action followed the disintegration of a completely depraved court, in which even Hamlet—sulky, sullen, entirely self-absorbed—was a part of the brutalization process. Only Ophelia preserved her innocence. A witness to every vicious action, including Hamlet's premeditated murder of her father, she fell into a degenerative psychosis—mutilating her hair with a dangerous pair of shears and distributing heavy iron nails as if they were flowers. She ultimately appeared as an angelic presence at her own funeral.

The final scene, a stunning *coup de théâtre*, superimposed a simile coda on an essentially metaphorical conception. Up to that point, the action had occurred in an unknown European country during an indeterminate period. With the entrance of Fortinbras, accompanied by the earsplitting sounds of rock music from a ghetto blaster, the setting became site specific. Outfitted as a Central American military leader in beret and jackboots, and leading soldiers wearing Korean riot helmets and brandishing machine guns, Fortinbras ordered his men to throw all the stage corpses into a pit, then take Horatio off and shoot him. His speech over Hamlet's body—lying on a crude platform—became a photo opportunity in front of klieg lights, a microphone, a hand-held video camera. The final line of the play—"Go bid the soldiers shoot"—was punctuated by deafening machine-gun blasts.

It was a scene of ferocious intensity that penetrated the audience's soul like a stab wound. It also managed to reinvent the meaning of catharsis for our time. It is true that Bergman's *Hamlet* evoked more terror than pity, but then so does our century. By reconceiving Shakespeare's tragedy as a bleak prophecy of the totalitarian future, Bergman managed to shake his audience to its very being while preserving the basic outline of the play.

One cannot argue that such interpolations are faithful to Shakespeare's original intentions—or use the glib defense that we don't have the playwright's telephone number. Still, charges of "desecration" are meaningful only if you subscribe to the idea of a "definitive" production. I don't. The specialness of theatre—alas, the poignance of the theatre, too—is its impermanence. Culture is a series of echoes and responses, and a "desecrated" classical text can always be reproduced again on stage in versions closer to the purist's heart. Texts develop fullness of being only through the continuing intervention of collective minds. They are not frozen in time, they are subject to continuing discovery, and each new production generates others in response. It is the proper role of theatre to let us look at plays through a variety of perspectives rather than in a single authorized form. It is also the function of criticism. Both act as prisms through which to view the limitless facets of great works of art.

Obviously, metaphorical reinterpretation is a process more appropriate for classics than for new plays, and living playwrights are often resentful of the director's growing privileges. Still, it was a playwright, Luigi Pirandello, who best defended the intruding director: "The Theatre is not archaeology," he wrote. "Unwillingness to take up old works, to modernize and streamline them for fresh production, betrays indifference, not praiseworthy caution. The Theatre *welcomes* such modernization and has profited by it throughout the ages when it was most alive." If our own theatre is once again showing signs of life, it is partly because of such bold investigation, such interpretive daring, on behalf of reinvented classics.

(1988)

Three Years after "1984"

(1984)

The New York stage, normally a pretty cold and unfriendly platform on Broadway and off, is beginning to show a degree of hospitality toward theatre from other cities, and this has added a touch of variety to its traditionally monochromatic mix of musicals, comedies, and British imports. The preferred season for these visitations is the summer, when, business being slow, even the most arcane offerings can be marketed under the rubric of a "festival." The "festival" known as PepsiCo Summerfare at Purchase this year has concerned itself largely with opera and dance, most of its pieces (perhaps in order to inspirit our AIDS-demoralized sexuality) inspired by the Don Juan motif. At Alice Tully Hall in Lincoln Center, the festival concept revolves around "Serious Fun"—a variety of avant-garde actors, dancers, mimes, and performance artists, mostly in one-person shows, entertaining uptown audiences with some of the turns and techniques evolved in the lofts of SoHo and San Francisco. Among its other benefits, the series has given us critics the opportunity to reflag old arguments about whether or not experimental theatre is being assimilated (and weakened) by the Establishment.

The Joyce Theater in downtown New York is running another form of festival this summer, and for the third consecutive year. Calling itself the "American Theatre Exchange," the Joyce management has invited four nonprofit theatre companies to the city for three-week runs, the laudable purpose being to expose New Yorkers to some of the productions being created in other parts of the country. Like the resident theatre movement itself in recent times, most of the companies have been hugging the middle of the road with rather unadventurous play selections—a Dickens adaptation from the Berkeley Repertory Theatre, a domestic drama from the Long Wharf—though these choices may have been dictated by the Joyce's small budget and limited playing space. Still, this is a worthy way of expanding New York theatrical horizons, and because the visit is restricted to a brief summer period when resident theatres are usually dark, a far less damaging method of showcasing out-of-town work than moving nonprofit productions to Broadway for open-ended commercial runs.

The most interesting offering to appear at the American Theatre Exchange is *1984*, Pavel Kohout's adaptation of George Orwell's novel, as produced by the Wilma Theatre of Philadelphia under the direction of Jiri Zizka. Zizka and his wife, Blanche (the theatre's artistic/producing director), are both Czech, which explains the Kohout connection. It also explains the theatre's interest in political plays of an anti-totalitarian nature (Orwell's *Animal Farm* was also on the Wilma's schedule in a recent season). You'd think by this time we'd had enough of *1984*. Aside from stage adaptations, there have been at least two movie versions, the most recent starring Richard Burton, not to mention the republication and reassessment of the novel in its eponymous year. Still, the material retains its power to shock and illuminate, and the Wilma company, despite weaknesses in its acting, has managed to open up access to some of its darker corners in a fresh, invigorating manner.

In 1987, be it noted, *1984* is no longer a work of terrifying prophetic power so much as an expression of hindsight. It's unnerving to realize that we are now three years past that celebrated anti-utopian date when Orwell (writing in 1948—reverse the last two digits) predicted the future would collapse on us with the force of a juggernaut. Some of Orwell's prognostications about tyranny (the prohibition on sexual activity, for example) have not materialized yet. Others (like the way the ordinary citizen would be manipulated by language and the media) have been realized in ways more subtle than even Orwell imagined. Orwell's vision of three mighty supernations locked in an endless war involving unacknowledged shifts in alliances was probably inspired by the period after World War II when the Cold War immediately followed a few years of American-Soviet friendship featuring kindly "Uncle Joe" Stalin. But it is equally relevant to a time when interdicted Red China becomes a tourist stop and the Reagan Administration makes secret overtures to Iran. The only thing Orwell failed to foresee was that the collective memory could be effaced and deadened without *official* use of drugs, unless he was predicting the narcotic effect of television.

Zizka is correct to note, in his program commentary, that Orwell's novel is a warning against all mass governments and not simply a monolithic assault on Stalinism. The climax of *1984* is undoubtedly inspired by the Moscow show trials, using "Room 101" as a metaphorical explanation for the otherwise inexplicable series of confessions extracted from hundreds of innocent people. Similarly, the concept of the "memory hole" is a brilliant way of suggesting how history is rewritten by totalitarian governments—how, for example, Trotsky (Emmanuel Goldstein in the book), like all who opposed Big Brother Stalin, could be transformed into an "unperson." But Orwell saw clearly—as did Hannah Arendt—that the greatest threat from totalitarianism was its contagiousness. It was capable of infecting not only the societies it controlled but potentially even those dedicated to combating it. *1984* takes place not in Russia or China but in an English-speaking country called Oceania—presumably an imaginary compound of England and the United States. Noting that Orwell objected to the "US Republican newspapers" who interpreted *1984* exclusively as an attack on tyrannies of the left, Zizka reminds us that one of the pretexts used by mass societies in suspending democratic procedures is the obligation to undermine real or imagined enemies. Which brings us right up to Ollie North and Admiral Poindexter.

The Wilma production of *1984* is highly visual. The set is a pile of junk sculpture tinged with green light, and a center screen bombards us with images provided by motion pictures and multiple projections. Zizka's Czech influences include not only playwrights, novelists, and directors, but also Joseph Swoboda, the great lighting designer whose Lanterna Magika was among the earliest manifestations of mixed media on stage. There are times when Zizka overworks these visual effects, when he seems to be auditioning for a directing job at Orion Pictures. This is a shame, because his stagecraft is firm. But with the screen making more powerful appeals to our eyes than the live actors, he often distracts attention from the continuity of the story.

Still, the action manages to force its way through, especially after a rather sluggish first act. Surrounded by a chorus of robots, and two particularly malevolent Hitler Youth types who function as "spies," Winston Smith (played by John Shepard as a hangdog wimp with bent knees, tired back, and lowered eyes) is a humanist in an inhuman society. Smith's job in Oceania is to reduce Newspeak to 999 words—Hamlet's soliloquy, for example, will be rendered as "To be or to unbe; that is the unanswered." For the Newspeak office is devoted to expunging all words that might allow Big Brother's subjects to escape control (a reflection of Orwell's lifelong belief that politicians gained power by mutilating language). Winston stubbornly polices his own small corner of freedom—partly by clinging to the conviction that two and two make four. He also believes that in a man named O'Brien he has met a high-placed ally. When he meets a woman with a lively sexual appetite named Julia, and rents a small room to make love to her, he has broken irreparably with the puritan system of Big Brother.

It is in the second act, after O'Brien has revealed he is the Minister of Love and tricked Winston into exposing himself as a traitor, that the production goes into gear. The first act has been devoted to exposition, simulated bomb attacks, many (too many) nude love scenes, and low-pressure acting. The second is essentially an extended torture scene, with Winston suspended on a rack, his agony reflected in mirrors. Still, it is here, through the shocks that accompany Winston's interrogation, that some electricity begins to spill out into the audience as well. O'Brien administers these shocks with weary compassion (Evan Thompson plays the part like a younger Patrick Magee), lecturing Winston on the inevitable shape of the new society and the controlling image of the future—"a boot stamping on a human face—forever." Finally confronted in Room 101 with his worst possible fear (different for every victim—for him, a ravenous rat eating at his face), Winston denounces Julia and is received back into the consoling arms of Big Brother, a sweet avuncular figure robed all in white.

Orwell's vision of the future is totally gloomy, and Zizka seems to share that vision sufficiently to make the last part of this production truly powerful. Using the sadomasochistic acting contortions of Grotowski, he bends Winston Smith into a question mark of pain, reawakening our appreciation of pleasure—just as Orwell reawakened our dormant love of freedom by imagining life without it. *1984*, on the page and on the stage, remains a beautifully articulated shriek of warning against what the author elsewhere called "the smelly little orthodoxies that are nowadays contending for our souls."

(1987)

A Tribute to Robert Penn Warren

(*All the King's Men*)

Robert Penn Warren's *All the King's Men*, like the novels of Thomas Wolfe, is a work that made a powerful impression on members of my generation when we were young. Unlike Wolfe's adolescent whimperings, however, Warren's book managed to maintain its hold on us through the decades. Now, forty years later, Adrian Hall is paying homage to its author with a faithful dramatic adaptation at the Trinity Repertory Company in Providence. *All the King's Men* is written in that terse punchy style originally patented by Hemingway before being expropriated by Dashiell Hammett and Raymond Chandler as the hard-boiled idiom of Sam Spade and Philip Marlowe. It is a style which, reinforced by a strong narrative, makes highly readable an essentially intellectual historical novel. But, along with its literary momentum, *All the King's Men* possesses a lyric, elegiac quality that signals the presence of an inspired poet who is also a brilliant social philosopher, acting as nostalgic witness to the lost promise of America. Warren's writing is permeated with a deep mournfulness, a pervasive sense of grief, that begins in the political realm and then grows metaphysical. He clearly set out to write an American tragedy, and in Willie Stark—his fictional version of the Louisiana demagogue Huey Long—he succeeded in creating a genuinely tragic hero.

The conscience of the book (he is also the author's spokesman) is the narrator, Jack Burden. Both a victim of the tragedy and its chief interpreter, Burden is arguably as important a figure in the book as Stark: "The story of Willie Stark and the story of Jack Burden," writes Warren, "are, in one sense, one story." Nevertheless, Burden has played a curiously subordinate part in previous dramatizations, including the one Warren wrote himself—an early play version which subsequently served as inspiration for the novel. In the movie, Burden was played by John Ireland, a hulking actor of no intellectual weight, who lurched around the office more like one of Stark's bodyguards than his chief political advisor and future chronicler. Burden is not just a smart reporter enticed into Willie's entourage by the promise of power. He is also a former doctoral candidate in American history, the author of a scholarly monograph (on Cass Mastern, a nineteenth-century Southern aristocrat), which occupies a discursive chapter of the book. Hall included this section in an earlier version of the play produced in Dallas, but it made the evening extremely long. In Providence, the play runs three hours without it. Nevertheless, even without this digression, the Trinity production is the first to give Burden the emphasis he deserves by moving him from the outskirts to the center of the action.

Hall is a director who works extremely well with novelists. Indeed, though eminently theatrical, his epic style is probably more congenial to narratives than dramas. So are the talents of his designer, Eugene Lee, who has devised for the production a sprawling, fluid set which keeps the action in continual motion. Seated on both sides of the stage—the flexible Trinity theatre has been rearranged as an arena—the audience alternates between observer and participant. On one side, Lee has built a weatherbeaten shack festooned with 1930s signs and logos, on the other an official stone building that doubles as courthouse and Burden's mansion. The rest is abstract space, decorated with ice-cream chairs, pool tables, rotating fans, bunting, and office furniture, where most of the action takes place, to the accompaniment of rousing songs by Randy Newman.

This action includes virtually all the central episodes of the book, both Stark's history and Burden's, moving nonsequentially through time from Willie's pinnacle as the Boss, back to his humble beginnings as a redneck idealist, and then forward again to the creation of his proudest achievement, the Willie Stark Hospital. Paralleling the story of Willie's gradual corruption—signaled not only by his power lust but by sexual betrayals, first of his schoolteacher wife and then of his pockmarked mistress, Sadie Burke—is the story of Burden's moral deterioration as well, which culminates in his exposure of the seemingly incorruptible Judge Irwin. Willie, who has a primitive instinct about human fallibility, needs to know Irwin's weakness so as to ensure his endorsement or neutrality. Using his research talents, Jack finds it: the Judge rose to eminence through bribery and the suicide of the man he displaced. This knowledge leads in turn to Irwin's suicide and to the revelation that the Judge is actually Jack's own father. After such knowledge, what forgiveness? Jack's penance is to withdraw from the world, to marry Anne Stanton, to finish the story of Cass Mastern, and, presumably, to chronicle the history of Willie Stark. Only then will he prepare—in the lovely concluding words of the book—to "go into the convulsion of the world, out of history into history and the awful responsibility of Time."

Stark's history is even more convulsive, the unfinished story of a man who might have made a difference—a man who had the brains, the imagination, and the power, but not, alas, the character to realize his dreams. Beginning as a corn-fed dupe of ruthless politicians before developing his own brilliant political instinct, Willie has a genuine desire to become the savior of his redneck class by wresting the reins of government from the "high-minded men in knee breeches and silver buckles" who run the world. But as his power becomes more absolute, so does his lust and ambition, and it is not long before his principles are being engulfed by political expediency and sexual athleticism. Only when his son is paralyzed in a football accident does he resolve to reaffirm his marriage vows and social idealism. But before he can exercise his new resolution, he is gunned down on the courthouse steps by Anne's brother, Adam, one of those "high-minded men" he has displaced. "It might have been different," says the dying Willie, and both Burden and the author are half inclined to believe him.

Hall's production sketches these episodes through direct address to the audience, rowdy barbecues, mass rallies, and costume balls, in a cinematic style that includes actual film footage (the director's debt to Federal Theatre and Living Newspaper techniques is tangible). In one of the strongest moments of the evening, a crude screen is lowered from overhead to show Willie—exhorting his followers against the background of a flaming torch—announcing his determination to smite his enemies, hip and thigh, with a meat ax. Actors bring on the props and furniture, Willie his bed, Judge Irwin his own coffin, and scenes are concluded with boisterous choruses of hymns and political songs.

There are weaknesses in this production, some of them in the acting. The two Stantons are badly performed and, more seriously, the central part of Burden, as played by Peter MacNicol, is miscast. MacNicol was young Stingo in the movie of *Sophie's Choice* and he still seems a youthful Southern innocent. His rustic ebullience makes the character seem somewhat callow, when what Burden needs is maturity, irony, and intellect. (MacNicol has his moments, however, particularly when he is exposing Burden's corruption and self-loathing, his mouth twisted into a kind of palsied grimace.) Furthermore, the adaptation moves too fast to capture the mournful, legato rhythms of Warren's writing. By including so much, the evening loses shape, sacrificing focus and concentration. As of now, there seem to be at least five or six endings, and this drains the play of emotional power. Still, there are fine performances in the show: Peter Gerety as Willie, with his shrewd eyes and barrel-chested strut; Richard Kneeland as the noble Judge Irwin, a white-headed stoic speaking in resonant cadences; Barbara Orson as Burden's oft-married mother, screaming, "You did it. You killed him. Your father," as an off-the-hook phone beeps its loud protest; Becca Lish as a lisping debutante; and, above all, Candy Buckley as Sadie Burke.

Miss Buckley is a handsome, redheaded dynamo from Texas who, on the basis of this one performance, establishes herself as a major actress. Possessed of a strong singing voice all the more potent because of her capacity to *act* her songs, she plays Sadie as a kind of female Mack the Knife, a sleek, sizzling street broad fresh from the city jungle. Crouched to spring, her jaws snapping in fury and defiance, she shows a set of teeth which could be the fangs of a puma. The character is dangerous, clearly a worthy mate for Willie Stark, and credibly vindictive enough to cause his death. Miss Buckley is an actress willing to take risks—risks that can be unsettling to those who prefer a more decorous theatre but highly appropriate for the big female roles: Medea, Lady Macbeth, Anna Christie. She brings high voltage to a production that sometimes tends to run on alternating current.

But the evening really belongs to Red Warren. It is his ringing language that fills the stage in Providence, his historical imagination that shapes the contours of the action. Our greatest living poet, he has presented us not only with some of our finest verse, but with an extraordinary body of fiction, and this novel is his crowning achievement. *All the King's Men* has weathered the decades like its author, still displaying, after forty years, the same wisdom and beauty and tough-minded decency. It was probably an impossible task to put this huge canvas on the stage, but we owe a debt of gratitude to Trinity and Adrian Hall for thus paying tribute to one of America's most gifted and beloved artists.

(1987)

Headline Hunting

(*The Front Page*)

Yet another revival of *The Front Page*, Ben Hecht and Charles MacArthur's 1928 play about Chicago newspapermen covering an execution, would not appear to be a particularly original theatrical idea or an especially bold choice to open Gregory Mosher's second season at Lincoln Center's Vivian Beaumont Theater. The play has already enjoyed three movie versions—one of them macerating this hard-nosed farce into a gender-reversed romantic comedy, with Rosalind Russell as a female Hildy Johnson and Cary Grant doing one of his incomparable comic turns as her editor-lover, Walter Burns. It is, besides, a regular feature of resident theatre schedules in this country, and in 1972 was even memorialized by the National Theatre of Great Britain in a version which, stretched to three hours and groaning under labored American accents, was treated with as much reverence as the Wakefield Mystery Cycle.

This new production under the direction of Jerry Zaks is far from reverent. It lasts only two hours and sweeps along like one. From the moment the lights come up on Tony Walton's massive rendering of an improvised press room, with its parquet floors, twirling fans, broken-down chandeliers, overstuffed wastebaskets, old Royal typewriters, and upright telephones—all backed by the silhouette of a Chicago courthouse—I was captured by the show, refreshed as if by a new play. This is one of those happy occasions in the American theatre when a familiar work of secondary reputation asserts its claim to classic status. Mosher believes *The Front Page* to be the finest American play ever written. I'm hardly prepared to go that far with him, but the Lincoln Center production certainly makes the play seem important.

The Front Page doesn't have a soft bone in its body. We are told that the authors originally conceived the work as a satire on ruthless reporters and sensationalistic journalism, only to end up with a valentine to the whole newspaper profession. I'm not so sure. These reporters certainly have their engaging side—so do the hack politicians and corrupt cops who serve as foils for their banter. But for all the double crosses, competitive dodges, sardonic backbiting, good-natured chicanery, and idiomatic wisecracks (expressed in authentic urban argot that O'Neill kept trying, unsuccessfully, to recapture), the play provides a glimpse into the seamy side of American politics and press practices that is ferociously contemporary. Earl Williams, a radical in an age of "Red Menace" hysteria, is going to the gallows because he has jeopardized the Mayor's bid for re-election; he has shot a black policeman and the "coon" vote in Chicago is crucial. When the governor sends a reprieve in the last days of the campaign—God knows what *his* motives are—the Mayor bribes the messenger to say he never delivered it. When the prisoner escapes, he orders him shot on sight.

The fact is that nobody gives a damn about Earl Williams—not Walter Burns, who only wants an exclusive for the *Examiner*, not the reporters who tailor the facts to suit their purposes, not even Hildy Johnson, who helps to hide him in Bensinger's desk. Apart from Mollie Malloy, the sentimental hooker who jumps out of a third-story window rather than testify, Williams has no value to anyone except as an opportunity for greed, ambition, vanity, or worse. For the press, the highest premium is "the great big Scoop"; the reporters want Williams hanged at five in the morning instead of seven, in time for the city edition. For the politicians, whose only motive is perpetuating themselves in office, ideology, conscience, even human life itself are hostages to expediency. *The Front Page* dramatizes Darwin's survival theory with a breezy sangfroid equaled before only by Ben Jonson and John Gay, and only by Brecht and Mamet in our own time.

Under Zaks's meticulously detailed direction, the play zips along like a hound dog with cans on its tail. Obviously, Zaks responds to plays with an edge (he is equally good with Durang), and this is a remarkable recovery after the blatant audience-fondling of *The House of Blue Leaves*. He has cast the newspapermen with performers in the tradition of 1930s character actors—such as Allen Jenkins, Edward Brophy, Edward Binns, the old broken-nose school of working stiffs—who lounge at their desks playing poker or hugging phones, "sitting here all night waiting for them to hang the bastard." They recall a livelier time in American life, when it was energy not efficiency that flowed from ruthless careerism.

The casting of the major roles (with one debatable exception) is also impeccable: Jerome Dempsey as the rotund, orotund Mayor, equipped (by the costumer Willa Kim, whose period designs are characterizations in themselves) with tailcoat and fez, bouncing languorously about the stage like a huge beach ball on the surface of a pond; Richard B. Shull as the persistently deflated Sheriff Hartman, a klaxon-voiced pol with a permanent sore throat; Bill McCutcheon as Mr. Pincus, the messenger with the reprieve, a sleepy little pink mouse with a passion for peanuts; Jeff Weiss as Bensinger, the fastidious hypochondriac who sprays his telephone receiver for germs; Paul Stolarsky as the pathetic goofball Earl Williams, appealing vainly to be recognized not as a Bolshevik but as an anarchist; Jack Wallace as Woodenshoes Eichorn, the bull-headed cop with phrenological theories of crime; Julie Hagerty as Peggy, the girl who competes with Walter Burns for Hildy's affections, a thin, nervous, high-pitched hysteric in a cloche hat; and, of course, John Lithgow as Walter Burns.

This is surely one of Lithgow's finest opportunities as a character actor, and although he doesn't enter until late in the second act, he makes the part, if not the play, his personal property. Bearing himself like a Junker general with brush mustache and military haircut, he towers over Hildy with the authority of one accustomed to absolute power (at one point, he wraps his arm around Hildy's head and pulls him around the stage like a cowboy breaking a steer). This is a considerably more ruthless Walter Burns than his predecessors in the role (Adolphe Menjou, Osgood Perkins, Walter Matthau)—menacing and dour for all his charm—whose passion for his newspaper leaves him indifferent to any weaknesses that aren't exploitable. To an ailing reporter, he shouts, "To hell with your diabetes, this is important." "I was in love once," he says in an uncharacteristic moment of Andrew Aguecheek-like tenderness, only to add, ". . . with my third wife." Like the play, he has a cartilaginous heart, and by the time he barks the play's famous last line—"The son of a bitch stole my *watch*!"—he has created a comic scoundrel unique in the annals of deception.

The casting flaw I suggested earlier is Richard Thomas' Hildy Johnson. When he first appears on stage, a slight youthful figure in a camel's-hair coat, it looks as if a stripling has been called to do the work of a man. Paradoxically, however, Thomas ends up contributing one of the most detailed performances in the production, precisely because he *has* been miscast. Like a repertory company actor challenged by a part for which he has to stretch, he builds his character piece by piece, and with such commitment he stakes out the role, even if he doesn't finally claim it. His hair slicked down, his accent washed with a Chicago rinse, dancing about the stage like a cocky young torero making passes, Thomas brings a crackling energy to Hildy that almost makes you forget he lacks the seasoning and the grit. He's the only alloy in an evening of tempered metal. In the way it takes a beady look at human corruption, *The Front Page* suggests how soft we have since become as a people and as a culture.

(1987)

Clowns and Vaudevillians

(*The Comedy of Errors*)

Milton Berle and Bill Irwin recently had a mild confrontation over the nature of comedy which had the ring of cultural commentary. In the course of making distinctions between the comic and the comedian, Berle, an old vaudevillian of the classic school, turned to Irwin, a rising young mime artist, and asked how he would define his own craft. "I'm a clown," replied Irwin. Berle acted as if he had been stung by a hornet. "Don't say that!" he sniffed, and turned away.

The way Berle reacted to Irwin's identifying himself with an honorable circus tradition was somewhat testy, but I think I know what was bothering him. It bothers me, too. The current phenomenon called the "New Vaudeville"—of which Irwin is a founding member—really belongs more to the tent than to the theatre, being a source of easily digestible entertainment that leaves no aftertaste. Like his brothers in this movement, Irwin is an affable and charming individual, but his performance rarely probes the inner spaces of human character or the membrane of social circumstance. To see him emerge from a box or catapult himself offstage or assume a variety of shapes is to be in the presence of technical wizardry rather than dramatic insight. The clown appeals to the child in us through artful and zany antics. Confronting us with the absurdity of human behavior, the comedian delights the child, but not at the cost of sedating the adult. All great comedy finds its basis in pain; it is tragedy's kissing cousin. Great clowning, even the mournful tradition of Emmett Kelley, is essentially an art of drollery. Comedy looks out on the world, clowning turns back on the performer, which is why the related art of mime—unless performed by supreme artists, Chaplin or Barrault—provokes violent impulses in comic actors: Dustin Hoffman in *Tootsie* knocking a performing mime off his pins in the park; Harvey Korman on *The Carol Burnett Show* assassinating the pasty-faced mutes who wander serially into his apartment.

I was half inclined to reach for firearms myself recently when watching a New Vaudeville version of *The Comedy of Errors* at the Vivian Beaumont Theater. The artistic director of Lincoln Center, Gregory Mosher, helped create this show some years ago when he was running the Goodman Theatre in Chicago. It must have seemed a good idea then to entrust this early Shakespeare farce to the manic talents of a vaudeville juggling troupe called the Flying Karamazov Brothers and a mime known as Avner the Eccentric. The play, based on Plautus' *Twin Menaechmi*, was hardly a piece of Scripture, and the artists involved were attracting substantial interest from the public and the critics. How better to unite the traditions of classic theatre with the media-made popularity of the New Vaudeville?

The results are winning for a while, and I should report that the audience I was with seemed to enjoy itself immensely. But after forty or so minutes of miming, tightrope walking, fire-eating, belly and tap dancing, pratfalling, trapeze acts, acrobatics, knife- and pie- and tomato-throwing, drag acts, brass and woodwind interludes, and, preeminently, juggling, I found myself longing for even the most conventionalized presentation of this play. It's not the irreverence that's irritating but rather the remorselessness of the irreverence, not to mention the air of self-congratulation that accompanies every topical reference, every piece of vaudeville shtik. "In Ephesus," says one of the characters (no doubt inspired by Antipholus' remark about "nimble jugglers that deceive the eye"), "you juggle or die," but in this Ephesus you can drop dead from the juggling. What wears you down finally is the uninterrupted physicality of the proceedings, and the vainglorious way the performers assume that the author (represented on stage by a bearded actor in a ruff) must be turning in his grave.

About the only thing I learned from this *Comedy of Errors* is that even minor Shakespeare must be acted: the major limitation of the evening is the absence of performers who can speak the lines. Sophie Hayden plays Adriana with spunky energy (she also twirls a mean baton); Gina Leishman has moments as her sister, Luciana; and Ethyl Eichelberger does outrageous transvestite turns ("God, it's great to be back from Betty Ford's") doubling as Luce and Emilia. But the others seem incapable of uttering a word without doing a pratfall or flipping plates. It's all rather like *Hellzapoppin* without the genius of Olsen and Johnson, a marathon circus clown act without the respite of elephants and tigers. Yes, the production induces nostalgia for childhood—it seems, in fact, like another of those well-intentioned civic efforts to prove to school kids that Shakespeare can be painless—and doubtless many will find the evening entertaining in its good-natured way. But I hope I don't come off as humor-impaired when I say that, like other manifestations of the New Vaudeville, this *Comedy of Errors* is essentially a yuppie phenomenon. It skirts the surface of experience, offering amusement without involvement, laughter without discovery, technique without depth, and the name of that game, my friends, is escapism.

(1987)

The Longest Journey

(*The Mahabharata*)

At the conclusion of the first part of Peter Brook's monumental production of *The Mahabharata* at Brooklyn's newly renovated Majestic Theatre, more than two hours into this nine-hour evening, a dice game occurs which determines the fate of all the characters and causes the great battle of Kurukshetra, in which eighteen million die. It is just about the only dramatic moment in the entire production. I mean *dramatic* as distinguished from theatrical, for no one could possibly fault Brook for being short on spectacular theatrical values. In *The Mahabharata*, however, he and his literary colleague, Jean-Claude Carrière, have undertaken the intractable task of reconstituting for the stage a huge Sanskrit epic—approximately fifteen times the length of the Bible—and while the effort is noble, it is also doomed. This saga of history, mythology, genealogy, philosophy, and religious dogma is simply too comprehensive, too diffuse, too linear—and ultimately too alien to the Western mind—to find a coherent, arresting dramatic form.

In his useful introduction to the published text, Carrière tells us that *Maha* in Sanskrit means "great" or "complete" while *Bharata* is the name of a legendary clan. Noting that *Bharata* also means "Hindu," he translates the title loosely as *The Great History of Man*, and in the opening sequences, the poet Vasya describes what he is about to unfold as "the poetical history of mankind." But *Hindu* does not mean "man" any more than the two warring clans recall any identifiable species from our own history or myth. The play breaks on the brow much the way a demonstration of Hindu kathakali once struck Brook—as "something mythical and remote, from another culture, nothing to do with my life." The first forty minutes of the evening are entirely devoted to pedigrees—an excessively ramified family tree—which is about as enthralling as watching a dramatization of the Book of Genesis, with all the "begats" included. After being introduced to the fifteen main characters, not to mention at least thirty supernumeraries, and learning how each was ushered into the world (one family sprang from the hundred shattered shards of a huge stone), we remain as estranged from their exotic (and erotic) exploits as from the numerous mythological deities who rule their lives.

Brook and Carrière work hard to universalize this Hindu epic, largely by hinting that the terrible weapon possessed by the archer Arjuna, as well as the one "launched" by his enemy Aswatthaman ("a white heat" that shrivels the earth to ashes), is actually the H-bomb. Brook affirms that the eighteen different nationalities gathered together in his cast help "to celebrate a work which only India could have created but which carries echoes for all mankind." But the only universal echoes I could hear were appeals for a sane nuclear policy. At the risk of sounding culture-bound, I'm compelled to say that these well-meaning efforts to erase international and ethnic boundaries— and Brook's work over the past seventeen years has been largely devoted to that worthy goal—have something forced and hortatory about them. Having wandered through the primitive nations of the earth to see his work performed before African natives, Iranian tribesmen, and Aborigines, Brook speaks fervently of a "third culture . . . a culture of links" which he hopes will counteract the fragmentation of the world: "It has to do with the discovery of relationships where such relationships have become submerged and lost—between man and society, between one race and another . . . between categories, languages, genres." This is the voice of the would-be world citizen, a theatrical Gary Davis, speaking through the larynx of a self-appointed international matchmaker.

For years, some of our most gifted theatre artists have been claiming for the stage an evangelical, even apocalyptic purpose in an effort to reestablish its original function as the trunk between God and the *polis*. First it was the Living Theatre, returning from exile to evangelize the nation in the name of messianic anarchism. Then Grotowski abandoned his experimentation with texts at the Polish Theatre Lab in order to engage in "paratheatrical experiments" (people performing yoga, chanting and walking in wide ellipses, chasing the vernal equinox). And, at the same time, Peter Brook was working, with his International Centre of Theatre Research at Les Bouffes du Nord in Paris, to develop a universal language for the stage that would halt its degeneration into an empty bourgeois entertainment. These efforts were informed by honorable, sometimes even heroic, motives. They were also sad evidence of how firmly rooted our theatrical messiahs were in their own cultural topsoil.

The Mahabharata, at least in its New York incarnation, carries this melancholy message throughout its entire nine-hour length. It may be one thing to see it outdoors in Avignon, at ten dollars a ticket, with the sun rising over the concluding rites. But at $96 a seat, in a production estimated at $6 million, and in a Brooklyn theatre renovated at the cost of another $5 million in order to replicate the battered and unpatched conditions at Brook's Bouffes du Nord, this costly "poor theatre" begins to take on some of the same bourgeois grandiosity (for all its feigned seediness) that made Nietzsche rage so rabidly against Wagnerian opera. It is painful to say this about a production fifteen years in the making, but to me *The Mahabharata* demonstrates not so much international harmony and interethnic bonding as the seductions of cultural imperialism. With the Majestic exquisitely transformed into an Etruscan ruin (and it now may very well be the most beautiful theatre in all five boroughs), it has essentially become an expensive colonial outpost for Peter Brook, created and equipped to serve his personal needs. It also conforms to his personal idiosyncrasies. The newly installed benches are designed for maximum spectator discomfort (in comfortable chairs, he writes elsewhere, "you are in danger of falling asleep"). And the long sit—nine hours, if you don't choose three hours on three successive nights—is another form of control, an implicit way of forcing homage.

None of this would mean much if *The Mahabharata* held one truly fast in its grip. But apart from the splendid theatricality (some of it familiar from Brook's previous work with the Royal Shakespeare Company), the evening is a bit of a yawn. Where the director's dedication shows through is in the physical training of the international cast. Like the Living Theatre, and like the Polish Theatre Lab, these actors are superb-looking creatures and never more impressive than when they are working with their bodies. It is quite another thing when they begin to speak. Difficult as it is to understand the unpronounceable Hindu names (Dhritarashitra, Ghatotkatcha, Djayadratha, Duryodhana), it is even more frustrating to try to identify phrases in a tongue familiar to us but foreign to most of the cast. Some of these performers, like the East German Andrzej Seweryn or the Italian Vittorio Mezzogiorno or the Trinidadian Jeffery Kissoon, succeed in making the dialogue comprehensible (though the Englishman Bruce Myers as Krishna makes us pay for his clarity with a display of cuteness). But to watch the legendary Polish Grotowski actor, Ryszard Cieslak, engage in a losing struggle between the English language and his guttural plosives is to recognize that there are certain cultural barriers that even goodwill cannot overleap.

No, the beauties of the evening are largely visual, starting with Chloe Obolensky's exquisite Oriental costumes—a palette of rich dyes alternating with saffron shifts and bleached robes and Afghan finery—and her deceptively simple setting—the three bare walls of the proscenium, framing a sandpit, a river, and a small pond. Brook is a master of this space and creates startling juxtapositions that always preserve an air of intimacy between actors and spectators. The battle scene, though it goes on too long, is vibrating with crashing bodies and simulated weapons of war. And Brook knows well how to suggest large objects with a simple symbol or prop—a wheel representing a chariot, a red ribbon a gush of blood, a circle of fire the contours of a battlefield.

What falls on the ear, however, is somewhat less propitious. The bizarre Oriental instruments, though beautifully fashioned, make the kind of music you hear in Indian restaurants between the pappadom and the shrimp vindaloo. And the Brook-Carrière dialogue is assertive, flat, prosaic, lacking the poetic resonance that compels attention. As for the story, like the dialogue it rarely reveals character. An elasticized tale of rivalry between two feuding clans, frequently broken by narrative asides, the play is a long gallop across an endless landscape with no pit stops to develop depth (or to water the horse). It is a surface ride. We are yanked too abruptly from anecdote to anecdote, from story to story, to settle into the characters or care about their fates, which is why the epic form is designed for leisurely reading rather than for stage adaptations, however reduced in length. The power of drama lies in compressing events into a nuclear plot whose explosion scatters insights into character and theme. But if plot is the soul of drama, *The Mahabharata* lacks a soul.

It doesn't, however, lack for discussion of the soul. This epic includes within its vast recesses the *Bhagavad-Gita*, a repository of Indian theology, which the play dispenses in digest form. There is some desultory discussion of *dharma*—an ineffable concept suggesting the road of truth or the order of life (and I won't stick my neck out trying to define it). There are tantalizing references to the way of Krishna and the meaning of death. And the play ends with the saintly Yudishthira, reunited with his dead brothers at a banquet, learning that paradise, like hell, is an illusion. Perhaps it's because these snippets of wisdom are pelted at us so fast that the only coherent theme I could retrieve from the fusillade was Krishna's perception that "no good man is entirely good—no bad man is entirely bad." If that strikes you as profound, so will the play. But those hungry for Hindu philosophy in Western dramatic form would be better off staying home and reading Strindberg's *A Dream Play* or *The Ghost Sonata*.

Would that Peter Brook had produced them! This supremely gifted director has now spent almost a third of his life on projects to which he is superior, whether *Orghast at Persepolis* or *The Ik* or *L'Os* or *The Conference of the Birds*. Like *The Mahabharata*, all were inspired less by interest in a text than by a humanitarian sentiment "to establish new relations with different people." The sentiment is moving; the texts are increasingly inflated and hollow. In his new book, *The Shifting Point*, Brook reveals, along with his passion for universal brotherhood, the unmediated love for Shakespeare that informed his earlier triumphs, his penetrating *King Lear*, his irreverent *Midsummer Night's Dream*. How many great plays still await his attention while he is acting out messianic ambitions and his own Western self-hatred. It is a smug and facile thing to offer advice to a master about his future course. Anyone willing to risk error or absurdity in the pursuit of large goals must be respected. Still, I wish the few inspired theatre artists in our midst would leave the salvation of the world to the swamis and the gurus, and return to the more achievable, if rather more humble, task of fashioning dramatic truths.

(1987)

Breaking the Frame

(*The Mistress of the Inn*)

A favorite Orson Welles process, when he was running the Mercury Theatre, was something he called "breaking the frame," whereby actors shattered the imaginary fourth wall to create a more direct relationship with the audience. There was nothing particularly novel about this theatrical device—it formed the essence, for example, of Elizabethan theatre, with its monologues, asides, and choral speeches. But the conventions of nineteenth-century realism and the box set had somehow managed to segregate the stage from the auditorium, turning the audience into mute witnesses, if not voyeurs. The extent of audience involvement in a play was one of the issues dividing Stanislavsky and Meyerhold, as it later divided Stanislavsky and Brecht, and the conflict was vigorously pursued by their followers in the United States. In the thirties, Welles took up the anti-realist banner in opposition to the rival Stanislavsky-oriented Group Theatre. In the forties and fifties, critics led by Walter Kerr and playwrights led by Thornton Wilder began to blame the proscenium arch for all the woes of the American stage. And in the sixties, the Living Theatre (following Pirandello) so erased the dividing line between actors and spectators that it was arguable whether the playing area was on the stage, in the house, in the lobby, or out on the street.

To this day, experimental theatre is mainly characterized by "breaking the frame," while mainstream Broadway drama continues to be a social-realist expression glimpsed through a proscenium by an audience cast as Peeping Toms. Carlo Goldoni's *The Mistress of the Inn* at the Roundabout Theatre is a classical play that breaks the frame, though for purposes of entertainment rather than experimentation. This pleasant if slight eighteenth-century prose comedy is a little gem of bourgeois theatre—like a Shakespeare romance without the poetry, or a Da Ponte libretto without Mozart's music. Goldoni's chief rival in Italy at the time was the aristocratic Carlo Gozzi. Both playwrights were indebted to the tradition of *commedia dell'arte*, but drawing deeper from the wells of fantasy and myth, Gozzi has proved much closer to our contemporary sensibility. Nevertheless, *The Mistress of the Inn* has its small charms, enhanced in this production through the labors of an attractive cast under Robert Kalfin's direction.

The play concerns the enticing Mirandolina, who runs a small inn in Florence. An independent woman with "an implacable will" that puts her in the line of feminist heroines, she is beloved by her customers (two aging noblemen), and by her steward, Fabrizio. Only one man ignores her, the misogynistic Cavaliere di Ripafratta, so naturally she sets her cap for him: "Bit by bit I shall domesticate this beast . . . If he doesn't fall in love tomorrow, may my nose fall off." In due time, Ripafratta is hooked and becomes the most jealous of lovers, fighting a mock duel with one of his rivals, using the other's broken sword. To everybody's surprise, she ultimately rejects him, along with her other two aristocratic suitors, and accepts the hand of her servant, Fabrizio.

The play is full of democratic sentiment—Mirandolina marries down rather than up in class, and refuses to go for money, because she values her freedom too much. Aside from her use of guile to manipulate men (she sometimes seems like a middle-class version of the Marquise in *Les Liaisons Dangereuses*), Mirandolina is bursting with moral health. This relentless healthiness can get a little tiresome, it's true, but as performed by Tovah Feldshuh in a curly red wig, yellow shoes, and layers of skirts, the heroine is as irresistible as she claims to be. Miss Feldshuh speaks the part with a hoarse whiplash voice vaguely tinted with the inflections of Yentl, whom she also played under Kalfin's direction. She has the spirit, speed, and mischievousness of Mozart's Suzannah, along with strong support by other members of the cast. Philip Kerr, playing Ripafratta with an odd Middle European accent, has the arthritic dash of an aging musketeer; Gabriel Barre, looking like a young F. Murray Abraham, is wily and inventive as Fabrizio; and George Ede and Edward Zang, as the two aristocrats, bring a nice relaxed exhaustion to their parts, though Zang occasionally seems a bit unfocused.

Kalfin's production is fast and stylish. The set design, by Wolfgang Roth, is a simple wooden structure with a white muslin curtain stretched between the scaffolding, decorated with a gouache backdrop and three frequently slammed doors for farcical effect. The Mozart and Vivaldi transition music is appropriate. And the adaptation by Mark A. Michaels is terse and speakable, retaining a few Italian phrases to localize the atmosphere.

What disturbed me a little about the enterprise is a habit that delighted the matinee group I saw it with: the way the performers, by breaking the frame, are encouraged to ingratiate themselves with the spectators. Miss Feldshuh's relationship with the audience is particularly winky and intimate. She draws applause from the women by telling them she adores making fun of men. She flirts with them, saying: "I really enjoy making men do everything I want—so do you." She fawns on the front row by confiding her plans. She peeks through the curtain at the beginning of the second act to notice "You're back." And finally, after vowing to change her ways, she throws the audience a bouquet of flowers, begging it to "remember kindly the mistress of the inn." All of this is perky, impish, and intimate, but also somewhat abject—the independence she wins from her suitors she abandons to the paying customers. By flattering the audience with excessive attention, *The Mistress of the Inn* turns the audience into potential publicists for a long-running show.

(1988)

The Definitive Production

(*A Midsummer Night's Dream; The Cherry Orchard*)

The generative impulse of classical theatre in our time is still the deconstruction of sacred texts by conceptual directors, but purists continue to be incensed by what they consider the ego trips of vandalizing barbarians. Still, culture is a series of echoes and responses, and a "desecrated" classical text can always be reproduced again on stage in a version closer to the purist's heart. Theatre, to use Jonathan Miller's useful terms, is more allographic than autographic, meaning that texts develop fullness of being only through the continuing intervention of many collective minds.

Purists won't be happy with either of the productions under review, and my own feelings toward them are far from undivided. Neither can be called "definitive," but that's not the reason. The more I reflect on theatre, the more I'm convinced that "definitive" production is only a trick of memory, reinforced by a stubborn nostalgia. Anyone who's recently seen Olivier's *Uncle Vanya* on cable—a production once considered the definitive English-language version of that play—has witnessed a dry antique gone moldy with age. Oddly enough, it's usually the most provocative revolutionary production of one generation that becomes the definitive production of the next, which was the paradoxical fate of Peter Brook's athletic *A Midsummer Night's Dream.*

Directors have been staging *A Midsummer Night's Dream* ever since in an effort to claim the play for other visions, other generations. Like *Hamlet*, it reflects the form and pressure of an age. After Brook rescued it from gossamer and stardust, Alvin Epstein made it a locus of combat and contention in medieval Europe, James Lapine restored it to the bosom of nature in Central Park, Liviu Ciulei explored its feminist implications in an abstract China-red surround—and now A. J. Antoon (in a production staged at the New York Shakespeare Festival Public Theater) has invoked its magical and supernatural properties in a multiracial South American country.

Abetted by his designers Andrew Jackness (sets) and Frank Krenz (costumes), Antoon has located the play in the Bahia province of Brazil—the European colonialists (courtiers) lounging in white suits and long dresses against pink, beige, and aqua terra-cotta slats, the forest people (fairies) cavorting in a steaming jungle, populated with native women carrying baskets on their heads, half-caste tom-tom players, and an amply endowed voodoo mama practicing macumba rituals with a whisk and an effigy doll. An ecstatic chorus performs sinuous dances, including the samba, to the accompaniment of Michael Ward's flute, marimba, and percussion rhythms; Oberon's magic flower becomes a hallucinatory drug provoking manic visions. To accommodate this hemispheric switch, Antoon has excised many (oddly not all) references to the Greek city-states, and altered the text wherever it makes mention of "fairies" ("women away" instead of "fairies away," the "very kingdom" instead of the "fairy kingdom," etc.). What he has substituted for sprites and spirits are black priests and priestesses of the Umbanda cult, practicing their dark arts through what a program note calls "hypnotic trances, spells and spirit possessions, using drum rhythms, chants, magical herbs and cigar smoke to summon up desired spirits."

It is an appealing enough concept, responsible for a lot of local color and smoky atmosphere—but it is essentially cosmetic. Shifting classical texts in place and time can be illuminating. The danger is to become too easily satisfied with altering the environmental surface of the play, letting visual analogies usurp the need to penetrate character or enliven theme. To be sure, *A Midsummer Night's Dream* is hardly Shakespeare's most profound work, and it lends itself easily to a variety of approaches. But this one seems more like an attractive pageant than an original reworking, and the performances sometimes lack concision and amplitude. I liked most of the lovers, though, especially Elizabeth McGovern's tall, leggy, red-haired Helena, and Carl Lumbly is an athletic Oberon matched well against Lorraine Toussaint's powerful Titania, levitating in her bower. As for the rustics—Athenian mechanicals transformed into Brazilian working stiffs—they are delightful in their merry and tragical, tedious and brief interlude (sounds like a fair description of Beckettian post-modernism, no?)—particularly F. Murray Abraham as a smug but curiously unhammy Bottom, squeezing Thisbe's lips and getting his pants pulled up his crotch in retaliation.

Back to Peter Brook, who started all this, and who has now remounted his Paris production of *The Cherry Orchard* at the Majestic Theatre (BAM) with a mostly American cast. This piece has been widely celebrated (along with *The Mahabharata*) as a formal breakthrough. But like that protracted Hindu marathon, Brook's Chekhov must have suffered a sea change during its ocean voyage; I found it a singularly colorless ordeal. No doubt, my response is influenced by having had to sit for two-and-a-half intermissionless hours on those padded benches with which the Majestic (otherwise a marvelous theatre) has been uncomfortably equipped. Perhaps the puritan Brook wants his affluent Brooklyn audiences to share the same Spartan conditions as his audiences in Iran and Africa. Still, his production scheme for *The Cherry Orchard* is equally Spartan. We may sit on benches, but the cast usually sits on the floor, like Turkish beys at supper, protected from lumbago only by the warp and woof of a Persian carpet.

This is Chekhov without walls, and its one original feature is the way it abstracts space by minimizing furniture and props. The lovely Persian carpets—the central one bleached and aged—are the central visual images. They are the only images, in fact, apart from a sheet-draped armchair, some fabric-covered screens, and a bookcase. Brook has had the admirable idea of rescuing Chekhov from all those overstuffed, overdecorated drawing rooms inherited from Stanislavsky realism, to let the audience focus on language and action. Stripped and simplified, and offered in a serviceable translation by Elisaveta Lavrova, this *Cherry Orchard*, nevertheless, often seems as heavy and upholstered as anything produced at the Moscow Art Theatre, and almost as lacking in surprise.

The production is clean enough, but it is also denatured. Occasionally, Chekhov's unheard music comes through sweetly, poignantly. Usually, the stage is full of familiar sounds, pedestrian melodies. And why is this music so penumbral? Chekhov, disputing Stanislavsky's morbid readings, called the play "a comedy—in places, even a farce." But the buffoons of this production—and Yepikhodov, Dunyasha, Pishchik, Lopakhin, even Trofimov, all have clownish qualities—don't reveal much capacity for comedy; and without some lightness of spirit, the play seems somber. Brook is perfectly aware of the comic nature of *The Cherry Orchard*; he alludes to it in a program note. But his characters lounge around the stage in a nerveless state, sometimes even listening to the sound of gypsy violins—all that patented Slavic mood machinery that alienated audiences from Chekhov for decades.

Brook is a daring director with a high intelligence. What accounts for the flatness of this interpretation? Well, by having us concentrate on language and action, he also makes us concentrate on acting, and the acting is plagued by serious casting errors, not to mention the director's inability to coax consistently textured work from a majority of his company. Writing the word "company," I realize that's a root problem, too. The actors fail to create a unified world. It's not just the international mix (Lyubov is English, Gaev Swedish, Yepikhodov Czech, the rest American, and all with pronounced—in the case of Yepikhodov, impenetrable—accents). It's the pickup nature of the cast. In the parts of Anya and Dunyasha, Brook has put the offspring of two warring writers—Rebecca Miller (daughter of Arthur) and Kate Mailer (daughter of Norman). Although Miss Miller has a gentle, limpid quality that ultimately makes you forget her inexperience, it is harder to forget that she and the less effective Miss Mailer are celebrity children who may owe their parts to qualities other than native talent.

Miss Mailer's bland Dunyasha, in fact, seems even paler when compared to Meryl Streep's languid, self-dramatizing ninny in the considerably more radical Andrei Serban production some years back. Stephanie Roth is much too sleek for the nun-like Varya, played by Serban's Priscilla Smith with exactly the right repressed ill temper. Nor is Natasha Parry's curiously stagy Lyubov—performed in the imperious manner of British grand dames—any match for the gyrating melancholia of Irene Worth in the Serban version. I saw Mike Nussbaum do an infinitely funnier, seedier, more hangdog interpretation of Pishchik in the Mamet/Mosher Goodman Theatre production than the elegant gentleman he is playing in Brooklyn. And although David Pierce's Yasha (looking like the young Strindberg), Roberts Blossom's Firs (looking like the old Mr. Dooley), and Linda Hunt's Charlotta (looking like the ageless Aunt Dan) are expertly and confidently enacted, you don't find yourself arguing with any interpretation, having been startled into a new conception of a familiar role (perhaps you might argue over Gaev's contempt for Lopakhin being totally directed at Yasha). As for Brian Dennehy's limber, relaxed Lopakhin, it is more a cinematic throwaway than a stage characterization—a demonstration that a big man can have physical grace and charm.

Without an attitude toward Lopakhin, *The Cherry Orchard* has no point of view, and I'm afraid the most disappointing thing to be said about this production is that it provokes no argument. Chekhov didn't take sides regarding the dispossession of his cultured aristocratic idlers by a middle-class developer, and he never moralized about the way a beautiful but useless garden spot was being torn up to make room for condos. But that's not because he was neutral. He saw both the sadness and the inevitability of progress, just as he saw that the dispossessor Lopakhin, who behaves like a villain from mortgage melodrama, was basically a sensitive and hardworking man. Brook's *Cherry Orchard*, however, *is* neutral, and that's why we end up feeling neutral about the play and the characters. For all the carpets, despite the lack of walls, regardless of discarded props, one always feels the production straining to be definitive—it only proves "definitive" is often a synonym for dull.

(1988)

The Limits of the Auteur

(*The Cherry Orchard*)

Among the most hotly debated questions of modernism is its relation to the past. Does modernist culture represent an unprecedented break with history? Has the modern artist confiscated the territory formerly occupied by tradition and authority? The sociologist Daniel Bell, one of the few American intellectuals still concerned with thinking about culture, has just written a paper on "The Contradictions of Modernity and Modernism" which may arouse the few Americans still interested in ideas about culture, for it is a closely reasoned attack on the most cherished assumptions of modernist art.

Defining "the modern" as a "readiness, if not eagerness, to welcome the new, even at the expense of tradition and the past," Bell goes on to excoriate a culture in which "the aesthetic separates itself from the moral, and the impulse to experiment and explore, to go to the depths of the new, knows no boundaries, the sensuous and the shocking have no restraints, there is 'nothing sacred.' " Bell charges the modernist artist with rejecting classical order, symmetry, and proportion. "The ego/self takes the throne as the center of the moral universe, making itself the arbiter of all decisions," and this results in the "diremption of *mimesis*, the shattering of the mirror of nature, particularly in art . . . What makes culture 'modern,' then, is the crossover from the external world and a copy theory of knowledge as primary, to the subjective standpoint of the knower, and the artist as the apex of imagination."

Bell's assault on modernism uses the artillery of philosophy, history, and politics, particularly (and curiously, considering his conservative cultural stance) the politics of liberalism. Arguing that liberalism could provide the basis for a culture that draws deeply on the ethical traditions of the West, he chides modernism for exercising rights without obligations. Bell concedes that rationalistic liberal culture is mundane and lacks a sense of the sacred, but nonetheless implores the artist to return to traditional roots: "It is the recognition by the individual that he does not come out of himself but is the son of his father, with the obligation to redeem . . . the inheritance he has received."

Bell is correct in noting that modernist art (regardless of the artist's private politics) is not often an expression of liberalism. But is he also correct to call the creations, say, of Joyce, Picasso, or Brecht—or of countless other modernists dedicated to reworking classical art—a breach with the world of our fathers? Quite the contrary, few artistic movements in history have been so deeply submerged in the literature and art of the past. Admittedly, these traditional works, whether Homer's *Odyssey* or Velázquez's *Las Meninas* or Gay's *Beggar's Opera*, are likely to reappear in radically revised forms—but artists do not redeem a paternal inheritance through mechanical imitation. It is true that *post-modern* art is often devoted to Bell's "diremption of *mimesis*" and "shattering of the mirror of nature," but even this highly independent movement has lately been giving way, in theatre at least, to a new involvement with classical texts.

A more relevant question to ask about these post-modern artists is whether the "ego/self" has transformed these texts beyond recognition. At what point does a director's approach to the classics merge into authorship? How much conceptual weight can a play bear before it loses its original shape and becomes another object entirely? Such judgments are entirely subjective, and complicated by the fact that some "interpretations" are clearly intended as fresh creative acts. But most auteur directors genuinely believe they are releasing the original impulses of the plays they direct from the conventions of traditional production, and would vigorously defend their concepts as "faithful" realizations of a playwright's intention, seen anew through modern eyes.

Lucian Pintilie's new production of Chekhov's *The Cherry Orchard* at the Arena Stage in Washington is an interesting case in point. Not one moment in this version emulates a previous staging choice by Stanislavsky, John Gielgud, Andrei Serban, Michael Blakemore, Peter Brook, or any other memorable production. It is completely original and yet—at least as far as interpretation goes—never violates the basic design of the play. Pintilie's *The Seagull* at the Guthrie some years back played havoc with Chekhov's structure by starting with the final act and making the rest of the play a flashback. This production, in Jean-Claude van Itallie's elegant translation, is so faithful to Chekhov's form and text that it includes an interpolation—a short colloquy between Firs and Charlotta ending the second act—which restores a scene that Stanislavsky (sensibly) cut.

Nevertheless, I found Pintilie's liberties with *The Seagull* often more faithful to the spirit of Chekhov's intentions than the constancies of his *Cherry Orchard*, and I believe the problem lies not with the concept but with the acting. Pintilie's approach to the play is visually striking, and his overall control is masterly. It is a production that continually stuns us into new thought—and makes the Brook version, by contrast, look like "deadly theatre." But as often happens with auteur creations (Lyubimov's *Crime and Punishment*, for example), the advances in concept and stagecraft are paid for at the expense of performance. The Guthrie *Seagull* had acting weaknesses, too; here, they are almost fatal. Shirley Knight's Ranevskaya is a dotty overweight *bourgeoise* with a high-pitched soprano only lapdogs could find tolerable—Shelley Winters crossed with Billie Burke. It is hard to remember that she (as Irina) was the one redeeming feature in the Actors Studio's otherwise ill-fated *The Three Sisters*. Rebecca Ellens's Anya proves her mother's daughter in one respect—her shrill vocal delivery. Otherwise, she plays the part like a hopped-up teenager preparing for a prom. Charlotta Ivanovna is performed by that spherical bantam who exorcised the spirits in *Poltergeist*; she's doing much the same thing here, using the same uninflected nasalities. The gifted Stanley Anderson, so compelling in Pintilie's *Wild Duck*, contributes the crudest Lopakhin I've yet seen, coarsened by a thick Slavic accent that alienates him from the rest of the non-accented American cast. Dunyasha is a splayed-out refugee from the chorus of *Oklahoma!*, Firs a plantation black with diction ("Dey knew how to do it; dey had a recipe") more appropriate to the announced sequel of *Gone With the Wind*. Only Richard Bauer's Gaev, Mark Hammer's Simeonov-Pishchik, Tana Hicken's Varya, and Henry

Stram's Trofimov manage to navigate their roles without losing the humanity of Chekhov's vision, though Pintilie's passion for perpetual motion makes even their seamanship shaky at times.

The best performances on stage are by Radu Boruzescu's setting and by Pintilie's control of the space—elements which sustain this production at a continually engrossing level, regardless of weak characterizations. The design, built in the round, is essentially a bare painted floor and ramps, with an armoire at one corner that serves as bookcase, storage area, and creche. When Beverly Emmons illuminates the floor with her luminiscent lights, it undergoes a mysterious transformation, dogs begin barking, and a child appears to blow on a toy horn. The child is the ghost of Grisha, the victim of Ranevskaya's indolence and irresponsibility, and he hovers near the action like a gentle rebuke. It is Pintilie's perception that not just the childish Gaev but all the characters of the play are stuck at some early stage of development, and when they gather in Grisha's nursery, they sit on miniature children's furniture and play with toys that materialize from the armoire and roll down the ramp.

In the second act, an exterior, sheaves of golden wheat appear through the floor, and the armoire is opened to reveal a huge Orthodox icon festooned with candles. Presiding over the wheatfield is an ominous scarecrow, almost human in a black mask, and at the sound of that eerie harp string, its head falls forward. During the third-act dance, that desperate party preceding Lopakhin's cataclysmic entrance to announce he has bought the cherry orchard, the celebrants wear false noses and party hats, while the ghostly child watches their antics through the armoire. And in the final act, a broken chandelier perches on the floor, a forlorn relic of past grandeur amid the detritus of packing boxes and suitcases.

The last moments are inspired (Pintilie's final images are always his best). The family has departed for the train station, the nursery is deserted. The child Grisha emerges from the armoire and surveys the room. Suddenly tremors on the stage begin to rattle a glass of Lopakhin's champagne, left behind on a table. The ancient and abandoned Firs enters to speak of the evanescence of life, his speech punctuated by ghostly taps. Firs lies down amid latticework shadows that now traverse the floor, and dies. The champagne glass rattles more violently, falls from the table, and breaks. Grisha displays a piece of string, and drops it. He blows his horn again, the doleful music of a passing age.

And then, as the floor opens, sheaves of yellow wheat rise up to gather Firs's body into the eternity of time.

Those soft, exquisite moments, and many other illuminating touches, often compensate for the screechy aural trials of the overactive performances. They also suggest that it's not conceptual audacity that defines the limits of auteur directing so much as a tendency to subordinate characterization—the humanistic element of production—to stage business and textual interpretation. Like many European directors, Pintilie probably expects the cast to do its own work while he does his, without realizing perhaps that most American performers regard directors as acting coaches and the rehearsal period as an exercise in relearning the elements of their craft. Whatever the case, I suspect that Daniel Bell and other critics of post-modern theatre might be less hostile to the explorations of auteur directors if they saw more focused acting on stage. Bell calls "the experimentalism of avant-gardes . . . the trivialized succession of fashion," and charges "the practitioners of post-modernism" with substituting "pastiche for form and cleverness for creativity." Watching more powerful performances, Bell and his traditionalist school might be brought to see that the motive of post-modern art is not cleverness but illumination, not a regard for fashion but the desire to let tradition breathe through a suffusion of fresh life.

(1988)

The Ultimate Broadway Transfer

(*Our Town*)

A reviewer of sequential works in a resident theatre, in my opinion, has two distinct obligations: first to evaluate the production and then to say what it reveals about the values of the institution. Isolated critical opinions serve the market needs of commercial theatre in determining hits and flops, but permanent institutions have an organic identity beyond the fate of a single show. It is defined by an aggregate of decisions, just as human beings are characterized by the sum of their actions rather than by a single trait. It is for this reason that I grouse about Lincoln Center. No one in theatre today has a better batting average than Gregory Mosher and Bernard Gersten, and pounding home runs for a sluggish theatre league is an important function. But it is a function shared with David Merrick or Cameron Mackintosh or any successful commercial producer, not with the mandated aims of subsidized theatre. While Lincoln Center's box score is dazzling, it has yet to be supported by any recognizable institutional purpose beyond winning, and that is why I sometimes find myself in the position of praising the team's plays while expressing doubt about the ball club.

Such is the case with *Our Town*, currently on stage at the Lyceum Theatre. This play is hardly the choice of an adventurous management. The reigning favorite of every high-school drama club, summer camp, and community theatre—already adapted to film and the subject of a projected musical—it seems as cozy as a comforter, as familiar as toast. Yet despite the misgivings with which I approached this familiar territory, I could not deny that Lincoln Center had staged a powerful production. Gregory Mosher, who directed, clearly loves the work, and his passion uncovers new values which make us see it as if for the first time. Like the Lincoln Center *The Front Page*, this production enhances our enjoyment of a popular if critically unappreciated American play.

Cynics have generally considered *Our Town* to be a slice not of life but of Bond bread, as close to contemporary reality as a faded daguerreotype or a knitted sampler. It is true there are no synagogues or Pentecostal churches nestled among the houses of worship in Grover's Corners—or any hint of unrest, though one belligerent audience plant makes passing mention of "social injustice and industrial inequality." It is also true that the soda-fountain courtship of George and Emily is vanilla-flavored enough to have been the inspiration for numerous teenage movie romances, beginning with the Andy Hardy series, just as the chitchat over the Gibbses' breakfast table probably informed countless family sit-coms (Little Rebecca: "Mama, do you know what I love most in the world—do you?— Money"). It was a habit of the author, who was a redoubtable scholar, to ruminate on the experiments of more serious artists and disgorge them as cottage cheese. Just as *The Skin of Our Teeth* is a homogenized version of *Finnegans Wake*, so *Our Town*, with its bare stage trappings and direct audience address, is a folksy reduction of Brechtian alienation techniques (the dialogue also cribs occasionally from Joyce's *Portrait of the Artist*).

And it is true that the play, or at least the first act, can be a little too smug about its small-town Philistinism. Mr. Webb, the newspaper editor, acknowledges that there's not much culture or love of beauty in Grover's Corners, though people enjoy watching birds and sunsets, and he tells us that this 86 percent Republican town is "hunting for a way the diligent and sensible can rise to the top and the lazy and quarrelsome can sink to the bottom" (eighty years later, New Hampshire's Governor Sununu is bringing this search to Washington). Domestic life is idealized, as if seen through the eyes of a child experiencing childhood without any night sweats. The real sexual issues of men and women remain unexamined; the worst family sin is a failure to complete chores. There is no deviation from the norm, nothing to trouble the constable except a drunken church organist, nothing to threaten the pastoral atmosphere except the presence of death.

But death *is* important to the play, and what distinguishes this production is Mosher's recognition that mortality is always leavening the sweetness. It's hyperbolic to suggest that Grover's Corners represents the world (the program cover is a photograph of the planet Earth), but it *is* true that *Our Town* is about the basic rituals of life: "This is the way we were: in our growing up and in our marrying and in our living and in our dying." Birth and copulation and death, all the facts when you come to brass tacks. Mosher hones this hidden edge of the play by casting Spalding Gray as the Stage Manager, thus removing the hat and pipe of the twangy, gallus-snapping philosopher portrayed by Frank Craven and injecting an element of post-modern irony. Although Gray is not yet one of our most accomplished actors—he is sometimes stumbling, sometimes hesitant—his experience as a monologuist has endowed him with a laconic, diffident way of delivering lines, partly out of the side of his mouth, which provides enough detached force to blow the mist off the borders of the picture. Gray makes no effort to charm. As he wanders around the stage setting up chairs and ladders ("for those of you who think you have to have scenery"), or serving imaginary sodas to George and Emily, or marrying them in a nervous ceremony, or introducing the cemetery society, he even appears somewhat derelict and dissipated.

And the rest of the company is impeccably cast. The domestic scenes work because the intentions are so clear, so unabashed, and because the actors realize them so well. Frances Conroy, a youngish lyrical actress, is not an inevitable choice for Mrs. Gibbs, but she plays the part with firmness covering the sentiment and sweetness softening the starch, just as Roberta Maxwell brings a tensile strength to Mrs. Webb. James Rebhorn as Dr. Gibbs is well matched by Peter Maloney as Editor Webb; and W. H. Macy, Jeff Weiss, and Bill Alton are strong in smaller parts. But the most penetrating performances of the evening are given in the thinnest roles: the lovers George Gibbs and Emily Webb, as played by Eric Stoltz and Penelope Ann Miller. Stoltz, a relaxed and forthright redhead, and Miller, a Rubens-complexioned blonde with a marvelous laugh, enact their somewhat hackneyed scenes together with absolute conviction, and with a kind of luminous innocence which is sustained throughout the fourteen-year span of the play.

In the final act, the chairs are arranged for the dead, and Emily's funeral proceeds under umbrellas (Wilder was one of the earliest writers to notice that it always rains at burials). It is here, where the central issue of the play is exposed, that we get the most potent writing and acting of the evening. Emily appears in a white dress, her hair tied in a ribbon like a little girl, to take a chair with the dead. She has died giving birth to her second child, and now she expresses her wish to rejoin the living just one more day. The day she chooses, significantly, is not one she spent with her husband or her children. It is a day she spent with her parents on her twelfth birthday. And returning to childhood with the eyes of an adult fills her—and us as well—with pain of extraordinary sweetness. So much was going on that she never noticed, so little was ever savored or appreciated. Enjoining us to live each day as if it were the last, she cries (in the play's most famous, curiously awkward line), "Oh, earth, you're too wonderful for anybody to realize you." One of "them" comes—it is the mute, grief-stricken George, who falls prostrate on Emily's grave, as the Stage Manager draws a curtain across the stage and sends the audience back to their homes.

The scene is as emotion-filled as the final act of *La Bohème* and has the same impact on our tear glands. Powerful as it is, however, the scene induces pity without terror, marking the play as a work not of classical tragedy but of American nostalgia. There's not much dread, no sting, in Wilder's prospect of death, since his view of the afterlife is much like a church service or a town meeting. And as a matter of fact, death in *Our Town* is really a metaphor for the abandonment of innocence and youth to the coarsening experience of adulthood—the loss of what Wordsworth called "the visionary gleam." It's no wonder *Our Town* retains an abiding appeal for a nation reluctant to grow up.

Nevertheless, as performed in the stark declarative simplicity of Mosher's production, it is irresistibly moving, and it is a deserved success, despite a sour notice in the *Times*. But a hit at Lincoln Center has come invariably to mean a reshuffling of productions, a reordering of priorities, a rescheduling of theatres. When the management has filled all its available stages with successful shows, it will presumably be forced to rent more Broadway houses or stop producing altogether. Planned for a limited run, *Anything Goes* is currently occupying the Beaumont for a second year. Planned for a limited run, *Our Town* will continue indefinitely at the Lyceum under a commercial Equity contract (*Measure for Measure*, which was to be the next scheduled course on the Lyceum menu, will be produced instead at the smaller Mitzi E. Newhouse). This makes *Our Town* the ultimate transfer. The show doesn't have to make a move to Broadway; it's already there. And the thin boundary line separating art from commerce, nonprofit practices from Broadway mechanics, has been reduced virtually to the vanishing point.

There are pressing reasons why Lincoln Center, in the face of growing subscriber displeasure and mounting press criticism, continues to make bottom line decisions—notably a monumental budget inflated by the failure of another commercial venture, the ill-fated national tour of *Anything Goes*, which has now lost almost two million dollars. It is the obligation of management to pare rather than expand the theatre's operations and the responsibility of the fund-raising board to relieve Lincoln Center's undue dependence on the box office. No doubt this is unwanted advice. Defenders of Gersten and Mosher charge that critics, second-guessing their decisions, are envious of their achievement. But it is possible to admire the producing savvy and artistic accomplishment of these men and still worry about the integrity of an important nonprofit theatre—not to mention the fiscal perils of gambling with huge sums of money on commercial enterprises. Previous Lincoln Center managements were done in by failure. The present management seems to be stumbling over success.

(1988)

Shakespeare with an American Accent

(*The Winter's Tale*)

Implicit in much of the criticism of Joe Papp's Shakespeare Marathon is a suspicion that American actors and directors are ill prepared to do classical plays. I believe with Papp that this assumption is false and that only a Tory culture besotted by British theatre could fail to appreciate the genuine performing talent in our midst. Admittedly, Public Theater Shakespeare over the last two years has not been without failure, but neither has the Shakespeare of the well-endowed English companies, which enjoy a sizable share of feeble productions and superficial interpretations. Papp's capacity to entice qualified American actors away from films—and American directors from comedies and musicals—ought to be honored for its effort to bring major artists back to the great plays. And if he has displayed no special inclination to form a permanent company with the people he attracts, Papp may simply be bowing to the exigencies of American careerism. I suspect a few will continue to return—those who haven't been too mauled and battered by the press—and, over time, a kind of improvised company will develop.

Papp gave James Lapine, for example, his first opportunity to direct Shakespeare some years back with a production in Central Park of *A Midsummer Night's Dream*. Before this, Lapine had staged only a few Off-Broadway musicals, his own plays, and *Sunday in the Park with George*. Lapine's *Midsummer*, though beautifully designed, was essentially the developmental work of a green talent (I called my review "Learning on the Job"). On the other hand, his production of *The Winter's Tale*, though far from flawless, represents a considerable advance, vindicating Papp's policy of building a classical theatre with native resources.

The Winter's Tale is a fearfully difficult play to stage. A late romance, written at a period when Shakespeare had apparently lost interest in consistent characterization and coherent plotting, it is packed with abrupt reversals and outlandish incidents ("Exit [Antigonus], pursued by a bear"). Yet, in Leontes, it features one of the most intriguing characters in all of Shakespeare, and the final scene is a haunting evocation of resurrection, reconciliation, and forgiveness. In his late period, Shakespeare—in language relatively bare of rich imagery or exquisite verse—is experimenting with the unexplored possibilities of the stage, just as Beethoven investigated the hidden reaches of music in his last quartets. Sixteen years go by in the intermission between Acts III and IV—this is not a playwright interested in the unity of time. Nor does he observe much unity of character. In the sudden, unmotivated jealousy of Leontes over the presumed infidelity of the chaste Hermione, Shakespeare is testing both the audience's capacity for empathy and its tolerance for the incredible.

Like Othello, Leontes is a man driven mad by suspicion, only his is self-generated. Without the insinuations of a Iago or the evidence of handkerchiefs, though also galled by conversations overheard, Leontes appears to be as great a potential tyrant as any Shakespearean villain. He orders the murder of his childhood friend Polixenes and his newborn daughter, Perdita. And his pre-Strindbergian paranoia about paternity is responsible for the near death of his wife, not to mention the actual death of his young son, Mamillius. Yet Shakespeare somehow manages to arouse indignation over Leontes' monstrous behavior without any loss of sympathy, this fulfilling Beaumont and Fletcher's definition of tragicomedy as a form that brings you close to catastrophe but stops just short.

But then he drops Leontes' story for most of the second part of the play, moving the action from Sicilia to Bohemia and creating a pastoral interlude wholly out of sync with the tragicomic mood of the first three acts. The roguish tricks of Autolycus, the shenanigans of the shepherdesses, Mopsa and Dorcas, the ritualistic sheep-shearing scene, the love affair of Florizel and Perdita, are hardly consistent with the dark colors Shakespeare paints in his earlier tale of jealousy and revenge, except for the parallel tyranny of Polixenes upon discovering his son's infatuation with a commoner. This disunity of tone makes the second part seem flaccid, as if the tragedy of *Othello* had been mistakenly collated with a few scenes from *As You Like It.* Yet the final episodes of the play, capped by the lovely Pygmalion ending, restore the unity of action, if not of character and tone, just when you thought the playwright's control was slipping away.

Lapine attempts to unify the play through a number of devices, including an interpolated prologue in which an intrusive Harlequin (played by Robert Besserer) cavorts through the action, dispensing flowers and scarves, and the way Mamillius hears the "sad tale best for winter" in storybook form from Hermione. This permits the dead child, the one discordant element in the resolution, to be resurrected at the end along with his mother and the devoured Antigonus. Yet Lapine, for all his ingenuity, is unable to bring any active life to the pastoral interludes. John Arnone's semi-Elizabethan setting transforms nicely from the somber Sicilian court, with its hidden upper alcoves and huge clock icon, to rustic Bohemia, decorated with a verdant Rousseau-like painting and a smiling sun that seems to be made of baked bread. Franne Lee's costumes place the characters in an Empire period, where the men look Napoleonic and the women slightly pregnant. And Beverly Emmons' lighting searches the remote corners of the elevated scrim area, ideal for plotting and eavesdropping on the events below.

But it is in the first part that the tension holds best, thanks to a riveting performance by Mandy Patinkin as Leontes. Patinkin emphasizes the Italianism of his character. Scowling from above as he watches Hermione plead with Polixenes to remain at court, he is in a rage from the first moment we see him, surly and sullen, sour as curdled milk. When Mamillius comes in with a toy, he almost strikes him, then tenderly washes a smudge off his cheek with spittle. Wagging his leonine hair, jabbing his index fingers in the air for emphasis, he tells a spectator his wife has also been "sluiced in his absence." Patinkin's face transforms into animal features, a wolf, a lynx, a marmoset. His gruff nasal tenor stammers over the *m* in "mercy," spits out the sibilant in "issue." And when his madness is gradually tempered by remorse over the multiple deaths he has caused, he who was preeminent in tyranny determines to be unmatched in grief. Touching the cheek of Hermione's living statue, he says in tones that have the vibrant ring of ecstasy, "Oh, she's warm."

Diane Venora, last seen on this stage as a female Hamlet (she has the mysterious, saturnine beauty of the dark lady of the sonnets), plays Hermione at first with wit and high spirits, then with open-eyed disbelief over her husband's pathological behavior. When Leontes confronts Hermione in her bedchamber and, charging her with adultery, pulls Mamillius from her arms, Venora's tone is conciliatory, but there's defiance and outrage beneath her lighthearted raillery. She appears before his judgment pale and enfeebled, in a gray worsted skirt and wrinkled satin shawl, as he hovers imperiously above her, hands behind his back like a merciless Javert. And returning to life wordless in the final scene (her last lines have been cut), she becomes an image of mute poignance and family unison, hugging Perdita to her bosom as snow falls from the flies.

Not all the roles are successfully executed. Christopher Reeve's Polixenes has a stately, aristocratic bearing, but also a muted naturalistic delivery which robs him of forthrightness and resolve. Alfre Woodard's Paulina lacks the requisite strength of this infuriated virago, and her "boundless tongue" is often twisted, when it is not singsong. Rocco Sisto's Autolycus, playing the gags instead of the situation, captures the cleverness of this "snapper-up of unconsidered trifles," but misses the coarse knavery that, say, Robert Newton might have brought to it. And while Jennifer Dundas' Perdita has a truly lovely adolescent innocence, she could use some voice training to deepen her teenage piping.

Many of the smaller roles, on the other hand, are sensitively played by MacIntyre Dixon, Michael Cumpsty, James Olson, Bertina Johnson, and others, and there is a common style to the performance which sustains its authority even when some of the acting flags. I also liked the witty, near-contemporary music of Michael Starobin and William Finn, Lapine's collaborators from musical comedy. Most of the time, the production is congenial to the play, and the company—the better actors trained at Juilliard—substantiates Papp's faith that Americans are capable of creating lively, intelligent classical work, if they could just spend some time on the job.

(1989)

Kid Coriolanus

(*Coriolanus*)

Although Shakespeare rarely displays affection for what he called the "beast with a thousand heads," his scorn for people's power is nowhere more evident than in *Coriolanus*. Bernard Shaw once defined democracy as substituting government by the incompetent many for rule by the corrupt few. Shakespeare's "few" are more arrogant than corrupt, but his "many" are not only incompetent but mindless and vicious. Representing the nobility they would curb, Caius Marcius (awarded the name of Coriolanus after his victory at Corioli) is a Roman general whose dauntless courage in battle against the Volsces qualifies him for election as a consul. But he is too proud to simulate the respect for the "voices" required to endorse his election or to grovel before this "common cry of curs." As a result, through the machinations of some jealous politicians, he earns the hatred of the masses and banishment from the country he helped to save. The timeliness of the play is almost too obvious to mention. Imagine his political rivals equipped with a couple of media experts, some well-placed sound bites, and a thousand points of light.

Steven Berkoff's muscular, energized New York Public Theater production never apologizes for the play's anti-majoritarian bias. Quite the contrary, it demonstrates how thin a line exists between populism and fascism, between democracy and demagoguery. In this radical adaptation, we are in a police state where an "ensemble" of citizens costumed in torn jackets and wielding baseball bats—they also treble as senators and citizens—rant, scream, threaten, and shout whenever its collective will is thwarted. It is during the scenes between Marcius and the citizens that the production gathers most steam. Advised by his mother and his friends to boast of his exploits and show his battle scars, Marcius responds by bidding the people to "wash their faces, / And keep their teeth clean." Christopher Walken adds an "Ugh." Walken turns Marcius' pretended humility into farce. Appalled at having to occupy the same space with these "stinking breaths," he mocks their power over him ("May I change these garments?"), supplicating in accents heavy with irony: "I pray, let me ha' it; I have *woooounds* to show you."

Walken is not the most patrician Coriolanus in memory. His manner often resembles that of the rabble he detests, and this makes it hard to believe that he and his mother, Volumnia, elegantly played by Irene Worth, came from the same family (they were better matched as Chance Wayne and the Princess Kosmonopolis in *Sweet Bird of Youth*). He rages against "the tongues of the common mouth," but his own gritty urban dialect marks him as a member of a similar class. Walken, furthermore, does not seem particularly comfortable inside Berkoff's highly choreographed production, which has him—and the rest of the cast—running, marching, riding, and fighting in a frenetic ballet (even the women sew in unison). Walken, a gifted dancer, sometimes seems purposely out of step, as if protesting the rigid boundaries of the concept. Still, what he lacks in nobility he more than compensates for in command and charisma. He is one of our most daring, unpredictable, and dangerous actors, and for most of the evening he is fascinating.

Walken plays Coriolanus less like a soldier than like a prizefighter. His hips in constant motion, he shambles, spars, feints, wriggles, and chops as if he were replaying his part in *Kid Champion*. Using imaginary weapons against the enemy, he slaps and kicks his own soldiers. With the rebellious plebeians he uses his fists, punching them out with well-placed chops to the face and body. In a fury from his first entrance, he stalks the stage like a sullen hood in a black leather long coat, edgy, ferocious, brutal, impatient. Always at top energy, he rasps, roars, yells, and snarls, then just as quickly lapses into a soft ironic smile. With his mother he is less the obedient child than the silken wooer. Irene Worth, lipping and tasting Volumnia's verse, comes on like a slightly dotty Madame Arcati in *Blithe Spirit*; Walken courts her like a lover, even leading her into a brief little dance. "There's no man in the world more bound to his mother," Volumnia tells us—and in the climactic scene Aufidius drives him into a fatal rage by calling Coriolanus a "boy of tears": "I / Flutter'd your Volscians in Corioli," he replies. "Alone I did it. Boy!" But Walken seems parentless. Among his "faults in surplus" one cannot count filial dependency.

Still, the performance is tumultuous and so is the production (sometimes to cover a little shallowness). On a black marbleized floor, decorated with twelve straight-back chairs (also black), the show moves forward with manic energy, punctuated by loud percussive music. The interracial "ensemble" of actors, in constant motion, change roles so fast that it's sometimes hard to identify them. They are in black, too; so are most of the cast. Tullus Aufidius, costumed in a synthetic black jumpsuit, Sam Browne belt, studded gloves, and jackboots, is played by Keith David as a mature and commanding African dictator, his spine arched with military stiffness, always standing at parade rest. Larry Bryggman and Andre Braugher as the scheming Roman tribunes wear the pinstriped suits and black slouch hats of Mafia henchmen (Braugher's shaved head and granny glasses also give him a marked resemblance to Malcolm X). Playing the Roman generals, Moses Gunn, stolid and saturnine as Cominius, and Thomas Kopache, wily and hooded as Titus Lartius, are friendly accomplices. And Paul Hecht plays Coriolanus' older friend, Menenius, as a dapper wit in a fur-collared overcoat and homburg, cogently speaking his "pretty tale" of the body's revolt against the head.

Nevertheless, this Rome is in a parlous political condition; even the graciousness of the three ladies, Volumnia, Virgilia, and Valeria, cannot redeem its overwhelming masculine brutalism. In Berkoff's production, it has been brought to this state by the lures and traps of democratic rule. "With every minute you do change a mind," snarls Coriolanus to the mob, "And call him noble that was now your hate, / Him vile that was your garland"—which is a pretty fair description of the press- and the poll-dominated electorate in our own country. Were Coriolanus chosen, he would hardly have been a judicious leader, but he was the only hope for peace. By the end of the play, the one possibility for political resolution—a Roman-Volscian treaty negotiated by Coriolanus after his mother prostrated herself before him—is abandoned on stage, a useless envelope lying inside a tattered briefcase.

(1988)

Much Ado about Something

(*Much Ado About Nothing*)

Much Ado About Nothing at the New York Shakespeare Festival is the fourth in Joseph Papp's Shakespeare Marathon, and it is running a strong race. Papp's former artistic director, Gerald Freedman—now head of the Great Lakes Theatre Festival in Cleveland—has given this romantic comedy a warm, intelligent reading with the aid of a strong company. Every line, every character, every action is cleanly interpreted; from the initial moment (a cannon blast, followed by a mock duel between Benedick and Claudio), we know we are in the hands of a decisive, thoughtful director. Freedman bases his interpretation on the ambiguous title—the noun "nothing" was once an Elizabethan homonym for the gerund "noting" (or watching). This is a play about eavesdropping—and the "ado" that results from misconstruing prearranged deceptions. Both Benedick and Beatrice are encouraged to express their dormant love when they overhear reports about being loved by the other; Hero is libeled after Don Pedro and Claudio mistake her for Margaret being visited by Borachio; Don John's schemes are exposed when the Watch eavesdrops on the drunken Borachio bragging about his villainy. Just as overhearing is the operative action of the play, so "to note" is the operative verb.

Any work with eavesdropping at the center needs a lot of windows, doors, and hedges, and these have been generously supplied by John Ezell's Sicilian village setting. Yet the physical element is the major disappointment of the evening. Freedman's associate director at Great Lakes, Ezell has collaborated in updating the play to Messina during the Napoleonic wars, but these stunted stucco buildings with their red slate roofs and pots of geraniums have a storybook quaintness appropriate less for housing the swashbuckling grenadiers of *Much Ado* than the Toon characters in *Who Framed Roger Rabbit.* I was not much taken either with John Morris's rather bland polkas and oompah band music, or the pastel Empire gowns of the women as designed by the usually more dependable Theoni V. Aldredge. These elements tend to ground the production in material banality, making it seem more conventional than it actually is, just as Central Park's reverberant amplification system makes it sound more hollow.

Still, a play like *Much Ado* rests on the back of actors. They mostly carry it well; Kevin Kline runs with it. Benedick makes no demand on his somewhat guarded interior resources, only on his considerable charm, and in a well-appointed uniform and corsair mustaches, he cuts an irresistible figure. Kline is in his maturity now, with a hint of gray in his hair. He brings weight to his role, but not at the cost of his athleticism, toppling over a hedge and through a window, almost falling from the tree where he has been eavesdropping on Don Pedro and Claudio while drinking a full bottle of wine. In a riot of blond curls, Blythe Danner's Beatrice has equal maturity, despite a voice that seems to be in shreds. She plays the part as if Beatrice were the kissing cousin of Katharina the shrew. Danner pricks Benedick with her wit and Hero with a sewing pin, throws lemons at her tormentors, and swings merrily on a trellis door. When she and Benedick finally decide to bury repartee and confess their tender feelings (Benedick has trouble kneeling, and stammers over the word "marriage"), their passionate kiss, repeated in the curtain call, is the rousing climax of a perfectly matched love.

Jerry Stiller's Dogberry shambles through the scenery in oversized green pants accompanied by the blind, halt, and enfeebled members of his Watch. He throws away his celebrated malapropisms with naturalistic New York inflections, all the while giving an invaluable lesson in relaxed comic acting. David Pierce is dour, pale, and fragile as the would-be villain Don John (he faints in outrage at another's reported happiness); Brian Murray plays Don Pedro with the sangfroid of a young Herbert Marshall; Phoebe Cates displays a ripening histrionic confidence as Hero; Don Reilly is an attractive Claudio; and most of the smaller roles are effectively filled.

Twenty-eight years ago, in the same park setting, Gerald Freedman directed the best *Taming of the Shrew* I've yet seen, creating a joyous, exuberant American farce style which drew on the Marx Brothers, Mack Sennett, and animated cartoons. This *Much Ado About Nothing* is not quite up to that standard, but Kline and Danner are able to display considerably more passion, if less elegance, than the frigid Derek Jacobi–Sinead Cusack performance sponsored by the Royal Shakespeare Company some seasons back. Admittedly, Freedman's new production is not very original or daring—Zefferelli's *Much Ado* at the

Old Vic in 1965 took a lot more risks—but it is consistently larky, and it captures all the epigrammatic wit, broad comedy, and melodramatic intrigue to be (over)heard in the play.

(1988)

Diderot's Yuppie

(Rameau's Nephew)

The Classic Stage Company, as its name suggests, is devoted to plays of the past. It has no permanent company at present. Along with most nonprofit theatres in a financial squeeze, it uses pickup casts for sequential productions. Nevertheless, producing in a modest space on a stringent budget, it has a growing potential to provide the classical theatre New York so sorely needs. Under the new leadership of Carey Perloff, the CSC has recently evolved from an amateur Germanic village into a center of rich cultural and intellectual activity. Like most Off-Broadway theatres, it has inherited remnants of the audience that used to patronize Broadway's serious plays, which means an audience of advanced age. Yet it is driven by youthful energy, and the recent repertory—Ezra Pound's version of *Electra*, Pinter's *The Birthday Party*, and now Diderot's *Rameau's Nephew*—is a mix of unconventional choices offered in free interpretations.

Rameau's Nephew is a literary anomaly. Written mostly in dialogue, it is essentially a philosophical disquisition on generational conflict between the author (identified as "Moi") and the disreputable nephew (identified as "Lui") of the great French Baroque composer Jean-Philippe Rameau. Denis Diderot was himself a dramatist, though not a very good one. Paradoxically, it is his nondramatic works that are earning him a place on the contemporary stage, largely because they have proved more appealing to the post-modern temperament: first *Jacques le fataliste*, which Milan Kundera dramatized as *Jacques and His Master*, and now *Rameau's Nephew* (unpublished at his death), which, under the spirited direction of the Rumanian Andrei Belgrader, has been adapted by the director and Shelly Berc.

My own company produced *Jacques and His Master* a few years ago, in a production directed by Susan Sontag. About fifteen years ago we also made a stab at *Rameau's Nephew*. This is a superior production because it is considerably more irreverent, an appropriate response to the irreverence at the core of the work. In a passage (sensibly included in the program notes) from *Sincerity and Authenticity*, Lionel Trilling mentions the appeal of the book to Hegel, Marx, and Freud, all of whom found confirmation of their own revolutionary positions in Rameau's bitter anarchism. For the intellectual drama of *Rameau's Nephew* consists of the conflict between two world-views—more accurately, one world-view and the nihilism of the youthful, venal, self-hating, self-absorbed hedonist who scorns having any world-views at all. Rameau is eaten up with envy for his more successful uncle. Reduced to eating scraps at other people's tables, he becomes, in Trilling's words, "the victim of an irresistible urge to offend those with whom he wishes to ingratiate himself. And stronger than his desire for self-respect is his appetite for demonstration; his ego . . . finds expression in a compulsive buffoonery, at once inviting shame and achieving shamelessness."

Rameau's credo is "Do your duty somewhat, always praise the boss, and let the world go its own way." Enraged by his own mediocrity, he is indifferent to patriotism, friendship, social obligations, the education of the young. Only money matters—and achieving success. This prescription, familiar enough to us, astonishes the older man, who cannot understand how Rameau could be so "finely attuned to the beauties of music and so deaf to the beauties of morality." In a prophetic passage which no doubt electrified Freud, he concludes that the savage created by Rameau's argument "would in time join the infant's reasoning to the grown man's passion—he would strangle the father and sleep with the mother."

At the CSC, this conflict between civilization and its discontented—between culture and anarchy—proceeds on a small stage decorated with a series of empty portrait frames and a shiny linoleum floor. After some lonely brooding on the risks of an artist outliving his fame, Moi (Nicholas Kepros) confronts his infamous antagonist Lui (Tony Shalhoub), a pseudo-artist with no hope for fame at all. Lui is a disheveled wreck in a disordered wig and torn stockings, unlaced, unbuttoned, lazy, gluttonous, "out of my mind." Possessed of a lacerating rage which Shalhoub often turns on the audience, Lui indulges anything that will help him forget his mediocrity: voracious appetite, derisive pranks, pernicious gossip (he is consoled to know that great men share his sordid habits). Lui has a little artistry, but not enough to appease his self-hatred. His greatest gift is a virtuoso cough, which he rehearses during an extended concert in major and minor keys. (In another virtuoso display, he downs countless glasses of wine, handed him by a stagehand, in a vaudeville riff worthy of the clowns in *Waiting for Godot.*) For him, the great produce of life is shit, a conviction he illustrates by squatting on the stage in a mock effort at defecation.

Vaguely bemused by his performance, involuntarily attracted by his nerve, Moi nevertheless takes refuge in moralistic pronouncements: "I believe you have brought the art of debasement to new heights." But Lui does possess a certain relative morality. He never lies when it is in his interest to tell the truth—and he draws negative precepts from the classics (from Molière he learns not to "show off your vices or you'll become an object of ridicule"). Nietzsche might have smiled over Lui's discourse on the need to excel in evil, on the superiority of the great criminal to the virtuous nonentity. Lui is Hobbes's natural man, and in Shalhoub's galvanic performance he becomes a curiously appealing figure—even a poignant one when he describes how Nature made a face when she belched him up ("But I feel!—I feel!").

Part of the interest in this character is stimulated by the way he anticipates so many modern malcontents to come: Dostoevsky's Underground Man, Camus's Rebel, Gide's Immoraliste. Critics will no doubt prefer to compare him to a Shaffer character, Mozart's enemy, Salieri, though he behaves more like a character in one of Mozart's operas, a jaundiced Cherubino, a self-hating Don Giovanni. Belgrader and Berc suggest Rameau's modernism with generous—perhaps overgenerous—anachronisms (Lui names the born geniuses as "Caesar, Copernicus, Trump"). Although Kepros, with his honeyed bel canto and basset-hound melancholy, is more inclined toward classicism, Shalhoub embodies this modernity by chasing female stagehands, laying his head in the laps of the older women spectators, doing stand-up comedy routines ("Thanks very much—you've been great—drive carefully"). Shalhoub's dark brooding lassitude movingly personifies the amusement and pain of this prophetic character, for whom the attractions of hope, the appeals of the future, represent "nada—zilch—zip—bupkis—not a goddamn thing."

(1988)

Phèdre with Pilaf and Pekoe Tea

(*Phaedra Britannica*)

Rameau's Nephew was enough to convince me that Ms. Perloff's broad learning and unconventional tastes were preparing us for a potentially important theatre, supplying a neglected repertory to culturally impoverished New Yorkers. Now that I've seen *Phaedra Britannica* I feel compelled to enter a caveat. Tony Harrison's Anglicizing of Racine's savage tragedy may have charm for English audiences, but combined with the relentless Anglicization of the production, it makes CSC momentarily look like a provincial British touring company. What we are asked to ingest is a French play populated with English characters impersonated by American actors, which is rather like eating a photo of a cardboard facsimile of a cassoulet. From the moment Thomas Theophilus (Hippolyte) enters to tell his tutor, Burleigh (Theramene), "Nyo, nyo, I *cahnt*," we know that the merits of this production will be more phonetical than theatrical. The program credits cite a "voice and text consultant" trained at the Central School in London, who may very well be responsible for the elocutionary emphasis of the evening. Whatever the reason, the actors presently on stage at the CSC, some of them very accomplished, all sound as if they had been taught the English language by Henry Higgins.

Ms. Perloff has made it her highly laudable mission "to rediscover lesser known or rarely produced classics in new translations." But Harrison's adaptation is less a new translation than a competitive effort that uses its poetic source for prosaic analogies. English audiences have traditionally had difficulties with classical French drama. Molière, for example, is generally disliked and rarely produced, unless he can be tarted up as a Restoration wit in lace and ruffles. Harrison himself did a post-Restoration comedy version of *Le Misanthrope* for the National in 1973, transforming Celimène into a bitchy Noel Coward hostess and Alceste into a sophisticated wit indistinguishable from his foppish adversaries. Come to think of it, Michael Frayn did much the same thing to Chekhov in *Wild Honey*, making *Platonov* march to the clackety-clack farce rhythms of his *Noises Off*. Perhaps it's time to start a society for the prevention of cruelty to Continental dramatists, before all the marrow is sucked from their bones by English adapters.

I would probably have more equanimity about this version were *Phèdre* a less powerful play and if we saw it more often. Composed by a great poet, it needs a great poet to put it into our language, and since our language is American, I wonder why the CSC didn't use the version Eric Bentley commissioned of Robert Lowell. Hardly faithful to the letter of Racine's text, that adaptation was unequaled in capturing the spirit of what Lowell called Racine's "hard electric rage." The Harrison, on the other hand, suffers from power shortages. Set in India during the period of the British Raj, it tries to substitute Anglo-Indian relations and Hindu theology for the mythical Athenian-Minoan world Racine sifted from Euripides and Seneca. Thésée, King of Athens, becomes the Governor of India; Phèdre, the lascivious Cretan, becomes his well-bred English wife; Hippolyte, the offspring of Thésée's union with an Amazon, becomes the half-caste Theophilus; the Athenian princess Aricie (Racine's invention) becomes the Indian Lilamani; and the monster who tears Hippolyte apart appears not through the intervention of Poseidon but through the Governor's appeals to Shiva. It's confusing enough to find a Hindu goddess responding to the prayers of one of the British colonials occupying her country, but by changing the nationalities of the principal characters, Harrison has totally muddled their motivations.

What is also lost in all this pukka-sahib attitudinizing is the political-sexual-mythological matrix of the play. In Racine's *Phèdre*, love is a "*funeste poison*" which turns people into monsters; *monstre*, in fact, is the operative word of the play. Thésée has vanquished the Minotaur; Hippolyte wishes to achieve *la gloire* by overcoming monsters himself; and Phèdre's family history is monstrous as well (she is related to Pasiphaë and Ariadne). Phèdre has every reason to hate Hippolyte, a rival claimant for the throne. But, in Racine, public ambitions have no power before private passions, and she cannot master her adulterous, incestuous love. The play is a brilliant psychological study of a lovesick woman: Phèdre is irritable, nervous, in love with death. The major obstacle is her marriage (another is Hippolyte's reputation for chastity); but when she is misinformed of Thésée's death, she is free to confess her feelings to her stepson, adding (in Lowell's words), "A worse monster threatens you than any Theseus fought and slew." Grabbing Hippolyte's weapon, she pleads in pulsing phallic imagery for "your sword's spasmodic final inch." Hippolyte resists, not just out of revulsion, but because he loves Aricie, another political rival. Burning with passion, fury, and self-loathing, Phèdre explodes on our ears like a cannon shot: "*Hippolyte est sensible, et ne sent rien pour moi*" (Lowell's rendering is equally powerful: "Hippolytus can feel, but not for me"). Only then does this self-characterized monster incite her husband to send a surrogate monster to kill him.

Racine displays his genius in the way he loads all the moral cards against Phèdre, yet makes her worthy of pity if not of absolution (legend has it that the play was written on a bet that a good poet could get crimes excused and even inspire compassion for the criminals). Harrison's Memsahib, by contrast, attracts neither pity nor interest. If Racine's Phèdre is a hot-blooded Cretan, the Governor's wife, as played by Caroline Lagerfelt, is a sharp-featured, henna-haired, starchy English housewife with a neurotic itch for extramarital adventure. And since the play has been updated to the mid-1850s, the incest motif between step-relatives is no more convincing than the sensuality. One can understand the fury of the Governor, but the extreme behavior of his wife seems excessive in a moral universe where hanky-panky behind the lattices of the colonial palace is almost commonplace.

Equally disappointing is Harrison's rendering of the French alexandrines. In place of Racine's rhymed couplets of twelve-syllable lines, Harrison substitutes couplets of iambic pentameter. These fall more gently on our ears (Lowell uses iambic couplets, too), but much of Harrison's version sounds like doggerel. Instead of Lowell's compressed "I want your sword's spasmodic final inch," Harrison gives us, "Get out your father's sword and thrust, thrust, thrust. / Kill the monster while it reeks of lust" (Theophilus' reply is also flat: "We've got to get away from here, we must,/I feel such nausea, such disgust"). Subordinate clauses are often force-fed to preserve the meter: "Whatever thoughts are passing through her head,/She seems, your Excellency, almost dead." And such terms as "uncouth," "catsup," "graffiti," "stepmother aggressiveness" too often cheapen the lexicon. Occasionally Harrison manages a resonant couplet—"It lumbers, lurking, from primeval slime/Where it's been lurking, biding its own time"—but usually his rhymes would sound better set to the music of Sir Arthur Sullivan.

Then there's the Anglo-Indian setting. I have previously tried to distinguish between reinterpretations of the classics based on metaphor and those based on simile. *Phaedra Britannica* seems to me a typical example of the second strategy, suggesting that the conditions of ancient Greece are analogous to those of imperial India before the Mutiny. The presentational style of Racine's *Phèdre* needs little more than a bare stage and some extraordinary actors. *Phaedra Britannica* is buried under excess colonial baggage and unnecessary Asian paraphernalia.

Ms. Perloff's production suffers much the same fate. Taking place within a pseudo-Calcutta surround consisting of columns, slats, potted plants, and ubiquitous Indian servants wearing lots of white linen, it is a curiously static staging that might have seemed less wooden in the abstract formal world of Racine's play. But in Harrison's near-contemporary setting, the production is stilted and actionless. The British strike and hold poses, as if they were having their photograph taken for the regimental yearbook, while the servants peek from behind lattices as if modeling for Indian drawings. As for the acting, it rarely touches the savage depths of the play. Richard Riehle as Burleigh, the pipe-smoking tutor, is—well—burly, a huffing Colonel Blimp; Sakina Jaffrey as Lilamani has a sari-clad beauty that would be more fetching in motion; Rajika Puri's Ayah (Oenone) is virtually inaudible; Jack Stehlin as Theophilus seems in a perpetual daze. And although Bob Gunton brings some blistering rage to the part of the Governor, even he is eventually tamed by excessive attention to diction. Every one of these actors is capable of performing a powerful part in the play. But artificial inflections make them sound as if they're speaking in another tongue and it's hard to muster much emotional strength in a language so far from your own.

Reading over these comments, I realize I've been harsh toward a theatre I admire. But one of the most disturbing things to me about our contemporary stage is its indiscriminate reverence for everything English. English acting can be wonderful, though its achievements are rarely seen here unless in television shows like *The Singing Detective* and *A Very British Coup*. What we prefer to import—and to imitate—is the Mayfair gentility once thought to be banished by the Osborne revolution. It is for that reason I am concerned about the CSC production of *Phaedra Britannica*. We don't need to repeat the mistakes of English theatre. We make enough of our own.

(1989)

Godot in LaLa Land

(*Waiting for Godot; Cafe Crown*)

It would be easy enough to satirize Mike Nichols's production of *Waiting for Godot.* I can imagine Nichols himself doing it with Elaine May. By casting two comedy superstars as Didi and Gogo, by setting the play in what appears to be Death Valley, and by calling this Lincoln Center offering "A Mike Nichols Production," the director invites charges that he has Hollywoodized an existential masterpiece—carbonated the philosophical heavy water, fizzed up the tragicomic metaphysics. This celebrity gathering features not only Steve Martin and Robin Williams as the tramps but F. Murray Abraham as Pozzo, Bill Irwin as Lucky, and Lukas Haas (the child in *Witness*) as the Boy. Since, for eight weeks only, they are occupying the 299-seat Mitzi E. Newhouse Theater (plans for a limited Broadway run fell through because of the stars' conflicting schedules), it can't even be argued that Hollywood names were needed to ensure a commercial success.

Indeed, subscribers are said to be incensed over the shortage of tickets. They're not missing a whole lot; the production expunges both the poetry and the pain of the play. Williams and Martin are very accomplished comedians. Under other circumstances, perhaps, they might have proved equal to their demanding roles (Williams, at least, has the vocal equipment). But either they've been encouraged to regard *Godot* as a scenario for improvisation or they've been living in California too long. Nichols's casting is no doubt inspired by the standard *Godot* criticism that the tramps have an affinity with the great clowns of silent films and music hall: Chaplin, Keaton, Laurel and Hardy. Without understanding a word of it, Bert Lahr played Estragon brilliantly in the first New York production with the more stolid E. G. Marshall cast as Vladimir, and Kurt Kasznar and Alvin Epstein as Pozzo and Lucky. But although the leading parts have roots in vaudeville, this is no reason to turn the entire play into stand-up comedy. Beginning with an ominous rumble and a rim shot, the evening realizes only the rim shot.

Abraham and Irwin, on the other hand, are very accomplished actors, and during their two scenes on stage the play begins to resonate. Abraham's voice was frayed the night I saw him, but he managed to turn that handicap into an asset, croaking a performance that exactly caught Pozzo's alternating imperiousness and helplessness. And Irwin was a consummate Lucky—prematurely aged, indifferent to the running rope-burn sores on his neck, sand-dancing on sand, creating a fanatically focused stoicism out of pain and bondage. Trained as a mime, Irwin has been growing into a fine actor, one I have previously underestimated. It's a shame his only opportunity for speech, Lucky's "Given the existence" monologue, was almost completely upstaged by Robin Williams' horseplay.

Williams, looking like a Western hobo under the turned-up brim of his derby, is a performer with a special relationship to the audience. It constitutes both his strength and his weakness. A number of his lines were delivered to the house, often embroidered with quotes from popular culture: he nasalized the theme from *The Twilight Zone*, twanged "Amazing Grace" on an imaginary Jew's harp, did macho John Wayne impersonations, turning a rusty automobile exhaust pipe into a machine gun. He's a very funny fellow, and one has to admire his nerve. But it's one thing to be irrepressible, another uncontrollable: his interruptions of Lucky's speech (Beckett calls for a "protest") were downright incorrigible. He not only threw Irwin to the ground, as the text requires, but emitted bored yelps while sitting in the audience and reading a spectator's program (at one performance, I'm told, he was asked to autograph it—an entirely appropriate response under the circumstances). Williams never touched Gogo's vulnerability or managed to convince us of his unhappiness. His anomie proceeded from irritability, not despair; the lyrical exchanges with Didi came off as arguments, not invocations. Gogo is a poet, but Williams' manic energy has its sources in prose.

Martin, on the other hand, was more subdued, but not nearly as interesting. His light voice provides his acting with no emotional ballast. Some touches were nice, such as when (like a Laker dunking a basket) he attempted to place a derby on Lucky's head without getting kicked or when he pretended to be Big Ben chiming the hours over Gogo's prostrate body or when he suffered a kidney attack after being libeled as a "critic." But Martin's inner and outer landscape, despite a growth of beard, are too cleanly contoured to accommodate the rough surfaces of this forlorn character and his persona is ultimately too California bland.

So is the production. It has been carefully calibrated, meticulously orchestrated. It is filled with precision, detail, clear choices. It never releases your attention. Yet somehow, the European penumbra has been illuminated in all its darkest corners by a sunny American disposition. Mike Nichols is working, as usual, with very gifted collaborators—Tony Walton on sets, Ann Roth on costumes, Jennifer Tipton on lighting—and what they have wrought on the tiny Newhouse stage is miraculous. But I fear that Nichols's specific behaviorist approach to his material, appropriate enough for American realistic writing, distorts a work that draws its strength from abstraction.

Beckett left his setting for *Waiting for Godot* deliberately unspecified ("A country road. A tree"). This production places us, as I mentioned earlier, in a California desert—to the point of changing references to "Macon" (and "Crackon") country to "Napa" (and "Crapa") country. There may be no vineyards bordering the premises, but there's an ocher-and-tan Western sky beaming over tons of sand, no doubt borrowed from Peter Brook's *Carmen* at the upstairs Beaumont. There is, besides, an abundance of identifiable hubcaps, automobile springs, license plates, bones, stones, and Georgia O'Keeffe cattle skulls—so many, in fact, that the amnesia of the tramps regarding whether or not they've visited this area before begins to verge on Alzheimer's disease. I am hardly in a strong position to criticize deviations from Beckett's published stage directions, when a production of *Endgame* at my own theatre, to the playwright's everlasting chagrin, was set in an abandoned subway station. But Beckett intended *Waiting for Godot* to be situated in a generalized purgatory. And whatever you think of California—even if you agree with Gertrude Stein that "there's no there there"—it still remains a little too site-specific to capture the abstract metaphysics of the play.

Finally, Nichols's impulse to prove the truth of *Godot*'s advertising claim (in the original Broadway production) to be "the laugh sensation of two continents" recalls his treatment of David Rabe's *Hurlyburly*, a migraine of a play which he softened into a comic anodyne. He remains one of the cleverest of American directors, with no peer in casting savvy, stagecraft, or skill in handling actors. What he lacks, either through indifference, shallowness, or cynicism, is the willingness to probe beneath the outer membrane of denser material.

Cafe Crown at the New York Public Theater is a pleasant if somewhat assimilated revival of Hy Kraft's dramatic memoir (written in 1940) about the waning days of Yiddish theatre. Although the play is weak, it is still a reasonably enjoyable way to spend an evening, especially for those old enough to feel nostalgic about the great actors—Jacob Adler, Boris Thomashefsky, Maurice Schwartz, Molly Picon, Menasha Skulnik—who consumed tea and stuffed derma between shows at a restaurant called the Café Royale. It is even more evocative of rude Jewish waiters, those terrorists of Second Avenue whose beady stares and acid tongues were usually a prelude to slammed plates and stained tablecloths. My father had such a waiter at a restaurant called the Grove. One day when he was scurrying past the table scratching his behind, my father asked him: "What's the matter, Peretz, you got hemorrhoids?"—to which the harried waiter replied: "Mr. Brustein, don't bother me, I'm in a big hurry—if it's on the menu we got it."

The major appeal of *Cafe Crown* is the way it stirs up such memories of a lost golden age. If you don't have access to such nostalgia, the evening may not be your glass of tea, since it's very weak on character and the plot turns are absurd. The story, for example, revolves around the efforts of the actor-producer David Cole (based on Jacob Adler) to mount a Yiddish version of *King Lear* set on Riverside Drive and starring an actor who is being tapped for Broadway. That's credible enough, given the appeal of *Lear* to all Jewish parents who think their children are ungrateful (i.e., all Jewish parents). Where credibility falters is in the fact that the actor cast as Lear, though famous for beard roles, is in his twenties. And when was the last time the Yiddish Actors Union admitted any actor into its ranks under the age of forty-five?

The plot and ensuing love complications are resolved in equally unconvincing fashion, but *Cafe Crown* is distinguished not so much for dramaturgy as for local color. In an affectionate reconstruction of bygone restaurant decor by Santo Loquasto, right down to pickles on the table and Yiddish newspapers on the racks (also a copy of *Time*!), the diners and pinochle players come and go, speaking of kreplach and onion rolls. Sam the waiter (Fyvush Finkel) maneuvers his way among the tables ("Hot stuff coming up"), while Hymie the proprietor answers the phone with cries of "Cafe Crown speaking— Who?" moaning about his daughter in "Bryn Mare—Ma?—More?" Eager to invest in any David Cole production so long as it isn't Shakespeare, Bob Dishy's Hymie is a particularly accurate embodiment of the mournful sobriety of this world—his shoulders slumped, his eyes half closed, lumbering through his establishment like an arthritic penguin.

Eli Wallach plays the famous Yiddish actor David Cole, plagued with financial woes, a quarrelsome wife, and an actress daughter (Stella Adler?) who prefers Broadway and Hollywood to the indigent charms of family enterprises. He performs the part with energy and flair, in a black slouch hat and fur-collared coat rakishly thrown over his shoulder. But the character is just a touch too flamboyant for Wallach's stylized realism; what it requires is a great Jewish ham. And where are the Yiddish accents in Martin Charnin's re-creation of this Yiddish world? Gone with the wind round the heart caused by the fried food. The play has a syrupy conclusion, with all issues happily resolved, including the means to let the play and the young hero go on—to Hollywood. But so what? If it doesn't sate your appetite for drama, it will certainly make you hunger for a good bowl of kasha and a couple of salt rolls.

(1988)

Jewish Metaphysics

(*The Tenth Man*)

Lincoln Center Theater is currently engaged, upstairs and downstairs, with plays deriving from Jewish metaphysics, which is to say with devils, demons, and dybbuks. This represents more unity than we've yet seen from this normally eclectic (I hesitate to say expedient) institution. Paddy Chayefsky's *The Tenth Man* at the Vivian Beaumont is thirty years old, while the two one-act pieces by David Mamet and Shel Silverstein, produced at the smaller Mitzi E. Newhouse under the collective title *Oh, Hell*, are brand new. It's nice to find Lincoln Center Theater back at the ranch house after sorties around various Broadway corrals, and even nicer to detect some consistent artistic direction following several early years of vagueness and improvisation. The emerging policy would seem to be American revivals in the larger theatre and new American plays downstairs, which pretty much reflects the aesthetic preferences of artistic director Gregory Mosher. The schedule will no doubt vary to accommodate the odd South African offering, possibly some classics, an occasional new play from abroad—but no one minds a few departures once you make some effort at self-definition.

This policy will not satisfy New York's need for a repertory acting company, but it may help to distinguish the goals of Lincoln Center Theater from the aims of current Broadway producers. Its production of *The Tenth Man*, on the other hand, evokes the ghost of Broadway past in the spectral shape of Paddy Chayefsky. Chayefsky is an enigma. His tough-minded screen writing—particularly movies like *The Hospital* and *Network* (and possibly even *Altered States*)—is far superior to his earlier writing for the theatre, which was invariably squishy, portentous, domesticated midcult. Having grown to admire Chayefsky from his movies, I was hoping to like this revival of *The Tenth Man* a lot better than Tyrone Guthrie's 1959 production, which gave me heartburn. Ulu Grosbard's is a stronger version on the whole, but it hasn't improved my dyspeptic condition. *The Tenth Man* remains an indigestible dose of mystical kitsch and boiled-cabbage cabalism.

The play was originally written to amuse a suburban audience with ambiguous feelings toward its immigrant forebears—the kind of assimilated Jews that Philip Roth satirized in his early stories. The action takes place in a ramshackle synagogue in Mineola whose Orthodox worshippers are full of disdain for Reform Jews who "sit around like Episcopalians, listening to organ music." Yet, perhaps in deference to these same Jews (who, after all, comprised his audience), the playwright has the congregation pray not in Hebrew but in English, put on "phylacteries" rather than *tefilin*, and seek out "quorums" instead of *minyans*. Chayefsky's version of Yiddish humor is also dispensed in assimilationist translation, most of it based on the bewildering impact of bustling New York on cloistered innocents from the Old Country. There are jokes about cemetery plots, the decline of Orthodoxy, and ungrateful daughters-in-law, the most successful being an extended vaudeville shtik concerning two Jews who never before strayed from Mineola trying to find the right subway to Williamsburg and always ending up in New Jersey.

Instead of being practical and realistic, in other words, Chayefsky's Jews are simple, lovable, and filled with mystical awe—suitable qualities for their role as affectionate Dwarfs to the play's hapless Snow White. Here Snow White is called Evelyn, a disturbed girl spirited from an asylum by her grandfather, while the Wicked Stepmother is Current Scientific Error in the shape of rational Freudianism. To accommodate the playwright's preference for supernatural explanations of psychological afflictions, the main plot is Ansky's *The Dybbuk* without tears, with Evelyn's paranoid hallucinations interpreted as demonic possession (the dybbuk being a vengeful Kiev whore named Hannah). When a young man enters—defeated, cynical, suicidal, an unbelieving analysand who doesn't believe in life or love—Evelyn offers to marry him.

In his presence, the girl's distemper takes a somewhat different form. She thinks she's a De Mille movie star. Not surprisingly, he thinks she's psychotic. When he finds the marriage impractical, she concludes he, too, is possessed of a dybbuk which will not allow him to feel. In the ceremony that follows, it is his demon that is exorcised, and capable now of love, he prepares to cure the girl with the strength of his passion.

"He still doesn't believe in God," observes the exorcist, "he just wants to love. And when you think of it, gentlemen, is there any difference?" This is the way that problems of madness, suicide, and anomie were cured in the theatre of the late fifties, no doubt along with coronaries, carcinomas, and the Cold War. Presumably, the rite of exorcism was also a simpler matter thirty years ago. Demons were more benign. The possessed heroine of *The Tenth Man* is hardly obliged to vomit green slime or rotate her head in 360-degree circles. In Paddy Chayefsky's symphonic metaphysics, diabolism is largely an occasion for romantic scherzos, with the orchestra playing variations on "All You Need Is Love."

Ulu Grosbard's Chagall-like production manages to capture some of the shmaltz-herring flavor of the play with the help of seasoned acting by Joseph Wiseman, Jack Weston, Sidney Armus, Ron Rifkin, Alan Manson, and Bob Dishy. Dishy—doing a variant of his sour waiter in *Cafe Crown*—is particularly endearing as a socialist-atheist who hangs out at the *shul* because he has nothing better to do; his hooded eyes, bent back, and grim-set lips add a note of reality to an otherwise fanciful evening. Peter Friedman also sours the pot a little in the part of the young man (the first of Chayefsky's suicidal heroes). But there's no particular electricity flowing between him and Phoebe Cates, who stumbles over the uncontracted dialogue of Evelyn and the Slavic flourishes of her Kiev dybbuk. I liked Santo Loquasto's set, though, with its grimy windows and linoleum floor flecked with traces of old paint, and the new thrust configuration of the Beaumont is a fine solution to a once forbidding space.

(1989)

Fairy Tailspin

(*Cymbeline*)

Cymbeline is the least performed of Shakespeare's mature plays, and for good reason. All his late romances are filled with absurdities, but *Cymbeline* lacks the compensatory inspiration, the charged vision of *The Winter's Tale* or *The Tempest.* Through much of the play, Shakespeare is nodding, his inertia suggested by the way he borrows characters and motifs from previous work, with sinew, blood, and nerves removed. King Cymbeline, the volatile British tyrant, is an anemic Lear; Iachimo slanders Imogen in the same way Iago slanders Desdemona; Imogen herself is a transvestite exile in the tradition of Viola and Rosalind; Cornelius, the physician, is a recycling of the Apothecary in *Romeo and Juliet*; and Iachimo's monologue in Imogen's bedchamber ("Our Tarquin thus / Did softly press the rushes") borrows imagery from *The Rape of Lucrece*. The only felt energy in the play is the rage of Posthumus Leonatus over Imogen's assumed adultery, and even these fulminations echo with lines from *Hamlet* and *Othello* ("Oh vengeance, vengeance," "I'll tear her limb-meal," "Let there be no honor where there's beauty," etc.). Still able to rouse himself over his constant theme of female inconstancy, Shakespeare is nonetheless suffering from temporary creative fatigue.

Shakespeare found in Holinshed the historical source for the conflict over tribute between the ancient Britons and the Romans; the outlines of Imogen's story he borrowed from Boccaccio's *Decameron*. Some important plot details, however, seem to have no formal literary source, which has encouraged scholarly conjecture on a link between *Cymbeline* and the tradition of fairy tale, particularly the story of *Snow White*. It is this link that JoAnne Akalaitis has emphasized in her controversial Public Theater production. Locating the play "in the midst of Celtic ruins" and calling it "a Romantic fantasy in Victorian England," Akalaitis has tried to force stylistic unity onto this messy sprawl through a theatrical metaphor designed to justify its vagaries of plot and distentions of character. I think she succeeds for the first part of the evening—until the play spins out of control and her production starts to splinter and break up.

But the opening scenes are lovely. Following the sounds of thunder and rain, and some perfunctory exposition in front of the curtain, we enter the fog-shrouded ruins of a garden, ravishingly designed by George Tsypin. (Tsypin's simple set pieces—two revolving boxed columns and a symmetrical moat—transform into locales as various as a wood, a bedchamber, a battlefield, through the agency of Stephanie Rudolph's exquisite projections.) We are in the bare ruined choirs of Wilkie Collins or the hidden enchantments of *The Secret Garden*, and with the entrance of Joan MacIntosh in flaming red wig and kimono, playing the Queen with extravagant hand gestures and exaggerated professions of sincerity, distilling deadly potions in smoking vials, we are also in the storybook world of Wicked Stepmothers. Joan Cusack, a healthily proportioned Imogen, will remind us of Cinderella, Sleeping Beauty, and Lewis Carroll's Alice. And George Bartenieff as the King, shambling about in side whiskers, dressing gown, and toque—later wearing a British redcoat over military Scottish kilts—resembles one of those sleepy imperial clubmen in Jules Verne's *Around the World in Eighty Days.*

Hovering on the edges of the stage are four gray apparitions who seem to have escaped from *The Turn of the Screw*—Leonatus' father, his mother, and his two brothers, who died before his posthumous birth. Their ghostly presence, and the melancholy arpeggios of Philip Glass's score (for synthesizer, percussion, and viola), lend a supernal quality to the play's early scenes which is sustained until well into the third act. Michael Cumpsty, puckering like Robert Goulet sucking lemons, turns Iachimo into a sour villain out of Victorian melodrama. He emerges from a trunk in Imogen's bedroom to check out the decor, steal her magic ring, and ogle the cinque-spotted mole under her breast—the potted proof, like Desdemona's handkerchief, that she's been false to her husband.

Leonatus' wager with Iachimo over Imogen's chastity is for modern audiences one of the sticking points of the plot. Who could respect a man who bets money that his friend can't seduce his wife? Among Shakespeare's romantic heroes, only Leontes in *The Winter's Tale*, and possibly Bertram in *All's Well That Ends Well*, have as many porcine male characteristics.

Like Leontes, Leonatus orders his wife's death on the strength of unsubstantiated evidence. This is the stuff of tragedy, but it is also what husbands do in fairy tales, and I suspect Akalaitis's Grimm Brothers strategy was partly designed to distance us from the discordant plot. For a while her strategy succeeds—until the fairy tale goes into a tailspin. She compounds Shakespeare's anachronistic blunders (his Britons are Jacobean Englishmen, his Romans Renaissance Italians) with the ridiculous *Duck Soup* costuming of the Roman forces, as well as by casting an Indian actress as their soothsayer, Philharmonus (in Victorian times, obviously, India was part of the British Empire, not an Italian colony). The Queen's son, Cloten, a minstrel-show clown in a large checked suit, whinnies like a black Pee Wee Herman. Imogen and Pisanio navigate the stage on a bicycle and a scooter. Belarius, the banished lord, is dressed as Robinson Crusoe, and Guiderius and Arviragus, his princely charges, are Indian braves, supplied with pigtails, decorated with warpaint, and given ample opportunity to display their bare behinds (Akalaitis seems to have a weakness for exposing male bottoms—even Iachimo shows a bit of tail emerging from his bath).

Following an impressive slow-motion battle scene—a percussive war fought between shafts of overhead light (choreographed by David Leong)—Akalaitis's concept trips on its own shoelaces. The ghostly family loses its spectral hold on us the moment they open their mouths (they become characters in Leonatus' dream, in a crude masque considered the work of another hand and usually cut). And what is arguably the longest—unarguably the dullest—recognition scene in Shakespeare is even further mauled through merciless camping. After this, Cymbeline's celebrated concluding lines ("Laud we the gods;/And let our crooked smokes climb to their nostrils/From our bless'd altars") suggest that odors of another sort entirely might be reaching those sacred olfactory organs.

The New York critics were almost uniformly savage in their treatment of this show, and my halfhearted defense must begin with the confession that JoAnne Akalaitis has twice directed in Cambridge with my own company. But the only other Shakespeare production that solicited an assault like this was Lee Breuer's equally unconventional *Tempest* (another Joe Papp production—in Central Park). That was a failure, too, but in each case, the director was trying to bring fresh eyes to Shakespeare's texts, not to trash them, as the critics charged. Breuer and Akalaitis are both affiliated with Mabou Mines, a group devoted to strong visual concepts, interracial casting, and performance-group techniques, and they bring these commitments to their mainstream assignments. Where their Shakespeare work may be faulted, I believe—and this is a weakness of many auteurs directing classical plays—is not for the interpretive chutzpah but for the acting, which sometimes descends to mannerist exaggeration.

Breuer encouraged his *Tempest* cast to impersonate Mae West, W. C. Fields, and Sid Vicious. Akalaitis, less dazzled by movies and rock music, creates histrionic distortion through feeble casting or broad performing. Michael Cumpsty manages to fulfill the director's concept without loss of skill, and Peter Francis James is a masterly Pisanio. Joan MacIntosh keeps her womanliness and power despite a wild-and-woolly characterization, and Don Cheadle and Jesse Borrego have a boisterous charm as the bare-assed Apache princes. But in central roles, Joan Cusack's Imogen is largely lost in sit-com, Jeffrey Nordling's Posthumus is pallid, and that Off-Off-Broadway legend George Bartenieff mumbles most of the King's lines into his side whiskers. Worst of all is the Cloten of Wendell Pierce, a comic part played by a humorless actor.

Since Mr. Pierce is black, critics were confused over how Imogen could mistake Cloten's headless trunk for her husband's corpse (eyebrows were also raised over how a white queen could have given birth to a black prince). This suggests, I think, a misunderstanding of nontraditional casting in classical plays. There are certain cases—the Goodman Theatre production of *Romeo and Juliet*, for example, where the Montagues and Capulets are engaged in racial feuds—that require consciousness of color. But the fundamental purpose of nontraditional casting—as implied in the phrase—is to be color-blind. Anyway, since the only dark flesh showing on this headless corpse is on the hands, it is even more unlikely that Imogen would have mistaken a short and pudgy Cloten for a tall and slender Leonatus—but let's not confuse the conventions of Jacobean theatre with those of realism. The real problem is Mr. Pierce's characterization, not his colored family tree.

Since criticism of this *Cymbeline*, whatever its artistic faults, seems more ideological than aesthetic, let me repeat what I wrote on the occasion of Breuer's *Tempest*: "Instead of savaging it and other productions like it, we might reflect on why the most violent reactions are usually directed not against what is conventional, mind-deadening, and banal, but rather against those very rare occasions when an artist dares to risk, and fails through a surplus of imagination and invention." The war on risk-taking is continuing to rage in critical circles, and it is continuing to drive our most inventive talents from New York. I salute Joe Papp for the courage to risk *his* reputation on their survival.

(1989)

The Hero of the Nursery

(*Peer Gynt*)

Ibsen's *Peer Gynt* is one of the great plays and great anomalies of modern theatre. Written, along with *Brand*, when Ibsen was living in Rome, drunk with sunshine, thawing out his imagination from frozen Northern constraints, it is a whopping poetic extravaganza that would seem to be unstageable in its original form. Two to three times as long as a conventional play, and roaming over most of the Western hemisphere, *Peer Gynt* requires at least two days to perform, besides innumerable set changes, a huge cast, and, most importantly, an actor capable of transforming from extreme youth to extreme old age in the course of a journey that spans not only continents but Time itself. Some productions (Ciulei's version, for example, at the Guthrie) manage to dodge this problem by casting three separate actors as Peer. The Hartford Stage Company version uses a single actor—Richard Thomas—who elects to ignore the aging process altogether.

Thomas attempts a character change in only one scene—the Act IV opening in Morocco, where, a coarse capitalist shrouded in cigar smoke, he hoarsely recounts his history as slave merchant and China trader to a group of equally venal international entrepreneurs. Soon after, however, he reverts to characteristic boyishness, and even in Africa he is dressed in his original costume, supplied with appropriate accessories (a white jacket and black bow tie added to his standard underwear top, red suspenders, black pants, and boots). Thomas wears the same clothes for fifty years—no wonder he smells a bit musty in the armpits.

The decision to keep Peer youthful throughout his life span is a bold choice, which is reinforced by John Conklin's ingenious scenic strategy. When the lights come up on the first scene, we see a child's nursery, complete with wooden crib, rocking horse, stuffed cat, rubber balls, and miniaturized buildings, including a little castle and a small house. In the background, a wooden boat is sitting on a swath of blue silk, and above hang a clock, a wheel, and a toy horse. All of these items will eventually play their part in Peer's odyssey; he carries his childhood with him wherever he goes. Scenes change largely through the agency of colored fabric—yellow silk represents the desert (with the toy castle downstage and a burning sun behind the backdrop), billowing black oilcloth represents the stormy sea. Asa is stranded on the roof of the toy house and dies in the crib; the ship that explodes in Act IV is the miniature vessel from Peer's nursery; the Sultan's steed is a giant version of Peer's toy horse; the tumbleweed is suggested by the rubber balls, rolling mysteriously onto the stage. For Peer, the nursery is the world. And the decay of this world, after his return to Norway as a young-old man, is symbolized by the decay of his childhood possessions, now in ruins and fallen out of the perpendicular.

This approach sacrifices some of the majesty and darkness and savagery of the play, so impressively realized in Patrice Chereau's 1982 Paris production. There the Great Sphinx and the statue of Memnon were almost the size of the originals; here, they are just a few more items from Peer's playroom. When Chereau's Peer wielded an ax, he hacked away at the proscenium, sending splinters into the audience; Thomas must be satisfied with a few whacks in the air. Paris provided the entire top deck of a ship, complete with rigging, lifeboats, and winches; Hartford's director, Mark Lamos, can afford only a miniature smokestack and a twirling helm. A number of Lamos' effects are similar to Chereau's—the black-drop storm, for example, and the *Marat/Sade* madmen with their pasty white faces. But American resident theatre economics dictate a considerably more simplified production scheme than that made possible in Europe by state subsidy.

The Hartford *Peer*, nevertheless, has qualities that compensate for Parisian size and grandeur, notably American playfulness and whimsicality. Chereau took an essentially Existentialist approach, which gave the play a post-modern bleakness at the cost of its folktale charm. Thomas, who has charm in abundance, brings a wholesome apple-pie sunniness to all his adventures. His scenes with his mother, played by Patricia Conolly as an affectionately cranky New England schoolmarm torn between spanking and hugging a truant charge, have the quality of domestic comedy, and her death scene, with Peer perched behind her crib-confined body on a rocking chair, riding her to heaven, is deeply affecting (characteristically, he doesn't stay for the burial).

The village scenes that follow are out of the Scandinavian exhibit at Epcot Center—stock choreography performed by twirling and clapping rustics (oddly dressed like Amish gauchos). But the episodes in the Troll kingdom are smashing. Peer abducts and rapes the bride Ingrid, who trails forlornly after him in a torn white wedding gown and one red shoe. When he hits his head on a rock, he has what may be a dream beginning with the seduction of the Woman in Green (the Troll King's Daughter), played by the same actress in a green wedding gown and one red shoe—plus two other elements, a pig snout and a tail. All the trolls he later meets are animalistic versions of the villagers, and their feast is a brutish rock-and-roll variant of the wedding party—a barbecue of beast and human heads by pig-snouted, monkey-eared guards carrying automatic weapons. If the villagers seem drawn from Disneyland, the trolls appear to have escaped from the island of Dr. Moreau. Grossest of all is the Troll King—played by Stephen Rowe as a sweating, slavering, pork-bellied Stanley Kowalski with horns—who garrots Peer with his tail, farts over his prone body, and forces him to drink his daughter's urine ("The thing that counts is it's homemade").

Peer refuses to have his eye cut and become a genuine troll, but he nevertheless accepts the troll's credo—not "To thyself be true," but rather "To thyself be—enough." (One of the quarrels I have with Gerry Bamman's and Irene B. Berman's otherwise witty adaptation is their misrendering of the Troll motto as "Be yourself and that's enough.") Peer pursues his Self throughout the play—in his encounter with the Great Boyg (oddly translated as "the Great Between"), in his temporary career as an Arab prophet, in his appearance before the Sphinx as a pith-helmeted tourist, carrying a Baedeker. Peer's failure to form a Self suggests the confusion of character and personality in the weightless modern world (today it would be called an identity crisis), and it is Ibsen's genius to crown him Emperor of Self in the madhouse, the one place where Ego reigns supreme. "Common sense met its demise" (no match for William Archer's version: "Absolute reason expired at eleven o'clock"), shouts the head doctor, madder than any of his inmates, as the strains of "Ode to Joy" pulse through the loudspeakers.

"To be oneself, the self must die," Peer is told by the Button Molder, preparing to melt him down in order to cast a new and better soul. Peer realizes, at the end, that his Self—and life—had always been preserved in the faith and hope of his innocent love, Solveig. But Solveig's forbearance and forgiveness remain, for modern audiences, the most problematical aspect of the play. Confirming this, the Hartford actress Tara Hugo reads her concluding lines less like a patient Penelope celebrating her Ulysses' return than like a resentful proto-feminist smoldering over Peer's fifty-year night-out in exotic places while she's been stuck at home with the sewing. (Why, she might also ask, has her husband remained ageless while her own hair has turned white in the interim?) It's a relevant contemporary touch, but it removes some of the emotion from the swelling mother-child resolution of the conclusion.

Actually the Hartford production—like the Bamman-Berman adaptation—doesn't rise often to the emotional heights of the play. The couplets and quatrains give the dialogue an arch contemporary tone ("Allow me to be your fond advisor / Drop dead—you'll make good fertilizer"), but the deeper darker chords come off sounding a little bland. Although Ibsen's first three acts (here called "Into the Mountains") have a unity of style and purpose well realized in the writing and the acting, the more difficult surrealist edge of Acts IV and V ("The Voyage") is not always consistently honed. Richard Thomas, so fresh and graceful in the first part, does not, I think, sufficiently reveal Peer's moral degeneration as the play proceeds. How could he when he shows no physical degeneration? Ibsen's hero has grown cruel and cranky by the time he returns to Norway; Thomas never seems to lose his wholesome disposition. Ibsen indicts Peer for the sin of *hahlveit* (half-and-halfness), for being a will-less mediocrity incapable of either great deeds or great crimes. The second part of the Hartford production shares some of those transgressions, attempting no daring leaps, no singular departures that could help it transcend a general competence. The only artistic excess is in the snow effects, which are visible even in the desert scenes.

Still, just to stage this awesome work and make it continuously engrossing over five full hours is a major achievement for an American theatre, and the Hartford Stage Company deserves a resounding salute for its accomplishment. Mel Marvin's well-orchestrated score—which owes something to Sibelius's tone poems, something to eighteenth-century Irish music, and a lot to Beethoven—provides strong reinforcement to dramatic climaxes and transitions—and Pat Collins' lighting design plays like a palette of colors and shadings on Conklin's imaginative set pieces. For all my cavils, I suspect the Bamman-Berman adaptation will now become the standard version (Bamman, coincidentally, was one of Ciulei's Peer Gynts at the Guthrie); and, for all my cavils, Richard Thomas should be warmly praised for his intelligence, commitment, energy, and endurance. The Hartford *Peer Gynt* may have lost some depth by making its hero a perpetual adolescent imprisoned in an eternal nursery. But most of this difficult play is there in all its amplitude and magnitude, confirming its important position as a bridge between the conventions of nineteenth-century German Romanticism and the thorny dilemmas of modern theatre.

(1989)

Transforming Actors and Star Personalities

(The Death of Olivier; *Twelfth Night*)

Laurence Olivier is dead, but the theatre values he so persistently represented expired long before his death. He was first and foremost a stage actor. Only serious illness could keep him off the boards. And in the last twenty years of his life he suffered a host of afflictions, including cancer and kidney failure. But I suspect the real *coup de grâce* came when he was summarily dismissed as artistic director of the National Theatre, at the age of sixty, just before the completion of the new complex on the South Bank. They gave his name, like a symbolic gold watch, to the largest of these theatres, and he accepted the sops and tributes with the natural grace of a theatrical nobleman. But he had led his followers to a peak in Pisgah only to be denied access to the milk and honey, and his bitterness was henceforth etched into the very set of his features, particularly in the lines about his mouth. One of the saddest things about Olivier's old age—a sadness recorded in his last films—was the way his sleepy, humorous eyes became a hooded death stare, the way his strong dimpled facial structure was frozen into a hollow-cheeked, narrow-lipped mask.

We're not supposed to regret the fact that the greatest actor of his age—the fateful Oedipus, the heroic Hotspur, the miserly Tyrone, the majestic Othello, the broken Shylock—was eventually reduced to playing second-rate villains in third-rate movies. Olivier pretended not to regret it—he had an obligation to feed his family—but his last book aches with regret over all those now inaccessible Shakespearean roles to which he had devoted his life. It was Olivier's decision, in the 1940s, to abandon a successful career as one of Hollywood's silken English stars and return to acting classics with the Old Vic. Of course he made movies during these years, but only to bring Shakespeare to larger audiences with his panoramic versions of *Henry V*, *Hamlet*, and *Richard III*.

Olivier's art belonged to the stage because it was an art of transformation. Much has been said about the way he worked from the outside in—first choosing a nose, a wig, or set of false teeth, and then discovering the inner character. This usually rankled American Method actors, who work from the self, if not from the personality. But the Strasberg Method rankled Olivier, not because he scorned Stanislavsky, but because he valued the actor too much to tolerate any fingering of his psyche. Stanislavsky himself abandoned emotional memory exercises, and probably for the same reason. They were not only an invasion of the actor's private life, they were an obstacle to transformation. How do you discover the thundering dimensions of Lear in the inner folds of your own narrow experience?

A story repeated in most of the obituaries epitomizes Olivier's attitude toward the Method. Watching Dustin Hoffman's elaborate preparations for his role in *Marathon Man*, he said: "My dear fellow, have you tried acting?" Hoffman is perfectly capable of acting, even of transformation. So are a number of his Method colleagues, as demonstrated by Brando's sclerotic Godfather and De Niro's ballooning Raging Bull. But however deep these performances, the Method usually limits an actor's range to contemporary proletarian types, which is why so few perform on the stage, much less in classical roles. Still, the conflict was not between classical and modern acting. Olivier was brilliant in contemporary plays (perhaps at his most brilliant in *The Entertainer* as the seedy vaudevillian Archie Rice). The issue was over how closely you need to fit the roles to your personality, whether you wear the mask of an actor or the face of a star.

Olivier, who had no qualms about exploiting his charisma, had no interest whatever in featuring his personality (indeed, he often said he didn't have one). That is why he was virtually unrecognizable in each of his parts. He put into acting terms what the Button Molder said to Peer Gynt: "To be yourself, you must slay yourself." Ibsen was describing the moral strength that separates the egotist from the artist, and Olivier embodied that strength throughout his career. He didn't just slay his personality with his makeup box. He did it through intelligent examination of the text, through the free exercise of his imagination.

His love of transformation was such that he had an absolute terror of repeating himself. Indeed, his passion for change even extended to changes in the direction of his theatre. Late in life, under the influence of his literary manager Kenneth Tynan, Olivier proved willing to adapt his aristocratic theatrical style to the roughneck world of Osborne, Wesker, Pinter, and Griffith—a Lord of the Realm playing working-class characters while his fellow knights, Sir Ralph and Sir John, were still employing old-laddie diction and received pronunciation. He also had the good sense to invite into his company many actors from the new theatre—Albert Finney, Robert Stephens, Colin Blakely, and Joan Plowright of Wesker's *Roots*.

His performance in Trevor Griffiths' *The Party* in the seventies was Olivier's last appearance on the stage. A series of four consecutive flops at the National, plus a few political shocks administered by Tynan, had convinced Lord Rayne to turn the theatre over to Peter Hall. Olivier had hardly been the most adventurous artistic director in Europe, but by contrast with Hall's cautious tenure he now seems almost daring. Most important, he made us believe that theatre mattered, having been responsible for productions that not only galvanized the past but (with Tynan prodding him) tried to reflect the form and pressure of contemporary life. Olivier, in Tynan's words, was "pragmatic, empirical, wary of grand designs or distant goals." He was at heart neither activist nor visionary but actually somewhat traditional, even conservative. Yet he understood as well as anyone in our time the social, aesthetic, and communal importance of theatre. He knew how closely it resembled society, how intimately its fate was connected to human development. He realized that the conduct of the actor was, in some way, a microcosm of the way people behave in their lives, and that an artist's dedication to his calling reflected a larger loyalty, which is the mucilage of the collective spirit. Great as they were, Olivier's stage performances may fade from memory, since theatre is ephemeral. What will never fade, I think, is his rare exemplary belief in the transforming power of the actor's art.

Would that example had informed some of the acting in the new *Twelfth Night* at the New York Shakespeare Festival in Central Park. For this, the tenth entry in his Shakespeare Marathon, Joseph Papp has engaged not a director but an acting coach, Harold Guskin, who is responsible for everything Olivier recoiled from in American theatre. Mr. Guskin, a program note tells us, has been conducting a Shakespeare workshop at the Public Theater "so that actors from stage, film and television would have a place to explore acting the great roles in classical plays." This procedure, worthy enough in theory, seems largely a pretext to attract vacationing celebrities, and the production has enough stars to decorate the dome of the Hayden Planetarium. The problem is that so few of these luminaries have the aptitude or experience to act in *Twelfth Night.*

I am disheartened by this production—and also a little bewildered. Papp doesn't need names to sell free Shakespeare, and even if he did, he has been in the business long enough to attract those with classical experience. Christopher Walken, Mandy Patinkin, Kevin Kline, Diane Venora, and others have lent considerable distinction to Papp's Shakespeare in recent months. Yet most of the people currently on the Central Park stage are distinguished only for demonstrating the difference between classical and personality acting. If most of the white performers seem to have been cast because they are movie stars (an exception is the stage-trained Mary Elizabeth Mastrantonio, a witty, attractive Viola), some of the black actors seem to have been cast because they are black (the exception is André Braugher, a virile Antonio). Papp's non-traditional casting policy is an admirable one, but too often it gets confused with affirmative action. I thought the purpose was to choose the best actor available for a role, regardless of race—not to cast classically unskilled talent for the sake of a more visible racial mixture.

What's happening on stage in this *Twelfth Night* suggests everything that denigrates the virtues of contemporary American theatre—a confusion of celebrity with artistry and art with sociology, a contempt for training, a fear of forceful ideas. Mr. Guskin's relationship to the actor in this production is what I imagine Paula Strasberg's was to Marilyn Monroe—shepherding a difficult temperament through the knotty undergrowth of collaborative projects without letting burrs stick to stockings. The text is not interpreted so much as hacked aside with a machete to make way for the progress of the stars, and every little speech is a turn. Some effort is made to place the action—John Lee Beatty's set is a garish playing area planted in front of an Exposition gambling casino in Monaco around the turn of the century. But since the entire show takes place in an exterior square, even the soliloquies seem to be public pronouncements. Worse, the historical setting is continually being undermined by Jeff Goldblum—who substitutes his own simpering Brundlefly vanity for Malvolio's foolish pomposity, garbling his most important lines when he is not misunderstanding them—as well as by the beauteous Michelle Pfeiffer's wide-eyed blankness as Olivia, and by Gregory Hines's compulsion to charm the audience rather than investigate the sour side of Feste (though Hines at least has a performer's instinct). As for Sir Toby and Sir Andrew, they don't seem to know what their lines mean, much less how to stress them, and the actor playing Sir Toby should not attempt a drunken scene again until he learns that drunks don't pitch from side to side, they walk with extra carefulness.

In order to avoid realizing the helter-skelter implications of its subtitle (*What You Will*), *Twelfth Night* needs a director, not a talent manager. It is the airiest of Shakespeare's comedies, but also the one with the deepest sexual ambiguities and erotic resonances. It requires actors experienced in verse-speaking, not untrained neophytes momentarily anxious to add a Shakespeare role to their résumés. It demands, in short, the kind of dedicated transforming stage actor that Olivier personified rather than a coterie of Hollywood tourists stuffing their marketable mannerisms into a suitcase for a visit to cultural New York.

(1989)

Actors Directing Actors

(*Macbeth*)

Joseph Papp's Shakespeare Marathon has had its successes and will undoubtedly have more, but it hit a kind of nadir with the New York Public Theater production of *Macbeth*. *Macbeth* is almost always ill-fated, which is why actors believe that identifying it by name, rather than by nationality as the "Scottish play," is only slightly less dangerous than whistling in the dressing room. It's not just that *Macbeth* productions are often accompanied by coronaries, broken limbs, falling flats, earthquakes, and similar "dire combustion and confused events"; *Macbeth*'s history includes not just natural catastrophes but also many artistic ones. The play is certainly a traditional butt of the most scathing criticism.

To avoid adding to these catastrophes, I'll try to resist a temptation to murder the sleep of the current perpetrators. But it occurs to me that the Papp version was doomed from the start for the same reason that *Twelfth Night* failed last summer and that the projected *Hamlet* with Kevin Kline, directed by Kline himself, faces such worrisome prospects. In each case, they have been staged by actors or acting coaches with little or no directing experience. I don't mean to say that actors are incapable of supervising classical performance. John Gielgud's *Cherry Orchard* still sits in my mind as among the most sensitive Chekhov productions I've ever seen. Laurence Olivier's work at the Old Vic, particularly his majestic, almost Elizabethan version of Arthur Miller's *The Crucible*, surely gave his company its special stamp; and his Shakespeare movies, of course, produced some of the finest performances and—in the case of *Henry V*—most stunning visual concepts available on film. Kenneth Branagh's movie of *Henry V*—so different from Olivier's medieval montages and chauvinist heroics, yet so powerful in its remorseless depiction of the deadening impact of war on human personality—was also the work of an actor.

Yet all these artists had classical training and experience, not to mention the opportunity to exercise their advantages in a healthy theatre. To his credit, Papp is trying to create the same conditions here, enticing major actors from Hollywood to perform in Shakespeare. But Shakespeare is not fast food, and it's merely one more example of our passion for instant culture to expect people to materialize overnight into an acting company when most of them have never met before, even if some can list a few classical roles on their résumés. It's not just that Hollywood offers no training in verse-speaking. An even greater obstacle to integrated Shakespeare performance is that performing in movies increases the actor's traditional suspicion toward directors. If on stage the actor feels manipulated for the director's conceptual purposes, imagine how the actor feels in the movies, where he's never in complete control of his performance, where his scenes are filmed out of sequence, and where his carefully prepared work can be chopped or cut or even redubbed according to a director's whim.

For that reason, I suspect, Papp manages to attract stars to his Shakespeare Marathon partly through assurances of a nurturing atmosphere and artistic autonomy. And who can understand the personal needs of the actor better than a director who is an actor himself—or, at least, an actor's coach? But as Harold Guskin unwittingly demonstrated in the course of squiring Jeff Goldblum and Michelle Pfeiffer through the thickets of *Twelfth Night*, even the best actors need something more than cosseting, flattery, and personal counseling. They need a firm directorial hand. Lee Strasberg proved this, too, when, in his preposterous production of *The Three Sisters*, he let the strongest stars of the Actors Studio indulge their weakest idiosyncrasies. If *The Three Sisters* was considered the standard of our classical acting when it opened to critical raspberries in London in 1965, it's no wonder that an American repertory company hasn't been invited there since.

Richard Jordan, the actor who directed *Macbeth*, is a cut above Strasberg or Guskin. He is an intelligent man who periodically returns to the stage, and who has some experience in staging modern plays, but the problems with this production are largely his doing. For once, most of the cast is classically trained. So is Mr. Jordan—as an actor. Why then is this *Macbeth* tepid and lifeless?

I must conclude that Jordan has pressed virtually nobody associated with this production beyond the minimal level of his talents, a conclusion which is early confirmed by John Conklin's setting. Since Conklin is one of our most accomplished stage designers, this set is an aberration. Consisting of a floor of pine planks, backed by a wall flecked with bloodstains, the space represents neither a bare platform nor a metaphorical statement, so the play comes off like a staged reading. The actors, doubling as stagehands, carry the furniture in and out laboriously. The weird sisters, continually reinforced by reverb acoustics and recorded thunder, play on triangles and tambourines, while toting a wagon that might have been rented from a suburban high-school production of *Mother Courage*. The banquet scene is played around a picnic table borrowed from a rest stop off a thruway. Macbeth's throne is an outsized baby's high chair. The boiling cauldron contains a hallucinogenic brew which acts on him like magic mushrooms. The apparitions that materialize during a puppet show conducted from the witch wagon would never increase his heart rate, much less sear his eyeballs. Macbeth is overcome by Macduff when he gets a cramp in his leg. The clumsy battles are fought amid a lot of yelling and trumpet blasts, right under our noses; yet Macbeth's death is hidden from the audience. So is his severed head, which has been severed only from the production.

This is poor theatre in all senses of the phrase, but one could forgive the penury of the circumstances were there the slightest hint of boldness in the performance or resolution in the staging. Raul Julia is invariably a strong presence on stage and screen, but he plays Macbeth like a man with a headache. He shows no anguish or despair, simply discomfort; his sleepy eyes and sardonic smile are those of an ironist, not a tragic sufferer. Julia reads his soliloquies like lectures to an anatomy class. The dagger speech costs him nothing. In a play riddled with occultism and superstition, the title character seems like a cynic and a secularist.

Julia's beard is grizzled since we saw him last; he also seems a bit advanced in age for Melinda Mullins' unripened Lady Macbeth. There's some heat in the relationship between this middle-aged man and his young wife, but the passion is largely uxorious. Little of it spills off into the conspiracy scene. The couple plot Duncan's death as if they were organizing a dinner party, with the wife displaying petulance over the placement of the guests and the arrangement of the silver; after Macbeth has done the bloody deed, she handles the daggers as though they were a pair of unwashed carving knives. Mullins speaks her role as if she's doing an exercise in scene study. There's no depth in her, no size; her voice is disembodied, when it should issue from her internal organs. In the production's single interpolation, Mullins' Lady Macbeth commits hara-kiri before her husband's eyes with a knife; curiously, he fails to notice her prostrate body until it's time for "Tomorrow and tomorrow and tomorrow."

The other roles are also played by able actors performing below the level of their gifts. With the exception of Dan Von Bargen's Ross, almost everyone seems at sea or relying on familiar comfortable habits. William Converse-Roberts' Macduff is stalwart and handsome, but occasionally given to harsh rant. Harriet Harris has genuine emotional strength, but her somewhat neurasthenic Lady Macduff sounds like a Tennessee Williams heroine. The gifted Harry S. Murphy turns the Porter into stock comedy, losing his pants, bumping into posts, engaging in so much stage business that he fails to build a character. Mark Hammer, more successful as the Doctor, plays Duncan like Father Christmas ringing a bell in front of Harrods. Larry Bryggman's Banquo is more nerd than nobleman, a lame-brained thane.

A less congenial director might have pressured, cajoled, harassed, tickled, wheedled, intimidated, frightened, entertained, irritated, encouraged, inspired these actors beyond the easily accessed limits of their known gifts. But Jordan, possibly in consequence of his own bad experience with intrusive directors, has merely contented himself with recruiting a good cast and leaving them to their own devices. The result is another in a long line of calamitous *Macbeth*s against which critics can aim their artillery, and I, abandoning all good intentions, seem to have unmuzzled my howitzers as well.

(1990)

Post-Modern Prophecies
(*Woyzeck; Baal*)

Georg Büchner is the great-great-granddaddy of the contemporary theatre, as well as one of the most curious figures in literature, writing post-modern plays a hundred years before his time. *Woyzeck*—at the Hartford Stage Company in a production directed by Richard Foreman—was unfinished at his death (at twenty-four!) in 1837, and not deciphered and published until 1879. The play is composed of a series of fragments, with unnumbered scenes, few stage directions, and very vague locations; yet it is an extraordinary work which has exercised an incalculable influence on neo-Romantic drama. Ferociously and precociously ironic, erratic, swampy, and strange, though composed just a few years after the heroic dramas of Goethe and Schiller, *Woyzeck* is completely unlike anything ever written before, even by Büchner. Its episodic structure, interspersed with songs, anticipates expressionism, and its ecstatic, rhythmic, tender-coarse prose (images from daily life juxtaposed with high-flown metaphors) leads directly to Brecht.

The play is based on a historical case—a barber-soldier who murdered his wife in a fit of jealousy. This resulted in the first public execution in Leipzig in over thirty years and engendered considerable debate over whether Woyzeck was mad or sane. Büchner resolves the problem by avoiding it altogether. Woyzeck is almost certainly mad, but then so is the entire world. In this cold, implacable, brutal environment, society is merely another form of Nature, and man is the cruelest of the beasts. Woyzeck himself is treated as an experimental object, and seems to be human only in his capacity to suffer. Examined by a doctor who could be a rough sketch for Mengele, Woyzeck is declared superior to other animals because he can control his urine, then urinates against the wall like a dog. Feeding him a diet of peas for three months, the Doctor is absolutely delighted with Woyzeck's "beautiful aberratio" and offers him a raise for going mad. When Woyzeck discovers his wife betraying him with a Drum Major, he expects to see blisters on her lips. Voices in his head urge him to "stab the bitch to death." When he responds, he is apprehended by the police, who admire the aesthetics of the crime ("a good genuine beautiful murder"), while his orphaned child rides blithely on a hobby horse.

Woyzeck would seem to be the quintessential ontological-hysterical play, then, and Richard Foreman would seem to be its ideal interpreter. The alienating techniques which are the signature of Foreman's theatre—suspended strings, groaning sound collage, harsh glaring lights, suspended skulls and chandeliers—create an atmosphere of searing intensity, like a fevered dream. And the final image—Woyzeck unsuccessfully trying to submerge the murder weapon into a series of shallow pools while washing the blood off his hands—is worth the price of admission. Foreman's design sets the play in an abstract gunmetal-gray hell, constructed of platforms and ramps and a wooden boardwalk along which Woyzeck runs like a rat in a maze. The characters wear the makeup of the madmen in *The Cabinet of Dr. Caligari*—white pasty faces with dark hollow eyes and black lips—and perform in the spasmodic style appropriate to a menagerie of the damned. There are touches, too, of vampire films, *Nightmare on Elm Street*, *Mad Max*, and *The Texas Chainsaw Massacre*—the whole repertory of snuff culture that has given such unappetizing new meaning to the concept of the pleasure principle.

David Patrick Kelly commits to the title part as if he were sitting on a razor. A short, stunted man whose skin is drawn tautly over his skull, he brings to the role a pervasive sense of stoical misery that identifies Woyzeck as the archetypal proletarian ("We sweat even in our sleep, us poor people . . . If we ever got to heaven, we'd have to help with the thunder"). He is abetted by a cast that conforms obediently to Foreman's vision of pain. The director's integrity and commitment never waver, and Hartford Stage should be commended for bravery in supporting a production so likely to repel its audience. But Foreman's *Woyzeck* is just a little *too* relentless, and thus eventually turns into another kind of fairy story—this one told by a man who teethed on *Struwelpeter* with all its bloody moral lessons for the German young.

Robert Woodruff's production of *Baal* at the Trinity Rep in Providence, like Richard Foreman's *Woyzeck* at the Hartford Stage, has subscription audiences reeling. The plays share many points of correspondence—one can trace a direct line from Büchner to Brecht in their nihilistic themes and episodic structures. The productions also resemble each other in the way Woodruff and Foreman manage to find post-modern equivalents for these ravaged German texts. *Baal* was Brecht's first play, written when he was only twenty-one, *Woyzeck* was unfinished when Büchner died at twenty-four. Youthful disenchantment scorches their pages like fitful lightning in an electrical storm. Sex, delirium, and death are inextricably linked. Only Wagner's *Tristan and Isolde* explores the fatal consequences of eroticism with such morbid fascination.

The sex in *Baal* is sadomasochistic, polymorphous perverse. The hero's insatiable appetites are nondiscriminatory—booze, food, poetry, virgins, whores, women in pairs, men, boys, his own body, all are consumed with the same animal hunger. Woodruff has chosen to heighten the transvestite aspect of the play, recognizing that homosexuality, though tolerated in Weimar Germany, is still the bane of fundamentalist America (also of Adolf Hitler, who featured Brecht in his Museum of Decadent Art). Jesse Helms's fulminations over Mapplethorpe and Serrano are required reading in the lobby; his recorded voice is heard on stage, rasping about obscenity and perversion. The production breaks all the senator's moral commandments and will doubtless inflame him further; it is certainly testing the limits of audience tolerance. Lipsticked male actors, in wigs, silk stockings, and garter belts, cavort on stage, and Baal's erotic relationship with his young friend Ekart is frontally exploited. The anger and discomfort in the house are palpable. Spectators leave the theatre telling Anne Bogart, Trinity Rep's new artistic director, they will never return.*

No question that Lester Prynne is flaunting his scarlet H, but the production transcends its provocative purpose. In Douglas Stein's punk high-tech environmental setting, a compound of neon, cellophane, and vinyl, Woodruff produces an anthology of 1970s experimentation—from Lee Breuer's shadowgraphs to Robert Wilson's slow-motion imagery. This provides the engraver's acid with which the actors etch their steel-cold characters. The itinerant poet Baal, in Mario Arrambide's massive, brutal performance, becomes a popular rock-and-roll performance artist, habituating decadent clubs. His celebrity is a source of erotic attraction for men and women alike, and love "is like biting into an orange with the juice squirting into your teeth." He gets more than his share of the pulp in this world of relentless pleasure-seeking. But Baal has no staying power. He tells the pregnant Sophie Barger (powerfully played by Anne Scurria) to throw her fat body in the river. Another jilted girl, Joanna, actually does manage to drown herself—in a Woodruff-interpolated fish tank—while Baal, indifferently watch-

* Following her first season, Miss Bogart didn't return. She resigned after a financial conflict with her board.

ing TV, improvises a watery poem (the haunting verses appeared later in Brecht's *Hauspostille* as the "Song of the Drowned Girl"). Having murdered his male lover Ekart, Baal finds himself "alone again, in my own skin." In a forest, woodsmen ominously sharpen their axes. Toothless, reviled, and spat upon by his enemies (he enjoys the taste), Baal dies amid urine and offal, having entered Nature as the excrement of God.

Strong stuff all right, and strongly delivered—especially in the first part, before the show gets jaded, along with its characters. Writing under Rimbaud's influence, Brecht is committed to a complete disordering of all the senses. Woodruff tries to disorder ours as well—not exactly what the average spectator seeks in an evening's entertainment. Yet, just as people are characterized by their decisions, so a theatre is characterized by its choice of plays. This degenerate, ecstatic *Baal* reaffirms the courage of the Trinity Rep.

(1990)

In the Midst of Death

(A Celebration of Samuel Beckett)

Some very talented people recently gathered on the stage of Lincoln Center's Vivian Beaumont Theater to celebrate the words of Samuel Beckett. The presentation—readings of live and taped selections from his plays, novels, letters, and interviews—suggested that this masterly dramatic artist, who died last year at the age of eighty-three, had been thinking about dying for most of his literary career. Beckett began writing as the poet laureate of Alzheimer's disease, of old age and paraplegia, memory loss, paralysis, apatheia, and aphasia. In his later years, he was writing more about the extinction of life as a reflection of a decaying terrestrial world and the demise of the human race.

The old age of the world was also the subject of T. S. Eliot, who, at forty, was already asking (in "Ash Wednesday"), "Why should the aged eagle spread his wings?" or speaking (in "The Song of Simeon") in the character of an old man "with eighty years and no tomorrow." Such premature superannuation made Edmund Wilson impatient: " 'Gerontion' and 'The Waste Land,' " he wrote, "have made the young poets old before their time." One can imagine what he would have said about Samuel Beckett, who, barely into his forties, personified himself as the aging, destitute Molloy and the even more ancient Malone, confined to his bed in what may very well be a nursing home. Eliot, along with Joyce and Proust, was one of Beckett's earliest literary models, and Beckett is Eliot's rival for the title of wasteland prophet of the modern world. But Beckett carried the idea of disintegration to new heights (or depths). "Joyce," Beckett wrote, is "tending towards omniscience and omnipotence as an artist. I'm working on impotence, ignorance."

The ultimate impotence, however, was death, and in retrospect, awareness and anticipation of death are the true motifs of his work. "They give birth astride a grave," he wrote in *Waiting for Godot*, "the light gleams an instant, then it's night once more." In his shortest work, *Breath*, he actualized this harrowing and beautiful perception through a single sound—the inspiration and expiration of air at the moments of birth and death. This swift passage of time's wingèd chariot is accompanied by a sense of its tedious progress—as in Chekhov (or in Proust), where life creeps along in an endless succession of days, yet is over in an instant ("My life has slipped by as though I'd never lived. Ech, you good-for-nothing"—Firs in *The Cherry Orchard*). In *Rockaby*—powerfully reprised at the end of the Lincoln Center evening by Billie Whitelaw, the actress for whom it was written—Beckett's metaphor is further compressed and refined. Using a minimalist, reductive prose of striking musicality, the playwright sketches an old woman in a rocking chair being whispered off to her closing labors by an offstage voice ("Time she stopped—going to and fro . . . Till the end—close of a long day"). Then, in a shocking conclusion ("Rock her off—stuff her eyes—fuck life"), she is yanked from the edges of consciousness into the final sleep of death—rocked, as it were, out of the cradle and into the grave.

Miss Whitelaw's legato reading of this play, coming over the audience like a caress, was the high point of the Lincoln Center celebration. Spoken from a lectern without the aid of rocker props, *Rockaby* reinforced one's belief that Beckett's plays were as appropriate to radio as to the stage. Despite his gift for generating powerful and expressive visual images (the bowler-hatted tramps near a single leafless tree in *Godot*, Nagg and Nell immersed in garbage cans in *Endgame*, Winnie buried up to her neck in the earth in *Happy Days*), Beckett's real genius was his feeling for language. Like that of the visually impaired James Joyce, his imagination was basically verbal, aimed toward the ear. It was, in fact, in an effort to tame his weakness for Joycean verbal splendor—"with the desire of impoverishing myself still further"—that he began to write his fiction, plays, and poetry in French. English, as he told Lawrence Harvey, "holds out the temptation to rhetoric and virtuosity." "It is easier," he added to Nicholas Gessner, "to write without style in French."

Like Hemingway's, Beckett's anti-style—simple, terse, ironic, repetitive, non-allusive, vaudevillian—soon became one of the most glorious verbal instruments in our literary orchestra. It is an instrument that can be played only by voices with the quality of good instruments themselves, which is why the Irish were among the best interpreters of the evening—Chris O'Neill thumping through *Embers* like a bass piano pedal, Barry McGovern vibrating like a cello in the lower registers in *Molloy*, the leprechaunish Jack McGowran (on videotape) honking *The Unnameable* like a tenor saxophone, and, best of all, Patrick Magee (on videotape) rasping through *Krapp's Last Tape* like a reedy bassoon, mournful, unshaven, hovering in mute despair over the detritus of his tape-recorded memories.

Considering the importance of the vocal organs in Beckett's theatre, it is not surprising that a disembodied mouth should play a solo part in one of his plays, *Not I*. In Lincoln Center's presentation of this work, the mouth belongs to Billie Whitelaw, recorded on videotape in a performance infinitely more frightening on screen than in the theatre. I'm told that Beckett, reluctant to allow *Not I* on television, eventually came to believe it was the best medium for the play. Close-ups certainly enhance its power. The stationary camera, scanning the mouth as if it were some unknown planet, explores the lips, the gums, the glottis, the peripatetic tongue, giving it the look, on the Beaumont's enlarged screen, of some obscene hybrid creature, a vagina with teeth, a grotesque set of comic clackers. It is this absurd apparatus that is responsible for speech, and in Beckett's notion of purgatory, it is doomed to eternal repetition.

Beckett's ambivalent attitude toward language and style concealed a profound hoarding instinct akin to Joyce's celebrated anal eroticism, which may explain the fascination of both these writers with the excretory functions. "It's hard to go on," Beckett wrote to his publisher, Barney Rosset, "with everything loathed and repudiated before being formulated." "To write is impossible," he said in another letter, "but not yet impossible enough." Like Didi's urine in *Waiting for Godot*, Beckett's words were squeezed out painfully, one drop at a time. The difficulty of writing made him an increasingly vigilant sentinel of his plays. He was compelled to do his own translation, he admitted, "by a foolish feeling of protectiveness towards the work." In the last years of his life, this took the form of an extremely protective feeling toward interpretations of the work as well. He successfully blocked a Comédie Française production of *Waiting for Godot* because it didn't conform exactly to the way he had conceived it. And in a highly publicized flap, he threatened court action to stop our American Repertory Theatre production of *Endgame* in 1984.

Endgame's director, JoAnne Akalaitis, influenced by the apocalyptic nature of the play, had set it in an abandoned subway station after a holocaust, using two black company actors in the parts of Hamm and Nagg. She also included a brief overture commissioned from Philip Glass. On the basis of hearsay (he never saw the production), Beckett protested that we had "musicalized" his play, and, objecting to what he had heard about the setting and the casting, asked first that we cancel the production, then that we remove his name from the program.

We refused both demands, but the conflict was finally settled when we agreed to include a facsimile of Beckett's original stage directions in the program, accompanied by a statement from the playwright. The statement read that "any production of *Endgame* which ignores my stage directions is completely unacceptable to me. My play requires an empty room and two small windows. The American Repertory Theatre production which dismisses my directions is a complete parody of the play as conceived by me. Anybody who cares for the work couldn't fail to be disgusted by this."

The controversy engendered a great deal of discussion about the supremacy of the playwright, the rights of collaborators, the difference between autographic art and allographic theatre. These were not unhealthy and there were persuasive arguments expressed on both sides. But it was sad that Beckett, who used to greet unorthodox versions of his work with a stoical shrug, was now instructing his licensing agents to refuse rights to any production that failed to follow his texts to the letter—demanding obedience not only to his stage directions but to virtually every pause and ellipse. I suspect, too, that his growing interest in directing his plays was another form of protectionism, an effort to safeguard the work from "parody." On the other hand, Beckett in rehearsal frequently made changes in the texts himself, a welcome sign that his grasp on his work was not inflexible.

Beckett spent his last years a feeble, sickly man in a nursing home, but the Richard Avedon portraits presiding over the Beaumont stage during the reading of his texts show the man as we like to remember him: healthy, lithe, vigorous, and dapper in a black suit and turtleneck sweater. His white tufted crest is fully raised above his sculpted forehead; his penetrating eyes frame his sharp eagle beak. He is gazing at us in one photo, looking down in the other, as if to say: This is my public and this my private self. But it was Beckett's generosity to expose his private pain to public view, and to do so with grace and power. He gave a voice to what he called "the irrational state of unknowingness wherein we exist, this mental weightlessness which is beyond reason." Some people think that this was a voice of despair, that it was morbid to lavish so much artistic attention on infirmity and death. But only the greatest souls have had the courage to stare so fixedly into the depths of the abyss. Like Lear, he gave us visionary suffering: "We that are young / Shall never see so much, nor live so long."

(1990)

How to "Serve" Shakespeare

(*On Directing Shakespeare*)

Foul weather rained me out of *The Taming of the Shrew* in Central Park, so I was forced to stay home with a good book. It is one that might interest you as well if you're wondering why Papp's director, A. J. Antoon, plunked down Kate and Petruchio in the Wild West. The volume is called *On Directing Shakespeare* (Hamish Hamilton) and consists of interviews conducted between 1973 and 1988 with twelve leading Shakespeare directors, many of them notorious for disregarding the place and time of the plays. The interlocutor is Ralph Berry, Professor of English at the University of Ottawa. Not only a scholar but a passionate theatregoer, Berry is fascinated by the alchemy with which frozen texts turn into live performance, and has closely followed the fierce storms thundering over the issue of directorial interpretation. Berry asks each subject "What is Shakespeare today?"—a question he says was inspired by Jonathan Miller's letter to *The* (London) *Times* in 1971, in which he defended Peter Brook's production of *A Midsummer Night's Dream* against the "Mandarin bardolatry" of its detractors. Miller's challenge—"What does a fairy look like and in what way does his utterance differ from those of ordinary mortals?"—immediately persuaded Berry of the correctness of directorial license. Still, Berry's conversion has not made him doctrinaire. He appeals to radicals and conservatives alike for answers to his query.

On Directing Shakespeare can be considered a companion volume to David Richard Jones's *Great Directors at Work* (in both books, coincidentally, the introductory essay is more satisfying than the subsequent material). While Berry is not as fanatical as Jones about the supremacy of the director, he does dispute the purist contention that a text should "speak for itself," a demand he believes impossible. The icon "Shakespeare" can be considered both a man and a body of work. If a man, he has certain authorial rights and intentions which it is the director's duty to obey and discover. But if Shakespeare is a text, then "we do not serve a man, we excavate or exploit a quarry. The plays cease to be expressions of intention, or attempts at communication; rather, they become 'material.' "

The idea that "Shakespeare" is material to excavate rather than a master to serve is inseparable from a belief that the plays are "a massive variable"—many exist in more than one version, most have only the barest stage directions, virtually all are too long to be played in their entirety. The English language, moreover, has changed radically since Shakespeare's day; it therefore becomes a director's obligation to "reactivate" the meaning of the play—not in the manner of a scholar or restorer (what Peter Brook calls the "footnoting attitude"), but in a way that allows the text to absorb the form and pressure of the time.

Berry proposes that every Shakespeare production involves at least three major interpretive acts before rehearsals begin. The first is selecting the play, since choice itself is a directorial statement (e.g., doing *Troilus and Cressida* in wartime). The second is cutting the play, for this helps the director decide among the many possibilities Shakespeare includes (whether to do *Henry V* as what Trevor Nunn calls the "National Anthem in 5 acts," or, in Michael Bogdanov's words, as the "great war play embedded in a greater anti-war play"). And the third is choosing the setting and the period. This last is more than a cosmetic option. It can influence and determine the whole directorial approach. Possibilities are limitless, ranging from period (Peter Hall's *Merchant of Venice*) to modern (Orson Welles's Fascist *Julius Caesar*) to period analogue (Miller's *Measure for Measure* set in Freud's Vienna) to an eclectic mix that ranges freely throughout historical time (Bergman's *Hamlet* or Brook's *Lear*).

The twelve directors encountered in this book differ widely in regard to how faithfully they feel obliged to "serve" Shakespeare. On one side is Peter Hall, pugnaciously insisting on uncut plays in Renaissance settings (preferably Caroline). On the other is the deconstructionist Peter Brook, whose attitude toward "serving" is a resounding *non serviam* resembling Lucifer's rejection of God ("There is only one service, which is to the reality which Shakespeare is serving"). Brook, who gives Berry his most provocative and suggestive interview, reveals a romantic revulsion to any form of artistic obligation. He is agonized by the notion that Shakespeare remains our model, believing that each generation must find its own way without reference to tradition. Brook, however, has as much chance of escaping from the embrace of Shakespeare as Jacob from the Angel, which may explain why he describes him in language reminiscent of Northrup Frye's definition of mythic heroes—a figure different not only in quality but in *kind*. "What he wrote is not interpretation," adds Brook, "it is the thing itself."

But Brook denies that Shakespeare represents a series of messages. He likens the plays, rather, to tea leaves in a cup. Every observer will perceive the patterns differently—a condition that may have inspired Orson Welles's forlorn remark: "We all betray Shakespeare." The plays are destined to be continually reinterpreted (or betrayed), yet will always remain intact. The real danger to Shakespeare, Brook believes, lies not in misinterpretation so much as in the pedantic impulse to fix him in time: "The great harm done by scholarship is to try to make choices . . . which is what the whole world of footnotes has been. Rather you want endlessly to come back to meeting this vibration in all its fullness and with all the ambiguity of something that does change through the ages."

"I cannot bear people who do Shakespeare with 'concepts,' " says Peter Hall. "They put blinkers on the play." Is this a criticism of his former associate Peter Brook? No, Brook's Socratic immersion in ambiguities has gradually disabused him of the kind of conceptual ideas he adopted as a *Wunderkind* of nineteen. Now he prefers the ideas evolved by actors during rehearsal. By contrast, some of the conceptual directors Berry interviews—Konrad Swinarski, for example—are as rigid about their ideas as any footnoting scholar. Consider Swinarski's unwittingly funny account of his *Midsummer Night's Dream,* where he interprets Quince's play as an allegory of governmental oppression, with the Lion representing federal power and the Wall as the older generation separating the lovers (the Duke prefers the danced Bergomask to the spoken epilogue because he is afraid to hear the truth!). Obviously, Shakespearean comedy does not always translate well into Polish.

Still, *On Directing Shakespeare* could have used a few more interviews with non-English directors for the sake of perspective. Giorgio Strehler offers some interesting reflections on Shakespeare's instinctual understanding of Italy, and Michael Kahn (under the influence of Susan Sontag) suggests an "against interpretation" theory, where characters like Shylock and Portia could express contradictory qualities in successive scenes. But what's missing from the book is the presence of truly radical and unorthodox Shakespeare directors from the Continent, such as Ariane Mnouchkine, Ingmar Bergman, and Peter Stein.

In their place, Berry invites (in addition to Miller, Brook, and Hall) the usual suspects from the English theatre: Trevor Nunn, Adrian Noble, Robin Phillips, Bill Alexander, and Michael Bogdanov. All have done distinguished work and each demonstrates in passing how a truly careful reading of a play in preparation for production can uncover original insights (as for example, Noble's perception that, as audiences grew more concerned with the failures of power than with subversive sexuality, the center of gravity in *Measure for Measure* shifted from Angelo to the Duke). Still, a truly wild card like Declan Donnellan of the Cheek by Jowl company in England introduces a frisky irreverent note this sober-sided assembly could use a little more of ("The most important thing to remember about Shakespeare is that he's dead and we're alive"). Donnellan's concept of Orsino as a raging queen who is actually in love with Viola *as a boy* ("So marriage is going to be some sort of therapy for him . . . ?" asks the straight-faced Professor Berry) could have been invented only by someone with no sanctified feelings whatever about the Bard—or about Art, Religion, or Life, for that matter. Donnellan's single criterion is that something be entertaining ("I'm sure the Crucifixion was entertaining")—his interview is at once the most outrageous and amusing thing in the book.

Obviously, tolerance for directorial license will vary according to the piety with which one regards Shakespeare, and there will always be those who insist that *A Midsummer Night's Dream* can take place only "in a wood near Athens" (actually the addition of an eighteenth-century editor). Peter Hall took "Memorial" out of the name of the theatre at Stratford-on-Avon—as Michael Kahn removed "Festival" from the marquee of the Stratford Theatre in Connecticut—largely in order to relax such starchy attitudes. But let the last words on the subject be those of Jonathan Miller—a man at times as critical of the directorial choices of others as critics are of his: "I think that fidelity is the job of forgers and of mapmakers, and of engineers and draughtsmen. The job of the artist in the theatre is illumination and reconstruction, and the endless task of assimilating the objects of the past into the interests of the present, on the understanding that the physical artifact which is the occasion for such an enterprise will be retained in some place in its original form, so that it is available for anyone who wishes to make a competitive reconstruction of his own." Only in that way, he implies—only by asking, "What does a fairy look like?"—can Shakespeare be truly "served."

(1990)

PART III

POLEMICS

INTRODUCTION

Reimagining the Process

Functioning both as an engaged theatre practitioner and as a semi-detached observer of the theatre scene, I sometimes find myself in contorted positions, juggling refractory problems. Perhaps the most knotty of these is how to preserve personal principles while trying to nurture a practical theatrical operation, congenial to all its members. From that perspective, it might be useful to explain why I, an artistic director of a resident repertory company who has watched some of its offerings move to the Broadway stage, find the present methods of transferring subsidized productions to the commercial theatre somewhat alarming. If I seem reluctant to give my regards to Broadway transfers, it's not, as some believe, that I wish to see Broadway collapse. I will admit to a certain disenchantment with a theatre system that puts financial gain before the creative fulfillment of its artists. But anyone interested in the health of a pluralistic culture has a stake in the survival of the New York commercial theatre. The problem is that Broadway's future seems to depend at present on the progressive destabilization of the resident theatre movement in this country, and possibly abroad.

I prefer the word "resident" to "regional," because this system was originally intended as an alternative to Broadway, not as a provincial tributary. When Zelda Fichandler created the Arena Stage in Washington and Tyrone Guthrie founded the Guthrie in Minneapolis, they were the forerunners of a movement—based on decentralization, subsidization, and consolidation—that subsequently spread to almost every major city in the nation. This movement wished to decentralize American theatre in the belief that it was unhealthy to originate so much stage activity in one cultural capital (New York) accustomed to feeding the rest of the country through pre-Broadway tryouts and tours. It sought partial subsidy—government and state grants, support from private foundations, corporations, and individuals—in an effort to free the theatre from undue dependence on the box office, with its celebrated timidity regarding unorthodox experiment and artistic aspiration. And it wished to consolidate itself out of a conviction that permanent ensembles of actors, directors, designers, and administrative staff, preserving the classical repertory and developing new plays, created a potentially more enduring theatrical art than pickup casts assembled for a single throw and dominated by star personalities. Although a collective idea, this concept was not incompatible with American traditions, however individualistic. Already proven in European and Asian countries, most of them blessed with permanent state theatres (partly if not totally supported by their governments), it had been fostered in this nation, albeit without benefit of subsidy, by a variety of companies, including the Group Theatre under Harold Clurman and the Mercury Theatre under Orson Welles.

The seminal branch of this decentralized movement was designed to be a seedbed for new plays, new forms, and new approaches to the classics. A later, more consumer-oriented branch—founded not by artists but by real-estate and business interests, and heavily dependent on Broadway or Off-Broadway product (the Kennedy Center in Washington, for example)—was more like a nonprofit equivalent of a tryout or touring house. Still, the original purpose of the resident movement in relation to Broadway was analogous to the now somewhat compromised early aims of the Public Broadcasting System in relation to commercial networks—to be an independent channel for presentations of a more adventurous, if usually less popular, nature. Perhaps its most radical idea was that theatre could develop the talents of artists and the imagination of audiences, not just be a source of profit and deals for backers, producers, and agents. My very manner of formulating these differences suggests that the profit and nonprofit systems might never be altogether compatible. Artistic directors and commercial producers would invariably be competing for the same talents, and the resident theatre was likely to attract people disgruntled with the way a once-aspiring art form had become a throw of the dice on hits and flops. But we never ceased to hope that these systems could live side by side in a mutually tolerant, even if mutually exclusive, manner.

What changed this relationship—and, in my opinion, threatens to corrupt the original goals of the seminal movement—was Broadway's increasingly desperate plight. With box office shrinking, with more theatres empty, with fewer plays and musicals being produced each year, the Broadway system of originating shows in New York rehearsals and then developing them through tryouts in out-of-town venues began to break down. Serious playwrights, who once distinguished the commercial theatre with such works as *Death of a Salesman, A Streetcar Named Desire,* and *Who's Afraid of Virginia Woolf?,* were no longer being assured of Broadway production, and even the giants of the American musical stage were finding success elusive. Broadway producers then tried a brand-new method of identifying potential hits—shopping for them Off-Broadway and on the stages of American resident theatres and British repertories, or trying out commercial plays and musicals under the umbrella of the nonprofit system.

On the face of it, this looked like a salutary arrangement. It helped to restore Broadway's failing health, it exposed New York audiences to otherwise inaccessible productions, and it brought some royalties to hard-pressed companies, as well as income and celebrity to its artists. One feels churlish about criticizing such a mutually satisfactory relationship. But over the years it has effectively changed the whole nature of the alternative movement. The first thing to go was the concept of permanent companies. When a production moved intact from a resident theatre to New York, its actors moved with it—and who was left to develop new projects at home? The Long Wharf Theatre's New York productions, for example, beginning with *A Long Day's Journey* and *The Changing Room,* effectively dissolved its permanent company in New Haven.

Seminal theatres were originally intended to create a large number of works over the course of the year, preferably in rotation, so that in a single week audiences could enjoy a variety of offerings (not just a hit show) and actors could play a variety of parts (and not just a starring role or a bit). In the new circumstances, theatres that once featured a permanent company were producing plays under the Broadway consumer system, sequentially rather than in rotation, using pickup actors whose bags were already packed for New York. This had the potential of transforming the resident institution from a theatre into a "house," indistinguishable from the Shubert or the Winter Garden in anything other than its nonprofit tax status. And it effectively reduced the membership of seminal repertory companies to the vanishing point (though the National Endowment for the Arts, through a special "Permanent Ensembles" grant, later tried to augment their number). Where once there were scores, there are now no more than six or seven major examples of this endangered species left in the land, and even fewer still perform in rotation.

Why do I cavil over what might seem to you merely superficial changes in the external structure of nonprofit theatres? Why cling so stubbornly to a puristic concept of company work in the face of such obvious advantages to both systems? It is because my own observation and experience suggest that the co-opting of resident theatres for the sake of Broadway transfers spells not only the end of a once-proud dream of alternative theatre but the abandonment of its animating ideals and the dispersal of its membership. It signals the dissipation of energies once devoted to developing talent and creating theatrical art into the marketing and merchandising of product.

These dangers were obvious at least as early as 1966, when I founded at Yale a version of the professional theatre I now lead at Harvard. At that time, we were preparing to mount, as our initial offering, the premiere of Jules Feiffer's *Little Murders*. The play never opened in New Haven because I discovered it was already encumbered with a commercial producer and I was reluctant to inaugurate our theatre as a Broadway tryout house. Over the years, a number of shows we initiated eventually found their way to New York, but usually with new actors and in new productions. More importantly, they moved without the prior involvement of commercial interests or our own administrative involvement in later commercial production. In that way, we could do the research and development for which we were founded without sacrificing our guiding principles, yet without depriving New York and other cities of our discoveries.

In Cambridge, where we took the name of the American Repertory Theatre, our commitment to these principles momentarily flagged. In the course of our years in Cambridge, we had a number of plays expropriated by New York producers—Feiffer's *Grownups,* Durang's *Baby with the Bathwater,* O'Neill's *Moon for the Misbegotten,* De Lillo's *The Day Room,* Marsha Norman's *'night, Mother*—occasionally with losses to our permanent company, though never with our cooperation. With Ms. Norman's *Traveler in the Dark,* on the other hand, we found ourselves on the verge of becoming a consumer theatre.

'night, Mother was a play about suicide, rejected as too morbid by every other theatre to which it was submitted. We cast it with two outside actors, because we couldn't fill the roles from our company. To our surprise, it found favor with critics and audiences, and moved to Broadway for a brief run under commercial auspices (not our own). *Traveler in the Dark* involved the same director, Tom Moore, and the same designer, Heidi Landesman—both former students of mine at Yale—but now it had a producer already preparing the show for New York with, as it turned out, an even larger cast of actors totally drawn from outside our company ranks.

I look back on this experience with a sense of defeat and not a little shame. From their point of view, it was perfectly understandable why the playwright, director, and producer should insist on name actors. I had an option other than to submit; it was to let another theatre stage the play. But I wanted to preserve the ART as a place for Ms. Norman's work, and to drop the play from our season would have disappointed audiences and exposed us to considerable embarrassment. I know now I should have done it anyway. The result of treating our theatre as a tryout station was to shake the company's faith in my support, if not to weaken my own sense of determination. It was not that our actors were unequipped to play the roles. Rather, we were being asked to function as a launching pad for a Broadway-bound show—one, in short, that needed stars—and our normally unpressured atmosphere was being subjected to considerable pre-Broadway jitters. Our theatre's contribution to this process—whether through advice, supervision, or personnel—was minimal. All we provided were four walls, a technical staff, and my own remorse.

Since the show was not a success and failed to transfer, we didn't even enjoy the modest residual royalties generated by such transactions (we do not, as a matter of policy, accept "enhancement" money). But the experience determined us never again to commit to a project not freely submitted to our company, without strings attached. Yes, one more show did come to us through what might be considered an "outside" source—*Big River*. This was submitted by another former Yale student, Rocco Landesman, not yet a Broadway producer and only later to become head of Jujamcyn. He had commissioned a stage adaptation of *Huckleberry Finn* by yet another former student, William Hauptman. I liked the work well enough to do it as a play, though Rocco always envisioned it as a vehicle for Roger Miller's music. I agreed to stage it as a musical; Rocco agreed to relinquish his interests in the project during the period of our production. And because of a long, friendly history with all participants, the ART *Big River* was happy and unpressured, cast entirely (one actor excepted) with members of our resident company. When Rocco decided to bring the musical to La Jolla for further development under its director, Des McAnuff, it was recast with new actors. And when he moved it to Broadway the next year, it was recast again. In this way, *Big River* managed to be an organic part of our own season, at the same time becoming available to audiences throughout the country without damage to our enterprise.

It is not the *Big River* pattern, however, but rather the *Traveler in the Dark* model that is frequently followed by resident theatres these days. And while few of these institutions have company actors to consider anymore, it is hard to see how they can retain much independence with Broadway producers hovering in the wings, often contributing front money to production and exercising control over artistic decisions, as was the case with the Old Globe Theatre's tryout of *Into the Woods* and the Yale Repertory Theatre's pre–New York airings of *A Long Day's Journey into Night* and *Ah, Wilderness!* It is true that some of these resident theatres occasionally control their own transfers—indeed, in a perplexing demonstration of confused purpose, Lincoln Center Theater has actually begun *originating* shows on Broadway (David Mamet's *Speed-the-Plow*). But in these cases, where we find nonprofit managements turning into commercial producers, it is their own artistic directors and managers who hover in the wings—the wings of Broadway houses. Transfers not only confuse the identity of resident theatres, they uproot their remaining personnel—who spend their time freelancing on other city stages rather than preparing new works at home. And while such worthy projects as *A Walk in the Woods, Ma Rainey's Black Bottom, Fences,* and *Joe Turner's Come and Gone* reach Broadway relatively unscathed, the excessive amount of time they require in New York and on the road is invariably stolen from local activities.

No one in a democratic country begrudges an underpaid artist's desire to freelance for high fees. But a theatre leader is not only responsible for his own career, he also serves as a model for others. And who provides the more inspiring model: the director who advances his own career, or the one who advances his company? The director who deposits his transfer royalties in a personal account or the one who returns them to the originating institution—as Dan Sullivan did after his production of *I'm Not Rappaport* moved East from the Seattle Repertory?

A good argument could no doubt be made for mounting popular products on the stages of subsidized theatres. But to be convincing, the argument ought to be artistic, not financial. It is one thing to move an occasional show to a commercial theatre in the hope of reaching larger audiences, or even bringing additional income to sorely underfinanced theatres: the classic example is *A Chorus Line,* developed in workshop at Joseph Papp's New York Public Theater. It is quite another to design a season in the expectation that a large percentage of offerings will be successful transfers. Such decisions may well be unconscious; they are subject more to suspicion than to proof. But they are nonetheless demoralizing to a theatre staff. And they are proving embarrassing enough in Britain to stimulate talk in the press and arts councils about limiting the number of shows a subsidized company can sensibly be allowed to transfer.

Such talk is rarely heard in our own newspapers and funding circles, where Broadway success is still considered the hallmark of theatrical achievement and Broadway transfers are the basis for endorsement and awards. But when such large, well-established, and generously subsidized institutions as the RSC and the National can suffer from commercial deprivations, imagine how vulnerable we are, being so much smaller and so much less well funded. American resident theatres rarely create a musical hit of the magnitude of *Les Misérables*. More often, they generate modest domestic plays in the realist tradition of Broadway's past mainstream drama. But the growing practice of circulating these works to a network of nonprofit franchises, their final destination being New York, has resulted in a subsidized version of the old Broadway farm system, with every resident theatre sharing the same play, the same production, the same style, the same kind of audience, and much the same cast—a McTheatre network resembling the franchising of McDonald's.

The result is not only the abandonment of company work by people once committed to advancing theatre art, it is the gradual transformation of theatres once devoted to risk and experiment into arenas of packaging and showcasing. Transfers from resident theatres now account for just about the only work on Broadway that can be called even mildly significant; and American playwrights certainly deserve the largest possible platform for their plays. A certain amount of theatrical circulation is inevitable, and probably even desirable. The real issues are frequency, prearrangements, commercial encumbrances. Surely a method can be found to satisfy New York's hunger for product without changing the nature of the whole resident theatre movement. The paradox is that by cannibalizing these theatres, Broadway is effectively reducing their capacity to generate innovative work. And by encouraging commercial transfers out of a shortsighted impatience for results, critics are helping to damage the slow, arduous process by which these results are achieved.

The nonprofit movement can continue to be a source of artistic product for the commercial theatre, but only when it is allowed to retain its early experimental thrust, its independent nature, its collective energy. I have no illusion that most nonprofit theatres will forgo their commercial ambitions, or resident artists their fees and celebrity, in order to preserve a fading dream. But I have stated the reasons why I believe it so necessary to pursue the original unrealized goals of permanent repertory companies, and to increase their number, without the distractions of careerism, marketing, and merchandising. If the commercial marketplace keeps pulling produce out of the ground before it has the opportunity to reseed, we will all find ourselves scratching in barren soil.

(1988)

The Legacy of the Group Theatre

Following the death of Harold Clurman, the thoughts of those concerned about serious American dramatic expression inevitably began to turn to the Group Theatre—the seminal company he helped to found in 1931—and how it both influenced and reflected the fate of later theatre collectives with similar ambitions. Clurman's passionate account of the Group's history, *The Fervent Years,* was written in 1945, but it is still our most penetrating analysis of the relationship between theatre and society; it is also a prophetic glimpse into the obstacles facing any collaborative effort in a country without a genuine commitment to the arts. The accuracy of Clurman's diagnosis has not led to a cure of what is by now an even more advanced disease; but reconsidering his book in the context of our current problems may be of consolation to those who feel such problems are singular only to our own times.

The most curious thing about Clurman's melancholy chronicle is that, while the Group is traditionally discussed as if it were a unique theatrical success, the author proceeds always on the assumption that it was a disappointing failure. Indeed, in his 1957 preface, Clurman refers to criticism of his "negative" and "self-deprecating" tone by friends and associates, particularly Irwin Shaw, who remarked that "the Group Theatre was a glorious crusade, not a funeral." Clurman hardly slights the signal achievements of his theatre: the development of an indigenous American acting technique based on Stanislavsky; the creation of a powerful acting ensemble with a unified realistic style;

the championing of lively social-minded playwrights, including Clifford Odets, John Howard Lawson, and William Saroyan; and, not least of all, the capacity to survive in a depressed society for ten years with most of its ideals intact. Still, I believe Clurman was correct in perceiving that, in some deeper way, the Group did fail to realize its original intentions. The reasons he gives are less an indictment of the Group than of the social and theatrical milieu in which it was forced to function.

In common with all such American efforts, the Group's most nagging and pervasive problem was financial. The basic aesthetic of the company was related to a sense of continuity; yet productions were continually being canceled, actors laid off, seasons shortened, as a result of a shortage of funds. It would be inconceivable, in any other country, for such a distinguished ensemble to be hobbled by economic constraints, but money was always raised, as Clurman wrote, "in dribs and drabs for individual productions. Never was any substantial sum set aside at one time for a carefully planned program on a long-term or at least a season basis." It was not the purpose of the Group to put on shows, but rather to build a theatre, one which would develop both its own artists and its own audience in order to "grow with the years and make a contribution to our social-cultural life in the manner of certain State theatres abroad." Without an endowment, however, or dependable support, the Group was forced to operate continually on the hit-or-miss system that characterizes Broadway, measuring the run of its plays by box-office receipts and critical reception. To rehearse a play for eight or nine weeks and then to close it after eight performances was the cause of Clurman's and the company's most dispirited moments—especially when the canceled works (including two or three by Odets) were among those the Group believed in most.

The Group, therefore, was mired in the commercial system, when all its instincts lay elsewhere. Still, as a permanent ensemble, the company was sometimes able to keep a play in its repertory that might otherwise have been destroyed by a perfunctory and thoughtless review. Such was the case with Odets' *Awake and Sing!*, which Brooks Atkinson of the *Times* had not much liked when it first appeared, but which, upon revival, he praised highly (when Atkinson thereupon asked whether the play had changed, Clurman replied, "No, you have!"). This change of mind inspired Clurman to write: "Now when no one ever mentions the possibility or desirability of a repertory theatre, it might be pointed out that there can hardly be any true theatre culture without it, since most judgments in the theatre are as spotty and short-sighted as those Mr. Atkinson confessed. Indeed, the judgment of any work of art on the basis of a single hasty contact would be as frivolous as most theatre opinion." Clurman's anger was often aroused against the New York press, and for similar reasons. The reviewer, he wrote, "cannot be held to anything, he represents nothing definite, he has no intellectual identity; his mind is a private affair, and his change of mind may be an accident . . . Unlike other people, our reviewers are powerful because they believe in nothing."

But the capacity to resurrect worthy plays after hostile notices was among the very few advantages the Group could claim under these self-limiting commercial constraints. The company, for example, never produced a classic—despite its love of Chekhov and its long-postponed plan to do *The Three Sisters* in a new version by Odets—because, as Clurman explained, "a first-class production of a classic can hardly be financed in New York without the support of a star name." Even the choice of new plays was sometimes influenced by what the directorship believed would excite the box office. "The basic defect in our activity," Clurman wrote, "was that while we tried to maintain a true policy artistically, we proceeded economically on a show business basis. Our means and our ends were in fundamental contradiction."

Subject to malign external pressures, the Group also buckled internally. The greatest threat to the nuclear stability of the company was the magnetic attraction of Hollywood. Clurman's attitude toward defections in the ranks of the Group was outwardly benevolent (he once spent a six-month period in Hollywood, too), but he was not happy to see the most talented members of his company being continually lured away, whether permanently or for short periods, by the promise of money and fame, or marriage with a movie star. The first to leave was Franchot Tone, followed soon after by Odets, John Garfield, Stella Adler, and most of the others. All had strong feelings for the company and argued constantly over its policy; all had accepted pitifully small wages and even small parts for the sake of a unified ensemble. But in the long run, there was no adhesive strong enough to keep the Group together on a truly permanent basis. Clurman was gradually coming to perceive that "the Group's situation was an impossible one, that we were carrying on a task that was almost against nature! . . . My idealism did not preclude my seeing that in a very real sense we were fools."

After the Group collapsed, Clurman saw the problem through a wider social perspective: "For a group to live a healthy life and mature to a full consummation of its potentiality, it must be sustained by other groups—not only of moneyed men or civic support, but by equally conscious groups in the press, in the audience, and generally in large and comparatively stable segments of society. When this fails to happen, regardless of its spirit or capacities, it will wither . . ." Quoting Robert Ardrey, he amplified this further: "The Group was destined to fail . . . because its premise went against the American grain. The Group aimed to cultivate the individual through a collective discipline and a collective approach to the individual's problems; and America's culture is fundamentally individualistic." No one spoke eulogies or sang dirges over the corpse of the Group, partly because it never officially announced its own death, partly because few recognized at the time what had been lost. The dissolution of what was arguably the finest company of actors ever to have been gathered together in America was, in fact, received with a certain "glee" by "the divisive forces of the New York theatre," as Clurman called them, "which through indifference, casualness, need for excitement, malice, and a miserable competitiveness dog the coherence and stability of all organic effort."

The artistic achievements of the Group Theatre, no matter how substantial, are not what have ensured its place in theatre history. Few of the plays it produced, not even those of Odets, were really of first-class quality, and great ensemble acting is too ephemeral to make a permanent impression on a culture. The offspring of the Group all ended up on Broadway or in Hollywood, or in the Actors Studio, training for Broadway or Hollywood. No, what was great and lasting about the Group was its Idea—and an unremitting devotion to that Idea on the part of Clurman and some of his colleagues. The Group defined the terms on which a serious American theatre would henceforth be approached, as well as identifying the conditions that would prevent such a theatre from enjoying a healthy life.

Alas, those conditions are unchanged, and Clurman's diagnosis remains as accurate today as when it was first written. The permanent theatre movement in America still faces the same indifferent culture, the same financial shortfall (exacerbated by the Reagan cuts), hence the same dependence on the box office and the critics, the same short-sighted press, the same lures to artists from more lucrative quarters, the same selfish individualism working like an acid on collective effort—and the same malicious divisiveness among competing theatrical entities. What is also the same, however, is an impulse Clurman recognized as the motivating quality of the Group, that however "against nature" such an activity might be, there is something fundamentally natural about it, too. It is the compulsion, in our lonely, isolating world, to discover community, to identify like-minded people, to create something precious that is not entirely personal and private. The hunger of the American individual, Clurman wrote in his concluding chapter, "for a cooperative interdependence (which is what I mean by the term 'collective') is slowly becoming greater than his slogans of self-preservation and self-aggrandizement. He begins to realize that his competitive sense tends to kill off not only his competitor but himself." He is talking here about the social ideal, and if it seems even more distant today than in 1945, it is still not entirely dead as a realizable goal. Clurman and the Group kept it alive by doing the impossible for ten years against the most fearsome odds; other theatre groups are still trying to continue the struggle in an equally cold and hostile climate. That effort is the true legacy of the Group. That effort is what transforms its apparent failure into enduring triumph.

(1984)

Notes on the Bottom Line

I had hoped to bring you a review of the Elizabeth Taylor *Little Foxes*, but I couldn't get into the show. A genial press officer informed me that she hadn't put aside any second-night tickets for me—or for a number of my colleagues on the magazines and out-of-town newspapers—and I couldn't buy my way in because the house was completely sold out. I probably could have begged a pair of house seats from the playwright, who is a friend of mine, but she was experiencing considerable discomfort as a result of a fall and I didn't want to disturb her in a time of pain. So . . . at least for the present, readers will be spared my wisdom on the subject of the new Lillian Hellman revival.

This minor incident has a wider significance. Along with a few other scratchy critics, I've occasionally been denied tickets to Broadway productions because either the playwright or the producer suspected I would have a negative reaction. This is the first time I have been banned because my reaction was considered of no importance whatsoever. The press office staff simply assumed (no doubt correctly) that small-circulation critics like myself were unlikely to affect the run of the play one way or another and, therefore, would be taking up expensive seats more profitably occupied with the warm bottoms of paying customers. The producers of *The Little Foxes* have secured the services of a glamorous movie star (Elizabeth Taylor) who guarantees a packed house as long as she stays with the show. Under these circumstances, who needs criticism that doesn't produce immediate financial returns? (By the way, *The Little Foxes* is an indictment of Americans who live by acquisitiveness and greed.)

Obviously, we are in a new phase as a society, where the value of things is determined less by their intrinsic qualities than by their impact on the bottom line. The social consequences of this for poverty programs, housing for the elderly, education, and all those other bothersome drains on the nation's exchequer are becoming clear enough, as our eminently personable and appealing President hacks away at anything unlikely to yield benefits to business or defense. Also becoming obvious are the cultural consequences of Reagan's bottom-lining: if Congress approves his proposed cuts in the budget of the National Endowment, the federal government will be spending more money on military bands ($89 million) than on the artistic activities of an entire nation ($83 million)—assuming, of course, that Reagan doesn't decide to eliminate arts patronage altogether. Not so obvious yet is how deeply our present-day bottom-line economics is influencing other aspects of society, including such traditionally liberal institutions as universities, nonprofit arts groups, and the press.

Let us, for example, cast an eye over the cover of a recent issue of *The New York Times Magazine*, where three gifted performers—Mickey Rooney, Jane Seymour, and Gregory Hines—have been caught in a moment of grotesque glee, presumably over what the cover article calls "The Box Office Boom: or How Broadway Sells Itself." Additional photographs decorating the body of the article feature four more stars of long-running Broadway hits displaying equally dazzling teeth, while the various producers responsible for this dental merriment line up on Broadway as "models of up-to-date entrepreneurs." It is true that an article of this sort appears in this newspaper annually, right before the Tony Awards, for the purpose of celebrating the financial health of the New York commercial theatre. This one, however, has been written by Margaret Croyden, whose previous contributions to the culture pages of the *Times* have usually chronicled such scourges of the box office as Peter Brook, Jerzy Grotowski, and the Living Theatre.

Rather than describe new theatrical techniques or artistic advances,

Miss Croyden has been asked to analyze box-office statistics: "Current predictions are that 200 million tickets will be sold for the entire 1980–81 season, and result in half a billion dollars' worth of business for the city." Miss Croyden is permitted a few asides on the quality of Broadway fare, which by common consent is declining every year. She is even allowed to quote a few dissenters (one of whom notes: "We have no plays that have anything to do with our lives"). But despite these few disclaimers, the most poignant conclusion of her article is that "artistic evaluations aside, the consensus among producers is that *business* has never been better" (Miss Croyden's italics).

And the business of America, as Mr. Coolidge once told us, is *business* (my italics), not artistic achievement. Reflecting the close relationship that exists between the health of the Broadway theatre and the economy of New York City, business seems to have become the chief business of the *New York Times* culture pages, too. Miss Croyden devotes most of her allotted space to press agentry and marketing techniques, including the impact of television advertising and credit-card purchasing, when she is not describing burgeoning real-estate values in the Times Square area. For all the concern with quality and aspiration, she might as well be writing about the underwear industry. As for the nonprofit theatre, originally designed as an alternative to pickup star casts, tourist audiences, safe choices, one-shot crap games, and a theatre centralized in New York, this enterprise is valued only for what it can feed Broadway, and anyone questioning this profitable partnership is written off as "small-minded." Meanwhile, there are not more than five or six major permanent acting companies left in America, and the dream of a decentralized American theatre, devoted to developing artists and expanding audience tastes, is rapidly becoming an abandoned relic that has fallen off the bottom line.

But why, when everyone is smiling, am I introducing this melancholy, "small-minded" dissent? Well, there is something in those photographs that scares me. The producers look natural enough, staring out at us from Duffy Square with the confident self-satisfaction of prosperous businessmen. But I'm a little worried about those actors, about their anxious effort to please. There's something unsettling here, a patently insincere rotogravure demeanor, a suggestion that spending your days on the bottom line can play havoc with the self. Stars are the meat and potatoes of the Broadway banquet (Elizabeth Taylor's temporary absence from *The Little Foxes* caused 90 percent of the audience to turn their tickets back and temporarily closed the theatre). But even the most undiscriminating diner will eventually reject synthetic food. The kind of look reflected in these photographs reminds me of Marx's descriptions of people alienated from the fruits of their labor.

Stars have always been regarded as commodities, but what happens when everything is esteemed according to how well it sells? Nobody can object to a healthy entertainment industry; what is truly alarming is when the demand for entertainment threatens to obliterate the conditions necessary for the process of art. In our depressed economy, where the sources of subsidized funding have virtually disappeared, the barriers protecting the desire for quality from the need for profit are disintegrating as well, and the most common standard of measurement becomes the balance sheet. It's not hard to predict the future in such a climate because it's already happening. Newspapers will estimate their value by circulation; universities will evaluate their courses by enrollment; publishers will rate their books by sales; theatres will measure their plays by the box office; galleries will appraise their painters by commissions—and society will assess its citizenry according to income. The Nielsen rating, designed to measure responses to mass entertainment, will soon become the technological determinant of every activity, no doubt producing the same level of culture one finds in network TV.

We stand to lose more than our culture from this bottom-line mentality; we are in danger of losing our young as well. Little more than ten years after this country experienced an unprecedented explosion of youthful idealism, the younger generation is drifting in cynicism, boredom, and anomie, seeking ever greater sensation, escaping into drugs, drink, rock concerts, and media narcotics. Conspicuously missing from their lives is purpose, heroic models, motivation, ideals—the very language one uses to describe the condition is now derided as old-fashioned. Meanwhile, the liberal intellectual community stands as a mute, bewildered witness to the dismemberment of our country's few remaining values. The smile on the face of our well-liked, good-natured, star President, like the smile on the faces of Broadway's box-office boomers, masks a profoundly unnatural condition. It is the condition of the bottom line, and it is already exacting an unexpected price.

(1981)

Theatre and the Individual Talent

There was a bit of a tempest recently when Actors Equity refused to permit Sarah Brightman to play her original role in Andrew Lloyd Webber's *The Phantom of the Opera* or Yvonne Bryceland her part in Athol Fugard's *The Road to Mecca*, in the projected Broadway transfers of those plays from London. Equity complained that neither actress was a "star of international stature," the one qualification, apart from actors' exchanges, that permits exceptions to the alien rules. The issue has now been positively resolved in the case of Miss Brightman, who will be allowed to act on the Broadway stage provided an American actor of equally dim candle power is invited to appear on the West End. But this old problem remains a continuing source of contention between acting unions on both sides of the Atlantic, with its overtones of job insecurity, chauvinism, xenophobia, and—in the case of American Equity members—bleeding egos.

Such growling no longer disturbs the resident theatre atmosphere, because Equity, in its contract with the League of Resident Theatres, will allow no foreign actors whatever to perform with nonprofit companies, unless they have a "green card" as resident aliens. This union prohibition gives Equity casting control—only American citizens or those in the process of naturalization are employable—which would be less oppressive if American actors had more lust for company work. It is a melancholy paradox that most abandon the stage at the first opportunity. Eager to become "stars of international stature" they accept frequently demeaning work in movies and television, while the great classical roles are proscribed for the English actors who want them. There are, of course, distinguished exceptions—gifted men and women who devote themselves to underappreciated company acting. But if you've been wondering why *Hamlet* or *The Master Builder* is not more often performed in nonprofit theatres—or why directors are currently taking center stage from actors—it is because a lot of those qualified to play the great parts are either working in movies or waiting by the phone for their agents to summon them to Hollywood for a comedy series.

The Equity prohibition on foreign actors smacks of protectionism, with artists at issue rather than microchips. And although neither the

Dramatists' Guild nor the Society of Stage Directors and Choreographers has thus far made a move to boycott foreign plays or foreign directors, this is not inconceivable in future if defensive labor practice rather than artistic necessity begins to dictate policy. Imagine a world in which Americans could no longer stage Beckett or Pinter, where English theatres would be denied rights to O'Neill, Williams, Miller, Shepard, and Mamet. Imagine Broadway without Stoppard, Frayn, and Shaffer! Would the prohibition extend to Shakespeare and Chekhov, Aeschylus and Pirandello? How long before we dropped the curtain on Pintilie and Strehler, Kantor and Grotowski? Come to think of it, the Immigration Department, having threatened to bar the brilliant Cracow Stary Theatre production of *Crime and Punishment* from our shores last summer because it had never heard of Andrzej Wajda, is again harassing the PepsiCo Festival at Purchase with questions regarding the "international stature" of the foreign companies invited. The very phrasing of the question suggests the department is being cued by the unions.

My own belief is that theatre, being an international forum, should keep an open door to international artists, applying no restriction whatever on free exchange except the qualification of the artist for the position—this to be determined not by government bureaucracies or labor unions but rather by the only agencies in a position to make such judgments: the theatres themselves. I am conscious that a theatrical open-door policy would prove threatening to a profession riddled with unemployment. But it is perfectly consistent with the American principle of free markets and, when reciprocated, would offer new opportunities to American actors in foreign venues. Inviting alien artists to our shores might even have the salutary effect of reviving our own performers' flagging interest in the stage. It would certainly provide models, singularly missing from our culture, of those who still retain some respect for acting.

In demanding that foreign performers qualify as "international stars," therefore, Equity helps to subvert one of the cardinal principles of the acting profession, which is the principle of ensemble. I don't mean to appear impervious to glamour or charisma. These are the qualities that distinguish the actor from the man on the street. But in an ideal theatre, every actor would have these qualities and take his or her turn with the others in displaying them to the public in leading roles. Although you'd never know it from our system of rewards, or the way our culture singles out individuals for praise, theatre is a collective art. It succeeds or fails in the way people interact with each other, in the way they realize their own needs without obscuring the superior needs of the group. No actor can fulfill a role without support from others, which makes the whole apparatus of Tony or Critics Circle Awards an absurdity.

I believe theatre will survive in this country precisely because few Americans can contemplate the idea of life without community—but it will need actors, not stars. It will need people who still believe in collective fulfillment, even when theatre tickets—not to mention newspapers and magazines—are sold only by identifying individual achievement. It will need men and women of warmth and generosity, qualities expressed through commitment and dedication rather than through the occasional benefit performance for a worthy cause on a night off from Hollywood. It will need artists willing to create a viable alternative to the increasingly mean-spirited world we live in.

(1987)

Lighten Up, America

A recent article in *The Economist*, a British magazine which admits to being "unashamedly Americanophile," looks with deepening concern upon what the anonymous author calls our "decadent puritanism." This condition is manifested in a number of ways, from America's weakness for euphemism (where the handicapped are now called "differently abled") to the killjoy national attitude regarding alcohol, diet, smoking, and health. But the author is mainly concerned with the subject of race. "There are few countries on earth," he writes, "in which people are generally less prejudiced about color than America. Yet there are few countries where the issue looms so large; where pressure groups are so quick to take offence at a careless remark, or where words are made to carry such a weight of meaning." Noting how easily American political careers can collapse because of a single reference that does not pass "some ideological litmus test," he concludes that we are being terrorized by "a conformist tyranny of the majority, an intolerance of any eccentricity," in a culture that would "rather bore than shock." The author concludes by urging us Americans "to lighten up a bit."

The Economist is correct in diagnosing this as a failure of humor. We live in a grim, censorious, supersensitive time. Consider the public humiliation of Andy Rooney and Jimmy Breslin, two wags who made careless remarks about gays and blacks (Rooney), Asians and women (Breslin)—or consider the precipitous collapse of H. L. Mencken's reputation as a result of a few sour notes in his diary about Jews (the thing to remember about Mencken is that, like his misogynistic comic cousin W. C. Fields, he hated everyone equally—with the possible exception of fundamentalists). *The Economist* sees the genesis of our oversensitivity to insult in the "warped idea" that the problem with America's underclass "is a lack of self-esteem." But the condition is hardly limited to the underclass. Today, virtually every race, religion, and ethnic group has some watchdog agency or anti-defamation league devoted to reducing the capacity for free expression or closing off the avenues of choice.

This pathology is common to all sides of the political spectrum—exacerbated (and sometimes generated) by the very print and broadcast media which should be guarding freedom of choice and expression. And it suggests why certain forms of American humor have now become so scabrous, extreme, and underground. How, for example, could conventional comedy do justice to Actors Equity's banning Jonathan Pryce from playing a half-Asian character in the musical *Miss Saigon* because he had the misfortune to be a white actor born in Great Britian? Equity claimed this was a "moral decision," a response to complaints by the playwright David Henry Hwang and the actor B. D. Wong (both associated with *M. Butterfly*) that Asian actors, like other minorities, have insufficient employment opportunities in the theatre. And it must have taken a certain courage for Equity to adopt such a pea-brained posture in the face of inevitable ridicule, not to mention the loss of thirty-four jobs for Asian actors when the irate producer canceled the Broadway production (responding to widespread outrage and economic practicalities, Equity has now reversed its position and the show will go on). Nevertheless, the flap exposed Equity's concept of "non-traditional casting"—an excellent idea in theory—as a form of reverse racism, selectively color-blind only when considering the casting of Caucasian roles.

Unlike Equity's protectionism preventing foreign actors from performing in Broadway plays unless they are "stars," this decision was based on decent, unselfish sentiments. Actors are generally good-hearted, generous people, especially when their interests are not at stake, and the American theatre has been a leader in integration. Still, the power of any organized group to coerce artistic choices is unacceptable for any reason. And Equity's reasoning would have retroactively blocked some of the greatest performances of our time (Olivier's Othello, Mirella Freni's Butterfly), as well as some of the most colorful (Peter Lorre's Mr. Moto, Warner Oland's Charlie Chan, Marlon Brando's Zapata), for the sake of placating minority groups. Even Equity's president, Colleen Dewhurst, would have had to cede her role in *The Good Woman of Setzuan* to an Asian actress—though Brecht's Shen Te is clearly less Chinese than Bavarian.

Brecht himself made a bizarre early contribution to nontraditional casting when he suggested that the black actor Canada Lee play the part of Bosola (in the playwright's adaptation of *The Duchess of Malfi*) in white face. Today, many would consider that racist, an inverted form of minstrel show. It is certainly unnecessary. We have learned that audiences have the capacity to suspend disbelief regarding the color—and even the sex—of actors playing roles for which they are not typecast. In the past few years, we've had not only a female Hamlet but a female Falstaff. It is an irony that while actors rightly despise type-casting, their union is insisting that racial roles be played only by minorities. But as Jonathan Pryce remarked upon suggesting that B. D. Wong's objection may have been opportunistic (Wong reputedly wanted the role for himself), "Changing our appearance is what we do as actors." Let's leave realistic acting to the movies. The art of the theatre is the art of imaginative transformation, regardless of racial or ethnic composition—and that is the true meaning of nontraditional casting.

Equity's prohibition regarding *Miss Saigon* represents suppression from the liberal left. It is hardly as threatening to the artist as the onslaught coming from the fundamentalist right. Still, it reflects a general mood of intolerance in the land which, if it continues to spread, will call for repeal of the Bill of Rights. What was once the freest country on earth is in danger of bowing down before the "decadent puritanism" of moralists and liberals alike. Mencken! Scourge of boobs! Thou shouldst be living at this hour!

(1990)

Designs for Living (Rooms)

(*The Theatre of Boris Aronson*)

It may seem curious that the first book-length study by *New York Times* drama critic Frank Rich should concern not a playwright, not an actor, not a director, not an overview of the New York stage, but rather a stage designer, Boris Aronson. Nevertheless, his handsomely illustrated coffee-table volume, *The Theatre of Boris Aronson* (written in consultation with Aronson's widow, Lisa, who supervised the visuals), is valuable not only for celebrating the career of one of America's greatest theatre artists but also for elevating the art of scenic design to its rightful place in the theatrical pantheon. Quoting generously from Aronson's own writings and interviews, interspersing cogent commentary on the designer's production history with innumerable color plates and photographs of his most inventive renderings, Mr. Rich positions his subject high on the ladder of the Broadway theatre he served so reputably throughout most of his career.

And served so sourly. His attitude toward Broadway was always adversary. Trained in the theatricalist tradition of the radical Russian director Meyerhold, deeply influenced by modernist art, and stimulated by the visionary designs of Gordon Craig and Adolphe Appia, Boris Aronson—arriving here (in the twenties) from the Soviet Union after a brief stay in Berlin—found little to admire in the mundane domestic realism which still dominates the commercial American stage. "Every production was *Life with Father*, or mother—or the uncles," he growled in his famous curmudgeon manner—"plays about relatives" more appropriate to television or radio. "I've done so many kitchens, I don't know how to do them anymore unless it's James Joyce's kitchen," he said, upon turning down a Gertrude Berg vehicle called *A Majority of One*, where, he crabbily concluded, "the whole Jewish problem is solved because she could make gefilte fish for a Japanese fellow."

The Broadway theatre responded with its own suspiciousness toward this foreigner who scorned its values, a rival, Lee Simonson, calling his design style "an exotic and transplanted thing," full of "Russian dogmas" that inadequately reflect "the current realities of the American stage." Nevertheless, Aronson, like other theatrical émigrés of the time, soon fell into lockstep with the demands of the job market. After a brief stint designing Constructivist settings for the Yiddish theatre, he then began doing living rooms for the Group Theatre (Odets' *Awake and Sing!* and *Paradise Lost*) and, in what the author calls his "Broadway breakthrough," for a variety of commercial plays and musicals, including *The Diary of Anne Frank*, *Detective Story*, *Bus Stop*, and *A Loss of Roses*. None of these designs was ever less than masterly, but—as typified in his magnificent setting (perhaps his masterpiece) for Archibald MacLeish's *J.B.*—they were usually for projects inferior to his talents, as if Picasso had been commissioned to decorate a lobby on West End Avenue. Only twice did he design a classic, the last being Olivier's *Coriolanus* at the Royal Shakespeare Theatre in Stratford, where, finally exposed to the virtues of the subsidized repertory system, he professed himself "flabbergasted . . . that there is such a thing as working without the pressures, without all the difficulties, without the deadlines."

It was not until the mid-sixties, when Aronson began collaborating on the "concept" musicals associated with the names of Harold Prince and Stephen Sondheim—*Company*, *A Little Night Music*, *Follies*—that he was able to escape the tasteless parlors of American drama and create sets equal to his epic imagination. Clearly, the presentational style and fluid staging of the musical appealed to his nonrealistic tastes, and just as clearly, the author believes it was through these open-stage opportunities that Aronson finally achieved creative fulfillment. The book does not record Aronson's opinions of Broadway musicals, which I suspect were just as jaundiced as his views of Broadway producers, audiences, and theatre people (we do know that this disciple of Marc Chagall admired *Fiddler on the Roof*, which he uncharacteristically petitioned to design). To the end, Aronson remained a much more acid critic of the commercial theatre than those who reviewed his productions. If this gracefully written book raises a question, it is not about the exhaustive treatment of its remarkable subject. Rather, it is why Aronson's artistic values have not rubbed off more visibly on Rich's own critical aesthetic, which, in my opinion, is often armored against the truly innovative, imaginative, questing voices in our midst today, though open enough to those conventional "plays about relatives" shouted out in those hideous kitchens and box-set living rooms that Aronson despised.

Where Aronson made his greatest impact, I believe, was not on Broadway but on the set designers who followed him, most of them working in an American version of that sensible theatre system he so much admired at the Stratford RSC. Ming Cho Lee, a gifted scenic artist who served an early apprenticeship with Aronson, is living testimony to the "range and possibility of theatre expression" he said this relationship opened up for him. And when Lee succeeded Donald Oenslager as design teacher at Yale, he went on to develop, with his associate Michael Yeargan, a string of talented, visionary designers whose artistry, variety, and commitment make them the unsung heroes of the contemporary American stage. Some, like Tony Straiges, the current designer of Sondheim's concept musicals, work primarily on Broadway; others, like Santo Loquasto, who designs for Woody Allen, have turned to film. But the majority—among them Heidi Landesman, Douglas Stein, Adrianne Lobel, John Conklin, Karen Schulz, Kate Edmunds, David Gropman, John Lee Beatty, Zack Brown, Eugene Lee, Derek McClain, and Andrew Jackness, not to mention the prolific Yeargan himself, who designs all over the world—are primarily associated with resident theatres, Off-Broadway, or opera companies. These, along with such non-Yale-trained designers as Robin Wagner, Robert Israel, Loy Arcenas, John Arnone, David Mitchell, Douglas Schmidt, George Tsypin, and countless others, form a cadre of theatre artists who make Aronson look less like a lonely dissenting influence on the American stage than the leader of a national movement.

I am surely not alone in my belief that such theatre designers are among a director's most cherished colleagues, not just because they help to realize an interpretation of a play, but because they help to formulate it. Design in the Aronson tradition is organic rather than decorative. Instead of functioning as environmental background for the action, an illusionistic enclosure for dialogue and gesture, the Aronsonian setting—like his circus universe for *J.B.*—is essentially a metaphor that encapsulates the poetic kernel of the production without hiding the instrumentalities of the stage. Today's most interesting stage directors try to realize a dramatic concept not just histrionically, through the actors, but visually, through the very tissue of the scenic surround, which at its best changes and develops very much like another character in the play. It is for this reason that so many conceptual directors are forming permanent relationships with designers: JoAnne Akalaitis and Douglas Stein, Andrei Serban and Michael Yeargan, Peter

Sellars and Adrianne Lobel, Martha Clarke and Robert Israel. The ideas they evolve are symbiotic, with the designer assuming as much responsibility for the directorial interpretation as the director does for the design. In the case of artists such as Liviu Ciulei or Robert Wilson or Richard Foreman, the director is usually his own designer, and the symbiosis is complete.

In my own experience, designers have proved not only among the most creative figures in the theatre but also among the most intelligent and broad-ranging. Not many American actors are devoted to reading, and fewer like to read plays. But when designers accept an assignment, they are trained to devour anything even remotely related to the work being produced. Their prodigious research embraces not only visual artifacts—paintings, architecture, and photographs of the era—but also literary and scholarly references, including stage history, other plays, novels, sociology, politics, and philosophy. They are well-educated, intellectually curious, and generous-minded. And being self-effacing, they have the opportunity and the tact to push the director deeper and deeper into the possibilities of the text.

The Theatre of Boris Aronson is especially valuable in documenting a great stage designer's questing, probing, inquisitive spirit. Among others, Harold Prince gives testimony there to Aronson's "crazy tenacity and impatience with compromise and second-rateness . . . He could poison me—he would make me no longer accept [the production compromises] that I'd planned to accept. He could make me pick the scab off when I'd been quite content to leave it there and go on with life." Discussions with Aronson could begin as early as two years before the musical was mounted, the designer encouraging the director to "say damn foolish things," to "free-associate." Prince and Aronson would talk about "characters, period, philosophy, the play in relation to its times, to these times. How were the politics of the time reflected in art? The mores? . . . The research is endless."

When applied to great plays, such investigation is arguably more deliberate and more penetrating than that done by the most rigorous scholars in the silence of their studies, because it is conducted collaboratively, word by word, by intelligences that are simultaneously analytic and artistic. It is certainly more satisfying than literary research, because discovery is invariably followed by a creative act. Not every designer is, like Aronson, the conscience of a production, but most of them have a considerably more important role in its evolution and development than is ever credited, and in their Aronson-like revolt against the artistic limitations of the living room, they have opened up the imaginations of audiences to theatre which is mysterious, dreamlike, and spiritual. Playwrights, actors, directors, and producers are the most conspicuous figures on the American stage and receive the lion's share of attention. But when the lights go up, the audience enters a designer's world, and it is the designer's images that implant themselves indelibly on the edges of its mind.

(1988)

An Actor Prepares

(*The 1988 Democratic National Convention*)

A new mini-series from Atlanta, called *Unity Village* or *The 1988 Democratic National Convention*, took up four days of prime time on CNN and all the major networks. Advance reports found it unlikely to displace reruns of *Dynasty* or *Falcon Crest* in the affections of American viewers. For one thing, the story lacked suspense, the climax was predictable. Even before the show started it was obvious that the presidential nomination would go to the Greek immigrant's son from Massachusetts. As played in a low-key style on a hydraulic lift by the relatively unknown Michael Dukakis, this was a daring bit of casting. But Dukakis was not considered a star of sufficient stature—some would say sufficient height—to guarantee the ratings. Perhaps conscious of this, the producers made every effort to introduce cameo appearances by bankable personalities, particularly the ever-popular Jesse Jackson in the part of a spellbinding Baptist preacher. But until Jackson electrified the audience with a fifty-minute monologue, only 32 percent of American television sets were tuned into this series and even the extras playing delegates were absent from the floor or dozing in their seats.

Part of the problem was the setting. The designer had devised a massive podium that might have been appropriate for the tomb of a pharaoh or a Nuremberg rally. But while it elevated the speakers, it dwarfed the delegate area, inspiring sour references to a "shoebox convention" or "the podium that ate the hall." Worse, in isolating the leading actors from the supporting cast, the playing area offered scant opportunity for dramatic conflict. The infinitely more exciting 1968 series from Chicago featured close-ups of Mayor Daly shouting obscenities at Abraham Ribicoff and documentary shots of bloody demonstrations in the streets. But the Omni Coliseum is familiar mainly as the home of the Atlanta Hawks, last seen being ignominiously defeated in the playoffs by the Boston Celtics—a stage, in short, associated less with roughneck politics or police brutality than with missed free throws and squeaking Reeboks.

Nevertheless, the mini-series had its surprises. One of these was the appearance of the three leading players before the show, pledging "unity" and exchanging words like "partnership," "participation," and "coalition" (disgruntled agents translated these as "sellout," "capitulation," and "surrender"). It is known that Jesse Jackson, an independent actor with no studio affiliation, had been miffed when the second lead was handed to a contract player from Texas, Lloyd Bentsen. Since Jackson had been encouraged by advance publicity to expect the part, the producers were concerned he might break from the show to start his own series. These fears were temporarily allayed by the "unity" appearance—which also provided a nice chromatic contrast for the color cameras: the Mediterranean swarthiness of Dukakis counterposed between Jackson's burnished brown facial tones and the vanilla-junket complexion of Bentsen. Color, by the way, was a continuing theme of the series. Thirty-eight percent of the delegates were non-Caucasian, women, or both, thus inspiring David Brinkley to inquire: "Is it all over for white males?"

Other interesting moments included a keynote speech by Ann Richards, playing a salty Texas grandmother no doubt modeled on Barbara Stanwyck's character in *Dallas*. Her spun-sugar hair crowning an Olympian head, her eyes as cold and hooded as a rattlesnake's, she poured ridicule on George Bush, the proposed lead in the rival series (scheduled in August). His performance she found a weak imitation of Ronald Reagan, another actor she scorned, the popular aging star of a long-running sit-com. The next episode featured debates over the platform scenario—Jackson's writers were trying to rewrite some themes in order to strengthen his role—which nonetheless remained close to the original seven-page shooting script. And then Teddy Kennedy, brother of the great superstar John F. Kennedy, rose to demonstrate the value of rhetorical repetition ("Where was George?") in satiric theatre. Not a leading man himself, Kennedy was ready to endorse Dukakis as the best available casting for the role his brother once played, and not just because he hailed from the same state and also had a Texas co-star.

Although the more discriminating critics believed the most convincing acting in the show was contributed by Walter Cronkite and Dan Rather pretending to like each other, there is no question that Jesse Jackson enjoyed the greatest popularity. Introduced by his immaculate, attractive children (a nonperforming Jackson Five), this personable and hypnotic actor initially seemed somewhat subdued, his delivery hampered by lip lethargy and a hoarse voice. Before long, however, his Rhett Butler sideburns, Kevin Kline mustache, and Bambi eyes had stirred the hearts of the supporting cast, while his Jeremiah oratory moistened its eyes. Jackson, who writes his own dialogue, got a little hung up on boat metaphors ("We're in the same boat tonight," "We got to go out, my friends, to where the big boats are"), and he violated the producers' prohibition against saying the T word (taxes) or the L word (liberalism) when he declared the rich and the powerful must "pay for the party." But by assuring his audience that he was only a newcomer to acting ("I wasn't always on television")—that he, too, was once an anonymous member of the mass audience—he managed at the same time to ensure his own celebrity and to promise future stardom to his fans.

Some jaundiced commentators remembered a few other magnetic political actors who spoke for the people and then acted for themselves (the name of Huey Long was charitably unmentioned). But whatever his future career, there is no question that Jackson is now at the peak of his histrionic powers, with a performance style drawn from strong internal resources. Rather than bolt from the show, he decided to steal it instead, thereby making sure he would soon have a series of his own.

Following this performance, there were dull spots and the ratings dropped again. Jackson withdrew from the cameras for a while and encouraged his followers to send their fan mail to Dukakis. After Governor Bill Clinton of Arkansas almost emptied the hall with a speech as long as one of Castro's, Dukakis was nominated by acclamation, and the crowd blew off their boredom with a noisy display of enthusiasm. The red JESSE! banners sank under a blue sea of DUKAKIS signs, and the way was prepared for the long-delayed acting debut of Dukakis in the final episode.

Critics had expressed doubt that Dukakis could carry the series, since he usually plays a passionless managerial type in a well-pressed suit—the only actor since Ben Gazzara who seems to be crying when he smiles. His capacity for handling temperamental cast members was known to be prodigious, but diplomacy is the gift of a director or producer, not a performer; and his mechanical delivery was considered appropriate largely for computer commercials. Still, the moment he entered the hall to the roars of the crowd—cheeks shining, hair glowing, eyebrows bristling—it was clear that the audience believed a star had been born.

But his forty-five-minute "American Dream" speech, interrupted ninety-nine times for applause, was hardly a model of great television writing. Though shrewdly bilingual, it managed to raise the art of generalization to a new plateau, and it had more than the usual share of platitudes ("We're all in this together," "Each of us counts"). Dukakis' story of his immigrant Greek parentage sounded a little like Kazan's *America, America*, and he tended to touch political bases so fast that we never got a close look at what was on or under them. Still, Dukakis represents a refreshing new kind of media performer—the direct, sincere, efficient, unglamorous Everyman who makes his effect without fanfares or flourishes. His writing was ragged, but if Dukakis manages to get rid of a slight touch of sanctimony in his performance, he just might have a chance to turn this pilot into an eight-year uninterrupted run.

(1988)

All in the Family Ties

(The 1988 Republican National Convention)

The biggest question about the four-day convention show sponsored by the Republican Party in New Orleans—*All in the Family Ties*—was whether it was going to be a continuing series or a one-shot pilot constituting an unsuccessful screen test for George Bush. With the pending retirement of the popular Republican superstar, Ronald Reagan, and the cancellation of his eight-year run as "The Great Communicator," the party was desperately in need of a new hit show with a bankable new leading man. It is true that Reagan's female lead,

Nancy, had earlier conceded the stage ("We've had a wonderful run, but it's time for the Bushes to step into the leads and for the Reagans to move into the wings"). But since Bush had performed only a dim supporting role in the previous series, critics were in doubt whether he had enough candle power to guarantee the ratings.

While Bush delayed his entrance, playing *I Got a Secret* regarding an important member of the cast, the party tried to compete with the successful mini-series the Democrats produced in July by trotting out a few studio celebrities for Dukakis-bashing. These included televangelist Pat Robertson as Elmer Gantry, Jeane Kirkpatrick as the Dragon Lady, keynoter Tom Kean as Betsy Ross restitching the American flag, and ex-series lead Gerald Ford as the Old Duffer. But the most sensational appearance of the evening was by "The Great Communicator" himself. Reagan has played that part for eight years, but he's been playing George Gipp for over forty. Using the Superdome, home of the New Orleans Saints, as a Warner Brothers set for the old Notre Dame football field, the Republicans staged a series of heartrending goodbyes to the Gipper which had the mostly white, mostly middle-aged stadium audience leaking with nostalgia. Jack Kemp, whose nostalgia is so powerful he wants to restore the gold standard, recalled the time Knute Rockne asked Reagan to run the ball down the field for a touchdown. And then the legendary quarterback himself appeared, his amputated leg miraculously restored, to speak of his pride in Nancy, in his "sweet country," and in George Bush, who was urged to "go out there and win one for the Gipper."

This suggests why Reagan will be so difficult to replace. It is not simply that he totally identifies with his roles; he can also convince an audience he writes his own lines. Each time he quoted John Adams (or misquoted, betraying his secret conviction that "facts are stupid things"), he looked down at a script—but he read his "improvised" lines off a Teleprompter. Showing up earlier as a mystery guest at Nancy's tribute, he joked, "I came on such short notice that I haven't had a chance to read my speech yet," threw away his prepared remarks, then "improvised" his heartfelt love from written notes on the lectern.

This was dynamite, daytime family theatre at its best, and Bush's greatest challenge was to persuade the audience that he, too, could play romantic-husband roles in public. In an effort to bolster his weak standing with female viewers, the Bush script came out unequivocally in favor of Family (also Fairness and Freedom), but his image as a doting husband was hardly reinforced when, in a pre-convention interview with Dan Rather, he exchanged affectionate slaps with his wife, Barbara, then dismissed her from the room with a pat on the rump when the discussion got down to politics. (Barbara's role in the series was confined to smiling, clapping, and waving a little American flag.)

Bush's problem is his limited acting equipment, particularly his voice. He has played key roles, not just as Reagan's understudy, but at the UN and the CIA. But despite his recent performance as a Texas wildcatter with a passion for pork rinds, he still comes on with the dry pinched tones of a New England banker patiently explaining why he's turned down your loan. Admirers cringe at his departures from the script ("deep do-do," "little brown ones"), but even with a well-written part, he projects an awkward image. Recognizing his limited appeal as a matinee idol, Bush stunned the audience on the second day of the series (and destroyed its only lingering suspense) by announcing he had chosen as his second lead a juvenile from Indiana, J. Danforth Quayle. Quayle is a relative unknown with only eight years' acting experience in the Senate, but enough family money to float his own TV series. Despite his opposition to abortion and ERA, his blond country-club good looks were expected to play well with the women who found Bush less than embraceable.

But Quayle was proving to have image problems of his own. In his first appearance beside a shirt-sleeved Bush on location at a Mississippi River dockside, he demonstrated plenty of Boy Scout energy and yuppie enthusiasm. (Later he confided to CBS's Diane Sawyer that becoming Vice President would be "a good career move.") But since both actors were known offstage as rich, right-wing golf players, people were saying the casting lacked dramatic contrast. Bush replied: "He's different from me—I'm sixty-four and he's forty-one." But it was clear that the man who had languished for eight years in the shadow of the most popular actor of our time was not in a mood to share the limelight with more experienced players.

Quayle stole the limelight anyway when it was revealed that he had no background in war movies, having used his wealthy family connections to join the National Guard and avoid combat in Vietnam. This was enough to take the focus off Bush's entrance, but the show was also suffering from technical difficulties. The $300,000 sound system was frequently on the fritz and the 87,000-seat Superdome ("the hall that ate the speeches") was proving inimical to intimate acting.

For most of the presentation, the studio audience was either snoozing or reading newspapers, and the lack of ethnic and racial variety in its ranks made for boring visual compositions, especially when virtually all the speakers, including the candidates, were wearing identical blue suits and red ties.

After Quayle's blow-dried performance, in which he expressed pride in Freedom ("the most precious commodity our nation has") and Family ("the very heart of civilization"), and just about everything else, the stage was set for the most important audition of Bush's career. Bush confessed that he had come to play the part of the Underdog, but in assailing the Democratic show (seriously distorting its script) he used lines like "You are history," "Read my lips," and "Make my twenty-four-hour time period" that made him sound more like Dirty Harry. Supporting the right to own a gun, capital punishment, and death for drug dealers, as well as prayer in the schools and anti-abortion laws, Bush went on to plead for a "kinder and gentler" nation. And in a daring innovation which invited audience participation, he concluded his speech by reciting the Pledge of Allegiance.

Although Bush admitted he wasn't a very good actor, his performance proved better than expected. His mouth is a bit frozen and his gestures mechanical, but with the aid of a shrewd scriptwriter, he managed to convince most critics the series had a chance of playing. The Democratic show suffered from excessive generalities. The Republican series was crammed with banality, cliché, sentimentality, and hypocrisy. But then so is most of television. If the producers are correct in their low estimate of viewer intelligence, then *All in the Family Ties* has a chance of becoming another cynical success.

(1988)

A Theatrical Declaration of Independence

Ever since the end of World War II, American audiences have been in thrall to the theatre emanating from Great Britain, often to the detriment of our own. Now that English imports not only constitute a significant proportion of "serious" plays on Broadway but dominate

Broadway's commercial musical offerings as well, our admiration for British playwriting, directing, composing—and particularly acting—has begun to resemble a national inferiority complex. The English have unquestionably been responsible for remarkable achievements in the past three decades, though nothing as advanced, in my opinion, as the rarely seen work being produced in Eastern Europe, Germany, France, and Scandinavia. Still, I am one of a small minority who believe English theatre is presently experiencing a decline. More heretically, I see American theatre, eclipsed in popularity, surpassing it in adventurousness, penetration, and power.

Admittedly, it is common wisdom that the English stage has never seemed more healthy or our own in more serious disarray. Apart from occasional anomalies like *M. Butterfly* and *The Heidi Chronicles*, few native American dramas have been able to survive on Broadway for more than a few months, and the success of *Jerome Robbins' Broadway*, an anthology of music-dance pieces from Broadway's golden past, only reminds us how desolate is the present state of our musical stage. Mainstream producers and critics now make annual pilgrimages to London in order to shop for the next season's offerings in New York. English plays sometimes outnumber American works in the schedules of resident theatres. And Actors Equity spends considerable office time and legal energy trying to prevent the incursion of British actors on our shores from becoming a full-scale invasion.

The most bankable musical-comedy director on Broadway, with two gigantic hits (*Cats* and *Les Misérables*) currently running there, is the Englishman Trevor Nunn. Broadway's most highly acclaimed musical performers are imported—Michael Crawford in *The Phantom of the Opera* and Robert Lindsay, formerly of *Me and My Girl*. All a producer needs to float a show like *Wild Honey* or *Breaking the Code* is Ian McKellen or Derek Jacobi or Jeremy Irons in the leading role. Andrew Lloyd Webber can guarantee a $17 million advance for his next musical just on the basis of *Cats* and *The Phantom of the Opera*. Peter Shaffer (*Amadeus*), Tom Stoppard (*The Real Thing*), and Michael Frayn (*Benefactors*) are assured of success with every new play. Slightly more marginal playwrights such as Simon Gray (*Butley, The Common Pursuit*) and Alan Ayckbourn (*How the Other Half Loves, Absurd Person Singular*) are staples of Off-Broadway and the resident theatres, while David Hare (*Plenty, The Secret Rapture*) and Caryl Churchill (*Top Girls, Serious Money*) have joined the stable of the once Anglophobic Joe Papp, through an exchange program with the Royal Court.

Of course they all deserve a hearing—Caryl Churchill, to my mind, is among the most interesting talents in the theatre today. What I am suggesting is that the undiscriminating critical adulation has begun to result in the virtual disenfranchisement of our own theatre artists, helping to feed the growing belief that they are not of the same professional quality. Implicit in much of the criticism of Joe Papp's Shakespeare Marathon, for example, has been the suspicion that Americans are not equal to acting or directing the classics, a suspicion that waxes (after *Cymbeline*) or wanes (after *The Winter's Tale*), depending on the critical reception of each production. Still, whenever a truly gifted film actor like Al Pacino or Martin Sheen returns to play Shakespeare, he is howled back to Hollywood with shouts of derision, and even Christopher Walken—to my mind the most galvanic actor of his generation—has had to endure a barrage of negative notices in classical roles until his triumph in *Coriolanus*.

In the face of such critical and public disapprobation—though that is not the only reason—many notable American actors have become reluctant to set foot on a stage. Years ago I wrote that, by appearing in a play, Marlon Brando could have revolutionized our theatre overnight, but his mutiny was put down by Hollywood's bounty. Today such rebellions seem more remote than ever. Meryl Streep, though trained as a stage character actress, has not played a theatrical role since *Alice in Concert* in 1980. Robert De Niro came East once to perform in *Cuba and His Teddy Bear*, but hasn't been seen here since. Dustin Hoffman's Willy Loman in a revival of *Death of a Salesman* was his first New York stage performance in decades (though he was later wooed back to play Shylock). William Hurt and Kevin Kline return from time to time, as do Mandy Patinkin, Sam Waterston, Raul Julia, John Lithgow, Morgan Freeman, F. Murray Abraham, Richard Thomas. But that doesn't begin to compensate for the hordes of fine stage-trained actors—George C. Scott, Robert Duvall, Willem Dafoe, John Glover, James Woods, William Daniels, Jill Eikenberry, Treat Williams, Max Wright, Walter Matthau, Gene Hackman, et al.—who, unlike their theatre-faithful English counterparts, prefer the fame and money offered by movies and TV.

The same Hollywood enticements are beckoning American playwrights, a breed traditionally more devoted to the stage. I'm not just referring to expatriated screenwriters (like Kevin Wade and Frank Conroy). Even our leading dramatist, David Mamet, is now preoccupied with writing and directing movies, possibly because his *Speed-the-Plow* could not survive on Broadway for more than a few months without the box-office magic of Madonna. Hollywood has totally ingested Sam Shepard, as film actor, writer, and director; once a prolific dramatist, he hasn't produced a play since *A Lie of the Mind* in 1985. Christopher Durang splits his writing between theatre and TV—when he is not acting in films, like another fine playwright, Wallace Shawn. And if we are to believe the notes appended to the published version of *Laughing Wild*, the talented Durang may stop writing plays altogether out of a sense that New York theatre is "an unfriendly and unaccepting place to work." Albert Innaurato and Marsha Norman have echoed this opinion publicly; many others privately. Taken in the aggregate, they demonstrate a growing loss of theatrical will among our most serious writers.

As for the older playwrights, Edward Albee and Arthur Miller haven't had a Broadway hit in years, and (apart from *Death of a Salesman*) even rare revivals of their work are unattended. In a reverse irony, Miller last season was the most popular playwright in London, with three highly acclaimed works in simultaneous production. Mamet's *Speed-the-Plow* will have had a longer run and more acclaim at the National Theatre than it enjoyed in New York. And Tennessee Williams, another playwright presently more honored in London than in his own country, is currently enjoying a great posthumous success through Peter Hall's production of *Orpheus Descending* with Vanessa Redgrave. To capitalize on this success, Miss Redgrave has brought this show to New York with an American supporting cast. But why wasn't the revival first done on Broadway under the same kind of auspices that originated it?

At the very moment that London is lionizing American writers, New York is on its knees before the English. The difference is that we can't seem to make room for a theatre from overseas without ignoring our own. Obviously, American producers are not going to fly in the face of critical and popular taste—issues of national pride have never had much force against the pressures of the marketplace. What puzzles me is how contemporary British theatre has achieved such exalted status in the minds of American theatregoers when it falls so short of past glories and, in many ways, of our own theatrical achievements.

Take playwriting. There was a time, in the sixties, when England was able to raise an army of spirited theatre revolutionaries—notably Harold Pinter, John Osborne, Arnold Wesker, Edward Bond, John Arden, Joan Littlewood, Shelagh Delaney, and David Rudkin. Lumped together under the generic name of "angry young men" (though some indeed were women), these were essentially regional, working-class artists, eager to create a vigorous alternative to the rather exhausted Mayfair tradition of Noël Coward and Terence Rattigan. In place of drawing-room accounts of adultery among the leisure classes or studies of anguished personal relationships in seaside resorts, they brought to the theatre a new social, political, and (with Pinter) metaphysical urgency. To American observers, the "angries" sometimes seemed to be rehashing subjects our own theatre had covered thirty years earlier in the activist drama, for example, of Clifford Odets and the Group Theatre. But this late awakening of class pride and social conscience was responsible for a theatrical resurgence of considerable power.

Today, few of these dramatists produce plays on a regular basis, and those that do seem to have moved to Mayfair themselves, made conservative by awards, honors, and upwardly mobile marriages. The same Pinter who created the savage working-class conflicts of *The Caretaker* and *The Homecoming* was soon to turn into the elegant craftsman of *Betrayal* and *Old Times*, while the radical incendiary John Osborne transformed himself into a conservative Colonel Blimp.

The playwriting stars of the current generation—Tom Stoppard, Michael Frayn, Peter Nichols, Peter Shaffer, Simon Gray—are surely more indebted to the glossy verbal wit tradition of Noël Coward than to the roughhouse style of the angries. Even their themes are interchangeable; each, for example, has written an Adultery Play about the sexual infidelities and moral failings accompanying worldly success. As for their attitude toward the dramatists that preceded them, this is symbolized by the custard pie that Stoppard's hero in *The Real Thing* throws in the face of a playwright from the working class. It is true that David Hare, Caryl Churchill, Howard Brenton, David Edgar, and others continue to work the social vein of their predecessors. But, apart from Churchill, they are usually lacking in subtlety or true dramatic power, and with his new play, *Secret Rapture*, even David Hare seems to have made a down payment on a Mayfair home.

English acting, too, seems to be afflicted, at present, by excessive gentility. The angry movement generated a slew of new performers—many of them from the provinces—who were unafraid to bring a new idiomatic diction to an English theatre previously dominated by the accents of Oxbridge and the BBC. They also brought a raw energy entirely appropriate to the volatile, if occasionally crude, plays they were enacting, though most of them were perfectly capable of playing in classics as well. Many of these actors—among them Kenneth Haigh, Ian Holm, Robert Stephens, Paul Rogers, Joan Plowright, Mary Ure, Alan Bates, Albert Finney—ultimately joined the large classical acting companies or started their own. And to his great credit, Laurence Olivier, the first artistic director of the National Theatre, not only assimilated many of them into his company but adjusted his own playing to suit the new style—most notably as the seedy vaudevillian Archie Rice in Osborne's *The Entertainer*, still one of his most memorable roles. In a sense, the marriage Lord Olivier contracted with Joan Plowright, the star of Wesker's *Roots* and later a leading actress at the National, symbolized the wedding of the old theatre with the new.

A marriage more symbolic of the reverse development in today's English theatre is that of Harold Pinter and Lady Antonia Fraser, if we construe it to represent the gentrification of radical energy in the eighties. In this country, avant-garde movements are inevitably dissipated when they are sucked into the mainstream of popularity and fashion; in England, new movements lose their force when their artists join the ranks of the dominant classes. The first is a matter of economic mobility, the other of social mobility. But British assimilation nevertheless reveals itself culturally and partly accounts, I believe, for the genteel state of the stage in Margaret Thatcher's England.

Clearly, English acting has currently reverted to the old-laddie diction of Garrick Club tradition and, with a few notable exceptions, has lost much of its sting as a result. Michael Gambon (seen here in the TV movie *The Singing Detective*) is one of those exceptions; he is an actor capable of bringing power, intelligence, elegance, poignance, and tragic depth to every role he plays. Vanessa Redgrave is a superb actress, though I don't share the critical ecstasy over her performance in *Orpheus Descending*, where a Polish accent in an Italian part seemed more a choice of Styron's Sophie than of Williams' Lady Torrance. And there are others, mainly women, such as Susan Fleetwood, Maggie Smith, Fiona Shaw, Diana Rigg, Judi Dench, Janet Suzman, and Helen Mirren, who sometimes break the cultivated surface with power and truth.

But the most highly acclaimed actors—Ian McKellen, for example, and Derek Jacobi—are conspicuous these days for flamboyant star turns. Instead of inhabiting their roles, they seem more interested in self-celebration. Personality acting is once again in vogue after disappearing in the sixties, when the English discovered Stanislavsky. In the American production of *Wild Honey*—a farcical reduction of Chekhov's *Platonov* by Michael Frayn—it was the American supporting cast that took the rap when it was McKellen's outlandishly hyperactive performance that capsized the play. Jacobi's appearances here—as the star of *Breaking the Code* and the RSC productions of *Cyrano de Bergerac* and *Much Ado About Nothing*—have also been singularly showy and superficial, though they have turned him into the reigning favorite of British acting.

Some years ago, as guest critic for a London newspaper, I offered the opinion that English theatre was often endowed with technique, wit, and intellectual insight, but rarely with emotional power, spiritual depth, or original imagination. Today, the situation has, if anything, worsened. Wit still reigns supreme and there are occasional displays of intellect, as in Alan Bennett's *Secret Spies* and the various philosophical exercises of Stoppard. But the technical polish that once made British classical theatre preeminent in the English-speaking world is losing its sheen. The major acting schools are apparently failing to place their customary emphasis on verse-speaking, with the result that the famed verbal skill of English theatre has begun to deteriorate. This is apparent at the two major companies, where actors are now breaking rhythms and garbling vowels, and has reached such a crisis that the RSC is making plans to initiate its own training program.

Where these skills are displayed by the more celebrated actors, they are not often informed by much power—"All pomp and no circumstance," as Humphrey Bogart tartly defined the British style in *Beat the Devil*. English upper-class speech is a highly civilized instrument, and it is elegantly employed in high comedy of the Wilde-Coward-Stoppard tradition. But being designed to conceal rather than express strong emotion, it waters down works of any depth. The same qualities that make this nation so courteous and civilized rob its stage of any real danger or surprise. It is for this reason that the English director Stephen Frears decided to cast American actors in his movie of *Dangerous Liaisons*. What Glenn Close, Michelle Pfeiffer, and John Malkovich may have lacked in style and smoothness, they more than compensated for in their capacity to excavate the suppressed feelings that lie beneath the polished surface.

And that is true of many of America's woefully underestimated actors—of our playwrights and directors as well. Eugene O'Neill was not an expressive writer and knew it—"Stammering," says his surrogate Edmund Tyrone in *A Long Day's Journey into Night*, "is the native eloquence of us fog people." But because language did not come easily to him, he substituted in his late plays an emotional eloquence of consuming power, writing round and round his subject until it exploded with centripetal force. (In a sense, the symbol of American theatre is Melville's Billy Budd, whose stammering makes him respond to Claggart's slanders with a similar emotional explosion.) David Mamet's plays are very carefully crafted, but one of his more impressive gifts is a capacity to render the stuttering, halting nature of American speech. The same is true of David Rabe. I'm not arguing, of course, that this kind of inarticulate poetry is comparable to the soaring verbal flights of Shakespeare and the Greeks; but it is certainly more penetrating than the brittle prose of most contemporary English playwrights. And, anyway, expressive language is not the primary touchstone of dramatic poetry or great theatre. Those who believe otherwise should take another look at Aristotle's *Poetics*, where semantics and diction rank fourth in importance among the elements of tragedy—after action, character, and theme.

It is precisely in those qualities that I believe American theatre now surpasses the English. Howard Korder, Craig Lucas, Glen Merzer, August Wilson, Ronald Ribman, Don DeLillo, John Guare, Wendy Wasserstein, Keith Reddin, Arthur Kopit are only a few writers not yet named who cut as deep or deeper than most English dramatists. And no one in England except Deborah Warner and the expatriate Peter Brook can match our best directors for daring and imagination. Because of New York's indifference, these have been working largely in resident theatres, where they explore the classics with considerably more originality than most of their British counterparts, who are usually content with modernizing the costumes and updating the sets. And no one can match the auteur Robert Wilson, unappreciated in England and the United States but an idol in Europe, for his capacity to create dream landscapes on the stage. Such visual-spatial tableaus as *Einstein on the Beach* and *The CIVIL WarS* conjure up a whole new universe of time and the unconscious, where no English writer or director has dared to follow him.

Admittedly, it is difficult to argue for the importance of American theatre when so many of our best actors shy away from the stage. Most actors still say they find their greatest artistic rewards in the applause of live audiences, and a number remain faithful to the theatre (particularly to resident companies) despite considerable personal sacrifice. But many of our more celebrated performers won't leave the physical and financial seductions of the West Coast for the uncertain rewards of acting in a play. No wonder. The glittering prizes in our society don't go to stage actors. The best they can hope for is not a knighthood but a Tony, not an OBE but an Obie—or, in the case of movie stars, an Oscar, a percentage of the gross, and a house in Malibu. Unlike London, New York is not a film center where actors can easily alternate stage work with movies and TV. And in a country that discriminates against actors in housing, credit-card applications, and telephone installation, we still have no respect for the profession, except when someone gets famous enough to be feted at the Kennedy Center.

And American actors will be wary of the stage as long as critics and audiences keep telling them the British do it better. For the same reason, we are now in serious danger of losing our playwrights and directors as well. To my mind, the American theatre has never been endowed with more talent, ambition, and originality than today; yet it has never been held in lower esteem. Until we draw up a theatrical Declaration of Independence from English rule and American-Tory endorsement, honoring the abundance in our midst, our talented stage artists will continue to be an endangered species of the American cultural ecology, wilting under the constraints of British domination.

(1989)

Dreams and Hard-back Chairs

Recently, I was invited to talk in the chapel of a private boys' school near Boston. The occasion was the inauguration of a new "culture center," consisting of painting and sculpture studios, photography labs, and a theatre auditorium in a former gymnasium. The boys were all between twelve and eighteen, neatly dressed in uniform blue blazers. They seemed as uncomfortable at this early hour as I was, their discomfort aggravated by the hard-back wooden pews in which they were jammed shoulder to shoulder like soldiers at a dress parade. As I improvised my remarks, my mind went back to the time when I was their age, in a Manhattan public school, attending assembly (as it was called) in my own school uniform of sneakers and corduroy knickers. Assembly was the only thing resembling "culture" provided those days by the New York school system. When the principal wasn't scheduled to give a speech about good conduct, one or the other of us was asked to recite poetry or play an instrument for the benefit of the assembled kids. My instrument being the clarinet, I got to play "Ding Dong, the Witch Is Dead" from *The Wizard of Oz*, a performance consisting more of squeaks than of notes.

I don't know why I mentioned this to the boys—perhaps to suggest how lucky they were to have a chance to perform and paint and take photos in appropriate spaces. But as I watched them squirming and wiggling uncomfortably, either because of my rambling speech or those hard-back seats, it occurred to me that things really hadn't changed that much over the years. Something in American schooling remains indifferent to the arts. Our institutional architecture, certainly, seems almost purposely designed to inhibit the play of imagination. The school I was talking at had been founded by a few Unitarian professors in the last century, to prepare their young children expressly for entrance to Harvard, where they would learn to be leaders of men. Those hard-back pews, I imagined, served the same function as the long poles used by beadles in Puritan churches to poke parishioners who might be dozing through the preacher's exhortations about moral purity.

These schoolboys were supposed to keep their minds alert for edifying instruction. And I began to wonder, noting that the new theatre was sitting in a former gymnasium and the studios in former classrooms, why American education, at its best, is capable of refining the intellect and training the body but remains completely indifferent to developing the imagination. Children attending this school—and other similar private institutions—are being encouraged in the competitive instinct by learning how to excel in courses and win at sports. But just as those hard-backed seats discourage the mind from wandering, so our schools make no provision for daydreaming, which is the stimulus of the noncompetitive imagination. They suppress the individual's capacity for fantasy, they inhibit the faculty of invention, they suggest that discomfort is intimately associated with achievement. Once these boys have entered the fast track at Harvard, they will major in social policy and economics, in preparation for careers as statesmen, legislators, stockbrokers, and corporate executives. But any vestigial passion they might harbor for music, theatre, poetry, or painting will be segregated to the patronizing category of extracurricular activity.

What is there about the imagination that stimulates so much distrust and so much indifference? Ever since Plato, who influenced our puritanism, we have been told that imaginative artists are out of touch with the "real world." Their fictions, at best, are a form of lying; at worst, a species of madness. Even Shakespeare is honored for his wisdom, for his language, for his understanding of character, for his comic instinct, and for a host of other attributes—yet rarely for his visionary invention. Recently, even Shakespeare's capacity for imagining has been under serious question.

I am referring to the spate of recent books—and especially to the television special lately shown on PBS—questioning Shakespeare's authorship of his plays. In the past, his works have often been attributed to other hands—Francis Bacon and Christopher Marlowe among them. At the moment, the reigning favorite is the Earl of Oxford. Since the man called William Shakespeare was the son of a glove maker and had never been to a university, the argument goes that he was an impostor. It is said that, having had an inferior education ("little Latin and less Greek"), he could never have imagined characters with the intellectual power of Hamlet, and being of inferior birth, he could not have been capable of understanding the thoughts of noblemen and kings. Alleging that very little is known about the historical Shakespeare, that he was an ignorant man who couldn't even spell his name consistently, the Oxfordians have concluded that he was simply a front for a gifted aristocrat reluctant to confess that he actually wrote plays.

As a matter of fact, a great deal more is known about the historical Shakespeare than about many past writers. He is referred to by name by a number of contemporaries—including the envious Ben Jonson, who would have been happy to unmask a literary fraud. Jonson famously called Shakespeare "not of an age but for all time" in his memorial poem, but he was not always so flattering. Having heard Shakespeare praised for never blotting a line, for example, he sourly remarked in *Discoveries*, "Would he had blotted a thousand." Yet, competitive as he was, Jonson knew and revered Shakespeare "this side idolatry."

What the doubts about Shakespearean authorship tell us, first of all, is that people find it impossible to believe in untutored genius. Great poets have to be wellborn and well educated. They must have aristocratic blood lines and sound classical learning. (Even Shakespeareans dispute Wordsworth's remark that he "warbled his native woodnotes wild," insisting that Elizabethan grammar schools were equivalent to modern universities.) But under the implied social and intellectual snobbery lies a basic incapacity to understand the workings of the imagination. For what makes Shakespeare supreme, though not untypical among great artists, is his ability to project himself into the minds of people different from himself—kings and commoners, heroes and villains, women and men. This is a faculty of the imagination, and it is no more open to logical explanation than the ability of Mozart to write musical composition at the age of four.

This faculty also suggests why the greatest artists, past and present, are so rarely realists. They are inventors, fantasists, fabulists who tap into their unconscious lives for inspiration. How many ideas for great works have come to artists in a dream? And how many times have they actually made dreams the stuff of their greatest works: Shakespeare's *A Midsummer Night's Dream* and *The Tempest*, Calderon's *Life Is a Dream*, Ibsen's *Peer Gynt*, Strindberg's *A Dream Play, To Damascus*, and *The Ghost Sonata*, even Robert Wilson's *CIVIL WarS*? Freud acknowledged that many of his psychoanalytical insights originally came from literature. It was only because he was a great artist himself that he was able to interpret dreams and the unconscious with the same imaginative genius as his literary predecessors. Sleep scientists have discovered that when you suppress the human capacity to dream, you stimulate depression or psychosis. The same must be true of schools and societies. The capacity to imagine belongs to us all; yet, in our culture, those who assert the primacy of dreaming are singled out as oddballs. If our art is not literal and straightforward, it risks being dismissed as fanciful. And those theatrical directors who try to invest Shakespeare production with the same imaginative impulses that originally inspired the plays are invariably the ones that take the severest critical beating. Fearful of invention, we demand a sound conventional realism. Yet, as a friend in the profession once said to me about a play written in the realistic style, "It may be real—but it isn't true."

For dreams are not lies; they produce deeper truths than those available to surface consciousness. Plato banished the artist from his ideal Republic because, since he believed material "reality" was only the imitation of an "idea," he thought artists who imitated "reality" were two degrees removed from the truth. Plato was wrong. More than any other human expression, great art provides a way of reaching that "idea" through the medium of dreams. But not in those hard-backed chairs.

(1989)

Dangerous Books

On the day the world was rocked with news that the Ayatollah Khomeini had put out a $3-million contract on the life of Salman Rushdie for committing blasphemy (only $1 million if the hit man is non-Iranian), I was in a classroom teaching Ibsen's *Ghosts*. Many contemporaries consider this play to be outdated because Oswald's fatal illness has now become curable. But Ibsen treated hereditary syphilis as a metaphor for all the ongoing diseases of modern life, among them the reaction of hidebound theologians to such "dangerous books" as *The Satanic Verses*. Pastor Manders has just rebuked Mrs. Alving for the reading matter he found on her table, and she replies:

MRS. ALVING: But what exactly do you object to in these books?
MANDERS: Object to? You surely don't think I waste my time exploring that kind of publication?
MRS. ALVING: In other words, you know nothing of what you're condemning?
MANDERS: I've read quite enough about these writings to disapprove of them.

(Tr. Rolf Fjelde)

Manders's know-nothing rejection echoes in John Cardinal O'Connor's expression of sympathy for Muslim grievances while refusing to read the book, in the fundamentalist attack on Martin Scorsese's film *The Last Temptation of Christ*, in the Catholic condemnations of Godard's film *Hail Mary* and Christopher Durang's play *Sister Mary Ignatius Explains It All*, and in countless other examples of religious proscription. Although the Church no longer consigns apostate authors to death or imprisonment—that's been left to totalitarian states—the past offers abundant examples of writers who were burned, crucified, stoned, and pilloried for their "dangerous books," generally by people who hadn't read them.

Some of these executions were for political reasons, but most were religiously motivated: there is no one more homicidal than a believer who thinks his sacred books have been altered or mocked. It wasn't always so. Ancient Greek literature, for example, incorporates a body of perpetually changing religious dogma in which the Homeric myths of Gods and heroes are subjected to considerable authorial variation. Athenians in the fifth century B.C., who worshipped in theatres as well as temples, and watched the Greek Chorus sing and dance around an altar, attended plays in which the sacred myths were treated in radically different ways. Euripides was just as inflammatory a writer as Salman Rushdie, and possibly even more skeptical of established religion. Yet, apart from being chased around the ecclesia by infuriated women in an Aristophanes play, he managed to survive in Athenian society without any known threats against his life.

It is true that Socrates, another heresiarch mocked in Aristophanic comedy, was forced to drink his potion of hemlock for exposing the young to dangerous religious ideas. But that was in the fourth century B.C., when endless war had frozen Athenian political and religious leaders into orthodoxy, making them increasingly sensitive to any departure from established opinion. Early religions such as Hinduism, Buddhism, and Islam (which accepted Moses and Jesus as Muslim prophets) were once remarkably open to divergent theological viewpoints. Even primitive Christianity was able to absorb such unorthodox creeds as the Arian heresy for a period before plunging headlong into the reflexive intolerance which inspired the Inquisition and dominated Europe for centuries. A similar intolerance infected Protestant reformers who, though also considered heretics in their time, invented a puritan strain of Christianity that was eventually to prove more sectarian than Roman Catholicism.

"He said Giordano Bruno was a terrible heretic. I say he was terribly burned," writes Stephen Dedalus in Joyce's *A Portrait of the Artist*, echoing a thought in Shakespeare's *The Winter's Tale*: "It is a heretic that makes the fire, / Not she which burns in 't." The need to scorch, singe, maim, perforate, and mutilate thinkers and artists whose opinions diverge from prevailing opinion or sacred Scripture is perhaps the most odious impulse in human nature. And while these Shiite clerics would plunge the world back into the Dark Ages, they have only reawakened a dormant strain of religious fanaticism that periodically reappears to poison history.

Hitler and Stalin were notorious for imprisoning and executing writers whose books were assumed to be heretical. And Stalin's assassination of Trotsky in Mexico is a famous example of how a dictator reached out to another nation to murder a dissident thinker. The engines of Nazism, Stalinism, and the Jihad are all driven by terror, as well as by a shared belief that even a single deviant idea is capable of wrecking the entire machine. When we are told by moderate Muslims that we don't understand the reaction to Rushdie's sacrilege because of our cultural differences, we are not being asked to recognize the nature of an unfamiliar religion so much as to forgive the excesses of a terrorist regime.

What binds the subjects of such regimes is absolute obedience to a single code—whether that code be the laws of the state or the canons of religion. When the regime offers the faithful a place in paradise in return for punishing heretics, unbelievers, dissidents, and other outsiders, it is providing authority for state-sanctioned murder. The same principle governs burnings in Spain and Salem, gas ovens in Nazi Germany, slave-labor camps in the Soviet Union, firing squads in Latin America, holy wars, book burnings, Klan lynchings (now called "Illuminations"), and all the myriad forms of rabid human behavior.

"Dangerous books," needless to say, have been responsible for virtually every advance in human history—whether scientific, religious, political, or artistic—while their authors, from Socrates through Galileo to Freud, have invariably been treated at first as enemies of the people. Except on rare and seemingly aberrant occasions like the McCarthy period, American writers are believed to be protected from political or religious vendettas by constitutional guarantees. Still, our record in regard to literary freedom is far from clean, and the admirable outpouring of support for Rushdie, while no doubt motivated by sympathy for a valuable artist menaced by mindless zealots, indicates a renewed awareness of how easily a dissenter's basic liberties, even his right to live, can be sacrificed to fanaticism and intolerance.

In our democracy, dangerous books (and plays and movies) have often been threatened by special-interest groups, representing both the right and the left of the ideological spectrum. Hawthorne's *The Scarlet Letter* was banned in 1852 after the Reverend A. C. Coxe fulminated against "any toleration to a popular and gifted writer when he perpetrates bad morals." The first edition of Walt Whitman's *Leaves of Grass* was purchased by only one American library when it appeared in 1855 and it was banned in Boston in 1881. Boston also banned Dreiser's *An American Tragedy*, Upton Sinclair's *Oil*, Sinclair Lewis' *Elmer Gantry*, Hemingway's *The Sun Also Rises*, Lillian Smith's *Strange Fruit*, Erskine Caldwell's *God's Little Acre*, and William Burroughs' *Naked Lunch*, among the more famous titles that scandalized this city's more straitlaced inhabitants.

But many other American states and communities have had their share of book bannings, most notably Philadelphia (Faulkner's *Mosquitoes, Sanctuary,* and *The Wild Palms*), Illinois (Sinclair Lewis' *It Can't Happen Here*), St. Louis (Steinbeck's *The Grapes of Wrath*), New Orleans (James Baldwin's *Another Country*), Detroit (Hemingway's *To Have and Have Not*), New York (Howard Fast's *Citizen Tom Paine*), and California (Hemingway's *The Sun Also Rises*, Allen Ginsberg's *Howl and Other Poems*). Attempts have been made to ban J. D. Salinger's *The Catcher in the Rye* ever since it first appeared in 1955 (in 1960, a Tulsa schoolteacher was fired for assigning the book to his class), and copies of Kurt Vonnegut's *Slaughterhouse Five* were not only banned but burned by an Iowa school board. Why, even a 1932 Mickey Mouse cartoon was once suppressed because it showed a cow resting in a pasture, reading Elinor Glyn's *Three Weeks.*

Dramatic works have been particularly vulnerable to the censor's red pencil and the puritan's blue nose. *Tobacco Road* was banned in Chicago, Detroit, St. Paul, and Tulsa in 1935 and was stopped by the mails in 1941. Sholem Asch's play *The God of Vengeance* was closed down in New York in 1923 and its leading actors were fined. In 1925, Eugene O'Neill's *Desire Under the Elms* was shuttered by New York police, and four years later *Strange Interlude* was banned in Boston (though not in Quincy, where it was first performed). O'Neill also received death threats from the Klan and its adherents during the production of *All God's Chillun Got Wings* because it featured a mixed marriage.

Perhaps the longest-suffering author of "dangerous books" is Mark Twain, whose greatest enemy has been not Mrs. Grundy but rather racially sensitive groups. Just as a dramatization of Harriet Beecher Stowe's *Uncle Tom's Cabin* was banned in Bridgeport in 1955 because of black protests, so Twain's *Tom Sawyer*, and particularly *Huckleberry Finn,* have been the recurrent victims of a mistaken interpretation of their contents. *Tom Sawyer* was excluded from Brooklyn and Denver libraries the year it was published (1876) and *Huckleberry Finn* was banned from Concord (Massachusetts) libraries in 1885 and Brooklyn libraries in 1905, as well as being dropped from high-school reading lists in New York as recently as 1955. Perhaps the most delicate examination of racial relations in all of literature, this great work continues to be a source of contention to this day, largely because of its use of a single offensive word ("nigger").

For much the same misguided reasons, American libraries were assailed by Jewish pressure groups in 1969 for stocking copies of Philip

Roth's *Portnoy's Complaint*, Italian-Americans protested against *The Godfather*, and blacks, feminists, gays, ethnics, and other minorities have all been involved in suppressive actions against books, plays, films, comedy acts, and ideas believed, mistakenly or not, to be offensive to their sensibilities. Needless to say, any powerful imaginative work is bound to prove offensive to somebody—otherwise it wouldn't be doing its job. The day artists are required to respect tender sensibilities, their typewriters will be covered, their ink will dry, all thinking will stop.

By forcing us to look into our own history, the Rushdie case obliges us to recognize that the First Amendment is not an iron-clad guarantee of free expression, and that artists will always be in jeopardy from powerful groups. Perhaps the best way to respond to this threat is not just by signing petitions or bearing witness, but by laboring to preserve an atmosphere of absolute toleration, even for ideas assumed to be hateful (providing they are not linked to hateful actions). Tolerance is not as instinctive to human nature as bigotry and prejudice, and our country is still racked by both the intolerant tyranny of the majority and a reactive effort by tyrannical minorities to suppress all points of view that affect their interests. In fact, America's commitment to free ideas remains surprisingly slack, even at the highest levels of leadership. It was not reinforced during the last election, when President Bush assailed the ACLU, one of the few neutral defenders of individual rights in this nation (he was characteristically unable to understand the civil liberties implications of the Rushdie case as well), or when Vice President Quayle called *The Satanic Verses* "obviously not only offensive, but I think most of us would say in bad taste." Quayle confessed that naturally he hadn't looked at the novel, thus endorsing the Pastor Manders definition of dangerous books as those you haven't bothered to read. But one can imagine the same criterion being applied to any work that raises the hackles of groups with political clout.

It is, of course, true that while sticks and stones will break our bones, names and words can hurt as well. But if we don't wish to see the Enlightenment repealed, we had better find some way to toughen our skins against affronts to religious, racial, ethnic, sexual, and political sensitivities. Peaceful protest and rational persuasion are perfectly legitimate forms of free expression, but any effort at forcible suppression lays our defense of Rushdie open to charges of hypocrisy. The best solution is tolerance, as practiced in fifth-century Athens and in most early religions, including that of Islam. The Ayatollah's death threat reminds us once again that dangerous books remain our best safeguard against narrowness and bigotry. We who love literature and ideas must be prepared to defend them not only when they offend others but also when they offend ourselves.

(1989)

Arts Wars

Disaster at the NEA

The first official act of John E. Frohnmayer, as chairman of the National Endowment for the Arts, was a disaster. By unilaterally withdrawing a panel-approved $10,000 grant to the Artists Space for an AIDS exhibition, he transformed the NEA, in one fell swoop, from chief advocate of the arts in this country into another of its philistine adversaries. Frohnmayer claimed he was not reacting to the homosexual content of the exhibit, though the language of his letter ("The message has been clearly and strongly conveyed to us that Congress means business") suggests how cowed he was by the legislative fulminations over the Mapplethorpe and Serrano exhibits and by the ensuing congressional measure which blocked NEA funds to materials "considered obscene, including sadomasochism, homoeroticism, the sexual exploitation of children or individuals engaged in sex acts" unless the materials have "serious literary, artistic, political, or scientific value."

This measure was intended to defeat a more radical proposal by Jesse Helms, but it is essentially the Helms amendment hedged by the Supreme Court test for obscenity. It was unclear about who was to make these judgments of value, nor did Frohnmayer assume the judicial role. Indeed, he objected not to what he called the "questionable taste" of the show but rather to the political content of the *catalogue* insofar as it criticized certain prominent people for their insensitivity to issues of art and sexuality—"a very angry protest," in Frohnmayer's words, "against the specific events and individuals involved over the last eight months in the most recent arts legislation in Congress. It's very inflammatory." Incredibly, Frohnmayer set out to penalize the Artists Space not for failing to meet the new obscenity tests but rather for conforming to them—for publishing a catalogue which fulfills the Supreme Court criterion of redeeming political value.

This is a curious development, to say the least, and it created a firestorm, which eventually led the chairman to reverse his decision and restore the funds. Nevertheless, Frohnmayer's action went well beyond the obscenity issue to become a fundamental breach of First Amendment rights. Restraint on creative freedom and dissenting thought—the name for that is censorship—was always the hidden agenda of congressional attacks on artistic license, so in a sense the chairman's gaffe was salutary in dramatizing the danger of enacting content restrictions in the first place. Clearly, the compromise measure was a mistake and should be tested in the courts. The well-intentioned Sidney Yates thought he was heading Helms off at the pass, only to let him in through a crack in the wall. As Ted Potter of the Southeastern Center for Contemporary Art put it, "We could see immediately that the compromise was a hunting license for ultraconservatives, but we didn't expect the first shot to be fired by the NEA."

By a single action, Frohnmayer managed to undermine his staff and the panel system which traditionally insulated the arts from government intervention. Following a barrage of protest, including Leonard Bernstein's rejection of the National Medal of Arts, he later tried to modify his stand, saying he regretted using the word "political" and offering to help overturn the anti-obscenity statute. But despite his decision to return the grant to the Artists Space, considerable damage had still been done. To protect their grants from controversy, many artists and institutions will become more craven, but some will surely grow more provocative. Does the NEA have enough thought police to monitor every production in the land? Will funds for oversight begin to exceed funds for the arts? And can our nation afford a reputation for cultural intolerance when Eastern Bloc culture is opening up? Clearly, the issue is no longer whether taxpayers should be required to contribute to obscene or unpopular expression but whether government funding is to be restricted to officially approved art.

It is highly likely that the National Endowment for the Arts will become a political football in the coming months, and there's a real question whether it will continue to survive. If it does, its structure will have to be fundamentally overhauled to protect its integrity and independence from external and internal interference. I have two suggestions. First, and most utopian, the NEA should become a true endowment with a large base of interest-bearing funds sufficient to support its grants. This would unencumber the NEA's money, thereby freeing the agency from undue reliance on annual congressional appropriations, not to mention uninformed congressional oversight. Admittedly, this plan would initially require a massive injection of federal seed money, but such an endowment could also attract private funds as well, in the manner of a university.

Secondly, discussion of NEA's accountability should be addressed by analogy not with an elective but with an appointive model, which was the intent of its enabling legislation. Elected representatives are responsible to the people and to consensus pressures. But the quality of art and artists cannot be properly evaluated by majoritarian rule any more than the public is qualified to vote on the products of science or intellect. The model for the NEA is not the legislature but the judiciary—the Supreme Court, for example, a body of trained Justices, proposed to the President by the Attorney General following the counsel of legal experts and then approved by Congress. The Court is hardly immune to the political process (Clement Haynesworth's recommendation was once defended with the argument that "mediocrity" deserved judicial representation), but in theory at least its seats are reserved for the finest legal minds in the nation.

Although the High Court also depends on "taxpayers' dollars," it, like the NEA, may very well make decisions unpopular with the vast majority—the flag desecration case is a recent example. But since Justices are accountable to the Constitution rather than to the people, they can formulate their judgments with more impunity. I would argue that artists are also accountable to a higher code than popularity (the intrinsic quality of the work, for example, which is evaluated by peers but determined ultimately by posterity) and therefore should be protected by a governmental model defined not by concepts of representative democracy but rather by ideals of leadership and excellence—nowadays called "elitism."

The fact that this word has today become an expletive suggests at least one reason why proposals like these are usually mocked or ignored. Another is the present climate of hostility toward the arts. In such an atmosphere, the NEA, if it survives, is more likely to become so hedged with strictures that no adventurous artist or arts institution would be willing or able to apply for grants. The nonprofit art world will either have to learn to live without government funding, which means severely curtailing its already diminished activities, or go under. The outlook is bleak—more bleak than I can remember since the founding of the NEA—and it is particularly disheartening following over thirty years of government-sponsored growth and achievement. We are now witnessing how what Yeats called "the mad intellect of democracy" can chew up a whole civilization and how what Ibsen called "the corpse in the cargo" can scuttle the entire ship.

The NEA Belly-Up

Bleeding from the most savage political bites in its twenty-five-year history, the National Endowment for the Arts is now foundering in the water with its belly up for all the cormorants to feed on. There couldn't be a messier time to consider congressional reauthorization. Drowning in controversy, the agency is now in serious danger of being dismantled; at the very least, it is likely to be fundamentally restructured. The most popular proposal—it was first floated by the National Assembly of State Arts Agencies—would distribute 60 percent of NEA funds to the states (at present they are receiving 20 percent) for the purpose of such peripheral activities as arts education, arts access, and rural and inner-city projects, with the remaining 40 percent of federal money going to the largest cultural institutions and even more arts education. The state agencies have now retracted their proposal, following shouts of betrayal and rank-breaking by the arts community, but since the proposed move placates various pressure groups and constituencies, it has found congressional favor, and the damage has been done.

The NEA is merely the crucible in which all the volatile issues of our time are boiling. In an article in the May *Commentary*, Samuel Lipman (a man with whom I seldom agree) has correctly attributed the problem to the fact that we have no national cultural policy—or we do have a policy by default. The absence of policy is reflected in a failure to define precisely what we mean by the arts. And this vacuum has created a policy biased toward affirmative action, multiculturalism, and the cutting edge. "Until now," Lipman adds, "our not having a cultural policy has meant no more than the tendency of our national leaders . . . to regard art as trivial diversionary pastimes, at best mildly amusing or sentimentally uplifting . . . But . . . our not having a policy has served to facilitate and consolidate the policy we do have—namely, the effort to exploit the vestigial prestige of art and culture to accomplish radical social and political goals."

Despite Lipman's tendency to see political subversives in every atelier, some of the points he makes are hard to dispute. The populist assault on "elitism," which began in the Carter years when the NEA was chaired by Livingstone Biddle, has now turned into a full-scale assault on "Eurocentric" culture as a white upper-class male-dominated expression. Lipman is reluctant to acknowledge the genuine contributions of non-European cultures—Asian and African art, for example, have had a profound and undeniable impact on modern Western forms—but there is justice in his charge that "multiculturalism" is now being widely used "as a device of political consciousness-raising." He is also correct in recognizing that current grant-making procedures are reflecting these motives. The NEA presently penalizes arts institutions that fail to hire enough minorities, while both the Rockefeller and the Ford Foundations have been channeling most of their arts funding to "Third World" and feminist projects—in the vain hope of resolving through culture the political inequities of the social system.

It is heartbreaking that the arts are being measured—even by the high-minded Mr. Lipman—according to purely political criteria, when the NEA was so carefully designed, in its enabling legislation, to insulate the artist from political intervention. Conservatives have grown obsessed with policing artistic expression for any evidence of deviation from norms of morality and patriotism, while liberals are pressing artistic expression into the service of social and political reform. One is reminded of poor Dr. Stockman, in Ibsen's *An Enemy of the People*, vainly trying to tell the community that its wells are poisoned, only to be drowned out by the deafening clamor of special pleading from the right and the left. In our pious climate, it is no wonder that the only issue on which everyone agrees is arts education, though, without the NEA, it is doubtful there will be much new art produced to be educated about. There's no sense in training riders when you're preparing to shoot the horse.

The crisis has forced the arts community into formulating its own political agenda. Just as the IRS has converted every citizen into an accountant, so recent events have turned many artists into marchers, campaigners, protesters, and First Amendment lawyers. Joe Papp has taken the radical step of refusing a $50,000 NEA grant for his Festival Latino because of the obscenity clause.* And while it is possible that he—unlike the rest of us—could continue to survive without his annual government grant to professional theatres (about 3 percent of the New

* A few months later, Papp refused an even larger grant, thus severing all ties with the NEA.

York Public Theater's budget as compared with 5 percent to 50 percent for small theatres), Papp's action puts pressure on all grantees to reconsider their relationship to the NEA. A letter-writing campaign originated by arts lobbies, designed to counteract an organized assault on the agency by such conservative groups as the American Family Association, has just begun to flood the postal boxes on Capitol Hill. But it is a sad commentary on our culture when the future of the arts in America is determined by a congressman's mail.

At the present time, it is certainly being determined by a congressman's bile. The same Helms-sponsored obscenity clause that impelled Joe Papp to refuse a grant has influenced the National Council on the Arts to cancel two more, while deferring another eighteen deemed to be controversial. According to one of its members, Jacob Neusner, the council thought that approving these grants would appear to be an act of defiance toward Congress: "We are listening to our critics . . . and we're not simply going to rubber stamp the decisions." Who said the NEA didn't have a policy? The policy is fear.

The fact is that, for a brief moment, America did have an arts policy. It was founded primarily on excellence, and administered by peer panels focused on artistic quality regardless (rather than *because*) of color, sex, ethnicity, or creed, whether "cutting edge" or Establishment. For that reason, the arts in this country, for a brief moment, were once a genuinely pluralistic expression. The concept of excellence—of meritocratic achievement within a democratic society—was not exclusive but embracing, and perfectly in harmony with our founding ideals. Excellence was a goal toward which any talented person could strive, and it was considered the function of government, rather than the obligation of the arts, to foster the social conditions that would help all qualified people attain it. Today, this concept is under general attack as racist, elitist, or discriminatory by those who have substituted relative values for absolute standards. As a result, respect for quality has become so alien to American life that a TV news special recently devoted a program to a Southern firm whose unusual distinction lay in trying to create a superior product. "The object," Chekhov said, "is to bring the people up to Gogol, not Gogol down to the people." Today, we placate the people not by trying to address their material needs but rather by turning culture into a populist wrecking ball, leaving Gogol buried under the rubble.

In his 1963 report to President Kennedy on the Arts and the National

Government—a report which preceded the founding of the NEA in 1965 by Lyndon Johnson—August Heckscher wrote that "the United States will be judged—and its place in history ultimately assessed—not alone by its military or economic power, but by the quality of its civilization." I am told that Kennedy, who read the report the same week he was assassinated, was preparing to use it as the basis for a major national initiative in the arts. At any rate, he replied to Heckscher: "I have long believed, as you know, that the quality of America's cultural life is an element of immense importance in the scales by which our worth will ultimately be weighed." I have always been skeptical of the Camelot mystique, but the tenor of this response is a far cry from Reagan's thin-lipped dismissal of the arts or Bush's halfhearted endorsement, and it is that change in tone that has strengthened the hand of those who would destroy the NEA.

Ultimately, despite its political form, the problem is a spiritual one. It is the result of American puritanism. This is clear enough in the fundamentalist religious attacks on anything that deviates from the purity and sanctity of some prelapsarian ideal. What is less clear is the puritanism of the left, which subjects the arts to utilitarian tests. For the same intolerant sectarianism that closed down English theatre for eighteen years (before seeking religious "freedom" in America) was also responsible for the belief that the doors of heaven are opened by charitable deeds. Thus, the arts today are valued not as good work but as "good works"—insofar as they can demonstrate their usefulness to the body politic through access, education, economic reinforcement, and social engineering. Or to use the bureaucratic language of a recently issued report, sponsored by both public and private granting agencies, it is the function of art to make "a profound impact on American society and the changes that are shaping it."

The function of art is indeed spiritual and formative, though not in the way our neo-Puritan friends believe. Great works of art suggest that humankind is capable of transcending its material needs, of penetrating to supernal depths, of remaking a badly fashioned world through the agency of the imagination. They do this sometimes through beauty and exaltation, sometimes through shock and provocation—at times in a traditional manner, at times through new forms—but always with the explicit or implicit purpose of rearranging consciousness and reordering the senses. The artist who creates this work may be a raging egotist, a moral idiot, a social misfit, a subversive scoundrel, but the work itself remains the ultimate measure of how he will be regarded in the future. For the artist may be answerable to society for his conduct. For his talent he is answerable only to posterity.

Let me complete this jeremiad with an anecdote from an ancient Chinese play (a variant can be found in the Book of Kings) which Bertolt Brecht used as the climax of *The Caucasian Chalk Circle*. In the adjudication of a maternity conflict, two women are asked to pull a child out of a circle in order to determine which is the true mother. The judge awards the child to the one who refuses, since she is obviously too fond of the boy to harm him. The opposing political forces now pulling the NEA to pieces are showing no such tender compunction.

Artistic Freedom and Political Repression

When the black smoke cleared after the Mapplethorpe and Serrano disputes over the propriety of awarding public funds to controversial art, an issue of vague concern had begun to take on clear and frightening definition: whether the independent arts enterprises of this country could continue to survive as autonomous creative entities in a political climate grown increasingly censorial. Contributed support, of course, has always been a critical problem for the nonprofit sector, which by definition depends as much on philanthropy as on earned income. What is significantly different today is the simultaneous convergence of social, political, economic, and moral constraints on the freedoms of our financially beleaguered arts institutions.

Pressures on the arts from the right and the left of the political spectrum first became apparent about thirteen years ago, during the early years of the Carter Administration. In the previous thirteen years, particularly in the Nixon Administration, the arts in America enjoyed a period of relative autonomy and growth. Sparked by W. McNeil Lowry's leadership at the Ford Foundation in the sixties and early seventies, when $80 million went to symphony orchestras and $25 million to resident theatres, large numbers of individuals, corporations, and private foundations began making significant grants to defray the operating costs of arts institutions. Most important of all was the creation of the National Endowment for the Arts in 1965—followed by subsidiary state councils—to provide small but stabilizing annual subsidies, along with important federal recognition, to the growing arts movement.

None of these sources of support was sufficient at the time to relieve our theatres, opera and dance companies, orchestras, and museums from the perennial need for annual fund-raising. Unlike more cultured nations, which provide between 60 percent and 100 percent of the budgets of arts institutions, our country has never been noted for its generosity toward collective nonprofit enterprises. It was, nevertheless, still possible for institutional art to keep afloat through a combination of federal, corporate, foundation, and individual giving, until these sources, one by one, began to dry up.

It was during the Carter years that private foundations began to withdraw from major arts giving, reducing their programs by as much as 80 percent and reserving the major portion of their grants for individuals rather than institutions. These foundations were never intended to be a permanent source of large subsidy, only a stimulus until other funding sources, particularly the federal government, recognized their obligation to the arts. This unhappily failed to materialize in a significant way, partly because the withdrawal of foundation money coincided with (and may have been caused by) an unfortunate dip in the economy which, in a liberal political administration, gave essential social services priority over "frills" like the arts. Under the chairmanship of Livingstone Biddle, the budget for the National Endowment, which had leaped encouragingly during the Nixon Administration, slowed to a crawl. Even more discouraging was the endowment's new "populist" stance in relation to "elitist" artistic expression, which subordinated standards of quality to criteria of social value, including geographical location, and ethnic, racial, and sexual status.

The politicization of the endowment from the left placed the arts in an increasingly embattled position over two related issues—funding and identity. A Theatre Communications Group (TCG) conference held at Yale in 1976 was almost entirely devoted to the question of arts advocacy, in preparation for mobilizing a lobbying group to stimulate increases in the federal arts budget. But McNeil Lowry's keynote address to the group identified an important and subtle issue: our obligation to define why the arts *deserved* to be funded. He appealed for a public policy which regarded artistic activity not as a useful extension of the educational or social process but as important in itself. Lowry also questioned the economic compromises of nonprofit theatre, particularly its increasing tendency to form an alliance with Broadway interests. Telling the conference that "it is very difficult to be just half-commercial," Lowry warned: "It is easier to popularize the arts away than to repress them."

In the mean-spirited climate later bequeathed us by Reagan, it is now clear that repression and popularization are *both* easy—indeed, may actually be the two faces of a market economy. Anyhow, nobody ever bothered to respond to Lowry's call for a public definition of the arts which would make excellence the primary criterion for support; and as a result, artists are now in the charming position of being subject both to liberal *and* conservative oversight, the one checking them for social and educational usefulness, the other monitoring their deviations from moral norms and religious pieties. Considering its ever-increasing reliance on Broadway for royalties and "enhancement money," the nonprofit theatre can even be said to be censoring itself. What is the celebrated "artistic deficit" but a hesitancy to produce projects considered too controversial to move to New York?

In the present decade, therefore, directors of theatres have been sharing decision-making with a number of unofficial co-artistic directors, all helping to determine their season's choices. Most corporate or foundation program directors, for example, can make grants to arts institutions only for narrow purposes determined by the social agenda of their parent organizations. One has an interest in women's theatre; another will fund projects involving the Third World; another is concerned with outreach programs in ghetto neighborhoods; another wants to develop young audiences; still another will underwrite programs for the handicapped. Compared with a time when corporations and foundations rewarded theatres primarily for their overall quality, even broader private programs today are relatively limiting—grants to comic plays, say, or to the development of musical theatre. The resourceful director of development knows that selling the theatre's track record is not enough. What he needs to attract funding is a musical comedy written by a blind black woman from Botswana, produced in a mobile unit capable of traveling to schools and underprivileged neighborhoods. With these grants in hand, an artistic director might even have enough surplus to underwrite a play he really wants to produce.

I do not wish to appear indifferent to the pressures on the private sector, which is charged with supporting social services now being neglected by government. Given the limited available funds, it is understandable why money to the arts would be expected to benefit other needy groups as well. But by pressuring the arts to help solve the problems of society, liberal funding agencies are helping to create an atmosphere in which artistic autonomy is virtually ceasing to exist. Worse, they are suggesting that the arts have no value in themselves except as a utilitarian agency of social change, which is rather like denying recognition to Shakespeare because he ignored the persecution of Catholics, or to Molière because he was indifferent to the plight of the Huguenots.

Of course, the theatre is equipped to deal with the evils of racism, sexual inequality, homelessness, anti-Semitism, and AIDS, as well as with cerebral palsy, muscular dystrophy, and mental retardation. But the social use of art has never been its major function, and it is safe to say that no problem was ever "solved" in the theatre. If you doubt this, watch homebound audiences, having been moved to tears by the plight of the poor in such plays as *Nicholas Nickleby* or *Les Misérables*, wending their careful way past the homeless lying on the nearby streets.

Constraints on the artist from the left today, however, are nothing to those now issuing from the right. The current assault on the National Endowment for the Arts by such Yahoo legislators as Jesse Helms and Alfonse D'Amato is surely a prelude to the extinction of everything daring, adventurous, and innovative left remarkable beneath the visiting moon. In our country, we don't sentence our artists to death, like the Ayatollah, or send them off to slave labor camps, like Stalin. Our more humanitarian method is to wave flags and brandish Bibles and remove their source of funding in the name of democracy and decency.

Helms and his like-minded cohorts on the Hill, along with such starched neoconservative critics as Samuel Lipman and Hilton Kramer, are simply reflecting the new reactionary ethos of our astonishingly retrograde society, and their message is clear—there will be no more federal support forthcoming for art that offends the majority. Hilton Kramer is too sophisticated to echo Helms's fundamentalist religious proscriptions, but his own position is not all that different. Although opposed to government intervention in the arts through systematic programs of censorship, he equates these with government intervention through systematic programs of support—citing such "antisocial" NEA-funded work as the Mapplethorpe and Serrano exhibits. Kramer's prejudices are moral and political, but he is subtle enough to cloak them in artistic judgments. He is opposed to all fads created by fashionable art-world establishments, including Richard Serra's morally neutral but (to him) aesthetically offensive *Tilted Arc*. What should the government support instead? Those artworks which Kramer calls "the highest achievements of our civilization." Invoking the same pious language, his colleague Samuel Lipman asks the NEA to reject "the latest fancies to hit the art market" and champion instead "the great art of the past, its regeneration in the present and its transmission to the future." Gradually, the real enemy begins to take shape—not a few "dirty" pictures, but the whole corpus of modern avant-garde art.

Senator Helms, citing the paintings of pastoral North Carolina scenes on his walls, says, "I like beautiful things, not modern art." The conservative preference for exaltation over provocation, for beauty over squalor, for the settled conditions of the past over the chaotic jumble of the present, seems a reasonable enough position—until we remember that much of the acceptable art today caused similar controversy when it first appeared. It is not the Congress but posterity that purifies works of art, and to limit federal support on the basis of moral health and social propriety is to impose conditions that will effectively halt the forward movement of creative expression. "It is not the function of art," said another political critic not too long ago, "to wallow in dirt for dirt's sake, never its task to paint men only in states of decay, to draw cretins as the symbol of motherhood, to picture hunchbacked idiots as representatives of manly strength . . . Art must be the handmaiden of sublimity and beauty and thus promote whatever is natural and healthy. If art does not do this, then any money spent on it is squandered." This is not Hilton Kramer or Samuel Lipman speaking—or even Jesse Helms or Alfonse D'Amato. It is from a speech made in Nuremberg by Adolf Hitler, inveighing against "degenerate" modern art.

Conservatives would probably reply that, unlike censors in Hitler's Germany or Stalin's Soviet Union or Khomeini's Iran, they are not calling for suppression of unpopular art, only for its exclusion from federal funding. Helms asserts that "if someone wants to write nasty things on the men's room wall, the taxpayers do not provide the crayons." A letter signed by twenty-seven senators and written on D'Amato's stationery says: "This matter does not involve freedom of expression. It does involve whether taxpayers' money should be forced to support such trash." And a D'Amato staff member adds that the senator was "absolutely opposed to censorship, but we are talking about taxpayers' dollars." The distinction between censorship and dictating the distribution of taxpayers' dollars on moral grounds is one that eludes me—but it reflects the American conviction that the marketplace should remain the unofficial censor of the arts.

In response to this congressional reaction, an independent commission in Washington—co-chaired by John Brademas and Leonard Garment—was charged with reevaluating the NEA in preparation for a report to Congress which would determine whether the agency will be permitted to survive, and if so, whether in its original form or with the restrictive anti-obscenity language enraging artists throughout the country. Among the questions posed by the commission to a number of witnesses were "whether the standard for publicly funded art should be different from the standard for privately funded art" and why the people of this country should be forced to contribute their "hard-earned tax dollars" to artistic projects they either ignore or despise.

I was one of the witnesses before the commission and my answer to the first question was an unequivocal no. There can be only one standard for arts funding and that is excellence, the artistic merit of the work (despite the current idea, recently endorsed by *The New York Times*, that "quality" is merely a buzz word for maintaining white male Eurocentric culture). As for the push to exclude the avant-garde from federal funding because it offends the majority, this would have effectively created a custodial culture, dedicated to preserving the great works of the past which have outlived their initial shock value.

The commission's second question seemed on the surface to be a fair one and harder to answer, though one might wonder why it was just now being raised, following the NEA's twenty-five-year success story. The question is also puzzling considering that the "hard-earned tax dollars" going to the NEA actually amount to 60 cents per person, representing an infinitesimal fraction of the national budget. Surely we taxpayers have very little direct say in how any of our dollars are spent. How much control do we have over expenditures for the infinitely more costly Stealth bomber, the funding of the Contras, the SDI program, or the multibillion-dollar S&L bailout?

The muddle arises, as Harvard's Kathleen Sullivan tells us, from confusing a constitutional with a majoritarian democracy. Not everything in this country is determined by polls and ballot boxes or by what Mencken called the "boobocracy." The Bill of Rights is specifically dedicated to protecting the rights of minorities, including artists, against the potential tyranny of the many. And a primary constitutional guarantee is the protection of free speech uttered by those whose views seem eccentric, unpopular, radical, shocking, or dangerous to organized groups. There are those, myself included, who believe the current assault on the NEA to be an infringement of First Amendment rights. People who disagree tell us that governments never fund their dissidents. Well, they did in Periclean Athens. Aristophanes won state prizes for anti-war and anti-government plays in the midst of a bloody conflict with Sparta. We are also told that denying federal subsidy is not the same as censorship, since the artist can always seek private support or fall back on the marketplace. What is not properly understood is that censorship in this country takes an economic as well as a political form. Here the marketplace can function as repressively as any Commissar of Culture.

Unless, as in the case of Karen Finley, publicity turns the defunded artist into a star, what usually flourishes in the marketplace is popular or majority culture: the television series, the rock concert, the block-buster movie, the Broadway musical. But even popular culture would have little future without the less popular arts—as Klee and Mondrian influenced advertising, Bach influenced the Beatles, and performance art influenced *A Chorus Line*. We subsidize this art, even if we don't like or attend it, for the same reason that we contribute our tax dollars to cancer research, though most of us fortunately don't have tumors. The results, immediately visible only to the few, will eventually spread their benefits to the many.

The major issue remains the question of choice. Those who find the Mapplethorpe or Serrano photographs disgusting and hateful, or don't like the way Karen Finley uses chocolate, can always see their 60 cents spent somewhere else. But branding these works obscene and banning them from federal funding is to deny others the option of deciding for themselves.

The question of whether the federal government should be funding art that a majority of Americans find unpalatable is, therefore, a red herring. The real question is whether federal arts funding is to be supervised by experts drawn from the field or by congressional overseers, in their role of representing the interests of the popular electorate.

This question was confronted in the original enabling legislation of the endowment, which was created precisely to prevent politicians from voting directly on artists or artistic projects. An unequivocal paragraph stated: "No department, agency, officer, or employee of the United States shall exercise any direction, supervision, or control over the policy, determination, personnel, or curriculum, or the administration or operation of any school or other non-federal agency, institution, organization, or association." In other words, the agency was intended to serve as a buffer between Congress and the arts, with the legislators responsible for approving the budget and professional peer panels responsible for approving grants. Congress was never empowered to be a watchdog on the endowment as it is, say, on the Pentagon. It was rather intended to guarantee the integrity of the grant-making procedure, however controversial. For twenty-five years, this pact was observed. The decisions of the panels were rarely, if ever, overruled; and only twenty grants out of a total of more than 85,000 were ever even questioned.

Today, Congress seems to have forgotten that the original purpose of the endowment was to support "free art and free expression," which clearly means to satisfy the needs of artists, not the tastes of the democratic majority. It was never the intention of the endowment to subsidize popular taste. No, the National Endowment was designed as a counter-market strategy, in the hope that by subsidizing cultural offerings at affordable prices the works of serious art could become available to all those normally excluded by income or education. This is a far cry from providing federal funding for "what the people want."

Critics like Kramer secretly acknowledge this argument and counter it by trying to discredit the credentials of professional panelists. "Professional opinion in the art world," he writes, "can no longer be expected to make wise decisions on these matters . . . There is in the professional art world a sentimental attachment to the idea that art is at its best when it is most extreme and disruptive." That may be true at times—and it is true that some artists like to flout prevailing codes of conduct. Still, the professional panel system, for all its flaws, remains the best we have, and it is clearly preferable to the punitive grant procedures being prepared by our elected politicians.

This political school of criticism has now proposed banning grants for five years to the Institute of Contemporary Art in Philadelphia and the Southeastern Center for Contemporary Art in Winston-Salem because they supported the Mapplethorpe and Serrano shows. It has dropped the School of Art Institute of Chicago from its customary $130,000 grant to a symbolic dollar because of a controversial flag exhibit. It has withheld funding from the Detroit Symphony until it hires a black musician, thus violating a time-honored tradition to hold auditions behind a curtain. It first canceled the entire funding of the Massachusetts Council on the Arts and Humanities, then relented and restored less than half of its previous $25 million appropriation. Other state councils are slashing their budgets. And the Congress has voted $100,000 to review the grant-making procedures of the National Endowment. The Bowdlers and Mrs. Grundys and Senator Claghorns are on the march, and unless the pendulum swings back to a position of reasonableness and sanity, nothing will stop their progress toward the promised land of moral purity.

Individual artists will survive this onslaught. They always have. T. S. Eliot could work in a bank; William Carlos Williams could practice medicine; Wallace Stevens could join an insurance firm in Hartford; Van Gogh could still paint in an asylum; Gauguin could go to Tahiti. But the institutions that publish and display and produce the works of individual artists are now faced with the prospect of ignoring controversial work and satisfying conventional tastes or going under. In the 1930s, a great experiment known as the Federal Theatre was killed by the political ax of an ignorant Congress. With government funding in jeopardy, and private funding dwindling, the great experiment of our own time that brought the arts in America to the forefront of world culture is also in jeopardy of being extinguished. To save it, we must seek concerted political action, we must write letters, we must arouse our audiences, we must scream, we must howl, we must stamp our feet. Otherwise, I do not think it apocalyptic to say that all that will be left of American culture will be sanitized versions of the classics and the North Carolina landscapes on Jesse Helms's wall.

(1989–90)

As the *Globe* Turns

Subterranean tensions have traditionally existed between the arts community of Boston and the city's newspaper of record, the *Globe*, regarding the nature of its coverage and the competence of its reviewers. Following the appointment of Lincoln Millstein as Living Arts editor in January 1989, these tensions erupted into open warfare. The latest salvo was a missile attack—thirteen articles and an editorial, occupying three days and over a hundred columns of newsprint, about the failings of Boston's museums, theatres, galleries, opera and dance companies, and musical organizations. "The Fine Arts: A World Without Color" said nothing about the quality of nonprofit institutions. The series' purpose was to charge them with "elitism," "exclusionism," and a lack of "multicultural diversity." I report this both as a witness of the *Globe*'s disciplining of the arts and as one of the alleged miscreants.

Not only was the American Repertory Theatre, where I am artistic director, among the many organizations chastened for failing to provide sufficient outlets for minority expression or employment opportunities for "people of color," but I was personally paddled last spring by *Globe* critics Kevin Kelly and Patti Hartigan, in two long, vituperative articles, for criticizing August Wilson's *The Piano Lesson* and the way it was brought to Broadway.

Recognizing that I am one of the players in this controversy, readers may choose to discount what follows as special pleading. The *Globe*, in fact, has already charged me with conflict of interest, not to mention envy, revenge, hypocrisy, prejudice, and paranoia, because I was the founding director of the institution that originated *The Piano Lesson*, the Yale Repertory Theatre. It is possible, too, that the flap may strike you as a parochial matter, of marginal interest to those living outside Boston. Still, the underlying issues strike me as sufficiently typical of the way a powerful newspaper can abuse its cultural influence—and how sociopolitical pressures are choking artistic endeavor—to warrant wider discussion, even from what might be construed as a subjective source.

Actually, the *Globe*'s hostile treatment of the arts had already come to wide attention last summer when Fox Butterfield, Boston bureau representative for *The New York Times*, wrote an article about the theft of paintings at the Isabella Stewart Gardner Museum. In the course of his report, he mentioned that the Gardner's new executive director, Anne Hawley (former head of the Massachusetts Council on the Arts and Humanities), had been threatened with retaliation by the *Globe*'s Living Arts editor when she didn't open a room, sealed by the FBI, to his reporter. "You can tell Anne Hawley for me," Millstein allegedly said to a museum aide, who relayed the conversation to the Boston *Phoenix*, "that she fucked up at the arts council and she's fucking up at the Gardner. I'm going to get her. I'm going to rip her to shreds." (Millstein denied making the remark but regretted using "bad language.") Soon after, the *Globe* published a long damaging article on the Gardner charging Hawley, among other derelictions, with permitting the collection to deteriorate, though she had been at the museum for only a few months.

When *The Village Voice* and the Boston *Phoenix* decided to pursue the story, both papers received calls saying Butterfield was bitter because his wife, a respected *Los Angeles Times* reporter, had been turned down for a job at the *Globe*. (In fact, the approach came from the

Globe, which couldn't match her salary.) The whispers were published; the *Globe*'s celebrated method of defaming the messenger discouraged Butterfield from writing a projected follow-up piece. The issue lay dormant until Maureen Dezell wrote a longer story in the *Phoenix* detailing the resentments of Boston's arts leaders toward the *Globe*. Fearful of retaliation, most refused to speak for the record. Being another recently defamed messenger, I also refused. But I did send a letter to Max Frankel at the *Times* saluting Butterfield's courage, attesting to his accuracy, and mentioning an article I had written in 1986, at the *Globe*'s behest. Then, a relative newcomer to the city and still untouched myself, I spoke of the malice I detected on the part of the newspaper toward virtually all of Boston's arts leaders (local expatriate hero Peter Sellars excluded): Seiji Ozawa of the Boston Symphony, Sarah Caldwell of the Opera Company, Bruce Marks of the Boston Ballet, David Ross of the Institute for Contemporary Arts, Anne Hawley as head of the Mass. Council—and later Christopher Hogwood of the Handel and Haydn Society.

Millstein later called our press office, saying he knew of this letter and wondering if the ART was dissatisfied with our coverage or with him. Actually, I had met him only once, when he first took over his position, to retail the litany of complaints that I, along with other arts people, had long been reciting to editors at the *Globe*. He seemed congenial enough at the time, and his colleagues attest to his loyalty and friendship. But he has no background in the arts ("I'm a journalist," he says) and shows little interest in culture other than movies and rock music (the *Globe*'s Sunday section, called "Arts Etc.," is mostly just "Etc."). In an address to a group of arts representatives, he told them his primary function was "to sell newspapers" (Millstein previously served on the *Globe* as Business Editor). Still, his editorship has not been used purely to promote circulation: he also has a generally recognized instinct for retaliatory strikes, which was thoroughly documented in Dezell's article. "One by one, he's attacked the arts leadership of Boston," said Larry Murray, chairman of the Midtown Cultural District Task Force, which had also suffered indignity at the hands of the *Globe*. "Millstein can't wait to write the obituary for the arts in this city."

Another figure willing to speak for the record is David Ross, recently appointed director of the Whitney Museum in New York after serving eight years as head of the ICA. Reported in the *Globe* as leaving Boston because he couldn't find enough "cultural diversity" here, he offered reasons in a recent *Phoenix* interview that sound a little more plausible: "The *Globe* is an unacknowledged co-conspirator in the malaise of Boston's cultural institutions . . . It's not taking a role as an educator or to provoke people to participate in Boston's cultural community . . . At the *Globe*, there's a know-nothing attitude, an anti-intellectual bias—an attitude of ingrown hostility toward the arts. In the arts community, there's a sense the *Globe* is our adversary." Or as a national foundation head recently put it, "The only trouble with the arts in Boston is the Boston *Globe*."

Given Millstein's provocative nature—and the fact that, despite his Jewish name, he's Asian-American—many now suspect that the recent series on the lack of "diversity" in Boston's cultural institutions was an effort to combine genuine minority concerns (he told me it was motivated by the flap over the casting of *Miss Saigon*) with some swipes at those who had been criticizing the *Globe*'s arts coverage. For this multiple purpose, he assigned Patti Hartigan, a reporter who had previously written articles criticizing Boston theatres for failing to hire enough local actors or minorities or women, assisted by Diane E. Lewis, one of the few blacks on the staff of the newspaper. Based on innumerable interviews with Boston's arts leaders, the investigation was essentially a statistical breakdown of the companies, staffs, audiences, and boards of all the major cultural institutions in regard to the way they employed "people of color" (the *Globe*'s preferred euphemism for anyone not pink). Hartigan's conclusion was that all these institutions, with the single exception of the Children's Museum (a "beacon of light"), were "dominated by middle-class and wealthy whites, with little representation from racial groups that are expected to make up more than 40 percent of the Boston population by the year 2000 and to exceed the white population two or three decades later."

The ART was the only local institution, under my instructions, that refused to supply her with statistics. This she mentioned more than once in the course of the articles, along with the fact that I, alone among Boston arts figures, had refused to be interviewed by her. This spared me the ignominy of wearing a hair shirt in public; I was rewarded instead with a scarlet letter. Though she had been told the reasons, off the record, in her interview with Managing Director Robert J. Orchard, both omissions were made to sound racist. Actually, I had determined not to talk with any reporter who had already misrepresented my views, and I wanted to protect my colleagues from racial inquisitions. Orthodox ACLU liberals were taught not to respond to inquiries into the racial, religious, political, or sexual background and preferences of people they worked with because these inquiries might be used for malevolent discriminatory reasons. Now, in the context of contemporary "political correctness," such inquiries were being used for more benign purposes of reverse discrimination—but considering the pendulum swings of history, who could tell what the future would bring?

As it happens, the ART is as well provided with minority company contracts on stage this year as any cultural institution in the city (perhaps in fact better)—but statistics cannot tell the whole story. Numbers change from season to season, partly influenced by production needs, partly by the willingness of skilled minority actors (who are much sought after) to join a resident company—or move to a racially tense city—at salaries considerably lower than they can make in movies or television. But to play this numbers game is to distract attention from the primary purpose of cultural institutions, which is to create works of art with high standards. This is not always identical with satisfying the requirements of social engineering. A member of a minority group himself, Seiji Ozawa properly identified racial discrimination as the biggest problem in America, but added that he wasn't hired as conductor of the BSO to resolve it. It was his job to make music. Challenged over whom he would choose between two musicians of equal quality—one black, one white—he replied: "The better one."

Although Boston is considered a racist city, no one I know in the liberal-minded Boston arts scene is indifferent to the pressing needs of minorities or less than outraged by the social inequities of the system. But there is a difference between equality of opportunity and equality of representation. It is simply no longer accurate to say that "blacks have to be better than their competition"—skilled black artists are now at a premium. And so the *Globe*'s attempt to equate the comparatively low number of minorities in high culture (as compared with the population) in 1991 with the way the great contralto Marian Anderson was prevented from singing in Washington in 1939 is historically specious. The doors of culture are open to everyone qualified to enter them, either as artists or as spectators. Yet the *Globe* invariably detects evidence of discrimination, blaming, say, the absence of black faces at the Museum of Fine Arts on the fact that everything there is white, from the marble on the floor to the staff, to the sculptures, to the paintings on the wall.

The *Globe* was particularly hard on the Museum of Fine Arts, an easy mark as a Brahmin stronghold, for reflecting what the series called "the values and Eurocentric art traditions of the city's elite" (racism was also detected in the very origins of dance as practiced by the Boston Ballet, in the very traditions of classical music as performed by the Boston Symphony). "There is almost no overlap," the *Globe* complained with astonishment, "between the audiences at mainstream organizations and the audiences at community centers." And while it stopped just short of asking the Handel and Haydn Society to stop playing eighteenth-century music, it did say that "the all white composition of the audiences . . . is a visual declaration of the increasing chasm." (For all the talk of accessibility, the *Globe* approvingly cited August Wilson and Lloyd Richards for rejecting the idea of inclusion in Western art as an affront to the integrity of black culture.)

Not only was the whole Western cultural tradition considered a source of discrimination, but the series even went on to impute racist motives to the fact that the museum has been forced, for financial reasons, to close its Huntington Avenue entrance ("What does that say to the urban population?") and to change its free hours from Saturday morning to Wednesday afternoon, while criticizing the failure of all Boston's cultural institutions to attract and support minorities in their training programs, or to subsidize underprivileged audiences.

These remarks suggest a kind of willed naïveté about the financial condition of the nonprofit world in the present day, particularly in Boston. For despite the city's reputation as the Athens of America, Boston has one of the worst records in the country for support of the arts, not only from the financial community, but from the media that might help change the situation (even well-endowed dinosaurs like the MFA and the BSO are hurting). The city ranks fiftieth among urban areas in corporate giving; the BSO is the only symphony in the nation that doesn't receive city money and the MFA is the only major museum not sitting on city land; virtually no private foundations support the arts; and the Mass. Council has lost most of its funding through legislative action. All but the largest cultural institutions in Boston are at the poverty level, which suggests why the *Globe*'s proposal for more minority representation in the arts is fiscally disingenuous. Even were the money available for additional staffing, outreach programs, and "multicultural" expression, affirmative action of the kind the *Globe* proposes would have little immediate impact on minority advancement in the arts. Twenty-three percent of Boston's population is black, but only a very small percentage is middle-class; and class not race drives the appetite for high culture. As Shelby Steele observes in *The Content of Our Character*, having noted a 74 percent dropout rate in the numbers of black university students, there will be no advantage to entitlements, preferences, and other sops to self-esteem if the society does not help blacks and other minorities develop the skills to enjoy them.

This is the task of families, the schools, and the media, all of which are failing in the crucial area of educating taste and developing appreciation for our arts (which, as Edward Rothstein notes, are deeply appreciated in Asia). It is certainly a failure of the *Globe*, which refuses to see a difference between high and popular culture, between the imperatives of the imagination and the need for prestige, between adding minority harpists to the Symphony and sniping at the "Eurocentric" classical repertory, between racial assimilation and self-segregation, between artistic homes and "multicultural" civic centers—or between an organization devoted to producing art and a community-driven museum for children. On governing boards, the proposed changes would be cosmetic. Though they also serve as bridges to the community, boards are formed not on the basis of racial or ethnic diversity but according to who is supportive enough to help raise money for needy institutions. As for staffs and companies, this is a situation which can and must be improved. The task is to find, or train, qualified members of minorities, and to find the means to afford them.

The problem is not that Western culture is closed to diversity but that it has been too intimidated to insist on standards. To do otherwise is condescending and patronizing. What Steele writes about universities is true of cultural institutions: they can never be "free of guilt until they truly help black students, which means leading and challenging them rather than negotiating and capitulating." The courage with which this idea is expressed almost restores one's faith in independent thought.

The *Globe*'s *Kulturkampf* against "elitism" may be a sincere ideological posture. But it fits in snugly with Millstein's declared mandate to increase circulation. Now that the Murdoch-owned Boston *Herald* is drawing away advertisers and subscribers, the *Globe* has apparently decided to attract a tabloid readership without losing its reputation as a liberal journal—through a little Brahmin-bashing. The paper (according to one of its jaundiced editors) has always been interested exclusively in "the indoor sport of politics and the outdoor sport of baseball"; the arts are a source of mystification and indifference to the higher echelon. This may account for the inferior quality of *Globe* reviewers (the exception is Jay Carr in movies, though Richard Dyer in music, while guilty of glaring prejudices, is at least literate). Long-ensconced and occupying well-fortified fiefdoms, unaccountable and impervious to the almost universal complaints of the cultural community, these reviewers add daily artillery to the unequal war between the city's culture and the city's paper of record.

The conduct of the *Globe* in regard to the arts, then, is not merely an instance of how one organ of the news can help to debase standards, lower morale, and ignore achievement. It is not even a story of how one idiosyncratic editor can use his power for purposes of intimidation. The storm was brewing before the arrival of Millstein—and will no doubt continue to rage after his rumored departure. Rather, it strikes me as a significant symptom of a germ that has begun to infest the mind of our entire country. The philistinism of the *Globe* is now taking a political form, reflected in a number of our institutions. It is influencing our art, our education, our very notions of progress. It is responsible for the perpetuation of unexamined ideas, thoughtless prescriptions, facile sentimental solutions. Martin Luther King, Jr., used to say he was less interested in the future of black people than in the future of America; it was just that America's future was intimately bound up with the resolution of the black problem. This majestic unifying insight could never be uttered today, when we have broken into dozens of isolated constituencies, each arguing for moral, social, and aesthetic supremacy. After King's death, the escalating protests on behalf of peace and civil rights turned to violence, separatism, and powerful assaults on intellectual authority itself; yet one could still believe, for all the youthful hysteria in the university, that the adult liberal centers were keeping their reason. Now that confidence is dwindling. The radicals who once occupied university buildings are inside the walls as members of the tenured professoriate, blocking dissent and political deviation, controlling hiring, monitoring the curriculum. They are also sitting at the heads of foundations, in the agencies of government—and in the newsrooms of powerful newspapers.

The intellectual atmosphere is filled with stifling vapors, and the gas is being expelled not just by Jesse Helms. The National Endowment for the Arts is beginning to penalize those grantees that cannot justify themselves on the basis of minority representation, and most of the private foundations are focusing on "multicultural" programs and audience development. This political agenda is being enforced on behalf of minorities, but there is one minority that's been excluded—the artist, who works on behalf of the imagination, unmindful of color, regardless of race, unused to being told precisely what and how to create. It is problematic whether this superficial approach to racial reconciliation will resolve our social conflicts or advance minorities. There is no doubt whatever that it will block the flow of free expression in the arts.

(1991)

Politics and Theatre

The relationship between politics and the arts, particularly in the context of the theatre, is a large issue which has been a matter of heated contention ever since Thespis first broke ranks with the Chorus, and it is alive in the American theatre today. The first to start these fevers roaring was Plato, who refused to admit the illusion-making dramatist, or any artist for that matter, through the portals of his ideal Republic. In less obdurate moments, Plato was willing to tolerate an art which held up ethical models of behavior for humankind to imitate—what he called *ethos*. Nevertheless, he maintained that the artist was a serious threat to a utopian politics.

Aristotle's *Poetics*, written not too long after Plato rejected the artist, may very well have been an effort to refute this argument. Rather than considering the dramatist a liar, Aristotle held that works of art, particularly tragedies, were among the highest forms of human activity. Far from masking reality, they had the capacity to bring us even closer to the truth than politics or philosophy. It is significant that, in listing the elements of tragic writing, Aristotle found *mythos*—variously translated as plot or fable or action—to be preeminent, while *ethos*, or character, he placed second in order of importance. Lower than these was *dianoia*—what a character says about the course to be pursued, what a person believes, his social morality—sometimes translated as "politics" or "thought."

In short, Aristotle considered the imagination to be not a source of fantasy or illusion but rather the supreme human faculty, and imitation, which Plato scorned, to be an important mode of understanding. He didn't exclude politics from the drama, but he most certainly subordinated it, and he seemed to believe that one's morality was of interest less for being right or wrong than for the way it illuminated action and character. In this regard, Aristotle's concept of *hamartia* assumes a crucial importance to our understanding of his tragic theory. Although sometimes translated as tragic flaw—medieval Christians appropriated the word to mean *sin*, suggesting a severe judgment on human morals and behavior—*hamartia* more accurately means *tragic error*, which is to say, a mistake that brings on tragedy. Oedipus' doom occurs not because of a character defect, not because he is proud or sinful, as some commentators describe his *hamartia*, but because he killed his father, Laius, at the crossroads, even though Laius provoked the act and Oedipus was ignorant of their true relationship. In other words, Aristotle believes that moral behavior and correct opinions are less relevant to tragedy than necessity. We suffer tragedy not because of our character or beliefs but rather because we have broken some inexorable law of the universe—like sticking a wet finger in a live electrical socket.

The disagreement between Plato and Aristotle concerning the function of art and the avenue to truth sparked twenty-five hundred years of contentious argumentation. Plato's assumptions permeated the medieval theatre, the seedbed for all Western drama; they influenced the Puritan hostility toward the stage, which led to the closing of English theatres for eighteen years; and they informed that utilitarian idea of art which, though it repelled Alexis de Tocqueville in his study of democracy in America, still dominates our culture today. The basic disagreement between Plato and Aristotle was whether the theatre has importance as an instrument of moral and political action, or whether it is an imaginative experience with no apparent usefulness beyond the purgation and exaltation (*katharsis*) of its audiences. But whereas Aristotelian theatre is an end in itself, complete and self-contained, designed to spend and discharge the passions of the audience, Platonic theatre is a means toward a future goal, not to be achieved until the audience, excited to passion by the spectacle before it, emerges into the world to resolve these tensions through some form of active intervention.

Platonic theatre, therefore, is political theatre, in the sense that it is intended to influence behavior, if not to change the world. It is political in a larger meaning of the word, because it offers to resolve ethical, moral, social, even religious issues through improvement and persuasion; it embodies a dynamic which continues to operate after the play is concluded. Theoretically, Platonic theatre carries the seeds of its own extinction, since it will have no function once the utopian state has arrived (a prospect that appalled such Aristotelians as Nietzsche, who believed that imaginative experience is a compelling human need, that we have art so as not to perish from the truth).

Still, this "anti-theatrical prejudice," as Jonas Barish calls it in a book of that title, is the motif underlying the Platonic political view of the theatre, and it dies hard. It can be detected even among some practicing dramatists in the modern age, where the conflict between the Aristotelian and Platonic, or aesthetic and utilitarian, views of the stage continues unabated. In Ibsen, the conflict is internalized, becoming the basis for his continuing quarrels with himself, not to mention persistent disagreements among his interpreters. For example, is *A Doll's House* Platonic or Aristotelian? What about *Ghosts*? Or *An Enemy of the People*?

Ibsen is deceptive because on the surface he seems to be embracing this responsibility. He has been claimed by both liberals and conservatives as an advocate of the women's movement, a proponent of euthanasia, a supporter of companionate marriages, a firm believer in social responsibility. Doubtless Ibsen was interested in these issues, and drawn into the orbit of social concerns, but he continued to insist that his interest was artistic rather than political, and therefore essentially analytical and descriptive. Addressing the Norwegian League for Women's Rights, he decisively repudiated any conscious ideological intent: "I am not a member of the Women's Rights League," he said. "Whatever I have written has been written without any conscious thought of making propaganda. I have been more the poet and less the social philosopher than people seem generally inclined to believe. I thank you for the toast, but must disclaim the honor of having consciously worked for the women's rights movement. I am not even quite clear as to just what this women's rights movement really is. To me, it has seemed a problem of mankind in general . . . True enough, it is desirable to solve the woman problem, along with all the others; but that has not been the whole purpose. My task has been the *description of humanity*" (tr. Evert Sprinchorn).

This is the answer Ibsen gave to every group that tried to expropriate him for its cause and explains why he always appeared so inconsistent to his progressive followers. "I shall never agree," he wrote to one of them, "to making liberty synonymous with political liberty. What you call liberty, I call liberties; and what I call the struggle for liberty is nothing but the steady, vital growth and pursuit of the very conception of liberty . . . The state must be abolished! In that revolution I will take part. Undermine the idea of the state; make willingness and spiritual kinship the only essentials for union—and you have the beginning of a liberty that is of some value. Changing one form of government for another is merely a matter of toying with various degrees of the same thing. Yes, my friend, the great thing is not to allow oneself to be frightened by the venerableness of institutions. The state has its roots in time; it will reach its height in time."

This is not a Platonist talking but an anarchist who would blow up even the ideal Republic in order to create breathing space and room for life. It is true that Ibsen occasionally grows tendentious, even propagandistic, on behalf of his individualist philosophy—particularly in *An Enemy of the People*—but it is not long before he is announcing a contrary point of view lest he settle into a single fixed position. The only permanent structure that Ibsen can long tolerate is the structure of his own art, because only there can he accommodate the contradictions and antitheses that for him constitute the fabric of truth.

Anton Chekhov is even less of a Platonist than Ibsen, because in his plays he seems to have virtually no formal beliefs of his own and displays scant respect for the beliefs of his characters as well. Ibsen wrote indignantly after *Ghosts*: "They endeavor to make me responsible for the opinions which certain of my characters express," but compared to Chekhov, this impersonal dramatist almost seems like a ventriloquist. No one has labored harder than Chekhov to keep the theatre free from political imperatives and utilitarian demands. "To hell with the philosophy of the great of this world," he wrote in an uncharacteristically rancorous mood. And even more pointedly: "I am not a liberal and not a conservative, not an evolutionist, nor a monk, nor indifferent to the world. I would like to be a free artist, and that is all."

"In my discussions with other writers," Chekhov wrote in a letter of 1888, "I always insist that it is not the artist's business to answer narrowly specialized issues. It is bad if a writer tackles a subject he doesn't understand. For specialized issues we have the specialist; it's their business to pass judgment about the peasant communes, the fate of capitalism, the damage of heavy drinking, boots, or women's ailments. As for the artist, he must pass judgment only about matters he can grasp; the artist's range is just as limited as that of any specialist . . . Anyone who insists the artist's domain covers all the answers and is free of any questions, has never written or has had no experience with images . . . You are right in requiring from the artist a conscious attitude towards his work, but you confuse two aspects: *the answer to a problem* and *the correct presentation of a problem.* Only the second is an obligation for the artist."

Chekhov was said by his contemporaries to have had an indefinite attitude toward what one of them called "the *burning questions* of the day," and he was proud that his characters were not created out of preconceived ideas or intellectual assumptions. But this does not mean that he excluded social and political questions from his plays. The debates over the future that permeate *The Three Sisters* were undoubtedly overheard by Chekhov in Moscow drawing rooms, and the original speeches of the revolutionary student Trofimov in *The Cherry Orchard* were said to have been so inflammatory that the play was threatened with suppression until he agreed to modify them. On the other hand, these opinions are never the personal property of the playwright; they belong to the people who express them, and exist, in Aristotelian fashion, to reveal character. In short, Chekhov introduced political, social, philosophical discussions into his work because these comprised the reality he was eager to present. But he was careful never to take sides or hint at solutions. As he put it in his favorite courtroom metaphor, "It is the duty of the judge to put the questions to the jury accurately, and it is for members of the jury to make up their minds, each according to his own taste."

Just as he tried to protect his characters from conventional moralistic interpretations of their behavior, so he tried to preserve their integrity as complicated human beings against narrow ideological interpretations of them as figures in a political chess game. Thus, Chekhov provided his characters with class roles, political convictions, and philosophic attitudes, but he never entirely defined them by these elements, even when they wished thus to define themselves. For Chekhov, the political animal and the suffering human often seem mutually incompatible.

It was because of their desire to protect the privacy of the individual from public imperatives that both Ibsen and Chekhov adopted, in their art, a stance aloof from civic responsibilities. Ibsen carried this posture so far that he elected exile in a variety of foreign countries rather than accommodate himself to the will of his countrymen. Although he never lost his love of his homeland, and never ceased to be primarily engaged with its problems, Ibsen maintained antisocial attitudes to the end of his life, practicing—like his Irish disciple, James Joyce—silence, exile, and cunning for the sake of an unmediated art. He paid a high price for this in homelessness and isolation, but it was, he believed, the only strategy by which he could preserve his commitment to the truth and his independence from causes, no matter how worthy. Living in prerevolutionary times, Chekhov and Ibsen were perhaps the last dramatists able to preserve a precious individualism without losing touch with social reality.

The concept of the "free artist," immune to political imperatives, ignoring any claims on him to be a mouthpiece for a movement or even a citizen of a state, was something Ibsen and Chekhov held in balance with a deep, abiding feeling for the human potential, a hatred of injustice, and a love of truth. This concept, however, was soon to find a more disembodied and fantastic expression in the work of modern poets, painters, novelists, and playwrights eager to divorce themselves entirely from the coarse reality of the modern industrial state. It animated the aesthetic movement of the late nineteenth century, perhaps the most extreme example we have of the separation of art from politics, if not from life. Villiers de l'Isle-Adam, the aesthete, announced: "As for living, our servants can do that for us"; Dada was devoted to an art of randomness and chance; and the Symbolist playwrights (especially Maeterlinck) took refuge from life in a world of supernal unreality.

The advent of aestheticism was bound to stimulate an adversary reaction from playwrights with a strong political conscience. And, sure enough, the drama of the twentieth century became dominated by two figures—Bernard Shaw and Bertolt Brecht—who not only held a more or less Platonic view of the stage but often scourged the Aristotelian tendencies of past and present writers.

Consider Shaw's attitude toward Shakespeare, a dramatist whose "romantic" theatre of lies and dreams, as he called it, he wanted to replace with a theatre of preachment and propaganda—"Plays for Puritans" was his significant subtitle. Calling himself an "artist-philosopher" rather than an artist, Shaw wished to scourge all art which relied on "mere" feeling instead of thought, and through the agency of artist characters like Marchbanks and Dubedat, he ridiculed the aesthetic tendencies of those who used poetry or painting for "mere" self-expression, or ruthlessly sacrificed the good of humanity for the perfection of their forms. Platonist though he was, however, Shaw continually tried to find ways to *include* the artist in his ideal Republic, if only by proving that the artist had utilitarian value. For at the same time that Shaw is a Platonic thinker, he is also an Aristotelian maker, whose ideas are only one element, and not always the most important one, in the body of his dramatic work. William Archer first came upon Shaw in the British Museum reading *Das Kapital* side by side with Wagner's *Ring* Cycle. And though Shaw tried to justify Wagner's aestheticism by interpreting *The Ring* as an allegory of the Industrial Revolution, the split in his own nature between the ethical and aesthetic ideals of art was never fully healed.

Bertolt Brecht couldn't heal that split either, but not for want of trying. Few in modern history worked harder to annihilate the Aristotelian theatre of feeling and replace it with a theatre of didactic thought devoted to promoting political change. Shaw's politics were always modified by the kindness of his own nature and the gradualism of his Fabian beliefs; Brecht's are intensified by his savage indignation and his harrowing vision of life. Shaw was a suppressed poet who rarely broke the skin of the unconscious, and while he called himself a puritan, he kept an abiding faith in human goodness and decency; Brecht was a lyric and dramatic poet of fierce intensity, and few Calvinist theologians have been more obsessed with the brutal, the satanic, the irrational side of behavior. Brecht's concern with the darker aspects of human nature grows out of his struggles with himself, but also characterizes his relationship to Communism. Shaw's Fabianism reflects his own genial personality; Brecht's Communism is a strict discipline imposed on an essentially morbid and sensual character.

Brecht's struggle against Nazism and his embrace of Communism are the central themes of his work from the early thirties until his death in the fifties, and it is not inaccurate to say that he is the first dramatist to define himself entirely in relation to modern totalitarianism. Having chosen one tyranny over another, he spent his later years trying to justify this decision to himself and others, but once having put his poetic genius in thrall to an ideology, he rarely flinched from the brutal consequences of his choice. In plays such as *The Measures Taken*, for example, which demonstrate the necessity to sacrifice the needs of the individual to the demands of the Party, he managed to embarrass the Party with the inexorable logic of his dialectic; his ideological writings are sometimes interpreted as some of the most effective, if unwitting, indictments of the whole Communist system because of that logic.

Brecht's instinct for survival, coupled with his pride about being more practical and committed than the most cynical Party hacks, sometimes makes his plays look like raw demonstrations of how the end justifies the means. But even in his crudest ideological works, there is a subtle and ironic dialectician quarreling with the would-be propagandist, a yogi arguing with the commissar. *The Good Woman of Setzuan*, for example, is designed to show how a person can be virtuous in a capitalist society only by becoming schizophrenic, splitting off charitable impulses from the venal, ruthless necessity to pursue wealth. But even in that work, Brecht manages to thwart his own thrust, concluding the action not with a call to revolution but rather with a characteristic note of irresolution. The three deaf gods, who have come to earth to reinforce their conviction that the current moral and social codes are perfectly compatible with the prevailing economic system, witness ample evidence that justice and survival are at odds, yet ascend to heaven still firmly believing in the status quo. "Should the world be changed?" they ask. "How? By whom? The world should *not* be changed!" To which the battered, anguished heroine can only murmur, "Help."

In short, while Shaw was able to imagine utopias, Brecht was too honest to do more than suggest why they were necessary. As a secret Aristotelian, a suppressed tragic writer, Brecht was compelled to examine the cruel exigencies of contemporary life, but his Platonic impulses were not strong enough to let him indulge in fantasies of the future. If Brecht was among the first to put his poetry at the service of the mass state, he was perhaps the last to find a channel—using a strategy of simultaneous engagement and detachment—past the Scylla and Charybdis of art and politics. After Brecht, we find the theatre more openly divided between the utilitarians and the aesthetes, between those who find an exclusively social-political function for the theatre and those who largely deny all interest in the public dimension.

Thus, in totalitarian countries, theatre is used primarily as a form of political consolidation, reinforcing the existing regime, or as a covert form of subversion and resistance, while the theatre of the capitalist countries, despite occasional eruptions of political consciousness, grows increasingly private, limited largely to escapist, domestic, psychological, even narcissistic subjects. As Philip Roth has put it: "In the East, nothing goes and everything matters. In the West, everything goes and nothing matters."

It is a generalization, of course, that admits of many exceptions in the Western countries. I am happy to acknowledge them, though few are particularly distinguished. America in the thirties, for example, produced a highly engaged political theatre (Clifford Odets, John Howard Lawson, the Federal Theatre, Theatre Union, etc.), vestiges of which would appear during the postwar years, especially in the drama of

Arthur Miller and August Wilson, while the anarchic Living Theatre, typifying the radical sixties in its Platonic scorn of imitation, tried to break down barriers between stage and audience altogether. The theatre of Great Britain, from the time of the "angry young men" in the late fifties until today, has featured a strong strain of radical consciousness, partly in reaction to the mainstream tradition of West End drawing-room comedies and seaside-resort dramas, from the plays of John Arden and John Osborne twenty years ago to the current work of David Hare, David Edgar, Howard Brenton, and Caryl Churchill. And there is probably no more committed political writer in the contemporary theatre than the Marxist Italian farceur, Dario Fo. Still, I believe that the split has widened between the Platonic and the Aristotelian approaches to the stage, in response to the pressures and exigencies of the mass industrial state. Political theatre has tended to become either official propaganda, on behalf of the socialist present, or polemical preachment in support of a fancied utopian future, while the mainstream aesthetic theatre has settled for those specious and mindless products of what Brecht called "the bourgeois narcotics factory."

At present, then, we seem to be caught between a theatre of ideology and a theatre of quietism, the one devoted to exhortation and outrage, the other to bright if mindless entertainment. Is there no way for drama to assume a public dimension without developing a dialectic form or falling into that "gray exacting realism" which Camus identified as the official aesthetic of totalitarianism? How can the stage address such critical contemporary questions as injustice, racism, inequality, inhumanity, war, and the threat of nuclear annihilation, not to mention the dwindling possibilities for freedom in the mass industrial state, while maintaining an individual style free of self-righteous melodrama? What is the dramatist's relationship to the political problems of his society, and how can his social responsibilities be combined with his own creative imperatives?

I believe there is a way for contemporary theatre to preserve both poetry and political responsibility, to synthesize its Aristotelian and Platonic functions, and that is through the medium of metaphor. Dramatists are still not equipped to solve problems—if they were, they would no longer be artists—but through imaginative metaphors they are certainly in a position to present them correctly. The advantage of metaphors is that they are suggestive rather than exact, reverberant rather than precise; they represent a poetic avenue to the truth. That metaphors describe rather than proscribe preserves the autonomous nature of theatre art; that they can permit a wider reality than domestic crises and marital woes allows the theatre artist to maintain his public function.

All great modern drama has been metaphorical, from Ibsen's metaphor of ghosts as a symbol of a rotting bourgeois social inheritance, to Chekhov's metaphor of the cherry orchard as a symbol of an aristocracy dying because it has lost its purpose, to Shaw's metaphor of a (heartbreak) house shaped like a rudderless ship as a symbol of Europe drifting aimlessly toward extinction, to Brecht's metaphor of Mother Courage's canteen wagon, collapsing under war's venality and carnage, through Beckett's metaphor of two tramps lost in a void decorated with a single tree. It is this metaphorical art that seems to me missing from minor contemporary drama, whether political or domestic; the common run of plays tend to be discursive, prosaic, simplistic, lacking the complications of a poetic structure. Still, the secret has not been wholly lost. The best of our theatre writers are continuing to mine a metaphorical vein, and it is to these writers that I turn for confirmation and illustration.

Consider, for example, Jean-Claude van Itallie's *America Hurrah*, particularly the final play in that trilogy, *Motel*. *Motel* is a monologue spoken by a female motelkeeper, an enormous aproned doll wearing a huge carnival mask, complete with hair rollers and granny glasses. Her speech drones on about rooms ("rooms of marble and rooms of cork, all letting forth an avalanche"), rooms throughout history, and specifically this motel room, with its antimacassars, hooked rugs, plastic Japanese flowers, TV set, automatically flushing toilet. As the motelkeeper catalogues the room's possessions, the door opens with a blinding flash of headlights and a young couple enters—two more mannikins on raised shoes, their huge heads obscenely bobbing, their bodies moving with the jerky menace of animated monsters. Slowly, they undress for the night, joining in a grotesque papier-mâché embrace, rubbing their cardboard bodies together—then turn on the TV and, to the accompaniment of deafening rock and roll, cheerfully proceed to demolish the room: ripping off the toilet seat, breaking the bedsprings, pulling down doors and windows, scrawling pornographic expletives on the walls with lipstick, and finally tearing the motelkeeper apart, head and all. Nabokov in *Lolita* used motel culture as an image of our squalor and rootlessness; van Itallie uses it as a metaphor of our violence, our lunacy, our need to defile.

Let me offer another American example, a work by Arthur Kopit called *End of the World (with Symposium to Follow)*. This black comedy is written in the style of a film noir and concerns a playwright approached by a mysterious stranger who wants to commission a play about doom. The playwright responds to this curious commission like a private eye hired to find a murderer, and in the course of the action investigates a number of witnesses with knowledge of our nuclear strategy.

What the playwright discovers is that our nuclear policy is insane, and what is more, *everybody knows it, including its architects*. The policy is a "closed loop system." Assured destruction and flexible response both lead to the same result. There's no way out unless you break the system itself. It is an Escher box—an illusion of reality. Though it looks feasible, it won't work, but because it looks workable, people can't stop working on it. The playwright concludes that writing such a play is impossible and abandons the project, along with all hope.

His final speech is the metaphor, and I would like to quote it at length. "Our son had just been born," he says. "We'd brought him home. He was what, five days old, I guess." (*Pause*) "And then one day my wife went out . . . And I was left alone with him . . . And I picked him up, this tiny thing, and started walking around the living room. We lived on a high floor, overlooking the river, the Hudson . . . And I looked down at this tiny creature, this tiny thing, and I realized . . ." (*Pause*) "I realized I had never had anyone completely in my power before!" (*Pause*) "And I realized he was completely innocent. And he looked up at me. And whatever he could see, he could see only in innocence. And he was in my power. And I'd never known what that *meant*! Never felt anything remotely like that before! And I saw I was standing near a window. And it was open. It was but a few feet away. And I thought: I could . . . *drop him out!* How easy to drop him out. And I went *toward* the window, because I couldn't believe this thought had come into my head—*where had it come from?* Not one part of me felt anything for this boy but love, not one part! My wife and I had planned, we were both in love, there was no anger, no resentment, nothing dark in me toward him at all, no one could ever have been more in love with his child than I . . . and I was thinking: I can throw him out of here! . . . and then he will be falling ten, twelve, fifteen, twenty stories down, and as he's falling, I will be *unable to get him back!* and I will feel a remorse . . . of infinite extent . . . and nothing will ever be able to redeem me from this, I will be forever outside the powers of redemption, if there is a God then with this act

I am forever damned. And I felt a *thrill!* I FELT A THRILL! IT WAS THERE! I FELT A THRILL AT THE THOUGHT OF DOING SOME ACT WHICH HAD NO REASON WHATSOEVER AND WOULD LEAVE ME FOREVER DAMNED! God will notice me with this, I said. And, of course, I resisted this. It wasn't hard to do, resisting wasn't hard . . . BUT I DIDN'T STAY BY THE WINDOW! . . . AND I CLOSED IT! I resisted by moving away, back into the room . . . And I sat down with him." (*Pause*) "Well, there's not a chance I would have done it, not a chance!" (*Pause*) "But I couldn't *take* a chance, it was very, very . . . seductive . . . If doom comes . . . it will come in *that* way."

I am reluctant to comment further on this passage, because it is so much more powerful than comment, which is precisely the power of dramatic metaphor. Without evading his responsibilities as a citizen under nuclear threat, indeed by frontally facing these responsibilities, Kopit has managed to understand our terrors and turn them into art.

Let me conclude with one more example, a work that embodies better than any I know the tensions between the Platonic and Aristotelian visions of reality: Jean Genet's *The Balcony*. Genet imagines bourgeois society through the metaphor of the brothel, in which the status quo is preserved by means of erotic fantasies. The agencies of power—government, the law, the army, the police, and the Church—prosper by being impersonated in the brothel by ordinary citizens. The threat to this system comes not from whorehouse imposture but from a rebellion which is raging in the streets of the city, dedicated to destroying all the masquerades through which the system perseveres. This is the purpose, at least, of the rebel leader, the proletarian Roger, who wants the rebellion to adhere to a chaste puritan ideal and put an end to role playing. Roger knows that if the rebellion does not begin by "despising make believe," it will soon come to resemble the other side. Everything must be aimed at utility. Skirmishes must be fought without gestures, elegance, or charm. Reason must prevail. And when the Great Figures of the regime are captured, their costumes must be ripped off.

But Roger is a dreamer, for the rebels cannot give up their hunger for emblems, heroes, banners, and a legendary figure to worship. Chantal, the La Pasionaria of this revolution, has learned "the art of shamming and acting in the brothel." Now she applies it to the revolution, becoming its female emblem. This dooms the rebellion, modeled by Genet on the French Revolution, which also began by despising artifice before developing its own ceremonies. The puritan Roger, with his devotion to Reason and Virtue, is obviously based on Cromwell or Robespierre, whose Platonic puritanism could not survive the people's love of flash and sensation. The need for change is undermined by the need to play a role; rebels adjust themselves to already defined characters; even the revolutionary leaders become play actors, their chaste, simple dress serving as another kind of costume. Thus, Robespierre introduces a terror much more bloody than the atrocities of the *ancien régime*; Stalin creates a bureaucracy far more murderous than the feudal hierarchy of the Romanovs. All progress is a dream, because reality is unattainable. For if real time moves forward, illusory time moves in circles, and humankind is doomed to repetition by its love of masquerade.

In Genet's vision, then, theatre and politics live uneasily side by side, and the concept of imitation, which Aristotle made the focal point of his *Poetics*, becomes a method of enshrining the status quo. Yet if Genet believes that the reality desired by Platonic revolutionaries is neither desirable nor achievable, he manages nevertheless to make a profound revolutionary statement of his own by means of theatrical metaphor. And ultimately, that is the most one can ask of dramatic art in regard to politics—not that it solve our problems, but rather that it increase our understanding; not that it accommodate the possible, but rather that it preserve our belief in the impossible. As I once wrote in another context: "Art encompasses politics but refuses to affirm it. The artist lives in compromised reality, but he lives in another world as well, the world of the imagination, and there his vision is pure and absolute . . . Politics demands resolution; dramatic art is content to leave us in ambiguity. The consequences are unreconciled opposites, tension, inaction—but also the metaphysical joy which comes from a pure truth, beautifully expressed." To that extent, and perhaps that alone, metaphor creates a bridge where politics and theatre meet, and it is there, at that imaginary junction, that Plato and Aristotle settle their ancient argument and join their venerable hands.

(1984)

ACKNOWLEDGMENTS

All of the reviews and articles in this book first appeared in *The New Republic*, with the following exceptions: "Reimagining the American Stage" is based on a talk given at Skidmore College and later printed in its *Skidmore Voices*. "Reimagining the Drama" is a revised version of an article first published in my book *Critical Moments*, under the title "A Crack in the Chimney." "Reimagining the Classics" and "Reimagining the Process" first appeared, under different titles, in the Arts and Leisure section of *The New York Times*. "An Actor Prepares" and "All in the Family Ties" were first published in the Op Ed section of *The New York Times*. "A Theatrical Declaration of Independence" and "Artistic Freedom and Political Repression" (included in *Arts Wars*) were first published, in different forms, in *American Theatre*. "Politics and Theatre" was commissioned by the Tocqueville Forum of Wake Forest University, then published as "The Theatre of Metaphor" in *Partisan Review*. "The Legacy of the Group Theatre" was commissioned by WGBH magazine. "Dreams and Hard-back Chairs," based on a talk given to the students of the Belmont Hill School, was later broadcast over National Public Radio. "Dangerous Books" appears here for the first time.

I wish to thank the magazines, newspapers, radio stations, and institutions that welcomed these articles, and the various editors—especially Ann Hulbert and Leon Wieseltier of *The New Republic* and Arthur Wang of Hill and Wang—who helped to improve them.

INDEX

Abraham, F. Murray, 144, 171–72, 242
Abundance (Henley), 104, 106–8
Accidental Death of an Anarchist (Fo), 40
actors, 14, 234–37, 242–48; British, 242–46; foreign, in American productions, 225–29. *See also specific actors*
Actors Equity, 225–29, 241
Actors Studio, 149, 191, 220
Adler, Jacob, 174
Adler, Stella, 219
Aeschylus, 226
Ah, Wilderness! (O'Neill), 214
AIDS, 257, 267
Akalaitis, JoAnne, 12, 13, 232; *Cymbeline*, 178–81; *Endgame*, 13, 200
Albee, Edward, 11, 32, 211, 243
Alceste (Gluck), 13
Alcestis (Euripides), 13
Aldredge, Tom, 48
Alexander, Bill, 204
Alexander, Jason, 77
Allen, Joan, 81
Allen, Woody, 71, 232
All My Sons (Miller), 23–24, 26
All the King's Men (Warren), 127–30
Alton, Bill, 153
American Buffalo (Mamet), 11, 51, 62, 63
American Expressionism, 104
American Hurrah (van Itallie), 289
American Place, New York, 37
American Repertory Theatre, Boston, 13, 200, 212–14, 273–76
American Theatre Exchange (Joyce Theater, New York), 123–26
Anderson, Kevin, 84
Anderson, Maxwell, 22
Anderson, Stanley, 149
Annie (musical), 47
Anouilh, Jean, 7
Antoon, A. J., 117, 143–44, 201
Anything Goes (musical), 44–46, 64, 155
Apocalypse Now (film), 49
Arcenas, Loy, 69, 96, 232
Arden, John, 243, 288
Arena Stage, Washington, 7, 149, 209
Aristophanes, 253, 269–70
Aristotelian theatre, 280–92
Aristotle, 280–81; *Poetics*, 247, 280, 292
Armus, Sidney, 177
Arnone, John, 157, 232
Aronson, Boris, 75, 230–34
Arrambide, Mario, 196
Artaud, Antonin, 118
Art Institute of Chicago, School of, 271
Artists Space, New York, 257–58
Asch, Sholem, *The God of Vengeance*, 255
Atkinson, Brooks, 218–19
audiences, 13–15, 141
Awake and Sing! (Odets), 218, 231
Ayckbourn, Alan, 241

Baal (Brecht), 13, 195–97
Babe, Tom, 11
Baby with the Bathwater (Durang), 212
Baitz, Jon Robin, 11
Baker, Russell, 54

Balaban, Bob, 92
Balcony, The (Genet), 13, 291–92
Baldwin, Alec, 96
Baldwin, James, 255
Ball, William, 10
Balm in Gilead (Wilson), 33–36
Bamman, Gerry, 184, 185
banned books, 252–57
Barnes, Clive, 71
Barre, Gabriel, 142
Bartenieff, George, 179, 181
Bates, Alan, 245
Battle of Angels (Williams), 81, 82
Bauer, Richard, 149
Beatty, John Lee, 189, 232
Beck, Julian, 74
Beckett, Samuel, 7, 20, 118, 197–201, 226; *Breath*, 198; *Embers*, 199; *Endgame*, 13, 198, 200; *Happy Days*, 198; *Krapp's Last Tape*, 199; *Lulu*, 13; *Molloy*, 199; *Not I*, 199; *Rockaby*, 198; *The Unnameable*, 199; *Waiting for Godot*, 171–73, 198, 199, 200
Belasco, David, 92, 93, 101
Belgrader, Andrei, 164
Bell, Daniel, "The Contradictions of Modernity and Modernism," 147–48, 151
Bennett, Alan, *Secret Spies*, 246
Bentley, Eric, 168
Bentsen, Lloyd, 235
Bergman, Ingmar, 204; *Hamlet*, 119–20, 202
Berkeley Repertory Theatre, 124
Berkoff, Steven, 159; *Coriolanus*, 159–62
Berle, Milton, 41, 134
Berlin, Irving, 77
Berman, Irene B., 184, 185
Bermel, Albert, 4
Bernhard, Sandra, *Without You I'm Nothing*, 71–72
Bernstein, Leonard, 76, 77, 258
Berry, Ralph, 201–3
Besserer, Robert, 157
Bettelheim, Bruno, *The Uses of Enchantment*, 46
Bhagavad-Gita (book), 139
Biddle, Livingstone, 261, 265
Big River (musical), 47, 213–14
Bishop, Kelly, 111
Bjornson, Maria, 55–56
black experience, in theatre, 25–27, 99–104
Blakely, Colin, 188
Blakemore, Michael, 149
Blessing, Lee, *A Walk in the Woods*, 64, 65–67, 68, 214
Blossom, Roberts, 146
Blue Velvet (film), 70, 94
Bock, Jerry, 77
Bogart, Anne, 12, 196 and *n*
Bogdanov, Michael, 204
Bogosian, Eric, 37; *Talk Radio*, 52–54
Bond, Edward, 243
book bannings, 252–57
Boruzescu, Radu, 150
Bosco, Philip, 108
Boston, 254, 255; press coverage of the arts in, 272–80; theatre in, 7, 81, 200, 212–14, 272–80
Boston *Globe*, arts coverage by, 272–80
Boston *Phoenix*, 273–75
Boston Symphony Orchestra, 274, 276, 277
Boys' Life (Korder), 64, 67–69
Branagh, Kenneth, 191
Brand (Ibsen), 21, 182
Brando, Marlon, 82, 187, 229, 242
Braugher, André, 161, 189
"breaking the frame," 140–41
Breath (Beckett), 198
Brecht, Bertolt, 7, 33, 57, 77, 97, 99, 118–19, 132, 141, 148, 152, 194, 229, 285–89; *Baal*, 13, 195–97; *The Caucasian Chalk Circle*, 264; *Coriolan*, 118; *The Duchess of Malfi*, 229; *The Good Woman of Setzuan*, 229, 287; *The Measures Taken*, 286; *The Threepenny Opera*, 118
Brenton, Howard, 244, 288
Breuer, Lee, 12, 180, 196; *The Gospel at Colonus*, 13, 58–59; *The Tempest*, 13, 180, 181
Bridge, Andrew, 57
Brightman, Sarah, 56, 57, 225
British theatre, 3, 7, 9, 44, 83, 84, 107, 117, 118, 123, 131, 156, 163–64, 167–70, 186–88, 191, 204, 215, 225–26, 228, 231, 240–48, 281, 288. *See also specific actors, directors, plays, playwrights, and theatres*
Brook, Peter, 3, 12, 57, 118, 149, 173, 202, 203, 204, 222, 247; *The Cherry Orchard*, 145–47, 149; *King Lear*, 118, 140, 202; *The Mahabharata*, 3, 136–40, 145; *A Midsummer Night's Dream*, 118, 140, 143, 201; *The Shifting Point*, 140
Brooklyn Academy of Music, 6, 13, 58, 119, 138, 145
Brooks, Mel, *2000 Year Old Man*, 41
Brown, Zack, 232
Bruce, Lenny, 71, 105
Bryceland, Yvonne, 225
Bryggman, Larry, 161, 193

Büchner, Georg, 52, 119, 194; *Leonce and Lena*, 13; *Woyzeck*, 13, 52, 194–95
Buckley, Candy, 130
Buried Child (Shepard), 11, 28–29
Burroughs, William, 254
Burton, Kate, 92
Burton, Richard, 124
Bush, George, 235, 237–40, 256, 263
Butterfield, Fox, 273–74
Byrne, David, 30

Caesar, Sid, 41
Cafe Crown (Kraft), 173–75
Caldwell, Erskine, 254
Caldwell, Sarah, 274
Caliban, Richard, 93
Camp, Joanne, 51, 81
Carrière, Jean-Claude, 136, 137, 139
Carter, Jimmy, 261, 264, 265
Cates, Phoebe, 163, 177
Cat on a Hot Tin Roof (Williams), 6, 38
Cats (musical), 9, 54, 55, 56, 109, 110, 241
Caucasian Chalk Circle, The (Brecht), 264
causality, theatrical, 19–31
censorship, issues of, 252–72
Central Park (New York), Shakespeare productions in, 89, 117, 143, 156, 162–64, 180, 188–90, 201
Champion, Gower, 75
Chaney, Lon, 55
Channing, Stockard, 111
Charlap, Moose, 77
Chayefsky, Paddy, 22, 176; *The Tenth Man*, 175–77
Chekhov, Anton, 90, 101, 119, 226, 262, 283–85, 289; *The Cherry Orchard*, 119, 145–51, 191, 198, 284; *Platonov*, 167, 245–46; *The Seagull*, 149; *The Three Sisters*, 149, 191, 219, 284; *Uncle Vanya*, 119, 143
Chereau, Patrice, 183
Cherry Orchard, The (Chekhov), 119, 145–51, 191, 198, 284
Chicago, 33, 130–33, 271; opera in, 7; theatre in, 13, 33–36, 51, 96, 134, 146, 181
Chorus Line, A (musical), 8, 215, 270
Churchill, Caryl, 241, 242, 244, 288
Cieslak, Ryszard, 139
Circle Repertory Company, 33, 69, 96
City Opera, New York, 7
Ciulei, Liviu, 119, 143, 182, 185, 233
CIVIL WarS, The (Wilson), 12, 247, 251
Clark, Bobby, 41
Clarke, Bill, 67
Clarke, Martha, 12, 72–74, 233; *The Garden of Earthly Delights*, 12, 73, 74; *The Hunger Artist*, 73; *Miracolo d'Amore*, 72–74
classical drama, 12–13, 21, 58–59; reinterpretation of, 115–205. *See also specific plays and playwrights*
Close, Glenn, 246
Clurman, Harold, 4, 81, 210, 217–21; *The Fervent Years*, 217
Coleridge, Samuel Taylor, 21
Collins, Pat, 81
Colored Museum, The (Wolfe), 26–28
Comedy of Errors, The (Shakespeare), 134–36
commedia traditions, 39–40, 141
Commentary (magazine), 4, 260
commercial theatre, 8, 9, 99, 155, 209, 211, 212–16, 218, 221–24, 242–43, 266. *See also specific plays and theatres*
Communism, 286–87
Congress, arts legislation in, 257–72
Conklin, John, 182, 185, 192, 232
Connection, The (Gelber), 33
Conolly, Patricia, 183
Conroy, Frances, 92, 153
Conroy, Frank, 242
Conroy, Kevin, 88–89
Converse-Roberts, William, 193
Coriolanus (Shakespeare), 159–62, 231, 242
Cosier, E. David Jr., 102
Coward, Noël, 244, 246
Craven, Frank, 153
Crawford, Michael, 57, 241
Cristofer, Michael, 22
critics, 3, 4, 14, 116, 221–23. *See also specific critics*
Critics Circle Awards, 227
Crosby, Kim, 48
Crouse, Timothy, 45
Crowbar (Wellman), 92–93
Croyden, Margaret, 222–23
Crucible, The (Miller), 191
Cumpsty, Michael, 179, 181
Cunningham, John, 111
Cusack, Joan, 179, 181
Cymbeline (Shakespeare), 177–81, 242

Dada, 285
Daedalus (magazine), 7
Dallas Theater Company, 10
Daly, Tyne, 87
D'Amato, Alfonse, 267, 268
dance/ballet musicals, 74–78

Dangerous Liaisons (film), 246
Danner, Blythe, 117, 163
David, Keith, 161
Day Room, The (De Lillo), 212
Death Destruction & Detroit (Wilson), 12
Death of a Salesman (Miller), 24, 26, 65, 211, 242, 243
Delaney, Shelagh, 243
De Lillo, Don, 212, 247
De Mille, Agnes, 75, 98
Democratic National Convention (1988), 234–37
Dempsey, Jerome, 132
Denby, David, *Theaterophobia*, 4
Dench, Judi, 245
De Niro, Robert, 187, 242
Dennehy, Brian, 146
designers, 230–34. *See also specific designers*
Detroit, arts in, 255, 271
Dewhurst, Colleen, 229
Dexter, John, 60
Diderot, Denis: *Jacques and His Master*, 164; *Rameau's Nephew*, 164–66, 167
directors and directing, 10, 12–13, 214–15; reinterpretation of the classics, 115–205. *See also specific directors and productions*
discrimination in the arts, 225–29, 275–80
Dishy, Bob, 177
Donnellan, Declan, 204
Dramatists' Guild, 226
Dreiser, Theodore, 254
Drinking in America (Bogosian), 37
Dukakis, Michael, 234–37, 238
Dundas, Jennifer, 159
Durang, Christopher, 11, 243, 252; *Beyond Therapy*, 49
Dutton, Charles S., 102

Eastern Standard (Greenberg), 78
Economist, The (magazine), 227, 228
Ede, George, 142
Edgar, David, 244, 288
Edmond (Mamet), 51–52, 62
Edmunds, Kate, 232
education, arts, 248–49, 251
Eichelberger, Ethyl, 135
Einstein on the Beach (Wilson, Glass), 12, 29–30, 247
Eisenberg, Deborah, *Pastorale*, 49
Eliot, T. S., 21, 61, 197–98, 272; *The Waste Land*, 28
Ellens, Rebecca, 149
Embers (Beckett), 199
Emmons, Beverly, 150, 158
"Empire Strikes Out, The" (*New York Times* article), 9
Endgame (Beckett), 13, 198, 200
End of the World (with Symposium to Follow) (Kopit), 13, 289–91
Enemy of the People, An (Ibsen), 23, 261, 282, 283
Engle, Debra, 35
Engler, Michael, 12
Ensemble Theatre Company, 49
Entertainer, The (Osborne), 187, 245
Epstein, Alvin, 143
Euripides, 253; *Alcestis*, 13
Evans, Peter, 51
Evita (musical), 57
Ezell, John, 162

Fast, Howard, 255
Faulkner, William, 255
federal arts funding, 8, 10, 109, 210, 212, 220, 222, 224, 257–72; and censorship issue, 257–72. *See also* National Endowment for the Arts
Federal Theatre, 272, 287
Feiffer, Jules: *Grownups*, 212; *Little Murders*, 212
Feldshuh, Tovah, 142
Fences (Wilson), 25–26, 65, 100, 101, 214
Fervent Years, The (Clurman), 217
Fichandler, Zelda, 7, 209
Fiddler on the Roof (musical), 75, 76, 231
films, 14, 69, 252. *See also* Hollywood; *specific films*
Finley, Karen, 270
Finn, William, 159
Finney, Albert, 188, 245
First Amendment rights, 252–72
Fitzgerald, Robert, 59
Flying Karamazov Brothers, 135
Fo, Dario, 37, 288; *Accidental Death of an Anarchist*, 40; *Mistero Buffo*, 38–40
Ford Foundation, 261, 264
foreign actors, 225–29
Foreman, Richard, 12, 13, 233; *Film Is Evil. Radio Is Good*, 52; *Woyzeck*, 194–95
Forest, The (Wilson), 30–31
Forsythe, Henderson, 92
42nd Street (musical), 44, 56, 75, 77
Fosse, Bob, 75
Foy, Kenneth, 86
Frankel, Gene, 104
Fraser, Lady Antonia, 245
Frayn, Michael, 167, 226, 244, 246; *Bene-*

factors, 241; *Wild Honey*, 167, 241, 245–46
Frears, Stephen, 246
Freedman, Gerald, 117, 162–63
Freeman, Morgan, 108, 242
French theatre, 13, 200
Freud, Sigmund, 22, 165, 202, 251, 254; *Moses and Monotheism*, 83
Friedman, Peter, 81, 177
Frohnmayer, John E., 257–58
Front Page, The (Hecht, MacArthur), 130–33, 152
Fugard, Athol, *The Road to Mecca*, 225
Fugitive Kind, The (film), 82
Funny Thing Happened on the Way to the Forum, A (play), 75, 77, 85

Gaines, Boyd, 81
Galati, Frank, 96–97, 98, 109
Gallo, David, 106
Gallo, Paul, 72, 73
Gambon, Michael, 245
Garden of Earthly Delights, The (play), 12, 73, 74
Garfield, John, 219
Gay, John, *Beggar's Opera*, 118, 148
Gelber, Jack, *The Connection*, 33
Genet, Jean, 10; *The Balcony*, 13, 291–92; *The Screens*, 13
Geniuses (Reynolds), 49–51
Gerety, Peter, 129–30
German Expressionism, 104
Germany, 7, 30, 104, 194, 195–96, 241, 253, 254, 268
Gershwin, George, 26
Gersten, Bernard, 151, 155
Ghosts (Ibsen), 29, 252, 282, 283
Gibson, William, 22
Gielgud, John, 7, 149, 191
Gilgamesh (Babylonian story), 30
Gilman, Richard, 4
Gilroy, Frank, 22
Glass, Philip, 7, 12, 179, 200; *Einstein on the Beach*, 12, 29
Glengarry Glen Ross (Mamet), 11, 62, 63
Goldberg, Whoopi, 37
Goldblum, Jeff, 189, 191
Goldenthal, Elliot, 61
Goldoni, Carlo, *The Mistress of the Inn*, 140–43
Goodman Theatre, Chicago, 13, 51, 134, 146, 181
Good Woman of Setzuan, The (Brecht), 229, 287
Gospel at Colonus, The (play), 13, 58–59
Gould, Morton, 77
Gozzi, Carlo, 119, 141
Grapes of Wrath, The (Steinbeck), 96–99, 109
Gray, Simon, 241, 244
Gray, Spalding, 37–38, 153; *Sex and Death to the Age 14*, 36–38
Great Directors at Work (Jones), 202
Greek drama, 12–13, 21, 58–59, 119, 247, 252–53
Greenberg, Richard, 22; *Eastern Standard*, 78
Gregory, André, 7
Greif, Michael, 12, 104, 106
Grimes, Tammy, 84
Grimm fairy tales, 47–48, 179
Gropman, David, 232
Grosbard, Ulu, 176, 177
Grotowski, Jerzy, 12, 137, 139, 222, 226
Group Theatre, 141, 210, 217–21, 231, 244
Guare, John, 11, 247; *Six Degrees of Separation*, 109–11
Gunn, Moses, 161
Gunton, Bob, 170
Gurney, A. R. Jr., 11
Guskin, Harold, 188–89, 191, 192
Guthrie, Tyrone, 7, 10, 116–17, 176, 209
Gutierrez, Gerald, 51
Gypsy (musical), 6, 77, 85–87

Haas, Lukas, 171
Hagerty, Julie, 132
Haigh, Kenneth, 245
Hairy Ape, The (O'Neill), 104
Hall, Adrian, 10; *All the King's Men*, 127–30
Hall, Peter, 9, 83, 102, 188, 202, 203, 204, 243
Hamilton, Hamish, *On Directing Shakespeare*, 201–5
Hamlet (Shakespeare), 117, 118, 119, 143, 178, 190, 202, 225
Hammer, Mark, 149, 193
Hammerstein, Oscar, 92
Handke, Peter, 20
Hansberry, Lorraine, 22; *A Raisin in the Sun*, 27
Happy Days (Beckett), 198
Hardwick, Elizabeth, 4
Hare, David, 241, 244, 288; *Secret Rapture*, 244
Harper, Tess, 106, 107
Harper's (magazine), 4
Harris, Harriet, 193
Harrison, Tony, *Phaedra Britannica*, 167–70

Hart, Charles, 55
Hartford Stage Company, 13, 182–86, 194–95
Hartigan, Patti, 273, 275
Hauptman, William, 11
Havel, Vaclav, 89–90
Havis, Allan, 11
Hawley, Anne, 273, 274
Hawthorne, Nathaniel, *The Scarlet Letter*, 254
Hayden, Sophie, 135
Headly, Glenne, 35
Hecht, Ben, *The Front Page*, 130–33, 152
Hecht, Paul, 161
Heckscher, August, 263
Heidi Chronicles, The (Wasserstein), 78–81, 109, 241
Hellman, Lillian, 11, 22, 100; *The Little Foxes*, 221–22, 223
Helms, Jesse, 196, 257–58, 262, 267–68, 272, 279
Hemingway, Ernest, 199, 254, 255
Henley, Beth, *Abundance*, 104, 106–8
Henry, William III, 3
Henry V (Shakespeare), 191, 202
Hines, Gregory, 189–90, 222
Hoffman, Dustin, 242
Hogwood, Christopher, 274
Hollywood, 8, 219, 220, 242–43
Holm, Ian, 245
Houston, opera in, 7
Howard, Sidney, 22
Huckleberry Finn (Twain), 213–14, 255
Hudson Review, The (magazine), 4
Hugo, Victor, *Les Misérables*, 5, 54, 215, 241, 267
Hunt, Linda, 146
Hurlyburly (Rabe), 11, 173
Hurt, William, 242
Hwang, David Henry, 11; *M. Butterfly*, 59–61, 110, 228, 241

Ibsen, Henrik, 19–23, 119, 260, 282–85, 289; *Brand*, 21, 182; *A Doll's House*, 282; *An Enemy of the People*, 23, 261, 282, 283; *Ghosts*, 29, 252, 282, 283; *The Master Builder*, 19–21, 225; *Peer Gynt*, 182–86, 187, 251; *Pillars of Society*, 23; *The Wild Duck*, 23, 119, 149
I'm Not Rappaport (play), 103, 215
Inge, William, 22, 82
In Living Color (TV show), 27
Innaurato, Albert, 243
Institute for Contemporary Arts, Boston, 274
Institute of Contemporary Art, Philadelphia, 271
Institutional Radio Choir, 59
International Centre of Theatre Research, Bouffes du Nord, Paris, 137, 138
Into the Woods (musical), 8, 46–48, 86, 214
Ionesco, Eugene, 20
Irons, Jeremy, 241
Irwin, Bill, 134, 171, 172
Israel, Robert, 12, 72, 73, 232, 233
Ivanovna, Charlotta, 149
Ives, David, 11

Jackness, Andrew, 144, 232
Jackson, Jesse, 234–36
Jacobi, Derek, 163, 241, 245, 246
Jacques and His Master (Diderot), 164
James, Peter Francis, 181
J.B. (MacLeish), 231
Jerome Robbins' Broadway (musical), 74–78, 241
Joe Turner's Come and Gone (Wilson), 100, 214
Jones, David Richard, *Great Directors at Work*, 202
Jones, James Earl, 101
Jonson, Ben, 250
Jordan, Richard, 192–93
Joyce, James, 152, 198, 199, 253, 284
Joyce Theater, New York, 37; American Theatre Exchange, 123–26
Juan Darien (play), 61–62
Julia, Raul 192–93, 242
Julius Caesar (Shakespeare), 116, 117, 202
Juniper Tree, The (Glass-Moran-Yorinks), 47

Kahn, Michael, 204
Kaiser, Georg, 104
Kalfin, Robert, 141, 142
Kauffmann, Stanley, 5
Kelly, David Patrick, 195
Kelly, Kevin, 273
Kennedy, John F., 262–63
Kennedy, Teddy, 235–36
Kepros, Nicholas, 165, 166
Kerr, Philip, 142
Kerr, Walter, 141
Kierkegaard, Sören, 22
Kim, Willa, 132
Kimmelman, Michael, 73
King Lear (Shakespeare), 13, 21–22, 118, 140, 174, 202

Kitchen, the (New York), 6
Kline, Kevin, 108, 117, 163, 189, 190, 242
Knight, Shirley, 149
Kohout, Pavel, 124
Kondoleon, Harry, 11
Kopit, Arthur, 11, 247; *End of the World (with Symposium to Follow)*, 13, 289–91
Korder, Howard, 11, 247; *Boys' Life*, 64, 67–69
Kraft, Hy, *Cafe Crown*, 173–75
Kramer, Hilton, 267, 268, 271
Krapp's Last Tape (Beckett), 199
Krenz, Frank, 144
Kroll, Jack, 3
Kundera, Milan, 164

Lagomarsino, Ron, 12, 107
La MaMa, New York, 6
Lamos, Mark, 183
Landesman, Heidi, 213, 232
Landesman, Rocco, 213–14
Lange, Anne, 81
Lapine, James, 46, 143; *Into the Woods*, 46–48; *A Midsummer Night's Dream*, 156; *Table Settings*, 49; *Twelve Dreams*, 47; *The Winter's Tale*, 156–59
Laurents, Arthur, 85, 86, 87
Lawson, John Howard, 218, 287
League of American Theatres and Producers, 108
League of Resident Theatres, 225
LeCompte, Elizabeth, 12
Lee, Canada, 229
Lee, Eugene, 128, 232
Lee, Franne, 157–58
Lee, Ming Cho, 232
Leishman, Gina, 135
Leroux, Gaston, 55
Lettice and Lovage (play), 109
Lewis, Marcia, 84
Lewis, Sinclair, 254, 255
Lincoln Center, New York, 6–7, 37, 44–45, 63, 64, 67, 90, 109, 123, 131, 132, 134, 151–55, 171, 173, 175–77, 197, 198, 199, 214
Lindsay, Robert, 241
Lipman, Samuel, 260–61, 267, 268
Lithgow, John, 35, 60, 133, 242
Little Foxes, The (Hellman), 221–22, 223
Little Murders (Feiffer), 212
Littlewood, Joan, 243
Living Theatre, 33, 74, 137, 138, 141, 222, 288
Lloyd, John Bedford, 92
Lobel, Adrianne, 107, 232, 233
Long Day's Journey into Night, A (O'Neill), 22–23, 211, 214, 246
Long Wharf Theatre, 211
Loquasto, Santo, 174, 177, 232
Lowell, Robert, 168
Lowry, W. McNeil, 264, 265, 266
Lucas, Craig, 11, 94, 247; *Prelude to a Kiss*, 94–96, 109; *Reckless*, 69–71, 94
Lulu (Beckett), 13
Lumbly, Carl, 144
LuPone, Patti, 46
Lynch, David, 94
Lynch, Tom, 81

Mabou Mines, 8, 12, 180
McAnuff, Des, 12, 67, 214
MacArthur, Charles, *The Front Page*, 130–33, 152
Macbeth (Shakespeare), 190–93
McCarthy, Mary, 4
McClain, Derek, 232
McDaniel, James, 111
McGillin, Howard 46
McGovern, Barry, 199
McGovern, Elizabeth, 144
McGowran, Jack, 199
Machinal (Treadwell), 104–6, 107
MacIntosh, Joan, 179, 181
McKellen, Ian, 241, 245–46
Mackintosh, Cameron, 152
MacLeish, Archibald, *J.B.*, 231
MacNicol, Peter, 129
Macy, W. H., 67, 153
Madonna, 64, 72, 243
Magee, Patrick, 199
Magnani, Anna, 82
Mahabharata, The (play), 3, 54–55, 136–40, 145
Mailer, Kate, 146
Maleczech, Ruth, 13
Malkovich, John, 33–36, 246
Maloney, Peter, 153
Mamet, David, 11, 67, 90, 132, 146, 226, 242–43, 247; *American Buffalo*, 11, 51, 62, 63; *Edmond*, 51–52, 62; *Glengarry Glen Ross*, 11, 62, 63; *Oh, Hell*, 175; *Sexual Perversity in Chicago*, 51, 67; *Speed-the-Plow*, 62–65, 69, 214, 242–43; *The Water Engine*, 52
Manson, Alan, 177
Mantegna, Joe, 64
Mapplethorpe, Robert, 257, 264, 267, 270, 271

Ma Rainey's Black Bottom (Wilson), 100, 214
Marat/Sade, 93, 183
Markell, Jodie, 106
Martin, Steve, 171, 172
Marvin, Mel, 185
Marx, Karl, 165, 224
Marx Brothers, 39, 40, 163
Mason, Jackie, *The World According to Me!*, 40–44
Massachusetts Council on the Arts and Humanities, 271
Master Builder, The (Ibsen), 19–21, 225
Mastrantonio, Mary Elizabeth, 189
Maxwell, Roberta, 153
M. Butterfly (Hwang), 59–61, 110, 228, 241
Measure for Measure (Shakespeare), 117, 155, 202, 204
Measures Taken, The (Brecht), 286
Medoff, Mark, 22
Mee, Charles Jr., 11, 73
Mencken, H. L., 228
Merchant of Venice (Shakespeare), 103, 202
Mercury Theatre, 140, 210
Merrick, David, 152
Merritt, Michael, 64
Merzer, Glen, 247
metaphorical theatre, 116–21, 288–90
Metcalf, Laurie, 35
Metropolitan Opera, New York, 7
Meyerhold, Vsevolod, 118, 119, 141, 234
Michaels, Mark A., 142
Michell, Roger, 90, 91–92
Midsummer Night's Dream, A (Shakespeare), 117, 118, 119, 140, 143–44, 156, 201, 203, 204, 251
Miller, Arthur, 11, 22, 23–25, 100, 226, 243; 288; *All My Sons*, 23–24, 26; *The Crucible*, 191; *Death of a Salesman*, 24, 26, 65, 211, 242, 243
Miller, Jonathan, 143, 201–2, 204, 205
Miller, Penelope Ann, 154
Miller, Rebecca, 146
Millstein, Lincoln, 272–79
Minneapolis, theatre in, 7, 209
Miracolo d'Amore (play), 72–74
Mirren, Helen, 245
Misanthrope, Le (Molière), 167
Misérables, Les (Hugo), 5, 54, 215, 241, 267
Miss Saigon (musical), 9, 228–29, 275
Mistero Buffo (Comic Mystery Play) (Fo), 38–40
Mistress of the Inn, The (Goldoni), 140–43
Mitchell, David, 232
Mnouchkine, Ariane, 204
modernism, 20, 147–48
Molière, 31, 39, 119, 166, 167, 267
Molloy (Beckett), 199
Moon for the Misbegotten (O'Neill), 212
Moore, Tom, 213
Moran, Robert, 47
Moscow Art Theatre, 145
Mosher, Gregory, 12, 51, 64, 131, 134, 146, 175; *Our Town*, 151–55
Mozart, Wolfgang Amadeus, 117, 141, 142, 166, 251
Much Ado About Nothing (Shakespeare), 117, 162–64, 246
Müller, Heiner, 20
Mullins, Melinda, 193
Murphy, Harry S., 193
Murray, Brian, 163
Museum of Fine Arts, Boston, 276–77
musicals, 44–48, 54–62, 74–78, 85–87, 211, 215, 231–32, 241. *See also specific musicals*
Music-Theatre Group, 61

Nation, The (magazine), 4
National Assembly of State Arts Agencies, 260
National Council on the Arts, 262
National Endowment for the Arts, 8, 109, 212, 257–72, 279; and censorship issues, 257–72; cuts in, 222
National Theatre (Great Britain), 7, 9, 117, 131, 167, 186, 188, 215, 243, 245
Nazism, 253, 254, 286
Nelson, Richard, 11, 92; *Some Americans Abroad*, 90–92, 109
New Leader (magazine), 4
New Republic, The (magazine), 4
Newsweek (magazine), 3
New Vaudeville, 134–36
Next Wave Festival (BAM), 13
New York magazine, 4
New York Review, The (magazine), 4
New York Shakespeare Festival, 7, 13, 143, 155–62, 178–81, 188–93, 201, 242
New York theatre, 3–15, 33–111, 116–17, 119–26, 130–47, 151–81, 188–93, 197–201, 209–29; and British theatre, compared, 240–48; decline of, 4–10, 211; resident movement, 8–10, 99–104, 109, 151, 164, 209–16, 223, 225, 241, 247, 266. *See also specific productions and theatres*
New York Times, The, 3, 4, 7, 9, 73, 99,

154, 218, 222–23, 230, 269, 273, 274
New York Times Magazine, The, 222
Nichols, Mike, 11; *Waiting for Godot*, 171–73
Nichols, Peter, 244
Nietzsche, Friedrich Wilhelm, 22, 23, 138, 166, 281–82
'night, Mother (Norman), 212, 213
1984 (Orwell), 123–26
Nixon, Richard M., 264, 265
Nixon in China (Sellars), 118
Noble, Adrian, 204
nonprofit theatre movement, 8–10, 99–104, 109, 151, 164, 209–16, 223, 225, 241, 247, 266, 273–76
Nordling, Jeffrey, 181
Norman, Marsha, 11, 243; *'night, Mother*, 212, 213; *Traveler in the Dark*, 212–13, 214
Not I (Beckett), 199
Nunn, Trevor, 9, 202, 204, 241
Nussbaum, Mike, 146

Obolensky, Chloe, 139
obscenity issues, in the arts, 257–72
Odets, Clifford, 11, 22, 100, 218, 219, 220, 244, 287; *Awake and Sing!*, 218, 231; *Paradise Lost*, 231; *Waiting for Lefty*, 97
Oedipus at Colonus (Sophocles), 13, 58
Oh, Hell (Mamet, Silverstein), 175
Oklahoma! (musical), 47, 75, 98
Old Vic (Great Britain), 7, 117, 164, 186, 191
Olivier, Laurence, 7, 143, 186–90, 191, 229, 231, 245
On Directing Shakespeare (Hamilton), 201–5
O'Neill, Chris, 199
O'Neill, Eugene, 11, 22–23, 25, 100, 102–3, 131, 226, 255; *Ah, Wilderness!*, 214; *All God's Chillun Got Wings*, 255; *Desire Under the Elms*, 255; *The Hairy Ape*, 104; *A Long Day's Journey into Night*, 22–23, 211, 214, 246; *Moon for the Misbegotten*, 212; *Strange Interlude*, 255; *A Touch of the Poet*, 100
one-person shows, 36–44
On the Town, 75, 76
Ontological/Hysterical Theatre, 12
opera, 7, 60; reinterpretation of, 117–18, 123
Orpheus Descending (Williams), 81–85, 243, 245
Orson, Barbara, 130
Orwell, George, *1984*, 123–26
Osborne, John, 243, 244, 245, 288
Other People's Money (Sterner), 85, 87–89
Our Town (Wilder), 38, 151–55
Overmyer, Eric, 11
Ozawa, Seiji, 274, 276

Pacino Al, 242
Papp, Joseph, 7, 8, 10, 52, 89, 116, 155–59, 162, 180, 181, 188, 189, 190, 191, 201, 215, 241, 242, 261 and *n*, 262
Parker, Ellen, 81
Parker, Mary-Louise, 96
Parry, Natasha, 146
Partisan Review (magazine), 4
Patinkin, Mandy, 158, 189, 242
Peaslee, Richard, 12, 72, 74
Peer Gynt (Ibsen), 182–86, 187, 251
PepsiCo Summerfare, Purchase, New York, 123, 226
Perloff, Carey, 164; *Phaedra Britannica*, 167–70
Peters, Bernadette, 48
Pfeiffer, Michelle, 189, 191, 246
Phaedra Britannica (Harrison), 167–70
Phantom of the Opera, The (musical), 5, 54–57, 88, 93, 225, 241
Phèdre (Racine), 167–70
Philadelphia, 255, 271; opera in, 7; theatre in, 7, 124, 125
Phillips, Robin, 204
Piano Lesson, The (Wilson), 99–104, 109, 273
Pierce, David, 146, 163
Pierce, Wendell, 181
Ping Chong, 12
Pinter, Harold, 32, 164, 226, 243, 244, 245
Pintilie, Lucian, 119, 226; *The Cherry Orchard*, 148–51
Pirandello, Luigi, 20, 33, 120–21, 141, 226
Plato, 249, 251, 280
Platonic theatre, 280–92
Platonov (Chekhov), 167, 245–46
Plautus, *Twin Menaechmi*, 135
playwrights and playwriting, 10–12, 13, 242–47. *See also specific playwrights and plays*
Plowright, Joan, 188, 245
Plummer, Amanda, 106, 107
Poetics (Aristotle), 247, 280, 292
Polish Theatre Lab, 137, 138
politics, 234–40; and arts censorship, 252, 257–72; and theatre, 89–93, 123–26, 280–92
Porgy and Bess (musical), 26

Porter, Cole, *Anything Goes*, 44–46, 64
Posner, Kenneth, 106
post-modernism, 148
post-naturalism, 33–36
Prelude to a Kiss (Lucas), 94–96, 109
Prince, Harold, 57, 231, 233
Prosky, Robert, 67
Proust, Marcel, 198
Providence, theatre in, 10, 13, 127–30, 195–97
Pryce, Jonathan, 228, 229
Prynne, Lester, 196
Public Theater, New York, 7, 13, 52, 155–59, 188, 190

Quayle, J. Danforth, 239–40, 256
Quiroga, Horacio, 61

Rabe, David, 247; *Hurlyburly*, 11, 173
Racine, Jean Baptiste, *Phèdre*, 167–70
Raisin in the Sun, A (Hansberry), 27
Rame, Franca, 37, 39
Rameau's Nephew (Diderot), 164–66, 167
Rape of Lucrece, The (Shakespeare), 178
Rattigan, Terence, 244
Reagan, Ronald, 237–38, 263, 266
Real Thing, The (Stoppard), 241, 244
Rebhorn, James, 153
Reckless (Lucas), 69–71, 94
Reddin, Keith, 11, 247
Redgrave, Vanessa, 84, 243, 245
Reeve, Christopher, 158
Reilly, Don, 163
reinterpretation of classical drama, 115–205
religion, and artistic censorship, 252–53
René, Norman, 12, 69, 96
Republican National Convention (1988), 237–40
resident theatre movement, 8–10, 99–104, 109, 151, 164, 209–16, 223, 225, 241, 247, 266, 273–76
Reynolds, Joshua, *Geniuses*, 49–51
Ribman, Ronald, 11, 247; *Sweet Table at the Richelieu*, 13
Rich, Frank, 5, 230; *The Theatre of Boris Aronson*, 230–34
Richards, Ann, 235–36
Richards, Lloyd, 99, 102, 103, 277
Riddell, Richard, 67
Rifkin, Ron, 177
Rigg, Diana, 245
Robbins, Jerome, 74–78, 87
Robertson, Cliff, 81
Rockaby (Beckett), 198
Rodgers, Richard, 77
Rogers, Paul, 245
Romeo and Juliet (Shakespeare), 178, 181
Rooney, Andy, 228
Ross, David, 274–75
Roth, Ann, 173
Roth, Michael S., 67
Roth, Philip, 176, 255–56, 287
Roth, Stephanie, 146
Roth, Wolfgang, 142
Rowe, Stephen, 184
Royal Shakespeare Company (Great Britain), 7, 9, 117, 138, 163, 215, 231, 232, 246
royalties, 5, 8, 211, 213, 214–15, 266
Rudkin, David, 243
Ruehl, Mercedes, 89
Rumanian theatre, 119
Rushdie, Salman, *The Satanic Verses*, 252–57
Russian theatre, 118, 119

Saint Louis, opera in, 7
Salinger, J. D., *The Catcher in the Rye*, 255
Santa Fe, opera in, 7
Saroyan, William, 218; *Time of Your Life*, 36
Satanic Verses, The (Rushdie), 252–57
Schmidt, Douglas, 232
Schneider, Alan, 4
Scurria, Anne, 196
Seagull, The (Chekhov), 149
Search for Signs of Intelligent Life in the Universe, The (Tomlin), 37
Seattle Repertory, 103, 215
Secret Rapture (Hare), 244
Secret Spies (Bennett), 246
Seitz, John, 106
Sellars, Peter, 12, 117–18, 233, 274; *Nixon in China*, 118
Serban, Andrei, 12, 13, 119, 146, 149, 232
"Serious Fun" (Lincoln Center), 6–7, 123
Serra, Richard, *Tilted Arc*, 276
Serrano, Andreas, 257, 264, 267, 270, 271
Sex and Death to the Age 14 (Gray), 36–38
Sexual Perversity in Chicago (Mamet), 51, 67
Shaffer, Peter, 226, 241, 244
Shakespeare, William, 7, 9, 13, 21, 108, 116–17, 118, 201–5, 226, 247, 250, 267, 285; *All's Well That Ends Well*,

179; and authorship question, 250–51; *The Comedy of Errors*, 134–36; *Coriolanus*, 159–62, 231, 242; *Cymbeline*, 177–81, 242; *Hamlet*, 117, 118, 119, 143, 190, 202, 225; *Henry V*, 191, 202; *Julius Caesar*, 116, 117, 202; *King John*, 89; *King Lear*, 13, 21–22, 118, 140, 174, 202; *Macbeth*, 190–93; *Measure for Measure*, 117, 155, 202, 204; *Merchant of Venice*, 103, 202; *A Midsummer Night's Dream*, 117, 118, 119, 140, 143–44, 156, 201, 203, 204, 251; *Much Ado About Nothing*, 117, 162–64, 246; *Othello*, 178; *The Rape of Lucrece*, 178; reinterpretation of, 116–17, 119–20, 134–36, 140, 143–44, 155–64, 178–81, 186–93, 201–5, 242; *Romeo and Juliet*, 178, 181; *The Taming of the Shrew*, 117, 163, 201; *The Tempest*, 13, 178, 180, 181, 251; *Troilus and Cressida*, 117, 202; *Twelfth Night*, 117, 186–90, 191; *The Winter's Tale*, 155–59, 178, 179, 242, 253
Shalhoub, Tony, 165–66
Shaw, Bernard, 89, 159, 285–87, 289
Shaw, Fiona, 245
Shaw, Irwin, 22, 217
Shawn, Wallace, 11, 243
Sheed, Wilfrid, 4
Sheen, Martin, 242
Shepard, Sam, 11, 28–29, 31, 226, 243; *Buried Child*, 11, 28–29; *A Lie of the Mind*, 243; *True West*, 11, 34
Sherwood, Robert, 22
Shull, Richard B., 132
Shulz, Karen, 232
Sills, Paul, *Story Theater*, 47, 48
Silver, Ron, 64, 109
Silvers, Phil, 41
Silverstein, Shel, *Oh, Hell*, 175
simile theatre, 116, 117, 118
Simon, John, 4
Simon, Neil, 5, 6, 8
Simonson, Lee, 230
Sinclair, Upton, 254
Sinise, Gary, 34, 98
Sisto, Rocco, 158
Six Degrees of Separation (Guare), 109–11
Skin of Our Teeth, The (Wilder), 152
Smith, Lillian, 254
Smith, Lois, 98
Smith, Maggie, 109, 245
Society of Stage Directors and Choreographers, 226
Socrates, 253, 254
Some Americans Abroad (Nelson), 90–92, 109
Sondheim, Stephen, 46, 76, 78, 231, 232; *Gypsy*, 85–86; *Into the Woods*, 46–48, 86; *Sunday in the Park with George*, 46, 47, 86
Sontag, Susan, 4, 164, 204
Southeastern Center for Contemporary Art, Winston-Salem, 271
Soviet Union, 253, 254; theatre in, 118, 119
Speed-the-Plow (Mamet), 62–65, 69, 214, 242–43
Stanislavsky, 141, 145, 149, 187, 217, 245
Stapleton, Maureen, 81
Starlight Express (musical), 9, 54
Starobin, Michael, 159
Steele, Shelby, *The Content of Our Character*, 277–78
Stein, Douglas, 196, 232
Stein, Peter, 204
Steinbeck, John, 22, 255; *The Grapes of Wrath*, 96–99, 109
Stephens, Robert, 188, 245
Steppenwolf Company (Chicago), 33–36, 96–99
Sterner, Jerry, 85; *Other People's Money*, 87–89
Stewart, Ellen, 6
Stiller, Jerry, 163
Stinton, Colin, 92
Stolarsky, Paul, 132
Stolz, Eric, 154
Stoppard, Tom, 226, 244, 246; *The Real Thing*, 241, 244
Story Theater (Sills), 47, 48
Stowe, Harriet Beecher, *Uncle Tom's Cabin*, 77, 255
Straiges, Tony, 48, 232
Stram, Henry, 149–50
Strasberg, Lee, 191–92
Strasberg Method, 187, 191–92
Strauss, Edward, 46
Streep, Meryl, 146, 242
Strehler, Giorgio, 204, 226
Strindberg, August, 20, 23, 104, 140, 251
Styne, Jule, 76, 77, 85, 86
subsidized theatre. *See* federal arts funding
Sullivan, Brad, 84
Sullivan, Dan, 80, 103, 214–15
Sunday in the Park with George (Sondheim), 46, 47, 86, 156
Suzman, Janet, 245
Sweet Bird of Youth (Williams), 83, 160
Swinarski, Konrad, 203–4

Swoboda, Joseph, 125
symbolism, 285

Talk Radio (Bogosian), 52–54
Talley, Ted, *Coming Attractions*, 49
Taming of the Shrew, The (Shakespeare), 117, 163, 201
Taylor, Elizabeth, 221–23
Taymor, Julie, 12, 61
television, 14, 234–40
Telson, Bob, 59
Tempest, The (Shakespeare), 13, 178, 180, 181, 251
Tenth Man, The (Chayefsky), 175–77
Theaterophobia (Denby), 4
Theatre Communications Group (TCG) conference (1976), 265
Theatre of Boris Aronson, The (Rich), 230–34
Theatre of Living Arts, Philadelphia, 7, 8
Theatre Union, 287
Thomas, Richard, 133, 182, 183, 185, 242
Threepenny Opera, The (Brecht), 118
Three Sisters, The (Chekhov), 149, 191, 219, 284
ticket prices, 5, 6, 77, 78, 108, 210, 223
Time magazine, 3
Tipton, Jennifer, 173
Tobacco Road (play), 255
Toller, Ernst, 104
Tomlin, Lily, *The Search for Signs of Intelligent Life in the Universe*, 37
Tom Sawyer (Twain), 255
Tone, Franchot, 219
Tony awards, 41, 108–9, 222, 227, 248
Touch of the Poet, A (O'Neill), 100
Toussaint, Lorraine, 144
Traveler in the Dark (Norman), 212–13, 214
Treadwell, Sophie, *Machinal*, 104–6, 107
Trilling, Lionel, *Sincerity and Authenticity*, 165
Trinity Repertory Company, Providence, 10, 13, 127–30, 195–97
Troilus and Cressida (Shakespeare), 117, 202
True West (Shepard), 11, 34
Tsypin, George, 179, 232
Turner, Kathleen, 108
Tutta Casa, Letto e Chiesa (It's All Bed, Board, and Church) (skits), 39
Twain, Mark, 255; *Huckleberry Finn*, 213–14, 255; *Tom Sawyer*, 255
Twelfth Night (Shakespeare), 117, 186–90, 191
Twelve Dreams (Lapine), 47
Twomey, Anne, 84
Two Trains Running (Wilson), 103
Tynan, Kenneth, 38, 188

Uhry, Alfred, 11
Uncle Tom's Cabin (Stowe), 77, 255
Uncle Vanya (Chekhov), 119, 143
Uncommon Women and Others (Wasserstein), 49, 79
Unnameable, The (Beckett), 199
Ure, Mary, 245

Van Itallie, Jean-Claude, *American Hurrah*, 289
Variety (magazine), 4
Venora, Diane, 158, 189
Village Voice, The, 4, 72, 273
Von Bargen, Dan, 193
Vonnegut, Kurt, *Slaughterhouse Five*, 255

Wade, Kevin, 242
Wagner, Richard, *The Ring*, 286
Wagner, Robin, 232
Waiting for Godot (Beckett), 171–73, 198, 199, 200
Wajda, Andrzej, 226
Walken, Christopher, 160–61, 189, 242
Walk in the Woods, A (Blessing), 64, 65–67, 68, 214
Wallace, Jack, 132
Wallach, Eli, 174–75
Walton, Tony, 45, 131, 173
Warner, Deborah, 247
Warren, Robert Penn, *All the King's Men*, 127–30
Washington, theatre in, 7, 149–51, 209, 210
Wasserstein, Wendy, 11, 78, 247; *The Heidi Chronicles*, 78–81, 109, 241; *Isn't It Romantic*, 79; *Uncommon Women and Others*, 49, 79
Waste Land, The (Eliot), 28
Waterston, Sam, 67, 242
Webber, Andrew Lloyd, 6, 44, 75, 85; *Cats*, 9, 54, 55, 56, 109, 110, 241; *The Phantom of the Opera*, 5, 54–57, 88, 93, 225, 241
Wedekind, Frank, 13, 119
Weidman, John, 45
Weiss, Jeff, 132, 153

Welles, Orson, 116, 140–41, 202, 203, 210
Wellman, Mac, *Crowbar*, 92–93
Wesker, Arnold, 243; *Roots*, 245
Weston, Jack, 177
West Side Story (musical), 75, 76, 85
Whitelaw, Billie, 198, 199
Whitman, Walt, *Leaves of Grass*, 254
Wild Duck, The (Ibsen), 23, 119, 149
Wilder, Thornton, 31, 141; *The Skin of Our Teeth*, 152; *Our Town*, 38, 151–55
Wild Honey (Frayn), 167, 241, 245–46
Williams, Robin, 171, 172
Williams, Tennessee, 9, 11, 22, 23, 74, 226, 243; *Battle of Angels*, 81, 82; *Cat on a Hot Tin Roof*, 83; *Orpheus Descending*, 81–85, 243, 245; *A Streetcar Named Desire*, 211; *Sweet Bird of Youth*, 83, 160
Wilson, August, 8, 11, 22, 25–26, 247, 277, 288; *Fences*, 25–26, 65, 100, 101, 214; *Joe Turner's Come and Gone*, 100, 214; *Ma Rainey's Black Bottom*, 100, 214; *The Piano Lesson*, 99–104, 109, 273; *Two Trains Running*, 103
Wilson, Lanford, 11, 22; *Balm in Gilead*, 33–36; *Hot l Baltimore*, 36
Wilson, Robert, 12, 13, 29–31, 196, 233, 247; *The CIVIL WarS*, 12, 247, 251; *Death Destruction & Detroit*, 12; *Einstein on the Beach*, 12, 29–30, 247; *The Forest*, 30–31
Winter's Tale, The (Shakespeare), 155–59, 178, 179, 242, 253
Wiseman, Joseph, 177
Without You I'm Nothing (Bernhard), 71–72
Wolfe, George C., 11, 26–28, 31; *The Colored Museum*, 26–28
Wolfe, Thomas, 127
Wong, B. D., 60, 228, 229
Woodard, Alfre, 158
Woodruff, Robert, 12, 13; *Baal*, 195–97
Wooster Group, The, 8, 12, 38
Working Girl (film), 80, 87
World According to Me, The (Mason), 40–44
Worth, Irene, 146, 160, 161
Woyzeck (Büchner), 13, 52, 194–95

Yale Repertory Theatre, New Haven, 7, 99, 103, 212, 213, 214, 273
Yale School of Drama, 78, 232
Yeargan, Michael, 232
Yeats, W. B., 32, 89, 260
Yorinks, Arthur, 47

Zaks, Jerry, 12, 45, 111, 131, 132
Zang, Edward, 142
Zefferelli, Franco, 117, 163–64
Zizka, Jiri, 124–26
Zollo, Frederick, 53

Robert Brustein is the founder and artistic director of the American Repertory Theatre at Harvard University, where he is also professor of English. He is theatre critic for *The New Republic* and the author of many distinguished books on theatre, among them *The Theatre of Revolt, Making Scenes,* and *Who Needs Theatre.* Mr. Brustein is the former dean of the Yale School of Drama and the founder and director of the Yale Repertory Theatre. He has twice been awarded the George Jean Nathan Award for dramatic criticism, in 1962 and 1987, and has also received the George Polk Memorial Award for outstanding criticism.

ELEPHANT PAPERBACKS

Theatre and Drama

Robert Brustein, *Reimagining American Theatre,* EL410
Robert Brustein, *The Theatre of Revolt,* EL407
Irina and Igor Levin, *Working on the Play and the Role,* EL411
Plays for Performance:
  Aristophanes, *Lysistrata,* EL405
  Anton Chekhov, *The Seagull,* EL407
  Georges Feydeau, *Paradise Hotel,* EL403
  Henrik Ibsen, *Ghosts,* EL401
  Henrik Ibsen, *Hedda Gabler,* EL413
  Henrik Ibsen, *When We Dead Awaken,* EL408
  Heinrich von Kleist, *The Prince of Homburg,* EL402
  Christopher Marlowe, *Doctor Faustus,* EL404
  The Mysteries: Creation, EL412
  August Strindberg, *The Father,* EL406

Literature and Letters

Stephen Vincent Benét, *John Brown's Body,* EL10
Philip Callow, *Son and Lover: The Young D. H. Lawrence,* EL14
James Gould Cozzens, *Castaway,* EL6
James Gould Cozzens, *Men and Brethren,* EL3
Clarence Darrow, *Verdicts Out of Court,* EL2
Floyd Dell, *Intellectual Vagabondage,* EL13
Theodore Dreiser, *Best Short Stories,* EL1
Joseph Epstein, *Ambition,* EL7
André Gide, *Madeleine,* EL8
John Gross, *The Rise and Fall of the Man of Letters,* EL18
Irving Howe, *William Faulkner,* EL15
Aldous Huxley, *Ape and Essence,* EL19
Aldous Huxley, *Collected Short Stories,* EL17
Sinclair Lewis, *Selected Short Stories,* EL9
William L. O'Neill, ed., *Echoes of Revolt: The Masses, 1911–1917,* EL5
Ramón J. Sender, *Seven Red Sundays,* EL11
Wilfrid Sheed, *Office Politics,* EL4
Tess Slesinger, *On Being Told That Her Second Husband Has Taken His First Lover, and Other Stories,* EL12
Thomas Wolfe, *The Hills Beyond,* EL16